Interpersonal Criminology

Revisiting Interpersonal Crimes and Victimization

Interpersonal Criminology

Revisiting Interpersonal Crimes and Victimization

Edited by
K. Jaishankar
Manonmaniam Sundaranar University
Tirunelveli, Tamil Nadu, India

CRC Press
Taylor & Francis Group
Boca Raton London New York

CRC Press is an imprint of the
Taylor & Francis Group, an **informa** business

CRC Press
Taylor & Francis Group
6000 Broken Sound Parkway NW, Suite 300
Boca Raton, FL 33487-2742

First issued in paperback 2020

ISBN-13: 978-1-4987-4859-9 (hbk)
ISBN-13: 978-0-367-59626-2 (pbk)

Visit the Taylor & Francis Web site at
http://www.taylorandfrancis.com

and the CRC Press Web site at
http://www.crcpress.com

To my mentor, Professor K. Chockalingam, who instilled in me the culture of excellence and quality consciousness.

K. Jaishankar

Contents

Section II

INTERPERSONAL CRIMES AGAINST CHILDREN AND YOUTH

Section III

CULTURE CONFLICT AND VICTIMIZATION OF GROUPS

Section IV
INTERPERSONAL CYBER CRIMES

Foreword

During January 11–13, 2013, the second international conference of the South Asian Society of Criminology and Victimology (SASCV) took place in Kanyakumari, India, and I had the privilege to participate in it as the chief rapporteur. The first conference, in Jaipur (2011), was very successful and has been instrumental in promoting research and exchange of knowledge in the fields of criminology and victimology. The editor of this book, Professor K. Jaishankar, is the driving force behind the South Asian Society of Criminology and Victimology (SASCV). As founding president of the SASCV, he has demonstrated a remarkable ability to energize researchers in the relevant areas and to build bridges between the established names in criminology and victimology—in both South Asia and other parts of the world—on the one hand and young fresh talent on the other. That in itself is commendable, looking at the vast potential of scholarly talent available in South Asia.

The current volume contains some pivotal and rigorously peer-reviewed papers that were presented during the second international conference of the SASCV. The overarching theme was carefully chosen, that is, revisiting interpersonal crimes and victimization. All contributions are written by international scholars and chapters are chosen to represent all parts of the world, making it global. The focus of the book covers a number of issues that are highly topical in the state of the art in criminology and victimology.

There are solid reasons for opening the book with a section on interpersonal crimes against women. The various contributions in this section confirm the great urgency of academically dealing with this problem. Women are particularly vulnerable in various ways and means. They are being attacked, harassed, and assaulted on the streets as well as in the places they are employed and in their own homes—where they are supposed to be well protected and cared for. The record shows that in most regions of the world, women face many obstacles in accessing the criminal justice system. This is, *inter alia*, evidenced by the low reporting rates. All of these aspects are covered in the various papers collected in Section I.

Section II is devoted to crimes against children and youth. Again, we are talking about a particularly vulnerable group of victims. The number of chapters under this heading is relatively small, but they suffice to give us a clear picture of what is at stake here. They demonstrate how we can find our way to other victimological findings leading to a better understanding of how we can reduce the prevalence of this phenomenon (prevention) and how to deal with it when it does occur (restorative justice).

In the following Section (III), attention is focused on group victimization. Tribes and other kinds of minorities quite often deserve our special attention in criminology and in victimology. Collectivities play a special role when viewed from the perspectives that we are so used to. All the key concepts that are central to the main theories in our field acquire a special dimension when applied to groups of people instead of individuals.

The final Section (IV) of this volume is about cyber crimes. Cyber criminology and cyber victimology (both terms coined by Professor K. Jaishankar) are rapidly gaining academic attention. The social media nowadays are abused on a massive scale. Sexting and revenge porn are good examples of a kind of behavior that can have a lasting impact on the lives of the persons involved. Other kinds of cyber crime redefine parts of our social life because of the uniquely huge scale of their impact. It is obvious that this relatively new branch of research is definitely here to stay.

It is my solemn conviction that the chapters collected in this volume will enrich the knowledge of the reader. I would hope that one day there will be more regional societies of criminology and victimology organizing (peer-reviewed) international conferences and publishing their main results. In this respect, the South Asian Society of Criminology and Victimology (SASCV) stand out as an example to be emulated by other peer groups. I commend the organizers, and the editor of this volume, for their efforts.

Professor Marc Groenhuijsen
President, World Society of Victimology (WSV) &
Professor of Criminal Law
Tilburg University
The Netherlands

Acknowledgments

I sincerely thank the reviewers of this book: Kushal Vibhute, Mark David Chong, Michael Bacchman, Michael Pittaro, Muzammil Quraishi, Thomas Holt, Tina Patel, Uri Yanay, Natti Ronel, and Yuning Wu. Without these people, the quality of the book would not have been ensured.

For the organization of the Second International Conference of the South Asian Society of Criminology and Victimology (SASCV 2013, Kanyakumari), I received great encouragement from my previous university (Manonmaniam Sundaranar University [MSU], Tirunelveli, India). Professor A. K. Kumaraguru, the then vice chancellor, was the patron of the conference, and Professor P. Govindaraju, the then registrar (in-charge), was the co-patron of the conference. Both evinced keen interest and provided significant support. I sincerely thank both of them.

I also thank my colleagues, research students, and master's students of the Department of Criminology and Criminal Justice, MSU, for providing monumental support for this conference. I earnestly thank all the keynote speakers, plenary speakers, and panel chairs of SASCV 2013. I thank all the sponsors/advertisers and knowledge partners, who provided great support for the conference. Without their support, it would not have been possible to organize such a mammoth event.

A. Ravisankar, the official designer of SASCV conferences, had several sleepless nights, and I sincerely thank him for his dedication, patience, and passion. Ravisankar also designed the text on the cover of this book on the Image by Naturals available at www.pixabay.com, which is released to the public domain under Creative Commons CC0. My heartfelt thanks are due to Periyar, Sivakumar, and Neethu Susan Cherian, the editorial assistants, for their dedicated and sincere support in bringing about this publication.

Professor Marc Groenhusjen, the president of the World Society of Victimology (WSV), was the chief rapporteur of SASCV 2013. I asked him to write a foreword for this book, and he was glad to accept my request. I sincerely thank him from the bottom of my heart. Also, Natti Ronel, Bar Illan University, Israel, the programme chair of SASCV 2013, wrote a compelling epilogue, and I earnestly thank him for the dedicated support he has provided for all my academic ventures.

My past and present employing institutions, the Manonmaniam Sundaranar University, Tirunelveli, India, and the Raksha Shakti University, Ahmedabad, India, provided excellent working environments, which enabled me to put my full energy into this publication. Without their support, it would not have been possible to bring out this publication on time.

Introduction

Contemporary criminologists and victimologists have moved far beyond a basic understanding of crimes and victimization. Most criminologists have moved beyond the core of criminology, that is, the causation of crimes, and have focused more on the issues and problems of the criminal justice system, as contemporary society urges them to become more applied, rather than to remain theoretical. The same is the case for victimologists, concentrating more on the rights of the victims, leaving the roots of victimization. Notably, only a handful of researchers work in the areas of interpersonal crimes and victimization. Also, the patterns of interpersonal crimes and victimization have changed in the contemporary globalized society, and need to be understood from an altogether different dimension. Interpersonal crimes and victimization need to be revisited and the Second International Conference of the South Asian Society of Criminology and Victimology (SASCV), January 11–13, 2013, at Kanyakumari, Tamil Nadu, India was a platform to return to the roots.

Second International Conference of the South Asian Society of Criminology and Victimology (SASCV 2013)

The South Asian Society of Criminology and Victimology (SASCV) is an international association founded in 2009 to nurture the study of criminology and victimology in South Asian countries. Academics, researchers, and practitioners worldwide have joined hands to establish SASCV and share best practices in the context of South Asia. SASCV hosted its second international conference (SASCV 2013) in January 11–13, 2013, at the Hotel Singaar International, Kanyakumari, Tamil Nadu, India. The website of the conference is http://www.sascv.org/conf2013 and online submission of abstracts as well as registration was facilitated on this site.

The theme of SASCV 2013 was "Revisiting Interpersonal Crimes and Victimization." The major subthemes were (1) Interpersonal Crimes against and by Women, (2) Interpersonal Crimes against Children and Youth, (3) Men as Victims: Myths and Realities, (4) Culture Conflict and Victimization of Groups, and (5) Interpersonal Cyber Crimes: Problems of Social Networking. The mission of SASCV 2013 was to revisit the roots of crimes and victimization in a domain where people now only look at the branches and have forgotten the roots, which are the reasons for most contemporary crimes and victimization.

The organizing committee of SASCV 2013 was general chair—K. Jaishankar, vice chair—R. Jayachandran, programme chair—Natti Ronel, chief rapporteur—Marc Groenhuijsen, administrator—Debarati Halder, treasurer—R. Sivakumar, and senior associate—E. Enanalap Periyar. Apart from the organizing committee, an international advisory committee composed of members of the SASCV international advisory board was formed to assist the organizing committee.

The second international conference showcased the academic thoughts of professors, practitioners of criminal justice system, professionals in related fields, and students of national as well as international origin from various backgrounds such as criminology, victimology, law, human rights, digital technology, socio-health sectors, etc. The conference was inaugurated by opening keynote speaker Vesna Nikolic-Ristanovic, the president of the European Society of Criminology and professor at the Department of Prevention and Treatment of Social Disorders, University of Belgrade, Serbia; she spoke on discrimination and violence against women in the workplace. The panel of other keynote speakers included Distinguished Professor Janice O. Joseph, Stockton University, Galloway, New Jersey, who spoke about gender-based street harassment; Professor S. Chandramohan, School of Law, Singapore Management University, who presented on underaged sex workers; and Dr. Dana Pugach, founder and director, Noga Center for Victims of Crime, Ono Academic College, Israel, who deliberated on child victims of crime. Also, there were plenary speakers such as Lorenn Walker, JD, peace-making lawyer, Hawai'i, who spoke on the utility of restorative and solution-focused interventions to address crime and offenses against and by youth; Professor Srisombat Chokprajakchat, Department of Criminology, Mahidol University, Thailand, who discussed children, violence, victimization, and punishment; Professor Doroval Govender, Department of Criminology and Security Science, University of South Africa, who deliberated on issues in policing domestic violence; and Dr. Michael Bachmann, Department of Criminal Justice, Texas Christian University, Fort Worth, Texas, who debated on the current status of cyber criminology, the new science of cybercrime, founded by Professor K. Jaishankar, the editor of this book. The conference concluded with the chief rapporteur's report by Professor Mark Groenhujsen, President of the World Society of Victimology (WSV), a closing keynote presentation by Professor Natti Ronel, Bar Illan University, Israel, and a valedictory address by Professor P. Madhava Soma Sundaram, Department of Criminology and Criminal Justice, Manonmaniam Sundaranar University. More than 250 participants were present at the conference and 100 paper presenters attended. The conference was a great success.

SASCV conferences are unique as a rigorous peer-review process forms the crux and ensures quality. With the continued tradition of excellence like the previous conference at Jaipur (SASCV 2011), the abstracts were reviewed (blind review) by two international experts of the programme committee chaired by Professor Natti Ronel, Bar Illan University, Israel, and the abstracts were selected following stiff competition. The rate of acceptance of papers was 62.1% and the rate of rejection was 37.9%.

After the conference, an expert committee was constituted to select quality papers based on the extended abstracts and presentation of the authors at the conference and revised papers were invited from the selected authors. Papers were rated as A and B. Papers that were rated A were selected to be published in this book as chapters and papers that were rated B were published in a special conference volume of the *International Journal of Criminal Justice Sciences* (the official journal of the SASCV, an open access journal available at www.ijcjs.com). After a rigorous peer review, out of 120 papers presented at the SASCV 2013 conference, 18 papers were rated A and 7 papers were rated B and were selected for publication. The peer-reviewed papers selected for publication as chapters of this book attempt to further establish our understanding of crime as an interpersonal, complex event that affects known and less-known vulnerable populations. All the chapters are diverse in nature from contributors across the globe and are a blend of theoretical and empirical perspectives.

Contents of this Edited Volume

This book is divided into four sections. I. Interpersonal Crimes against Women, II. Interpersonal Crimes against Children and Youth, III. Culture Conflict and Victimization of Groups, and IV. Interpersonal Cyber Crimes. Four major themes of the conference discussed in the following sections form the major content of the chapters of this edited volume.

Interpersonal Crimes against Women

Traditionally, women have suffered not only from discrimination, but also from behaviors that have only recently become known and defined as criminal. Battered by intimate partners, forced sexual activities, abuse at any social level, are a few illustrations of how the interpersonal experiences of women are widely affected. However, in a growing number of countries these are considered offences and are subject to law enforcement, and in many cultures they are no longer accepted. Changing social, cultural, and personal attitudes toward women, which changed their role and status in societies, also changed their role concerning criminality. On the one hand, women may now act differently to stop any attempt to victimize them and may encounter a different, more positive social reaction than a few decades ago. On the other hand, the new social role of women has opened new social opportunities, and has also increased the opportunities for crime. Women, traditionally less involved in crime, are now presenting new forms of criminal activities, which have to be studied in depth. Should the social reaction toward female criminality follow the known one toward male criminality? Or, based on gender difference, should the social reaction follow different lines? These are examples of new topics for study and practice.

There are six chapters under the section, Interpersonal Crimes against Women. In Chapter 1, Janice Joseph analyses a common form of gender harassment, that is, street harassment. Joseph analyses this issue from an international perspective and provides detailed occurrences of street harassment and its responses in various countries such as the United States, Poland, Belgium, South Korea, Japan, India, Egypt, Yemen, and Israel. In this chapter, the responses to street harassment are discussed from the perspective of legal and modern reforms. Modern reforms in various countries, such as patrols, women-only transportation, use of technology, and activism (campaigns), both in offline and online circles are examined. This chapter concludes with a message that street harassment should not be viewed as a trivial problem, but as a symptom of larger issues of crimes against women in society. Also, this chapter calls for a change in attitude and policies and advocates a multidimensional approach to prevent street harassment.

In Chapter 2, Akansha Singh touches on a contentious issue in the Indian scenario, that is, marital rape. While many countries have criminalized marital rape, India has not criminalized it. Section 375, Indian Penal Code (IPC), has a clause "Sexual intercourse by a man with his own wife, the wife not being under 15 years of age, is not rape." In this chapter, a detailed overview of the situation in other countries vis-à-vis India in relation to marital rape is provided. The author argues that laws should criminalize marital rape and society's attitude toward marital rape should change. Also, a discussion on the pros and cons of criminalizing marital rape and the social reasons for underreporting are provided. The chapter concludes with recommendations for various reforms.

In Chapter 3, Helena Menih and Catrin Smith present base-level findings of a much larger study on female homelessness in Brisbane, Australia. The authors feel that there is a significant increase in female homelessness in Australia and they also feel that there is a gap in the current literature and that it is gender blind. Also, this chapter emphasizes that even though previous studies suggest a strong link between violence and homelessness, there are no in-depth studies to understand how women are victims of violence and how they become homeless. Although violence is one of the contributing factors for female homelessness, there are many factors that contribute to such victimization. This chapter provides the findings of a study that utilized qualitative methods, where women victims shared their experiences in relation to their victimization and the impact of victimization. The chapter concludes that the stories provided by the women victims "demonstrate that the experiences of women's reasons for, and pathways into, homelessness tend to be complex, individualistic and gendered." Also, the authors suggest gender-specific social policies to mitigate female homelessness and policies to prevent domestic violence, which is one of the leading factors for female homelessness in Australia.

In Chapter 4, Johnson Ayodele "examines the impact of crime involving market women on their crime reporting practices in Oyo town, Oyo State, Nigeria." In this study, the author utilized mixed methodology to examine the victimization of market women in Nigeria, the impact of crime, and their reporting behavior. The study found that market women tend not to report their victimization to police for fear of losing business and certain culture issues. Instead of reporting their victimization to police, the market women reported their victimization to traditional dons or to religious organizations such as churches or mosques. The author feels that market women in Nigeria have great potential and they contribute more to the economic growth of the country and it is the duty of the state to provide enough security to market women, so that they will continue to contribute to the growth of the economy.

In Chapter 5, Vesna Nikolić-Ristanović, Sanja Ćopić, and Bejan Šaćiri discuss the prevalence and characteristics of discriminatory practices and victimization of women in the workplace in Serbia. Such discrimination and victimization in the workplace is commonplace across the globe. In this chapter, the authors attempt to analyze most of the international documents that examine discrimination of women and prohibit it. The authors further attempt to utilize a research work to understand the prevalence of discrimination and victimization of women in the Serbian workplace. The research suggests reforms in legislation and policies to prevent the discrimination and victimization of women in the workplace in Serbia.

In Chapter 6, C. Hannah, G. Subbaiyan, and T. Srinivas discuss the different forces at play that affect a woman's concern for safety, concentrating on transit spaces such as bus shelters. The authors describe their experiment as an attempt to study the impact of the built environment surrounding bus shelters on the spatial behavior of women and their perception of security during their waiting time. The findings of the study show that most women have distinct safety and security needs. The authors claim that this is one of the earliest studies to be conducted in the context of developing countries such as India. The authors are confident that the results of the study can go a long way in helping town planners and architects design transit spaces that are more women friendly.

Interpersonal Crimes against Children and Youth

To continue the foregoing discussion on women as victims of crime and as criminals as well, children and youth provide a topic with even newer understandings. The abuse of children and youth was traditionally considered legitimate and socially accepted. Sometimes, in the name of education or that of maintaining family roles in traditional societies, and even in ultramodern societies, children and youth, as vulnerable individuals, still suffer from various degrees of abuse. Some children and youth belong to social groups that might be in conflict with the law, based on their personal characteristics. Although most children and youth who experience some conflict with the law spontaneously overcome their rebellious, law-breaking tendencies, the social reaction they increasingly encounter may lead them into greater law breaking. How do we better act toward children and youth who are in conflict with the law? How can we practice the innovative "positive criminology" perspective with them?

There are three chapters under the section Interpersonal Crimes against Children and Youth. In Chapter 7, Lorenn Walker attempts to explore the restorative practices for juveniles in Hawai'i. She emphasizes that "Hawai'i has been experimenting and successfully providing restorative practices for youth in a variety of areas including "ohana conferencing" (its version of family group conferencing), youth transition planning circles, reentry circles for incarcerated youth and for youth with incarcerated parents, solution-focused planning for homeless youth, and diversion for juvenile law violators and status offenders, from traditional justice interventions." This chapter provides novelty as it is written in story form and gives a deeper focus to understand the restorative practices adopted in Hawai'i.

In Chapter 8, John Christopher and Johan De Tavernier provide a roadmap to prevent interpersonal crimes and violence among children and youth through virtue education. The authors believe that a strong focus on virtue ethics, especially in a school environment, will prevent youth becoming offenders. The authors discuss the perspective of virtue ethics and its contribution to virtue education and how it can prevent violence in schools. The authors also propose three unique orientations on the perspective that they have developed on the contribution of virtue ethics to virtue education: "education that outshines from knowing to doing and to being; an education that transcends from information to formation and to transformation; and finally an education that transforms from curriculum-centered and teacher-centered to person-centered." The authors confidently conclude that violence can be curtailed by virtue education in schools.

In Chapter 9, Chandra Mohan analyses a novel issue in relation to a new legal amendment that has prosecuted innocent men in Singapore for their involvement in underage commercial sex. A new amendment in 2007 to the Singapore criminal law criminalized utilizing sexual services from girls under 18 years of age. In 2011, it is reported that at least 51 men who were purportedly lured by an Internet advertisement that wrongfully stated that the girls were above 18 years of age, were prosecuted under this new amendment. The author empathizes with the men who are victims of this draconian law and he further suggests that this new law not only victimizes the men but also their families. The author is also surprised to note that, in Singapore, the legal age of sexual intercourse is 16 and prostitution is not criminalized. This chapter further discusses the nature, effect, and enforcement of the new law and the many questions that arise from a victimological perspective.

Culture Conflict and Victimization of Groups

The complexity of crime as an interpersonal event is mostly revealed when we focus on culture and group conflicts. Through history, the change of power between groups has created lasting cultural narratives of victimization and struggle; unfortunately, sometimes also narratives of resentment and aggression. Regrettably, we see it almost everywhere. Rapid globalization creates more areas of intercultural meetings. On the one hand, it reduces tension by constant mutual exposure. On the other hand, however, old narratives of cultural or racial discrimination do arise, sometimes as counter forces of globalization, and less-privileged groups still pay the toll. The process of abusing "the other" based on cultural excuses finds new targets in the new order of the global world. Is it preventable, or does it lie within our human fate?

There are five chapters under the section, Culture Conflict and Victimization of Groups. In Chapter 10, Doraval Govender examines issues in policing domestic violence in South Africa. In South Africa, the police are responsible for preventing, combating, and investigating statutory and common law offences related to the Domestic Violence Act 116 of 1998. The author argues that, to effectively and efficiently police domestic violence, it is important to understand the causes of domestic violence, the types of violence and abuse experienced by victims of domestic violence, and the response by the police to domestic violence complaints. The aim of this chapter is to evaluate the policing of domestic violence through interviews and documentary study. Based on the findings of the study, the author proceeds to make recommendations for innovations in policing domestic violence.

In Chapter 11, Vesna Nikolić-Ristanović and Ljiljana Stevković examine the domestic violence legislation and its application in Serbia. This chapter is a research work, which adopted a mixed methodology. It relied on court files for the research. This chapter explored some good practices in relation to the effective management of abusers of women victims. The authors are confident that the identification of good practices and their dissemination will be helpful to criminal justice managers such as police, prosecutors, and judges. This study also found lacunae in the files of criminal justice managers and argued how these lacunae will be detrimental to women victims.

In Chapter 12, Dattatary Bhandalkar analyses the process of labeling the Ramoshis who are denotified tribes in Maharashtra, India. The Ramoshi tribe in Maharashtra is one of many tribes in India who were declared 'criminal tribes' during the British period and later reclassified as 'denotified tribes' postindependence. The author argues that the Ramoshis remain deprived of their rights and opportunities and continue living life with stigma and discrimination even today. This chapter attempts to bring to the forefront the voices and experiences of the Ramoshi tribesmen about being 'denotified' in society. The research investigates the origin of labeling among the tribe, the process of continued labeling over years, and the effects on the tribe. The findings of the study show that the process of labeling began with the enactment of the Criminal Tribes Act 1871, which played a significant role in the lives of the Ramoshis.

In Chapter 13, Pavithran Nambiar and Suhas P. Nambiar examine case studies of women victims of trafficking in Gujarat, India, who later became offenders of sex trafficking. This chapter is unique in nature as there are very few studies on victim turned offender. Women victims of trafficking have later become either pimps or owners of prostitution rackets and they have played a great role in the perpetration of trafficking in the state of Gujarat. The chapter is based on a qualitative study and has mostly relied on the firsthand experiences of the lead author who had a long stint in policing and dealt with various cases of sex trafficking in Gujarat. The chapter also relied on the secondary data collected from police files. This qualitative chapter provides some recommendations on mitigating trafficking for sexual purposes and some on the rehabilitation measures of such victim turned offender of sex trafficking.

In Chapter 14, Natti Ronel presents a new concept to the field of victimology, that is, positive victimology. The author earlier provided the concept of positive criminology and now he is proposing the new concept of positive victimology. The author argues that "positive victimology focuses on empowering the victims as well as assisting him or her grow on a personal and social level despite being hurt as a result of a negative traumatic event." The author feels that this new concept will expand the scope of victimology. He has presented this new concept to several international conferences including the Third SASCV, Kanyakumari (2013), which serves as the base for this volume. The author expands the new concept in this chapter and feels that this is only a starting point of the concept and many future researches needs to be done in this new area.

Interpersonal Cybercrimes

Cyber society regularly invents and opens new social opportunities. The interpersonal arena is increasingly more cyber focused than direct. But new arenas are also new opportunities for old acts of abuse, and the high accessibility of the new social networking creates innovative methods of attracting possible victims. There is a need to provide a state-of-the-art knowledge base for preventing cyber victimization, for educating safer use, and for immediate intervention when needed.

There are four chapters under the section Interpersonal Cyber Crimes. In Chapter 15, Philip Ndubueze explores the vulnerability of young Internet users in Nigeria and their online victimization. The author feels that contemporary youth, who are mostly referred as "Generation Y," are technology driven and have become slaves to the Internet/mobile technology. Also, they are daring to meet people in real life whom they have met online. This situation puts them in a very vulnerable position. The author feels that this issue needs to be analyzed in detail and more studies have to be done in this area. Also, the author provides various suggestions to mitigate the vulnerability of young Internet users and their online victimization.

In Chapter 16, Debarati Halder and K. Jaishankar examine the issue of sexting from the perspective of teens. There are numerous examples of the misuse of sexted images and the victimization of children who are involved in sexting. This prompted the judiciary to treat sexting as a "felony" from the perspective of circulating online child pornography. However, if sexting is seen from the viewpoint of adolescents' right to sexual fantasy, then laws meant for curbing online pornography and regulating the creators, producers, and distributors of said material may not be successful in yielding effective and expected results on adolescent teens who may have participated in sexting out of sexual fantasy. Should the teens involved in sexting be seen as offenders or victims? Why is it necessary to regulate sexting among teens? The authors argue that teens who involve in sexting should be treated as victims and not offenders. This chapter delves into these questions from legal and criminological angles. This chapter also emphasizes building up effective socio-legal mechanisms to control the issue.

In Chapter 17, Thomas Holt, Grace Chee, and Esther Ng analyze the problem of cyber and mobile phone bullying victimization among youth in Singapore using quantitative techniques. The authors have also tried to adopt the application of Routine Activities Theory to this issue, collecting data from a sample of youth in Singapore. The authors found that the online behavior of individuals and their exposure and proximity to the motivated offenders increased their risk of bullying victimization both in the Internet and on mobile phones. The authors justified the application of Routine Activities Theory to their study; however, they have not included guardianship, which is one of the key components of the Routine Activities Theory and they have mentioned that as a limitation. The study has opened vistas to new research in the field of cyber criminology.

In Chapter 18, the last chapter, Brie Diamond and Michael Bachmann provide an overview of the current state of cyber criminological study with regard to theory, research, and teaching. The authors argue that, in contrast to the vast knowledge about technical aspects of cybercrimes, behavioral research on these offenses is currently still in its infancy with few data sources or publication outlets. This chapter details the fundamental issues and problems facing researchers involved in the young discipline of cyber criminology, ranging from definitional to methodological problems. There remains argument among cybercrime scholars over how best to define the focus of the field and numerous theoretical explanations compete for preference with the scholarly community. These issues pose significant obstacles and need to be addressed for the discipline to advance. Suggestions of how to address some of the primary issues are provided and potential solutions are presented in the chapter.

The book concludes with a fitting epilogue by Natti Ronel. Natti Ronel is confident that the "chapters of this book will contribute to our understanding of new opportunities to prevent crime and victimization that represent the old—our old and lasting ability to be fully human."

Editor

Professor K. Jaishankar is presently a professor of criminology and the head of the Department of Criminology at the Raksha Shakti University, Ahmedabad, Gujarat, India. Prior to this position, he was a faculty member at the Department of Criminology and Criminal Justince, Manonmaniam Sundaranar University, Tirunelveli, Tamil Nadu, India. He has published more than a hundred publications, including peer-reviewed articles in journals such as the *British Journal of Criminology*, editorials, book chapters, and books. He is the recipient of the prestigious National Academy of Sciences, India (NASI)—SCOPUS Young Scientist Award (2012)—Social Sciences and ISC—S.S. Srivastava Award for Excellence in Teaching and Research in Criminology. He is the founding editor-in-chief of the *International Journal of Cyber Criminology* (www.cybercrimejournal.com) and editor-in-chief of the *International Journal of Criminal Justice Sciences* (www.ijcjs.com). He is the founder president of the South Asian Society of Criminology and Victimology (SASCV) (www.sascv.org) and founder executive director of the Centre for Cyber Victim Counselling (CCVC) (www.cybervictims.org). He was a discussant in the "Opening discussion: Focusing on victims of crime—Comparing crime patterns and improving practice. Researchers' advice to policy" of the Stockholm Criminology Symposium held June 11–13, 2012, in Stockholm, Sweden, and responded to questions from Beatrice Ask, Swedish minister for justice, and Paula Teixeria da Cruz, the Portuguese minister for justice. He was a keynote speaker at the 14th World Society of Victimology Symposium held May 20–24, 2012, at The Hague, the Netherlands, and the 15th World Society of Victimology Symposium held July 5–9, 2015, Perth, Western Australia. He was a member of the United Nations Office of Drugs and Crime (UNODC) core group of experts (15 member group) on identity-related crime (2007–2008). He is a member of the Membership and Advancement Committee, World Society of Victimology (WSV), an international advisory board member of the Center for the Research and Development of Positive Criminology, Department of Criminology, Bar Illan University, Israel, an advisory board member of the Center for Cybercrime Studies, John Jay College of Criminal Justice, New York, and a member of the International Cybercrime Research Centre, Simon Fraser University, Vancouver, Canada. He was a Commonwealth Fellow (2009–2010) at the Centre for Criminal Justice Studies, School of Law, University of Leeds, UK, and has completed a research project on victims of cyber crimes. He is a member of the scientific commission of the International Society of Criminology (ISC). He is a fellow of the African Center for Cyberlaw and Cybercrime prevention. He was recently appointed as an international ambassador of the British Society of Criminology (BSC). His areas of academic competence are victimology, cyber criminology, crime mapping, geographic information systems, communal violence, policing, and crime prevention.

E-mail: drjaishankar@gmail.com; URL: http://www.jaishankar.org.

Contributors

Johnson Oluwole Ayodele is a lecturer and faculty member, Department of Sociology, Lagos State University, Ojo, Nigeria. He holds a PhD in sociology from the University of Ibadan, Nigeria. His research interests include criminology, victimology, social problems, social work, sociology of education, and sociology of mass communication. He is passionate about victims' crime reporting practices to both informal structures of crime control and the police. He has done extensive work on these in Lagos, and some in the Ogun, Oyo, and Osun States of Nigeria. His work focuses on social responses to victimization, police attitudes to victims, women as victims of widowhood, fuel subsidy withdrawal injustice, and marital rape. Ayodele has had some of his works published in reputable local and scholarly international journals.

Michael Bachmann is an associate professor of criminal justice at Texas Christian University, Fort Worth. His research spans all facets of the intersection of high technology and the law, ranging from computer hacker subcultures and ethics to the facilitation of crime investigations through geospatial mapping applications. He is the author of several book chapters and articles on cyber crimes, such as Internet piracy, fraud, espionage, malicious code releases, and the use of Internet technology by human trafficking and terrorist organizations. His work has been translated and published for international audiences in four languages. Dr. Bachmann's current projects include two Department of Justice–funded grants with a total volume of $800,000. He is developing a comprehensive database on the involvement of organized crime syndicates in human trafficking operations and is employing crime mapping technologies to combat gun and gang violence. Outside of Texas Christian University, Dr. Bachmann serves as a U.S. Agency for International Development consultant to help combat the rampant crime of extortion in developing countries by advising on issues pertaining to cyber crimes and cyber investigations, cyber forensics, and electronic search and seizure procedures, as well as cell phone interception, surveillance, and tracking techniques. He also serves as a member of the advisory boards of the South Asian Society for Criminology and Victimology and the Graduate Cyber Security Program at Henley-Putnam University, San Jose, California.

Dattatreya Bhandalkar is a PhD scholar at the School of Social Work at Tata Institute of Social Sciences, Mumbai, India. He received his master's degree in social work from the University of Pune, India, in 2008 and MPhil in social work from Tata Institute of Social Sciences in 2011. His research interests include criminalization, labeling, stigma, and discrimination. He received the Indian Council of Social Science Research Fellowship to conduct his PhD research.

Grace Chee is a PhD student focusing on child development in the Human Development and Family Studies Program at Michigan State University, East Lansing. She is a sixth-year PhD candidate (all but dissertation), and she plans to defend her dissertation soon. She has varied research interests including elder abuse, bullying, grandparenting (particularly among immigrant and minority groups), adolescents, Chinese families, and immigrant families.

John Christopher belongs to the Research Unit Theological and Comparative Ethics at the Faculty of Theology and Religious Studies, Katholieke Universiteit Leuven, Belgium. He has his master's and advanced master's in theology and religious studies from Katholieke Universiteit Leuven. He defended his doctoral dissertation entitled "Character, Virtue and Education: Rehabilitating and Exemplarist Virtue Approach (*Gurukul*) to Moral Education" in November 2015 from Katholieke Universiteit Leuven. He was a founding member of Bethany Navajeevan Higher Secondary School and Bethany Navajeevan College of Education at Vencode, Kanyakumari, Tamil Nadu, India, and served as principal and correspondent of these educational institutions, respectively. His research areas are ethics, education, children and ethics, crime and violence, moral education, character formation, and virtue ethics.

Sanja Ćopić is a research associate at the Institute of Criminological and Sociological Research in Belgrade, Serbia, and a researcher and president of the Executive Board of the Victimology Society of Serbia. She has participated in numerous research and action-oriented projects on victims of crime, discrimination, domestic violence, and human trafficking, as well as on reconciliation, victim support, and restorative justice. The main focus of her recent work has been the use of restorative justice in criminal matters and the victim's position in restorative justice programs, as well as the position of female offenders in prison in Serbia. Sanja is the deputy editor of *Temida*—an academic journal on victimization, human rights, and gender, published by the Victimology Society of Serbia. She is an author and coauthor of numerous books and papers published in Serbia and abroad.

Johan De Tavernier is a professor of theological ethics and vice dean for education at the Faculty of Theology and Religious Studies, Katholieke Universiteit Leuven, Belgium. He is director of Ethics@Arenberg (Science, Engineering and Technology Group, Katholieke Universiteit Leuven). He served as the academic secretary and vice dean for education at the Faculty of Theology and Religious Studies for nine years (1996–2002 and 2005–2008) and as vice dean for international relations for two years (2012–2014). He teaches courses in Christian ethics, personhood, environmental ethics, and bioethics, mainly to theology students, and introductory courses in Christianity to engineering and bioengineering students. His research interests focus on fundamental moral theology, especially the history of the personalist tradition, the distinctiveness of Christian ethics, evolutionary biology and ethics, a reinterpretation of the natural law tradition, and the use of scripture in ethics. He is also specialized in three fields of applied ethics: food ethics, engineering ethics, and animal ethics. He is a member of many scientific boards: Member Executive Board European Society for Agricultural and Food Ethics (2001–2014), Member Internationale Vereinigung für Moraltheologie und Sozialethik, Member Board IST—Flemish Parliament (2011–2014), Member Research Group European Ethics Network, and Member Ethics Committee Animal Experiments, Katholieke Universiteit Leuven.

Brie Diamond is an assistant professor of criminal justice at Texas Christian University, Fort Worth. She completed her PhD in criminal justice from University of Texas at Dallas

(2013). Her research interests include juvenile delinquency, corrections, program evaluation, and criminological theory, with an emphasis on advanced statistical methodologies. She has published several book chapters and articles in leading journals.

Doraval Govender is an associate professor in the Department of Criminology and Security Science (Program: Security Management) at the University of South Africa, Pretoria. He has been a member of the South African Police Service, where he served operationally and at different management levels in both the uniform and detective divisions. He retired from the South African Police Service at the end of 2008 with the rank of assistant commissioner (major general). He underwent many educational, training, and development programs both nationally and internationally, including the FBI program for international students in Quantico, Virginia (199th session). He has an MTech degree in forensic investigations and was one of the first two students internationally to obtain his doctorate in criminology, specializing in security risk management. In 2009, he joined the University of South Africa as a lecturer in the Department of Criminology and Security Science. Since 2009, he has published several articles in national and international journals. He is also the subeditor of the *Acta Criminologica Journal*, editor for the *Policing Organization of Southern Africa Journal*, and member of the editorial board of the *African Criminal Justice Journal*. He has chaired several sessions at different conferences and has presented papers both internationally and nationally on policing and security-related issues.

Debarati Halder is an advocate and legal scholar. She is the managing director of the Centre for Cyber Victim Counselling (www.cybervictims.org). She received her LLB from the University of Calcutta, Kolkata, India, and her master's degree in international and constitutional law from the University of Madras, Chennai, India. She holds a PhD degree from the National Law School of India University, Bangalore. She has coauthored a book titled *Cyber Crime and the Victimization of Women: Laws, Rights and Regulations* (IGI Global, Hershey, Pennsylvania, 2011). She has published many articles in peer-reviewed journals and chapters in peer-reviewed books. Her work has appeared in scholarly journals, including the *British Journal of Criminology, Journal of Law and Religion, Victims and Offenders, Murdoch University E-Journal of Law, ERCES Online Quarterly Review, TMC Academic Journal* (Singapore), and *Temida and Indian Journal of Criminology & Criminalistics*, and edited volumes *Crimes of the Internet, Trends and Issues of Victimology*, and *Cyber Criminology*. Debarati's research interests include constitutional law, international law, victim rights, cyber crimes, and laws. She has presented her research works at many international conferences, including the Stockholm Criminology Symposium held during June 11–13, 2012, and the International Conference on Social Media for Good, held during May 15–16, 2015, at Istanbul, Turkey.

C. Hannah is a doctoral research student in the Department of Architecture, National Institute of Technology, Tiruchirappalli, Tamil Nadu, India. She completed her BArch from the National Institute of Technology, Tiruchirappalli (gold medalist) and her MDes from the Indian Institute of Technology, Mumbai. Her areas of research include environmental psychology, virtual environment, simulation, and their applications in urban planning and design for security.

Thomas J. Holt is an associate professor in the School of Criminal Justice at Michigan State University, East Lansing, specializing in computer crime, cyber crime, and technology. He received his PhD in criminology and criminal justice from the University of Missouri–St. Louis in 2005. His research focuses on computer hacking, malware, and the role that technology and the Internet play in facilitating all manner of crime and deviance. Tom is also the project lead for the Spartan Devils Honeynet Project, a joint project of Michigan State University, Arizona State University, Tempe, and private industry, and a member of the editorial advisory board of the *International Journal of Cyber Criminology*.

Janice Joseph is a distinguished professor of the Criminal Justice Program at Stockton University, Galloway, New Jersey (earlier, Richard Stockton College of New Jersey). She earned her MA and PhD from York University, Toronto, Canada. At Stockton University, she teaches courses on gangs, juvenile justice, corrections, and victimology. She has also taught in Canada, England, and Croatia and guest-lectured in Italy, Israel, Austria, and other countries. She is the editor of the *Journal of Ethnicity in Criminal Justice*, a scholarly criminal justice journal, and serves on the editorial boards of several criminal justice journals. Her broad research interests include gangs, youth violence, juvenile delinquency, violence against women, and women and criminal justice. She has more than 60 publications, including books and articles on delinquency, gangs, domestic violence, femicide, stalking, sexual harassment, and minorities and crime. She has also conducted research studies in Canada, the United States, England, and Montenegro, and has made more than 130 presentations in more than 25 countries. She is presently the United Nations nongovernmental organization representative for the Academy of Criminal Justice Sciences and executive council member of the World Society of Victimology.

Helena Menih is a lecturer in the School of Behavioural, Cognitive and Social Sciences at the University of New England, Biddeford, Maine. She is an anthropologist and criminologist and, as such, is well versed in qualitative research techniques and has considerable experience applying them to the study of vulnerable populations. She was recently awarded a doctorate in the School of Criminology and Criminal Justice at Griffith University, Brisbane, Australia.

S. Chandra Mohan is presently an associate professor of law (practice) in the Singapore Management University, Bras Basah. Chandra graduated from the law faculty of the then University of Singapore in 1967. In his third year at the university, he was cowinner of the Higgins Book Prize for the best undergraduate contribution to a legal journal. Upon graduation, he joined the Singapore Legal Service, where he held a number of senior posts, including senior judge of the district court, director of Legal Aid, official assignee and official receiver, and public trustee and director of Legal Policy (Ministry of Law). In 1972, he obtained an LLM from the University of Singapore, and in 1988, he was awarded a PhD by the University of London, United Kingdom, for his dissertation "The Control of Corruption in Singapore." He taught continuously at the University of Singapore law faculty as an adjunct from 1971 to 1981 and from 2003 to 2007, and at the Postgraduate Practical Law Course from 1972 to 1999. He was a visiting fellow at the United Nations Asia and Far East Institute for the Prevention of Crime and the Treatment of Offenders in Tokyo in 1996 and 2001 and is an academic counselor with the Asian Crime Prevention Foundation. Chandra has written widely on criminal law and procedure, evidence, family law, and insolvency law and practice.

Pavithran Nambiar is presently working as an assistant professor (R&D) at Raksha Shakti University, Ahmedabad, Gujarat, India. He has had 39 years of service in the Gujarat Police, and during this tenure, he worked in different divisions, that is, State Reserve Police, Communication, Intelligence, and CID Crime. Along with his job, he pursued his studies and secured a BA, MA, MPhil, and PhD in sociology. He was conferred the prestigious President's Medal for Meritorious Service in 2003. He has 14 years of research experience in the Police Research Center of State CID Crime, Gujarat. He has authored several books and published papers in national and international journals. He was a fellow at the Police Foundation, Washington, D.C., in 2011, where he produced a paper titled "Radicalization of Islam: A Historical Perspective and Homegrown Threat to the U.S." He is a visiting faculty at the Gujarat Forensic Sciences University, and his areas of interest include homeland security and police science.

Suhas P. Nambiar has an MA (first rank) and PhD in political science from Gujarat University, Gujarat, India. She possesses more than 13 years of research and teaching experience, wherein she worked as research assistant, research associate, and assistant professor at the Mahatma Gandhi Labour Institute, Ahmedabad, India; Gujarat Vidyapith, Ahmedabad, India; and Joan Kroc Institute for Peace and Justice, University of San Diego, California. As an Ambassadorial Scholar of Rotary International, she earned her postdoctoral diploma from the Joan Kroc Institute for Peace and Justice in 2001. She has published several articles in international journals and was a visiting faculty at Amity University, New Delhi, India. Her areas of interest are international relations, disarmament, and peace and conflict.

Philip Ndubueze is a lecturer in the Department of Sociology, Federal University Dutse, Jigawa State, Nigeria where he teaches criminology. He holds a PhD in criminology and criminal justice from the University of Nigeria, Nsukka, Nigeria. He has published several articles and book chapters in referred local and international journals and edited volumes on cyber crime and cyber security. He is a member of the Nigerian Anthropological and Sociological Practitioners Association and the Western Society of Criminology, Corona, California. His research interests include cyber criminology, crime prevention and control strategies, penology, victimology, and third-party policing.

Esther Ng is an art psychotherapist at MySpace Psychotherapy in Singapore, and works with children, youth, and adults. Esther has a MA in art psychotherapy and has provided art psychotherapy to young children, youth, and adults. Her work experience using art as a modality in psychotherapy includes populations such as children in transition, terminally ill patients, and teens and adults experiencing trauma, loss and grief, addition, self-harm, depression, and other psychiatric disorders. Prior to becoming an art psychotherapist, Esther received her bachelor's degree in early childhood studies from the University of Melbourne, Australia. Esther has worked with children, youth, and families over the past 28 years. She has designed and managed 17 centers for children's services in Singapore and overseas. These centers include childcare, student care, special needs inclusion, and hospice for children with cancer. In 2005, Esther founded the nonprofit organization Coalition against Bullying for Children and Youth. Her advocacy and research work has won her accolades from local and international organizations. In recognition of her continuous passion to advocate for children and youth, Esther received the Channel News

Asia Singapore Woman Award 2009. Currently, Esther is also a member of the panel of advisors to the juvenile court in Singapore.

Vesna Nikolić-Ristanović is director of the Victimology Society of Serbia and full professor of criminology, victimology, juvenile delinquency, and child abuse at Belgrade University, Faculty for Special Education and Rehabilitation, Serbia, and former president of the European Society of Criminology. Her fields of experience and research include victims of crime, violence against women, women's crime, war and crime, reconciliation, yoga, victim support, and restorative justice. She is the founder and editor in chief of *Temida*, the journal on victimization, human rights, and gender. She is an author and coauthor of a large number of books and papers published in Serbia and abroad, among which the most important are "From Victim to Prisoner: Domestic Violence and Women's Crime," "Domestic Violence in Serbia," "Social Change, Gender and Violence: Post-Communist and War-Affected Societies," "International Standards on Domestic Violence and Its Implementation in the Western Balkans," "Surviving Transition: Everyday Life and Violence in Post-Communist and Post-Conflict Societies," and "Discrimination against Women at the Labour Market in Serbia."

Natti Ronel is the head of the Department of Criminology at Bar-Ilan University, Ramat Gan, Israel. Natti is a clinical criminologist who incorporates clinical experience with research to develop theories on crime (criminal spin), recovery (grace therapy), and criminal justice. Natti introduced the positive criminology and victimology perspectives, and is currently developing the spiritual criminology concept. Natti leads continuous training courses for criminal justice and victim assistance professionals, and he is a recurring faculty member of the annual postgraduate Victimology, Victim Assistance, and Criminal Justice course in the Inter-University Centre, Dubrovnik, Croatia, where he lectures on therapy for recovering victims. His various writings reflect both his clinical and academic experiences in criminology. He has a special focus on the spiritual aspect of criminology and victimology—its values and impact on individuals and communities, spiritual-based intervention and recovery, moral transformation, and forgiveness and spiritual intelligence. He is head of the research group for the development and study of positive criminology at Bar-Ilan University. He has written and edited several books. He is a member of the advisory board of the South Asian Society of Criminology and Victimology and is the program chair of the Second International Conference of the South Asian Society of Criminology and Victimology held during January 11–13, 2013, at Kanyakumari, India.

Bejan Šaćiri is a PhD student at the Department of Psychology, Faculty of Philosophy, University of Belgrade, Serbia, and a researcher for the Victimology Society of Serbia. He is currently working on his PhD thesis, which is in the domain of clinical psychology and psychotherapy. As a volunteer, he is involved in supporting victims in the victim support service VDS Info and Victim Support, which operates within the Victimology Society of Serbia. His research activities, so far, have been mainly related to the issues of discrimination, peace building, reconciliation and restorative justice, professional ethics in psychology, domestic violence, and female offenders in prison. Bejan is a transactional psychotherapist in training and actively works in the field of individual and marital counseling.

Akansha Singh is an undergraduate student at the National Law Institute University, Bhopal, Madhya Pradesh, India.

Catrin Smith is a senior lecturer in the School of Criminology and Criminal Justice at Griffith University, Brisbane, Australia. She joined the School of Criminology and Criminal Justice in 2009, having previously been a reader in criminology at the University of Chester, United Kingdom. Prior to that, she was a lecturer in criminology and criminal justice and a member of the Centre for Comparative Criminology and Criminal Justice at Bangor University (Formerly the University of Wales, Bangor).

T. Srinivas is a professor in the Department of Architecture, National Institute of Technology, Tiruchirappalli, India. He obtained his BArch from the Jawaharlal Nehru Technological University, Hyderabad, India; master of city planning from the Indian Institute of Technology, Kharagpur; and PhD from the University of Sydney, Australia. He is actively involved in research and consultancy projects, in addition to teaching and academic research. Through his research, he tries to explore the dimensions of thermal comfort, safety in the built environment, and human behavior in urban open spaces and how they impact design. His other academic interests include functional design, the sustainable built environment, and energy-efficient buildings. He and his research associates have been cited with a few "best paper awards" at various conferences. His research work is shared through many presentations and publications. He is involved in various committees related to architecture education and has been an active member of various professional bodies related to the built environment.

Ljiljana Stevković is a teaching assistant at the Faculty of Special Education and Rehabilitation, University of Belgrade, Serbia, and a researcher volunteer for the Victimology Society of Serbia. She has participated in numerous international and national projects on crime victims, victims of domestic violence, juvenile delinquency, victimization of children, human and victims' rights, and protection of women victims of violence who are serving prison sentences. She has published numerous articles and book chapters on domestic violence, juvenile delinquency, the online victimization of girls, the victimization of children and the elderly, and trafficking in human organs. Ljiljana has also participated in many national and international criminological and victimological conferences and presented papers.

G. Subbaiyan is an associate professor of the Department of Architecture, National Institute of Technology, Tiruchirappalli, India. He completed his BArch, securing first rank, from the National Institute of Technology, Tiruchirappalli. He obtained his master's of city planning from the Indian Institute of Technology, Kharagpur, with the institute's silver medal for the highest cumulative grade point average and was awarded his PhD from the National Institute of Technology, Tiruchirappalli. He has about 26 years of teaching experience. He has also served as a member of various academic and administrative committees of the institute. His research interests include crime prevention through environmental design, architectural lighting, and architectural conservation. He has several journal and conference papers to his credit.

Lorenn Walker is a public health educator and restorative lawyer who develops, implements, researches, and publishes the results of social learning processes using restorative justice and solution-focused approaches. She has extensive educational, social service, and legal experience. Lorenn uses a public health approach with organizations and individuals in finding positive solutions for difficulties and increasing performance. Lorenn is an expert in designing and facilitating effective learning programs. Her recent work has focused on reentry for incarcerated people, substance abuse, violence prevention, and reconciliation for people harmed by wrongdoing and social injustice. She is on the Fulbright Specialist roster until 2018 for international peacemaking training, administers Hawai'i Friends of Justice and Civic Education, and teaches speech courses for the University of Hawai'i Honolulu Community College. More about her work can be found at www.lorennwalker.com.

Interpersonal Crimes against Women

I

Gender-Based Street Harassment
An International Perspective

1

JANICE JOSEPH

Contents

Introduction

Gender-based street harassment (street harassment) is perhaps the most pervasive form of harassment that is an everyday occurrence. It usually constitutes the harassment of both men and women, but the most common form is the harassment of women by men. Any woman, regardless of age, size, or subjective attractiveness, can experience street harassment. This form of harassment is sexual in nature and can be either verbal or physical, or both. Unfortunately, it is often viewed as complimentary and trivial. However, like other forms of sexual harassment, street harassment is deplorable. There is considerable research on sexual harassment in the workplace and harassment that is perpetrated by strangers in public places, such as streets, subways, shopping malls, and parks. There are very few comprehensive academic studies on the subject matter. However, more attention is now being placed on the phenomenon, so the number of studies on this phenomenon will increase. Using an international perspective, this chapter focuses on the harassment of women by men. It examines the concept, nature, extent, context, and responses to gender-based street harassment.

Gender-Based Street Harassment: Conceptual Definition

There are several terms that have been used by different researchers for this phenomenon. Gardner (1980), for example, refers to the behavior as street remark, and Lord (2009) identifies it as gender-based public harassment. Other researchers categorize it as stranger harassment (Fairchild and Rudman, 2008; Fairchild, 2010; Wesselmann and Kelly, 2010; Macmillan et al., 2000). It is referred to as eve teasing in India and sometimes Pakistan, Bangladesh, and Nepal, with "eve" being a reference to the biblical Eve. Bowman (1993, p. 524) states the following:

> Although street harassment encompasses a wide variety of behaviors, gestures, and comments, it has some defining characteristics: (1) the targets of street harassment are female; (2) the harassers are male; (3) the harassers are unacquainted with their targets; (4) the encounter is face to face; (5) the forum is a public one, such as a street, sidewalk, bus, bus station, taxi, or other place to which the public generally has access but (6) the content of the speech, if any, is not intended as public discourse.

Davis (2002) has argued that there are three ways to define and understand street harassment. First, she has suggested that it is necessary to examine what acts constitute street harassment. Second, there are the characteristics of the act, such as where it took place, the gender of the victim, the relationship between the victim and the perpetrator, and which parts of the victim's body were targeted. Finally, she views street harassment as an "element of a larger system of terrorism" (Davis, 2002, p. 214). She also refers to street harassment as the genderization of the streets "by distributing power in such a way that perpetuates male supremacy and female subordination" (Davis, 2002, p. 216).

Understanding Street Harassment

Street harassment occurs within a variety of contexts. According to Kearl (2010), street harassment occurs within a culture of gender inequality, but it also reinforces the gender inequality that exists in many societies. She argues that when men harass women, it reminds women of their inequality. She further argues that it occurs within a rape culture that creates fear for women when they are alone in public. The threat or fear of rape restricts women's mobility to be alone in public places.

McKelle (2013) posits that street harassment occurs because of sexism, which is based on the perception of sexuality for both males and females. She has noted that street harassment is gender based because the power differences between males and females create the circumstances for street harassment to exist. Women have been socialized to dress appropriately and avoid danger and walking late night. Men, on the other hand, are taught not to be afraid of public spaces and women are sex objects, so commenting on their bodies is acceptable. These contradictory socialization patterns create the social atmosphere that allows for street harassment to exist. Consequently, street harassment will not end until sexism is ended (McKelle, 2013).

Lenton et al. (1999) identified three explanations of public harassment that demonstrate the unequal power between men and women. They are the social-structural, sociocultural, and social control perspectives. The social-structural approach views street harassment as an integral part of a larger structure in which men and women have unequal power, with men having access to more resources than women. The sociocultural perspective examines the social construction of gender that places males in a superior, dominant position to females, and women in an inferior position. As a result, women are viewed as passive and submissive sexual objects. They are, therefore, objectified in public places, sometimes to the point of blaming themselves for the behaviors to which they are subjected. Sexual objectification is clearly a component of street harassment. The social control argument focuses on street harassment as a means of controlling women and a way to maintain male dominance (sexual terrorism). It serves as a "means of social control that serves to reproduce and maintain the status quo of male dominance" (Lenton et al., 1999, p. 520).

According to Larkin (1997), sexual harassment in the public sphere reflects a redefinition of women as the public (as opposed to private) property of men. Kearl (2010) argues that street harassment is about power and not about sexual attraction. Davis (2002, p. 216) also refers to street harassment as the genderization of the streets "by distributing power in such a way that perpetuates male supremacy and female subordination." Benard and Schlaffer (1996) and Gardner (1995) suggest that street harassment is a form of male bonding because they tend to harass women in public when they are in a group.

Street harassment is a multilayered phenomenon that is affected by race, sexual orientation, socioeconomic status, nationality, disability, and other social statuses (Kearl, 2010). According to Nielsen (2004, p. 41), "street harassment certainly is a form of gender domination, but it represents a more complicated process because multiple hierarchies are in play at the same time." These statuses, when intersected, affect the nature and the extent of the harassment. Kearl (2010), for example, found that women of color were subjected to racist and sexist verbal slurs, although they experienced sexist comments more often than racist comments. She also found that street harassment is mainly interracial or interethnic (Kearl, 2010). Transwomen also face the multilayered characteristics of street harassment. They face street harassment because of their newly obtained gender as a woman but antigay sentiments as well because of societal attitude toward transgendered individuals (Kearl, 2010).

Extent of Street Harassment: A Global Analysis

Street harassment is a global problem. Kearl (2010) conducted an informal survey of more than 900 people from 23 countries and 45 states. Her research revealed that 80% of women were victims who experienced gender-based street harassment, such as sexually explicit comments and gestures, from unknown men. She also found that 75% had been followed, more than 50% had been groped, more than 33% had faced public masturbation, and 25% had been assaulted by a male stranger. She reported that several girls were harassed by men who were old enough to be their fathers or grandfathers.

Americas

Street harassment is a significant problem in the United States. On June 3, 2014, Stop Street Harassment (SSH) released the largest ever national report on street harassment. According to the report, 65% of women and 25% of men reported experiencing at least one type of street harassment in their lifetime. More than 57% of all women had experienced verbal harassment, and 41% of all the women had experienced physical harassment, including sexual touching (23%), following (20%), flashing (14%), and forced to engage in explicit sexual behavior (9%). The study also found that sexual harassment began at a very young age (before 17 years), occurred multiple times, and the victims became scared because they were concerned that it would escalate. According to this study, street harassment forced the victims to constantly assess their surroundings as a result of harassment (47% of women), stop walking alone (31%), and even quit their job or move away (4%). According to the report, 65% of women and 25% of men reported experiencing at least one type of street harassment in their lifetime. The study found that among all women, 23% had been sexually touched, 20% had been followed, and 9% had been forced to do something sexual. However, 25% had been street harassed (a higher percentage of lesbian, gay, bisexual, and transgender (LGBT)–identified men than heterosexual men reported this), and their most common form of harassment was homophobic or transphobic slurs (9%) (Stop Street Harassment, 2014).

In the United States, an Indiana University, Indianapolis, study found that all of the 293 women interviewed reported multiple incidents of street harassment (Gardner, 1995). A Northwestern University study in the early 2000s found 54% had been the target of offensive or sexually suggestive remarks on multiple occasions. Nielsen (2004), who conducted a study of 100 women in the California San Francisco Bay Area, found that 54% had been the target of offensive or sexually suggestive remarks. In 2007, the Manhattan Borough President's Office surveyed 1790 transit riders in New York City and found that 63% had been sexually harassed on the subway. The results of the study indicated that a large number of women experience problems on the subway system (Stringer, 2007; Chan, 2008). A recent study in Boston of 500 respondents indicated that 88% had experience street harassment (Hollaback, 2013a).

In Canada, Macmillan et al. (2000), who studied the impact of street harassment on women's perceived sense of safety, found that more than 80% of the women surveyed had experienced male stranger harassment in public. In 2013, an online study found that of the 350 respondents who were interviewed in Ottawa, 97% said that they had experienced street harassment in the previous year. Eighty-four percent of the respondents identified as women and 54% as LGBT (Hollaback, 2013b).

In Guatemala, more than one-third of the 1500 complaints received annually by the Association of Urban and Suburban Transport Users are abuses against passengers involving sexual harassment of girls and women. Men often groped their victims, verbally abused them, and even raped them (Valladares, 2011).

Europe

In a poll conducted by the End Violence Against Women (EVAW) Coalition in London, 43% of young women ages 18–34 had experienced street harassment during the year prior to the survey. The sample size was 1047 adults, and the poll was conducted in early March 2012 (End Violence Against Women, 2012).

In Poland, an informal online survey of 818 respondents found that 85% of female respondents had experienced street harassment in public spaces (49% more than once), compared to 44% of men. The study indicated that public harassment occurred in the street, on public transportation, and during mass events (such as at concerts and in pubs). They experienced more nonverbal harassment than verbal harassment (Roszak and Gober, 2012). In Croatia, an informal survey of 500 people found that 99% of the women had experienced some form of street harassment in their lifetime, and 50% experienced it at the age of 18 years old (Hollaback, 2012). In Istanbul, Turkey, street harassment is one of the most pervasive forms of gender-based violence. A study in Istanbul revealed that 69% of the respondents experienced street harassment regularly on a monthly basis. The most common forms of harassment included leering (75%), being honked at (60%), being whistled at (59%), having kissing noises directed at them (48%), and being sexually touched or groped (46%) (Hunter, 2011). Researchers from the National Institute of Statistics and Economics Studies in France found in a 2013 study that 25% of women aged 18–29 were afraid when they walked on the streets. Results from this study also indicated that 1 in 5 women had experienced verbal harassment on the street in the previous year, and 1 in 10 reported being kissed or caressed against their consent (Plank, 2013). In Belgium, a student filmmaker decided to secretly record her harassers and interview the men who took part in this behavior and the women who had experienced it. Her documentary, entitled *Femme de la Rue*, portrayed vivid and blatant firsthand accounts of street harassment in Belgium. Although the film was criticized for its focus mostly on immigrant men, it did highlight how common and pervasive street harassment in Belgium is. It identified the level of street harassment in Brussels, which included leers, catcalls, sexual propositions, and name calling, such as "whore," "slut," and "bitch" (Guardian, 2012; Charalambous, 2012).

Asia

In many Asian countries, street harassment is very prevalent. Street harassment is commonly known in India as eve teasing, and is almost an everyday problem in the major cities in India. While walking to college, traveling by bus, or shopping in a crowded place, women are targeted by eve teasers. According to Sharma et al. (2013), women often face daily aggressive sexual harassment in India, in public, ranging from catcalls on the streets, to groping and touching on public transport, to rape. While a few women do retaliate by filing a complaint with the police, most of the young girls tend to take lewd comments in their stride, as they believe there is little choice. One of the most serious forms of street harassment took place on December 16, 2012. On that day, a woman was attacked on a bus while she was traveling home from a visit to the cinema. She was beaten with metal bars and gang raped for an hour. She died from her injuries two weeks later (BBC News, 2012).

In 2010, a study of 828 salaried employees in a city in Korea found that 43% experienced harassment during their commute—on the subways, buses, and taxis. Of these, 79% were women (Lee, 2010). In Tokyo, Japan, groping on trains, subways, and transit stations is rampant. In 2008 in Tokyo, for example, there were 2000 reported groping cases (Fukada, 2009). In a 2004 survey of 632 women who traveled during rush hour in Tokyo, nearly 64% of the women in their twenties and thirties said they were groped while commuting (ABC News, 2005). A study of 200 youth in Gujranwala, Pakistan, revealed that 96% of the girls experienced street harassment (Bargad, 2005). Likewise, a 2002 survey of 200 citizens in Beijing, China, showed that 70% had been subjected to a form of sexual harassment, mainly on public transportation (Shanghi Star, 2002).

Middle East

The United Nations Entity for Gender Equality and the Empowerment of Women reported in 2013 that 99% of Egyptian women had experienced some form of street harassment. Almost 96% of women in the survey reported some form of touching, while 96% reported experiencing verbal sexual harassment (Daily News, 2013). In a 2008 study by the Egyptian Centre for Women's Rights, 83% of Egyptian women and 98% of foreign women reported being sexually harassed in several ways, including verbal abuse, stalking, groping, and indecent exposure. About 62% of Egyptian men admitted to perpetrating street harassment (Abdelhadi, 2008; Johnston, 2008). Ebaid (2013) reported that sexual harassment is commonplace on the streets of Cairo. Women reported that the sexual harassment on the street is inescapable, and a large percentage of the male population who harass women are repeat offenders. It appears that the number of sexual harassment cases increases during the summer, when there are more tourists and Gulf Arabs looking for excitement in Cairo.

The *Yemen Times* conducted a survey on teasing and sexual harassment and found that 95% of the women interviewed said their mobility was restricted because of fear of male harassment in public places, and 82% said the bus is the most unsafe mode of public transportation for them because of male harassers (Saeed and Al-Sakkaf, 2009). A study in Israel revealed that in Tel Aviv, 83% of Tel Aviv women reported being sexually harassed at least once in their lifetime. The highest incidence of harassment was against women aged 22–39 years old. The common forms of harassment included whistling on the street (64%), cars beeping horns (61%), unpleasant looks (45%), and suggestive remarks (40%) (Ilan, 2011).

Responses to Street Harassment

Legal Responses

There are very few countries that have legislation that addresses street harassment. In 2012, Sophie Peeters, a student at the Haute École Rits in Brussels, produced a documentary on street harassment in Brussels (Guardian, 2012; Charalambous, 2012). The showing of the documentary prompted the government of Belgium to introduce a new law that criminalizes harassment on the streets. This law makes it an offense to make a gesture or statement that is intended to express contempt for others on the basis of their gender or to make them feel inferior or that constitutes a serious attack on their dignity (Elphick, 2014). The new legislation in Belgium has given women the opportunity to fight street harassment, legally.

Recently, France passed a new sexual harassment law because the existing sexual harassment law was found to be unconstitutional on the grounds that it was too vague. The new law addresses sexual harassment inside and outside the workplace. Some female politicians have also complained about sexism in Parliament. Notably, on July 17, 2012, just days before the vote on the new sexual harassment bill, male lawmakers in the National Assembly hooted and made catcalls, whistles, and jeers because Housing Minister Cécile Duflot wore a floral dress (de la Baume, 2012).

Recently, Egypt introduced a drafted law against sexual harassment. The draft law defines a sexual harasser as someone who "accosts others in a public or private place through following or stalking them, using gestures or words or through modern means of communication or in any other means through actions that carry sexual or pornographic hints" (Mezzofiore, 2014, par. 4). The punishment includes imprisonment for at least one year, a fine of between LE 10,000 (£853) and LE 20,000 (£1,707), or both. This draft was approved after a female student was sexually harassed by a group of male students from Cairo University. A university dean blamed the victim's attire for the attack (Mezzofiore, 2014).

Although Indian law does not use the term *eve teasing*, it can be used to prosecute offenders of street harassment. Section 298(A) and (B) of the Indian Penal Code (IPC) sentences a person who makes obscene gestures, remarks, songs, or recitation to a maximum jail sentence of three months, a fine, or both. Under Section 509 of the IPC, indecent language, negative comments, and obscene gestures are punishable with simple imprisonment for a term that may extend to one year, a fine, or both. However, because of the complexity of the law, these provisions, and the proof that is required to get a conviction, many of the alleged offenders are never punished (Ahmad, 2011).

In Yemen, there is no specific law penalizing sexual harassment. However, there is a law penalizing "offending acts in public." Article 273, for example, of the Yemeni Penal Code criminalizes "any act which offends public morality or honor, exposes private areas or involves speaking indecently." In Article 274, for example, the punishment is imprisonment not exceeding six months or a fine for anyone committing an offending act. Because there is no clear definition as to what constitutes offending public morality, it is difficult to arrest street harassers in Yemen (Al-Absi, 2012).

The United States has laws against sexual harassment in the workplace and in schools, but there is no law in the United States specifically against street harassment. Because of the First Amendment and free speech rights in the United States, it is difficult to regulate verbal harassment, the most common form of street harassment. However, when the behavior crosses into a physical act, such as rape or sexual assault, perpetrators are subjected to criminal charges. In fact, it does appear that very few developed countries have legislation against gender-based street harassment.

Patrols

In 2008, Boston started a "grope patrol" designed to halt sexual harassment on the subways. This program consisted of undercover police officers who rode the trains with the intention of identifying inappropriate sexual behavior or touching on the trains. In addition, the city posted posters and signs urging victims to report their victimization (Cowles, 2008). In 2012, volunteers assisted the police in Egypt by patrolling the streets and subway stations, watching out for harassers. They assisted police with the arrests of several harassers each day (Kearl, 2012). India also created a women's patrol to patrol the main streets in Delhi in order to provide security for women as they traveled the city (*Times of India*, 2016).

Women-Only Transportation

There have been several responses to gender-based street harassment. In order to ensure women's security on public transportation, many countries have implemented transportation alternatives for women. One response is to provide women-only transportation, which is a service dedicated to providing safe transport for women because of the threat to their safety on the streets.

In cities in Brazil, Egypt, Indonesia, Mexico, Indonesia, and other countries, women-only rapid-transit and commuter-rail cars have been introduced as a way to counter groping and sexual harassment. In 2000, Japan restored its women-only trains to prevent women from being groped or subjected to other forms of abuse in public. Typically, one car per train is designated for the exclusive use of women. Some of these trains operate during rush hours, and others throughout the day or during rapid-service trains. Platforms and train doors are marked with signs indicating boarding areas for the cars, and the days and times when the cars are women only (Krieger, 2012).

Some cities have launched women-only buses to address the problem of street harassment (Dunckel-Graglia, 2013). Guatemala City's mass transit system started a pilot program on June 14, 2011, with several "For Women Only" buses that run from 6:00 to 7:30 a.m. and 5:30 to 7:00 p.m. Boys under the age of 12 years are allowed to ride the buses, and the only other males are the drivers. The new system has won over a large number of Guatemalan women (Valladares, 2011). Other countries, such as Pakistan (Khalid, 2014), India (Jaisinghani, 2013), Mexico (USA Today, 2008), and Brazil (Associated Press, 2006), have made women-only buses available to their female population.

There are also women-only taxis that can be found in cities in the Middle East, such as Lebanon, Jordon, Dubai, and Egypt (Jerusalem Post, 2010). Women in Mexico and India also have access to women-only taxis (Jean, 2012). In some cities in England, Russia, Australia, Lebanon, Iran, India, and the United Arab Emirates (UAE), there are women-only taxi cabs with women drivers. Most of the women-only taxis in these countries are pink (Kearl, 2009).

There are several problems with women-only transportation. Women-only buses and trains are not offered with enough frequency to allow all women to use them. It is not uncommon for men to still use the women-only train cars. Furthermore, men continue to harass women at railway or subway platforms or bus stops. More importantly, it does not address the root causes of the problem and why men are harassing women in public. Instead, these initiatives segregate women from men to provide them with temporary relief from the harassment, and critics have argued that segregating men and women on public transportation is likely to deepen the division between the genders (Associated Press, 2009). However, based on her research on Mexico City, Dunckel-Graglia (2013, p. 97) has suggested that "women-only transportation will likely reduce gender inequality embedded in the public transit system."

Use of Technology

Victims of street harassment have been utilizing social media to report street harassment. In an attempt to empower themselves, women in Egypt and elsewhere are using the HarassMap, which is an online service that enables women to report their experiences of harassment via Short Message Service (SMS). It is a volunteer-based, independent initiative that was launched in 2010. It combines online and SMS (6069) reporting and a mapping system. The main goal of HarassMap is to change the environment on the streets. It includes four main components. First, the women who are harassed on the streets are encouraged to send an anonymous text message or log onto the HarassMap website to report their experience. Second, HarassMap then sends automated information to each victim about how to access free services, such as filing a police report, getting legal aid or psychological help, or taking a self-defense class. Third, volunteers review reports and sort them into categories, such as "indecent exposure," "sexual invites," "stalking or following," "catcalls," or "groping." Finally, HarassMap then maps each incident online, collates the messages, and provides evidence that harassment did place and where it took place. The information is shared with women, organizations, and the police so that they can make the streets safer (Tavaana, 2014; Sharkey, 2013). In general, HarassMap allows victims to immediately report an experience of street harassment. The incident and its location are added to a map, which then shows problem hotspots. Women can check the map to avoid the areas. In the United States, victims are encouraged to send their stories to Hollaback, which uses these stories to identify on maps where the hotspots for harassment exist in the United States. In addition, victims are encouraged to take photographs of the perpetrators, which can then be disseminated (Hollaback, 2014; Cowles, 2008).

Activism

One attempt to address street harassment is to raise public awareness. As a result, there is a great deal of activism against street harassment across the globe. According to Reid and May (2010, p. xii), "street-harassment activism is at a tipping point. Over the past five years, we have watched as the issue moved from obscurity to urgency."

Hollaback is an international organization that exists in more than 79 cities and 26 countries and operates in 12 languages. As of June 2010, several other active branches of Hollaback exist in the United States and cities in England, Germany, France, Israel, Mexico, and India. The organization was founded by seven New York City residents in reaction to a well-publicized event in August 2005, when a man was photographed masturbating on the New York City Subway. It is dedicated to fighting street harassment by creating a global movement. It also provides a platform for victims to tell their stories. Hollaback has a number of local chapters around the world, and it holds many events, such as demonstrations, lectures, and film screenings, designed to raise awareness about street harassment. The organization has also created a street theater working group that performs songs, chants, and skits about street harassment (Hollaback, 2014). Stop Street Harassment (SSH) is a nonprofit organization that documents gender-based street harassment worldwide. It started as a blog in 2008 and slowly grew and became incorporated as a nonprofit organization in 2012 (Stop Street Harassment, 2014). Its website provides information about street harassment, including statistics, strategies to deal with street harassers, and the laws that can address street harassment. Individuals from more than 30 countries have submitted their street harassment stories to SSH (Stop Street Harassment, 2014).

On March 20, 2011, the first International Anti-Street Harassment Day was launched. In 2012, it was expanded into a week, and more than 20 countries and tens of thousands participated in the week. In 2014, it took place from March 30 to April 5 and involved rallies, marches, workshops, tweet chats, street theaters, and chalk walks and the use of fliers and posters to bring attention to street harassment (Stop Street Harassment, 2014). SlutWalk is an international movement of protest marches that began on April 3, 2011, in Toronto, Ontario. Since then, it has been occurring globally. Participants protest against street harassment, rape, and other forms of sexual violence. The activities include speakers, workshops, live music, sign-making sessions, leafleting, dances, martial arts, and receptions (Stampler, 2011).

There are also films and documentaries about street harassment. *War Zone* (1998) is based on women's experiences in New York City, San Francisco, New Orleans, Minneapolis, and Chicago and highlights men harassing women. In 2002, it was used by the U.S. Department of Defense as an educational tool to teach members of the military. In 2007, Tracey Rose created a short documentary entitled *Black Women Walking*, which was the result of interviews with women of color about street harassment. The documentary tried to examine street harassment from the perspective of women of color. Through personal stories of women interviewed, the documentary explored how the intersection of race and gender manifests into street harassment of black women (Rose, 2007).

Prevention

One major strategy to prevent street harassment is to teach men to respect women. This will require teaching them "healthy definitions of masculinity" (Kearl, 2010, p. 135). Organizations like Men Can Stop Rape, the Coaching Boys into Men program, and the global Man Up Campaign all focus on healthy definitions of masculinity and teach boys and men how to respect themselves—and women (Kearl, 2010). More of these organizations are needed.

Women need to be empowered so that they are not fearful in public places. Ignoring and avoiding street harassers changes nothing. It is disempowering and limiting. Therefore, women need to be taught assertive responses and how to report harassers. They need to be taught how to make harassers accountable for their actions and to avoid self-blame for the harassers' actions.

In general society trivializes street or public harassment of women by dismissing it as complimentary or minor. Society, therefore, allows street harassment to occur. This behavior is perpetuated by the media and policies that disrespect and discriminate against women. This needs to change. All forms of gender-based violence and harassment must be challenged because they are all interrelated. Society, therefore, needs to create a culture of intolerance for street harassment in order to eliminate the behavior.

More academic research is needed to determine the extent of this problem in order to control and prevent it. It is important, for example, to understand how the intersectionality of class, race and ethnicity, and sexual orientation affects victims of gender-based street harassment. Studies are needed to examine the nature and extent of street harassment in developed and underdeveloped countries. The effects of street harassment on victims should also be an issue for future research.

Conclusion

Gender-based street harassment is a manifestation of the gender inequality in many societies. It is a symptom of a greater problem in society. It is part of the continuum of violence against women that has been reinforced and sanctioned by many people and institutions in society that ignore, accept, and applaud this behavior. It often restricts a victim's mobility and her full participation in public life. A change in attitudes, policies, and institutions is vital in controlling and preventing gender-based street harassment. A multifaceted, multidimensional, comprehensive, and holistic approach is needed to eliminate gender-based street harassment. Women need to feel safe and secure in public places.

References

ABC News. (2005). Japan tries women-only train cars to stop groping. June 10. Retrieved December 5, 2013, from http://abcnews.go.com/GMA/International/story?id=803965.

Abdelhadi, M. (2008). Egypt's sexual harassment 'cancer'. BBC News, July 18. Retrieved December 2, 2015, from http://news.bbc.co.uk/2/hi/middle_east/7514567.stm.

Ahmad, F. (2011). Eve teasing under criminal law. October 23. Retrieved March 2, 2014, from http://aamjanata.com/eve-teasing-under-criminal-law/.

Al-Absi, G. (2012). Who is to blame? Street sexual harassment in Yemen. December 3. Retrieved April 12, 2013, from http://www.opendemocracy.net/5050/ghaidaa-al-absi/who-is-to-blame-street-sexual-harassment-in-yemen.

Associated Press. (2006). Brazil city ready to introduce women-only buses. Retrieved November 10, 2013, from http://www.nbcnews.com/id/15772398/ns/world_news-americas/t/brazil-city-ready-introduce-women-only-buses/#.Vt_ECYS4aLE.

Associated Press. (2009). Mexico's pink taxis cater to fed-up females. October 19. Retrieved November 10, 2013, from http://www.msnbc.msn.com/id/33385984/ns/world_news-americas/t/mexicos-pink-taxis-cater-fed-up-females/#.TqAr7XJltLc.

Bargad. (2005). Research study, street harassment against girls in district Gujranwala. Retrieved November 13, 2013, from http://bargad.org.pk/media/page-downloads/65.pdf.

BBC News. (2012). Shock and outrage over India Delhi bus gang rape. Retrieved June 12, 2013, from http://www.bbc.com/news/world-asia-india-20765320.

Benard, C. and Schlaffer, E. (1996). The man in the street: Why he harasses. In T. A. Verta, N. Whittier, and L. Richardson (eds.), *Feminist Frontiers* IV (pp. 395–397). New York: McGraw-Hill.

Bowman, C. G. (1993). Street harassment and the informal ghettoization of women. *Harvard Law Review*, 106(3), 517–580.

Chan, S. (2008). Subway harassment questionnaire garners a big response. *New York Times*, July.

Charalambous, E. (2012). Whistling, pinching, "sweetheart"—it's all harassment. August 9. Retrieved June 8, 2013, from http://blogs.independent.co.uk/2012/08/09/whistling-pinching-sweetheart-its-all-harassment/.

Cowles, I. (2008). "Grope patrol" in Boston curbs sexual harassment on the subway. May 28. Retrieved April 15, 2013, from http://www.findingdulcinea.com/news/Americas/May-June-08/Grope-Patrol-in-Boston-Curbs-Sexual-Harassment-on-the-Subway.html.

Daily News. (2013). 99.3 percent of Egyptian women experienced sexual harassment: Report. Retrieved November 10, 2013, from http://www.dailynewsegypt.com/2013/04/28/99-3-of-egyptian-women-experienced-sexual-harassment-report/.

Davis, D. (2002). The harm that has no name: Street harassment, embodiment, and African American women. In C. L. Mui and Julien S. Murphy (ed.), *Gender Struggles: Practical Approaches to Contemporary Feminism* (pp. 214–225). Oxford: Rowman & Littlefield Publishers.

de la Baume, M. (2012). France passes a tougher sexual harassment law. *New York Times*. July 31. Retrieved from http://nyti.ms/1f28f35.

Dunckel-Graglia, A. (2013). Women-only transportation: How "pink" public transportation changes public perception of women's mobility. *Journal of Public Transportation*, 16(2), 85–105.

Ebaid, N. (2013). Sexual harassment in Egypt: A neglected crime: An assessment for the Egyptian Government performance in regard to the sexual harassment in Egypt. Retrieved from http://www.culturaldiplomacy.org/academy/content/pdf/participant-papers/2013-05-iscd-hr/Neama_Ebaid.pdf.

Elphick, N. (2014). Belgium to ban sexist comments. March 17. Retrieved June 15, 2014, from http://www.dailylife.com.au/news-and-views/news-features/belgium-to-ban-sexist-comments-20140317-34w68.html.

End Violence Against Women. (2012). 4 in 10 young women in London sexually harassed over last year. May 25. Retrieved from http://www.endviolenceagainstwomen.org.uk/news/20/4-in-10-young-women-in-london-sexually-harassed-over-last-year.

Fairchild, K. (2010). Context effects on women's perceptions of stranger harassment. *Sexuality & Culture*, 14(3), 191–216.
Fairchild, K., and Rudman, L. A. (2008). Everyday stranger harassment and women's self-objectification. *Social Justice Research*, 21(3), 338–357.
Fukada, T. (2009). In anonymous packed train lurk gropers. *Japan Times*, August 18.
Gardner C. B. (1980). Passing by: Street remarks, address rights and the urban female. *Sociological Inquiry*, 50, 328–356.
Gardner, C. B. (1995). *Passing By: Gender and Public Harassment*. Los Angeles: University of California Press.
Guardian. (2012). Belgium film on street harassment strikes a chord across Europe. Retrieved from http://www.theguardian.com/world/2012/aug/03/belgium-film-street-harassment-sofie-peeters.
Hollaback. (2012). Croatia: Street harassment survey 2012. Retrieved from http://www.ihollaback.org/wp-content/uploads/2012/06/Hollaback-Croatia_Online-street-harassment-survey.pdf.
Hollaback. (2013a). State of the streets 2013: A report on street harassment in Boston. Retrieved from http://www.scribd.com/doc/171930576/State-of-the-Streets-2013.
Hollaback. (2013b). Study finds street harassment common in Ottawa. Retrieved March 11, 2015, from http://dailyxtra.com/ottawa/news/study-finds-street-harassment-common-in-ottawa.
Hollaback. (2014). Hollaback. Retrieved from http://www.ihollaback.org/about/.
Hunter, M. (2011). Street harassment in Istanbul. Retrieved from http://www.ihollaback.org/wp-content/uploads/2012/06/Street-harassment-in-Istanbul.pdf.
Ilan, L. (2011). Vast majority of Tel Aviv women report sexual harassment, survey finds. *Haaretz*, November 23. Retrieved from http://www.haaretz.com/print-edition/news/vast-majority-of-tel-aviv-women-report-sexual-harassment-survey-finds-1.397163.
Jaisinghani, B. (2013). 'Women only' buses to make commuting safer. *Times of India*. Retrieved from http://timesofindia.indiatimes.com/india/Women-Only-buses-to-make-commuting-safer/articleshow/18336991.cms.
Jean, L. (2012). Pink women only taxis. Retrieved from http://trndmonitor.com/pink-women-only-taxis.
Jerusalem Post. (2010). Women only taxis. January 3. Retrieved from http://womenofhistory.blogspot.com/2010/01/women-only-taxis.html.
Johnston, C. (2008). Two-thirds of Egyptian men harass women? July 17. Retrieved from www.irfi.org/articles2/articles_3801_3850/two-thirds%20of%20egyptian%20men%20harass%20womenhtml.htm.
Kearl, H. (2009). Women run taxi in Beirut. Stop Street Harassment. Retrieved from http://www.stopstreetharassment.org/2009/07/women-run-taxi-service-in-beirut.
Kearl, H. (2010). *Stop Street Harassment: Making Public Places Safe and Welcoming for Women*. Santa Barbara, CA: Praeger.
Kearl, H. (2012). Patrol against harassment in Egypt. Stop Street Harassment. Retrieved from http://www.stopstreetharassment.org/2012/08/patrols-against-harassment-in-egypt.
Khalid, F. (2014). Women-only bus service 'Tabeer' begins in Pakistan for first time. *News Tribe*, March 8. Retrieved from http://www.thenewstribe.com/2014/03/08/women-only-bus-service-tabeer-begins-in-pakistan-for-first-time.
Krieger, D. (2012). Why women-only transit options have caught on. Retrieved from http://www.theatlanticcities.com/commute/2012/02/why-women-only-transit-options-have-caught/1171.
Larkin, J. (1997). Sexual terrorism on the street: The moulding of young women into subordination. In C. Kitzinger and A. Thomas (eds.), *Constructing Sexual Harassment: Contemporary Feminist Perspectives* (pp. 115–130). Buckingham: Open University Press.
Lee, H. (2010). 4 in 10 salaried workers harassed during commute. *Korea Times*, December 7.
Lenton, R., Smith, M. D., Fox, J., and Morra, N. (1999). Sexual harassment in public places: Experiences of Canadian women. *Canadian Review of Sociology and Anthropology*, 36(4), 517–540.

Lord, T. L. (2009). The relationship of gender-based public harassment to body image, self-esteem, and avoidance behavior. Doctoral dissertation, Indian University of Pennsylvania, Pennsylvania. Retrieved from *Dissertations & Theses: Full Text* (Publication No. AAT 3369986). URI: http://hdl.handle.net/2069/186.

Macmillan, R., Nierobisz, A., and Welsh, S. (2000). Experiencing the streets: Harassment and perceptions of safety among women. *Journal of Research in Crime and Delinquency*, 37(3), 306–322.

McKelle, E. (2013). USA: Why sexism causes street harassment. Stop Street Harassment. Retrieved from http://www.stopstreetharassment.org/2013/04/sexism.

Mezzofiore, G. (2014). Egypt set to approve law on sexual harassment. April 10. Retrieved October 30, 2013, from http://www.ibtimes.co.uk/egypt-set-approve-law-sexual-harassment-1444153.

Nielsen, L. B. (2004). *License to Harass: Law, Hierarchy, and Offensive Public Speech*. Princeton, NJ: Princeton University Press.

Plank, E. (2013). 1 in 4 French women are afraid on the street due to sexual harassment. Retrieved from http://www.policymic.com/articles/32421/1-in-4-french-women-are-afraid-on-the-street-due-to-sexual-harassment.

Reid, O., and May, E. (2010). Foreword. In H. Kearl (ed.), *Stop Street Harassment: Making Places Safe and Welcoming for Women* (pp. xi–xiii). Santa Barbara, CA: Prager.

Rose, T. (2007). *Black Women Walking*. Short documentary. Retrieved from http://theblackgirlsclub.blogspot.in/2013/08/blackpowerisforblackmen-street.html.

Roszak, J., and Gober, G. (2012). Poland has the power to end street harassment: Research on harassment in public spaces in Poland. Retrieved from http://www.ihollaback.org/wp-content/uploads/2012/06/Harassment-in-public-spaces-in-Poland_Roszak-and-Gober1.pdf.

Saeed, A., and Al-Sakkaf, N. (2009). Sexual harassment deters women from outdoor activities. *Yemen Times*. 18 January. Retrieved from http://en.europenews.dk/Sexual-harassment-deters-women-from-outdoor-activities-104448.html.

Shanghi Star. (2002). Harassment rampant on public transportation. April 11. Retrieved March 8, 2014, from http://app1.chinadaily.com.cn/star/2002/0411/cn8-4.html.

Sharkey, J. (2013). A worldwide fight against street harassment. Retrieved January 10, 2014, from http://www.nytimes.com/2013/10/22/business/fighting-harassment-of-women-on-streets-worldwide.html.

Sharma, A., Mukherji, B., and Subramanya, R. (2013). On India's streets, women run a gantlet of harassment. February 27. Retrieved from http://online.wsj.com/news/articles/SB10001424127887324616604578302620513689386.

Stampler, L. (2011). SlutWalks sweep the nation. *Huffington Post*. Retrieved from http://www.huffingtonpost.com/2011/04/20/slutwalk-united-states-city_n_851725.html.

Stop Street Harassment. (2014). *Unsafe and Harassed in Public Spaces: A National Street Harassment Report*. Reston, VA: Stop Street Harassment.

Stringer, S. M. (2007). Hidden in plain sight: Sexual harassment and assault in the New York City Subway System. *New York Times*, July.

Tavaana. (2014). Taking back Egypt's streets: The HarassMap Campaign to end sexual harassment. Retrieved from https://tavaana.org/en/content/taking-back-egypts-streets-harassmap-campaign-end-sexual-harassment.

Times of India. (2016). Women beat marshals to patrol city streets. March 9. Retrieved from http://timesofindia.indiatimes.com/city/nashik/Women-beat-marshals-to-patrol-city-streets/articleshow/51322951.cms.

USA Today. (2008). Mexico City debuts women-only buses. January 24. Retrieved from http://usatoday30.usatoday.com/news/world/2008-01-24-mexicpcity-buses_N.htm.

Valladares, D. (2011). Women-only buses against sexual harassment. Retrieved from http://www.mediawatch.com/?p=420.

War Zone (1998). A film about sex, power, and what happens when men threaten a woman's right to walk undisturbed on the streets. Retrieved from http://www.mediaed.org/cgi-bin/commerce.cgi?preadd=action&key=213.

Wesselmann, E., and Kelly, J. (2010). Cat-calls and culpability: Investigating the frequency and functions of stranger harassment. *Sex Roles*, 63(7/8), 451–462.

Marital Rape
A Socially and Legally Warranted Crime in India

2

AKANSHA SINGH

Contents

Introduction

Marital rape is a wrong that has plagued the life of many women throughout the world, and "just as they are more likely to be blamed, they are more likely to blame themselves" (Russell, 1990, p. 198). Physical and sexual abuse of women has become widely recognized in India, with several legislations providing medicine for the scars inflicted by crimes such as rape, molestation, abduction, and cruelty. The noose has been tightened on these offenders, and the former legal requirements for conviction have been allayed. Reforms have been brought about in the 150-year-old Indian Penal Code (IPC), judicial activism has often rendered landmark judgments for the protection of the rights of women, and legislative intent, social organizations, and mass media have played an active role in bringing about an awareness regarding these issues. But amidst all this social and legal progress, a very heinous crime has percolated through the very fabric of matrimonial relationships and has established itself as a justified act. There is a curious silence surrounding the crime of marital rape or spousal rape. This chapter seeks to throw light on this latent reality, which is eating away at the very core of the institution of marriage, pointing out the lacunae in the laws enshrined in India regarding this issue and suggesting reforms to bring about a change in the society and the legal system.

Marital rape can be defined as any unwanted intercourse or penetration, vaginal, anal, or oral, obtained by force, threat of force, or when the wife is unable to consent (Bergen, 1999, p. 1). David Finkelhor and Kersti Yllo determined three forms of coercion that are generally applied by husbands in the act of marital rape—social coercion, which is the pressure women feel because of cultural expectations or social conventions; interpersonal coercion, which occurs when a husband threatens the wife into having sexual intercourse, but the threats are not violent in nature; and threatened or actual physical coercion, which is at the core of rape (Finkelhor and Yllo, 1985, pp. 37–60). Stereotypes about women and sex continue to be reinforced in our culture through both mainstream and pornographic media. Not just men and society, but also women refuse to give this nonconsensual form of sexual intercourse a name, and refuse to recognize it as a wrong against the individuality of women. It has been grossly overlooked in the country's legal literature on rape and sexual abuse. The social norms have established sexual relations between a husband and wife as an embarrassingly intimate subject. Despite women's progress in India compared to the earlier decades since independence, men still consider women to be their chattel, and the wives let themselves be crushed under this social mindset. This chapter recognizes the need for change.

Situation in Other Countries

It is important to study the situation of marital rape in other countries, before we dwell on the situation of India. There are 76 countries that have made this act a criminal offense, which includes the developed countries of the United States, the United Kingdom, France, Japan, Russia, Australia, and South Africa. India, Indonesia, and Vietnam are the only three nations that treat spousal rape as a form of noncriminal domestic violence. Among the 40 countries that have not yet criminalized marital rape are Afghanistan, Bangladesh, Pakistan, and most of the underdeveloped countries of Africa, like Ethiopia, Kenya, Uganda, and Yemen (Bureau of Democracy, Human Rights, and Labor, U.S. Department of State, 2008).

When it comes to the nations based on the English common law, the major countries of the United Kingdom, Canada, Australia, New Zealand, Hong Kong, and Israel have criminalized marital rape. In England, the judicial view on this issue until around the mid-1990s did not recognize the act as an offense. This was illustrated most vividly by Sir Matthew Hale, in his 1736 legal treatise, *Historia Placitorum Coronæ*, where he wrote that such an act could not be considered a criminal offense of rape since the wife "hath given up herself in this kind unto her husband, which she cannot retract" (Hale, 1800, p. 628). It was not until *R v. Clarence* (1888) that the question of this spousal exemption first arose in an English courtroom, but in this judgment the concept of implied consent was upheld. *R v. Miller* (1954) held that the wife must legally revoke her consent to sexual intercourse for the act to fall under the scope of the criminal offense of rape. However, in the year 1991, the House of Lords in the landmark case of *R v. R* (1992) set aside this marital rights exemption, stating that "the fiction of implied consent has no useful purpose to serve today in the law of rape," and the appellant was convicted for raping his wife.

In the United States too, there has been a gradual change in the law regarding marital rape. The principle of spousal exemption was formally embraced by the American legal system in the year 1857 in the judgment of *Commonwealth v. Fogarty* (1857). Before that time, the spouse was typically exempted from the state sexual assault laws, for reasons rooted in the historical views set forth above. The United States did not begin to criminalize spousal rape until the late 1970s. Women's rights advocates began efforts to change these laws, and by July 5, 1993, marital rape was a crime in all 50 states. The first state to abolish the marital rape exemption was Nebraska in 1976, and the last was North Carolina in 1993.

General Indicators of Women's Equality and Prevalence of Sexual Violence in India

To fully comprehend the inability of women to fight this injustice called marital rape, the issue necessitates the understanding of the condition of women via the general indicators of women's inequality and the prevalence of sexual violence in India. Numerous statistical and social science reports enlighten the masses of the equality, or rather inequality, of the women in India on a social, economic, and legal footing when compared to men. Women are suppressed in all spheres of public and private life. When it comes to violence against women, there will of course be a gap between the number of reported incidents and the number of actual incidents, on account of the several reasons that inhibit women from dragging the offenders to court, which will be discussed at a later stage in this chapter.

India's sex ratio is 940 females per 1000 males (Census Organization of India, 2011). The Central Statistics Office's publication (2011, pp. 21, 25, 26) lays down these statistics about women in India, which act as general indicators of the well-being, progress, and overall social and economic health of the fairer sex. India ranked 114 in 2009 among 178 countries in terms of the Gender Development Index. The mean age at marriage was observed to be 20.7 years for females in India. The female mortality rate in the age group 0–4 years is 16.1. Women are underrepresented in governance and decision-making positions. At present, women occupy less than 8% of the Cabinet positions and less than 9% of seats in high courts and the Supreme Court, and less than 12% of administrators and managers are women. Delivery at a health facility is an indicator of programmatic effort for safe motherhood. It is observed that only 47% deliveries took place at a health facility in India (Ministry of Health and Family Welfare, 2006, p. 68). According to National Family Health Survey–III, in the rural sector currently married women make 26% of the decisions regarding obtaining health care for themselves, and 7.6% in the case of purchasing major household items. Ten percent of the decisions are made by females with respect to visiting their family or relatives. For urban areas, these figures are 29.7%, 10.4%, and 12.2%, respectively (Ministry of Health and Family Welfare, 2006, pp. 83–94).

When we study the statistics of violent crimes against women in the country, we see a staggering trend. According to the National Crime Records Bureau's report (2011), 10.38% of the total crimes against women (which would include everything from cruelty to kidnapping, molestation, sexual harassment, and immoral trafficking) reported in the year 2010 were incidents of rape. The rape victims were mainly between the ages of 18 and 30, followed by the age group of 30–50, with 2.5% being under the age of 10. Around 43% of the victims were minors. In 7.5% of the cases, the offenders were related to the rape victims. Moving on from rape, 19.01% of the total number of reported crimes against women are incidents of molestation, and 44.02% of the total crimes against women fall under the category of cruelty by husband and relatives, indicating a disturbing amount of abuse of women in the private spheres of their homes. Only 1 in 69 cases of rape gets reported in India (Mathias, 2008). No statistics or data have been gathered specifically on the problem of marital rape in India, pointing at the lack of consciousness regarding this issue. The only relevant statistics on spousal rape have been provided by the research conducted by

Finkelhor and Yllo (1985) and Russell (1990) in the United States. Ten to fourteen percent of ever-married women have experienced at least one forced sexual assault by a husband or ex-husband. Studies of battered women staying in shelters and women seeking relationship help show that one-third to three-quarters of those asked reported sexual assaults by their husbands or intimate partners. Most of the women reported being raped on more than one occasion, and one-third of the women under study reported being raped more than 20 times over the course of their relationship.

Legal Framework for Addressing Marital Rape

Marital rape is not a recognized offense in India. The exception to Section 375 in the IPC, 1860, clearly states that "sexual intercourse by a man with his own wife, the wife not being under fifteen years of age, is not rape." This is referred to as "spousal exemption." This means that nonconsensual sexual intercourse with a wife, when the wife is above the age of 15, is not a criminal offense and the husband cannot be prosecuted for such an act, even if the intercourse was without her consent or against her will, which are two of the qualifying conditions for the offense of rape under the aforementioned section in the cases not involving a married woman under the age of 15. This is a blatant violation of a married woman's human rights. She is thus expected not only by society, but also by the legal system to renounce her right to refuse and let herself be at the mercy of her husband's sexual advances.

We must then study the punishment for rape under the various circumstances mentioned in Section 376 of the IPC. The offense of rape is punishable by imprisonment for a minimum of 7 years to a maximum of life, along with a fine. Marital rape is punishable only if the wife is below the age of 15. The law makes no exemption for the rape of a woman under the age of 12, whether she is a wife or not, and provides for a rigorous imprisonment ranging from 10 years to life. If the wife is between the ages of 12 and 15, the offender is mildly punishable with an imprisonment up to 2 years or with a fine or both. There is no imprisonment or fine for the rape of a wife above the age of 15, and the aggrieved wife cannot bring the husband to justice for the commission of this heinous act.

Section 376A of the IPC is another provision to be considered. This section criminalizes the rape of a wife during the period when the married couple has been separated by a judicial decree or under any custom or usage. The husband for the commission of this act shall be punishable with imprisonment, which may extend to two years, or with a fine, or both. This has been included in the Criminal Law Amendment Act of 1983 as a piece of advancement toward the goal of protection of women from sexual assaults, and is indeed a beneficial legislation for married women. But the fact that the amendment was effected to protect the sexual respect of only wives who are undergoing judicial separation and not to punish the rape of married women in general is reflective of the social mindset that wives cannot deny their husbands the fulfillment of their sexual urges if they are cohabiting and will remain a blight on the intention of the legislature, casting a shadow on the conviction of the lawmaking body to protect the married women of India.

Section 498A of the IPC criminalizes the subjection of a woman to cruelty by her husband or relatives of the husband. The relevant explanation of the section defines cruelty as conduct that is likely to drive the woman to commit suicide or to cause grave injury or danger to her life, limb, or health. This section thus protects the wife from the insistence of the husband on perverse sexual conduct and excessive and unreasonable demands of sexual intercourse (Mathur, 1996, p. 29). The wife can also seek divorce on this ground. But it still does not explicitly include marital rape in its scope of application. Moreover, the punishment laid down is mere imprisonment for up to three years, along with a fine.

Further, the occurrence of marital rape during cohabitation is not grounds for divorce. Section 13 of the Hindu Marriage Act of 1955, Section 27 of the Special Marriage Act of 1954, and Section 10 of the Indian Divorce Act of 1869 lay down the grounds based on which the wife can present a petition for divorce in the relevant court of law, cruelty being one of them. It is true that marital rape can come under the scope of cruelty if it has been accompanied by physical abuse, but if the case involved rape by the husband wherein the consent was obtained by the threat of hurt, which in a nonmarital relationship has been held to be the commission of rape (*Rahul Pundalik Birahade v. State of Maharashtra*, 2000), then the wife cannot seek divorce.

A relevant legislation to be considered is the Protection of Women from Domestic Violence Act 2005 (hereinafter referred to as the Domestic Violence Act). The act, which aimed to bring about a revolution in the gender laws, proved to be a disappointment to the issue of marital rape. It provides civil remedies to the offense of cruelty. It lays down the duties of the government, protection officers, shelter homes, police officers, and so forth. The act, according to Section 3, covers marital rape only under the circumstances of life-threatening or grievously hurtful conduct. So if the nonconsensual sexual intercourse is not accompanied by such behavior, the wife cannot seek any relief under this act. Moreover, by providing only civil remedies, it does not criminalize the offense.

Judicial Treatment of Marital Rape

There are not any cases dealing directly with marital rape in India. But a study of the judgments on rape given by the Supreme Court and high courts is important to understand the judicial perspective on the offense of rape and how it is the violation of a woman's right to sexual privacy. In the case of *Vikram Singh v. State of Haryana* (2003), which was a case of gang rape wherein the husband was also involved, the Punjab and Haryana High Court punished the husband with life imprisonment and a fine of Rs. 5000. The court stated that "a rapist not only violates the victim's privacy but also her personal integrity and such persons do not deserve any sympathy of law or society. The honour of a woman has to be protected." The Supreme Court in *Bodhisattwa Gautam v. Subhra Chakraborty* (1996) held that rape is the violation of a woman's right to life, which includes the right to live with human dignity. Every woman is entitled to sexual privacy, and it was not open to any and every person to violate her privacy when he wished (*Maharashtra v. Madhukar Narayan*, 1991). The spousal exemption from the offense of rape gives credibility to male superiority and transforms the marital bond into an ungoverned, arbitrary sphere where the state cannot interfere to bring about equality and justice (West, 1990, p. 71). In the case of *Rafiq v. State of Uttar Pradesh* (1980), it was held that "when a woman is ravished, what is inflicted is not mere physical injury but the deep sense of some deathless shame. The judicial response to human rights cannot be blunted by legal bigotry." The contention of this chapter is in conformity with the above judgments.

Social Reasons for Underreporting

There are a number of social reasons for the underreporting of the occurrences of marital rape by wives. Women themselves are afraid to raise the issue of the sexual violation of their bodies by their husbands because of the social stigma attached to it. The fear that society will look down upon her and her family prevents the wife from approaching the police for protection and the judiciary for redressal. Another factor is the concern that the issue of marital rape would adversely affect the fragile minds of children and impress upon them a negative concept of marriage and family values, leading to their social retardation and alienation. In most cases where the wife is financially dependent on her husband, there is a constant pressure from him and his family members upon the wife to not report the occurrence of such an incident, generally accompanied with threats of violence and the withdrawal of financial sustenance (Russell, 1990, p. 220). The mindset of the traditional Indian society that stresses implied consent, that is, the bond of marriage comes with an irrevocable consent on the part of the woman regarding sexual intercourse, instilled within the wife extinguishes the wife's knowledge of her right to resistance. This societal demand of submissiveness, along with the general taboo in the Indian social order regarding the discussion of marital sexual relations in the public sphere, makes it very difficult for the wife to fight for her physical rights, and hence the number of reported incidents of marital rape is less than it should be.

Arguments for Criminalization

There are nine commonly argued points in favor of the criminalization of marital rape. The first is the physical effect of the act on abused wives. The physical effects of marital rape generally include injuries to the vaginal and anal areas, bruising, soreness, torn muscles, fatigue, lacerations, and vomiting (Bergen, 1999, p. 5). Women who have been assaulted and raped by their husbands may suffer broken bones, black eyes, bloody noses, and knife wounds that occur during the sexual violence. Campbell and Alford (1989, p. 947) report that one-half of the marital rape survivors in their research sample were kicked, hit, or burned during the sexual acts. Second, spousal rape causes great emotional distress to the victim, which persists for a long period of time. Long-term effects often include disordered eating, sleep problems, depression, problems establishing trusting relationships, and increased negative feelings about themselves. Some marital rape victims undergo flashbacks, sexual dysfunction, and emotional pain for years after the incidents (Bergen, 1998, p. 153). Some of the short-term effects of marital rape include shock, depression, fear, suicidal tendencies, and posttraumatic stress disorder (Kilpatrick et al., 1988, pp. 335–344). Compared to women raped by strangers, wives who have been raped by their husbands report even higher rates of anger and depression (Koss et al., 1988, pp. 1–24).

The third argument is that there are certain anomalies in the IPC regarding the act of marital rape. Sexual intercourse with a woman under the age of 16 is statutory rape according to the clause sixthly of Section 375 of the IPC. And if the woman is above the age of 15 and married, then sexual intercourse between her and her husband will not be rape, according to the exception provided in the same section. But, if the woman is between the ages of 15 and 16, and her husband has sexual intercourse with her, be it with or against her will and consent, it will not amount to rape under any circumstance. This is an anomaly and it goes against the statutory rape provision enacted to protect young girls, the only reasoning being that the girl is married to her rapist. There is another anomaly in this provision. The legal age for marriage for women has been provided as 18 by the Child Marriage Restraint Act of 1929. This was enacted to protect the rights of young women under the age of 18. The commentary to this legislation states that "the object is to eliminate the special evil which had the potentialities of dangers to the life and health of a female child, who could not withstand the stress and strains of married life and to avoid early deaths of such minor mothers." But Section 375 of the IPC protects the right to sexual privacy of wives only until the age of 15. Thus, there is a very large bracket from 15 to 18 whose basic rights to life and health and reproductive freedom are being violated by this provision. There is a third anomaly in the law on rape, provided in Section 376 of the IPC, which provides for punishment for the offense of rape. Here, the punishment for the rape of the wife between the ages of 12 and 15 is imprisonment for a maximum term of two years, or fine, or both. Section 375 clearly excludes wives above the age of 15 from the ambit of rape. But, when it comes to determining the punishment, the wives under the age of 15, but above 12, get less justice than rape victims outside the wedlock or raped wives below the age of 12.

Fourth, Section 376A of the IPC protects wives from marital rape only if they have been judicially separated, and not if they have been living separately upon their own volition, even if for a long period of time. Fifth, Section 122 of the Indian Evidence Act of 1872 prevents communication during marriage from being disclosed in court unless one spouse is being prosecuted for a crime against the other. So this provision will provide for the disclosure of marital communications only in criminal cases, like cruelty and battery. The Domestic Violence Act provides for civil remedies for the sexual abuse of wives, and the communication, though relevant, would be inadmissible in a proceeding under this act. Hence, it is impossible to combine the Domestic Violence Act and the aforementioned section, unless marital rape is criminalized.

The sixth argument is on the basis of Article 21 of the Constitution of India, which provides for the fundamental right to life. The Supreme Court has in its judgments extended the scope of this right to life to the right to live with dignity (*Francis Coralie Mullin v. Administrator, Union Territory of Delhi*, 1981) and the right to health (*CERC v. Union of India*, 1995). Marital rape as discussed above violates these two fundamental rights of the wife. Seventh, Article 14 of the Constitution provides for equal protection of the law to each and every citizen of the country. Again, the noncriminalization of marital rape goes against this fundamental right, by legally differentiating between women who have been raped on the basis of the marital relation between the victim and the abuser. The eighth argument is that the international community has recognized the married woman's right to sexual privacy. The position of other countries on the issue of marital rape has already been discussed. The United Nations Declaration of Elimination of Violence against Women affirms that "violence against women constitutes a violation of the rights and fundamental freedoms of women and impairs or nullifies their enjoyment of those rights and freedoms, and concerned about the long-standing failure to protect and promote those rights and freedoms in the case of violence against women," and in Article 2 explicitly includes marital rape within the scope of physical, sexual, and psychological violence occurring in the family, which the article recognizes as violence against women. The Supreme Court has held that the international covenants and declarations as adopted by the United Nations have to be respected and regard must be had for them for construing domestic law (*Vishaka & Ors v. State of Rajasthan*, 1997). The meaning given to the words in the declarations and covenants has to be such that it would help in effective implementation. And lastly, if a wife refuses to have sexual intercourse with her husband over a long period of time, causing mental and emotional distress, the husband can seek divorce on this basis (*Samar Ghosh v. Jaya Ghosh*, 2007), and there is no justification for the husband forcing his wife to resume sexual relations against her will.

Arguments against Criminalization

There are some common arguments against the criminalization of marital rape in India that are generally put forth by family rights activists. The primary opposition is the idea that spousal sexual relations fall under the private sphere, and the revocation of the implied consent associated with the traditional concept of marriage by legislation or judicial activism would be an excessive interference with marital rights, and hence would corrode the fabric of marriage. This feminist demand of the woman's right to refuse sexual intercourse post marriage is often hailed as the violation of the procreation and conjugal rights of the husband. Another argument is that such a law will become an unfair weapon in the hands of the wife who can pin false charges of rape against the husband. Marital rape is said to be difficult to disprove on account of continued sexual relations and the often lack of bruises due to passive consent. The criminalizing law can then be misused by discontented wives wanting to hurt the social standing and the general well-being of the husband. The third rationale provided is that marriage stands for the coalition of the identities of the husband and wife. The wife belongs to the husband and the husband belongs to the wife, and hence the state cannot take any penal action against any sexual act of either spouse against the other.

Rebuttal to the Above

There is a rebuttal to each of the aforementioned arguments. First, the concept of marriage has been changed in India by amendments to our existing laws by the legislature and the judiciary. Concepts like judicial separation, divorce, divorce based on the irreparable breakdown of marriage, legal age for marriage as 18 for girls and 21 for boys, punishment for bigamy, maintenance provision for the spouse after divorce, and the recognition of rape during judicial separation have molded the traditional Indian concept of marriage into a modern, more liberal form followed by the progressive countries of the world. Hale's statement in *Historia Placitorum Coronæ* upholding the idea of marital exemption from the criminal offense of rape was overruled by the English judiciary in 1991, establishing lucidly in common law that the wife is not a chattel of the husband. Spousal rape itself has destroyed the sanctity of the marriage bond by violating the wife's right to her body. Marriage does not require the woman to sacrifice her human rights at the altar. Coercion of the wife into having sexual intercourse is in contravention with the basic principles of fundamental right to life. Second, regarding the abuse of the criminalization of marital rape, the primary rebuttal is that each and every law comes with the scope of being misused by the ones who can, but that does not mean that the law should not be passed. If there are no laws to check the actions of the people and penalize them for their wrongs, this would send society as we know it spiraling down into the state of nature where, in

Thomas Hobbes's words, life is "solitary, poor, nasty, brutish and short" (Hobbes, 2010, p. 126). If we take the example of Sections 354 (assault or criminal force to a woman with the intent to outrage her modesty) and 509 (word, gesture, or act intended to insult the modesty of a woman) of the IPC, which are concerned with sexual harassment, women can definitely misuse these provisions by registering false complaints, but there are numerous cases (*Rupan Deol Bajaj v. Kanwar Pal Singh Gill*, 1996; *Vishaka v. State of Rajasthan*, 1997; *Apparel Export Promotion Council v. A. K. Chopra*, 1999) that evidence that these laws, despite their loopholes, have aided women in their movement for their right to their bodies. It is the responsibility of the legislature and the judiciary to make considerations for the difficulty in collecting useful evidence, like the lack of bruises on the body and private parts may be because the wife could not resist the act of rape out of fear of grievous hurt. Courts have held in the past that even if there are no bruises on the genitalia of the woman to prove that the sexual intercourse happened and it was nonconsensual, the accused can be convicted for rape (*Rahul Pundalik Birahade v. State of Maharashtra*, 2000). "The assumption, and indeed the expectation, of resistance are predicated upon a number of stereotypes, family assumption and misunderstandings about sexual assault. According to this view, when suddenly confronted by a rapist, a woman will struggle, fight back, and vehemently resist the assault, thereby proving her lack of consent to the sexual contact. However, when assaulted, some women might choose not to physically resist because, for example, they might feel that their safety, and perhaps even their life, is better protected by not resisting" (Randall, 2010, pp. 418–419). The Supreme Court has in a number of leading judgments held that passive consent, that is, consent given under fear of injury or duress, does not exclude the act from the scope of rape (*Uday v. State of Karnataka*, 2003; *Pradeep Kumar Verma v. State of Bihar*, 2007). Also, the statute can establish a clear distinction between marital rape and domestic violence, so that a case that falls under the latter cannot be unjustly tried within the scope of marital rape. Third, the social progress of the country requires equality in marriage. The husband cannot coerce the wife into having sexual intercourse against her will. The Hon'ble Supreme Court in *State of Maharashtra v. Madhukar Narayan Mardikar* (1991) said that a "woman is entitled to right to sexual privacy and it is not open to any and every person to violate her privacy when he wished." There is no implied consent to sexual relations upon the whims and fancies of the husband. The Apex Court, extending the ambit of Article 21, held that mere existence is not the right to live. It is a right to live with dignity. It gives the women the right to health, the right to profession, the right to privacy, protection against sexual harassment, and the right to live with human dignity as part of her right to life (*Suo Moto v. State of Rajasthan*, 2005). The right to equality stipulates that express consent should be given by both the partners, whether they are married or not.

Law Commission Recommendations

The Law Commission of India laid down certain recommendations regarding changes in the law governing the offense of rape in its 172nd Report on Review of Rape Laws (2000). The report suggests that the definition of *rape* be substituted by the definition of *sexual assault*, so that the offense shall include all forms of penetration, and not just penovaginal. "It is also necessary to include under this new definition (sexual assault) not only penile penetration but also penetration by any other part of the body (like finger or toe) or by any other object" (Law Commission of India, 2000, para. 3.1). The Law Commission also recommends that it should be "open to the prosecution to request the court to provide a screen in such a manner that the victim does not see the accused, while at the same time providing an opportunity to the accused to listen to the testimony of the victim" (Law Commission of India, 2000, para. 6.1) so that the fear of the rape litigation process does not inhibit the victim from reporting the offense. If marital rape is criminalized, these recommendations shall benefit the abused wife. Another suggestion in the report is that Section 376A of the IPC should be amended. This section that provides a lesser punishment to a husband who sexually assaults his own wife living separately in the aforesaid circumstances, the advocates for Sakshi argued (*Sakshi v. Union of India*, 2004), is arbitrary and discriminatory. "In the circumstances, while recommending that this section should be retained on the statute book, we recommend enhancement of punishment under the section" (Law Commission of India, 2000, para. 3.3).

Suggested Reforms

There are certain reforms that need to be introduced in the Indian legal and judicial system. Foremost, Sections 356 and 357 of IPC should be amended to include the marital rape of the wife of any age within the scope of the offense of rape and to provide punishment equivalent to that which would be imposed upon a rapist under general circumstances. Practical mechanisms must be established for the proper registering of complaints. There must be special police units consisting of women to handle such complaints, so that the abused wives are not inhibited from lodging their complaints at police stations out of the fear of male authority. The Code of Criminal Procedure (Amendment) Act of 2008 provides that "any offence under Section 376 and Sections 376A to 376D of the IPC shall be tried as far as practicable by a Court presided over by a woman." The cases on marital rape can too be tried preferably by female magistrates to ensure that there is no bias toward the male abuser. Another reform can be establishing legitimate state-funded sexual assault services, especially for victims of spousal rape, to educate them about initiating criminal proceedings against their husbands, to dispel the fear of litigation and society, and to help them cooperate with the police in investigations. "Women who have become victims of violence should have a right to professional help. Cost-free phone hotlines for women are important for first contacts for providing information about victims' rights and for initial counseling. In order to be protected from violence, victims must also be granted the right to safe accommodation and adequate help" (Logar, 2008, p. 8).

The state can provide legal aid, financial aid, and alternate shelters to abused wives who are financially dependent on their husbands until the judgment has been passed by the relevant court, to prevent their relapse into their sexual abuse history by their withdrawing their complaints under family and monetary compulsion. Also, bruises or injuries to the body or private parts should not be the sole determining factor for conviction under the offense of marital rape. Since wives generally give into the rape by their husbands out of fear or societal expectations, it is difficult to obtain these physical signs as evidence of the lack of consent. Conviction under marital rape should also be included as grounds for divorce, so that the wife can have the option of severing her marital relations with her abuser. The offense of marital rape should be cognizable, nonbailable, and noncompoundable to convey the seriousness of the crime. The legal positions on marital rape, cruelty, and domestic violence should be clarified, so that there is no conflict or confusion. The rape of a woman by her husband should exclusively come under the ambit of marital rape, and not cruelty or domestic violence. Also, "the police and judicial authorities were not regarded as cooperating partners but from a feminist point of view they were rather part of the problem than of the solution, as they were dominated by men and showed little sensitivity or even hostility towards the interests and needs of women who had become victims of violence" (Logar, 2008, p. 3). Hence, the state should take measures for the sensitization of the judges and the police by organizing regular workshops and seminars wherein they would be formally educated with respect to the prevalence of sexual violence against women in India.

Conclusion

Marital rape reflects the perversity of not just the husband, but also the legislature and the criminal justice system and Indian society in general. It ravishes the dignity and sexual privacy of the victim. Wives in these abusive traps should be uplifted and given a position that is at par with men. The judiciary and the police must be sensitized toward this issue. The mere fact that the parties are married should not be the reasoning for imposing a lighter sentence. There is a need for change in the social outlook on the issue of marital rape and also the empowerment of women so that they can themselves fight for their personal rights. The law has until now pretended to be blind to the prevalence of this heinous practice, but the new progressive code of the international order requires India to mold its laws on women into ones that provide justice.

References

Apparel Export Promotion Council v. A. K. Chopra. AIR 1999 SC 625.

Bergen, R. K. (1998). *Issues in Intimate Violence*. Thousand Oaks, CA: Sage.

Bergen, R. K. (1999). *Marital Rape*. Harrisburg, PA: National Resource Center on Domestic Violence.

Bodhisattwa Gautam v. Subhra Chakraborty. 1996 1 SCC 490.

Bureau of Democracy, Human Rights, and Labor, U.S. Department of State. (2008). *Country Reports on Human Rights Practices: Introduction*. Washington, DC: U.S. Department of State.

Campbell, J. C., and Alford, P. (1989). The dark consequences of marital rape. *American Journal of Nursing*, 89(7), 946–949.

Census Organization of India. (2011). Census of India. New Delhi: Census Organization of India.

Central Statistics Office, Ministry of Statistics and Programme Implementation. (2011). Women and men in India 2011, 13th issue. New Delhi: Ministry of Statistics and Programme Implementation.

CERC v. Union of India. AIR 1995 SC 636.

Commonwealth v. Fogarty. [1857] 74 Mass. 489.

Finkelhor, D., and Yllo, K. (1985). *License to Rape: Sexual Abuse of Wives*. New York: Free Press.

Francis Coralie Mullin v. Administrator, Union Territory of Delhi. AIR 1981 746.

Hale, M. (1800). *Historia Placitorum Coronæ: The History of the Pleas of the Crown*. from the Original Manuscripts by Sollom Emlyn. With Additional Notes and References to Modern Cases Concerning the Pleas of the Crown. By George Wilson. A New Ed. And an Abridgment of the Statutes Relating to Felonies Continued to the Present Time, with Notes and References, by Thomas Dogherty 1, London: Printed by E. Rider, for T. Payne, H. L. Gardner, W. Otridge, E. and R. Brooke and J. Rider [and seven others in London], p. x, OCLC 645127647.

Hobbes, T. (2010). *Leviathan*. Calgary, AB: Broadview Press.

Kilpatrick, D. G., Best, C. L., Saunders, B. E., and Vernon, L. J. (1988). Rape in marriage and in dating relationships: How bad is it for mental health? *Human Sexual Aggressions: Current Perspective*, 528, 335–344.
Koss, M. P., Dinero, T. E., Seibel, C. A., and Cox. S. L. (1988). Stranger & acquaintance rape: Are there differences in the victim's experiences? *Psychology of Women Quarterly*, 12, 1–24.
Law Commission of India. (2000). 172nd report on review of rape laws. D.O.No.6(3)(36)/2000_LC(LS). New Delhi: Law Commission of India.
Logar, R. (2008). *Good Practices and Challenges in Legislation on Violence against Women*. New York: United Nations Division for the Advancement of Women.
Maharashtra v. Madhukar Narayan. AIR 1991 SC 207.
Mathias, P. (2008). A bill to help rape victims. *Deccan Herald*, November 25.
Mathur, K. M. (1996). *Crime, Human Rights and National Security*. New Delhi: Gyan Publishing House.
Ministry of Health and Family Welfare. (2006). National Family Health Survey–III 2005–06: Gender equality and women's empowerment in India. New Delhi: Ministry of Health and Family Welfare.
National Crime Records Bureau, Ministry of Home Affairs. (2011). *Crime in India: Statistics*. New Delhi: Ministry of Home Affairs.
Pradeep Kumar Verma v. State of Bihar. AIR 2007 SC 3059.
Rafiq v. State of Uttar Pradesh. [1980] Cr.LJ 1344 SC.
Rahul Pundalik Birahade v. State of Maharashtra. [2000] (5) BomCR 148.
Randall, M. (2010). Sexual assault law, credibility and ideal victims: Consent, resistance, and victim blaming. *Canadian Journal of Women and the Law*, 22(2), 397.
Rupan Deol Bajaj v. Kanwar Pal Singh Gill. AIR 1996 SC 309.
Russell, D. E. H. (1990). *Rape in Marriage*. Indianapolis: Indiana University Press.
R v. Clarence. [1888] 22 QBD 23.
R v. Miller. [1954] 2 QB 282.
R v. R. [1992] 1 AC 599.
Sakshi v. Union of India. AIR 2004 SC 3566.
Samar Ghosh v. Jaya Ghosh. [2007] (6) BomCR 834.
State of Maharashtra v. Madhukar Narayan Mardikar. AIR 1991 SC 207.
Suo Moto v. State of Rajasthan. RLW 2005 (2) Raj 1385.
Uday v. State of Karnataka. AIR 2003 SC 1639.
Vikram Singh v. State of Haryana. Criminal Appeal No. 583-DB of 2003.
Vishaka & Ors v. State of Rajasthan. AIR 1997 SC 3011.
Vishaka v. State of Rajasthan. AIR 1997 SC 3011.
West, R. (1990). Equality theory, marital rape and the promise of the Fourteenth Amendment. *Florida Law Review*, 42, 45–79.

Homelessness
A Consequence of Abuse of Women in Brisbane, Australia

3

HELENA MENIH AND CATRIN SMITH

Contents

Introduction

Chamberlain and MacKenzie (1992) argue that the definitions and kinds of homelessness are quite complex. Therefore, not only is it important to conceptually and operationally define homelessness, but also it is imperative to distinguish different experiences within homeless populations, for example, among gender-specific populations. Chamberlain and Johnson (2001) point out there will always be individual homeless people who are hard to classify. Currently, in an Australian context, there are three sections of the homeless population relevant to the official definitions: primary, secondary, and tertiary homelessness. Primary homelessness encompasses those without conventional accommodation, most commonly people living on the streets (Chamberlain and MacKenzie, 2009). Secondary homelessness includes people who move frequently from one form of temporary shelter to another (Chamberlain and MacKenzie, 2009). Tertiary homelessness encompasses people who live in boarding houses on a medium to long-term basis, operationally defined as 13 weeks or longer (Chamberlain and MacKenzie, 2009).

According to the Australian Bureau of Statistics (ABS), in 2011, the number of homeless people in Australia reached 105,237, which was 8% higher than five years previously. Further, women represented 44% of the overall homeless population, which enumerated to 45,813 homeless women, compared to 38,569 homeless women in 2006 (ABS, 2011). Moreover, a recent annual specialist homelessness services (SHS) report found that 229,247 Australians accessed SHS during 2011–2012, with females representing 59% of the overall number (Australian Institute of Health and Welfare [AIHW], 2012). Further data show that almost equal numbers of males and females were homeless when they began receiving support; however, the females at risk represented 68% of all the people at risk of becoming homeless (AIHW, 2012). The ABS data further suggest female homelessness in Queensland* rose from 7851 women in 2006 to 8504 women in 2011. This is a higher percentage rise compared to men; in 2006, there were 11,008 homeless men, and in 2011, 11,333 homeless men. From the 8504 homeless women in Queensland in 2011, 592 are considered to be primary homeless (the data are based on persons who are in improvised dwellings, tents, or sleeping out).

In response to this increase in the homeless population, the Australian government published a white paper proposing to halve the homeless population and offer supported accommodation to all rough sleepers by the year 2020 (Department of Families, Housing, Community Services and Indigenous Affairs [FaHCSIA], 2008). One of the main suggestions was to intervene early to prevent homelessness, yet in order to prevent people from becoming homeless, the reasons for and pathways into homelessness need to be explored and understood. In response to the white paper, the ABS developed a robust and evidence-based definition of homelessness that is used to enumerate homeless people; it focuses only on the homeless population, thus providing a more accurate picture of homelessness in Australia. The white paper also facilitated homelessness services rethinking their method of collecting data on homelessness. Thus in 2011, the SHS collection was established to collect data on people who are homeless and at risk of becoming homeless. Based on these ABS and SHS data collection mechanisms, it can be seen that not only is the number of homelessness in Australia on the rise and female homelessness increasing, but also there is an overrepresentation of women at risk of becoming homeless. Women also report family or domestic violence as either the main factor for homelessness or a contributing factor for seeking help to prevent homelessness (AIHW, 2012).

Early Intervention for Homeless

Within the field of homelessness, the terms *early intervention* and *prevention* have different meanings. As Chamberlain and Johnson (2000) explain, the definition of *early intervention* tends to relate to young people, and it can be implemented at any time until the shift to chronic homelessness. However, in the case of adults, early intervention cannot be implemented after the household loses its home; it needs to take place before homelessness occurs. On the other hand, prevention comprises of developing policies that are specifically designed to address the structural reasons for homelessness.† Yet, a review of the literature suggests that reasons for homelessness among adults tend to be more of an individualistic nature and less structural (Wright, 2009). Chamberlain and Johnson (2002, p. 36) explain that early intervention mechanisms focus on "preventing households from entering the homeless population."

They also point out that the intervention programs for adults tend to be different than the intervention programs for young people. In addition, for an intervention to be successful, there are four characteristics that are required: (1) assistance needs to be provided when a household is at risk before losing accommodation, (2) the workers in housing services need to have a high level of interpersonal skills to communicate with people from various backgrounds and in various situations, (3) the workers in housing assistance departments

* Research was undertaken in the city of Brisbane, which is located in Queensland.
† An example of prevention could be government-funded rental assistance through social welfare.

need to have an extensive knowledge of policy and public and private housing systems, and (4) there needs to be sufficient funding for agencies that provide early intervention strategies (Chamberlain and Johnson, 2002). In this instance, women who are experiencing domestic violence are considered an "at-risk" population. Yet, if the at-risk population is not being addressed appropriately, it can lead to the loss of current accommodation, consequently resulting in homelessness (Chamberlain and Johnson, 2002).

Chamberlain and MacKenzie (2009) explain that when homelessness occurs, it needs to be addressed as soon as possible; otherwise, it can lead to chronic homelessness, which can be very hard to exit. At this point, the emergency shelters offer women who are at risk a secure and safe accommodation. Currently, in Brisbane* the emergency shelters offer 46 beds for women, 30 for young people, and 200 for men. However, on any given night, there are around 4000 women experiencing primary, secondary, or tertiary homelessness; there is an obvious lack of available beds in emergency shelters.

Research on Female Homelessness

It was not until the late 1970s that female homelessness was recognized by researchers. However, while it was established that women experience homelessness as well as men, the research into adult homeless populations in the United States and the United Kingdom had predominantly focused on men (Tomas and Dittmar, 1995). In the mid-1980s, research on homelessness started to shift, and internationally, research started focusing on homeless women. Yet, despite this trend, the research tended to compare homeless women with homeless men (see Bassuk et al., 1984, 1986; Bassuk and Rosenberg, 1988; Breakey et al., 1989; Burt and Cohen, 1989; Calsyn and Morse, 1990; Crystal, 1984; Hagen, 1987; Maurin et al., 1989). Such studies identified the importance of understanding homelessness in the context of gender; women and men were studied separately to understand the differences in reasons for, and pathways into, homelessness. Studies on gendered experiences of homelessness also indicated that women are more likely than men to experience violence prior to homelessness, which in turn suggests that homeless women tend to have different needs than homeless men (see Martin, 2010; Mina-Coull and Tartinville, 2001; Roll et al., 1999; Tomas and Dittmar, 1995; Zugazaga, 2004; Wardhaugh, 1999).

Internationally, the literature on women's homelessness implies a strong link between violence at home and homelessness (e.g., Browne and Bassuk, 1997; Metraux and Culhane, 1999; Moss and Singh, 2015; Toro et al., 1995). The link between homelessness and domestic abuse in Australia has also been explored (Chung et al., 2000; Johnson et al., 2008; MacKenzie and Chamberlain, 2008; Tually et al., 2008). Healy (2002) explained that 45% of women in Australia named domestic violence or sexual, physical, or emotional abuse as the main cause for their homelessness. Moreover, 55% of women with children and 36.9% of unaccompanied women named domestic and family violence as the main reason to seek assistance (AIHW, 2008). Still, most of the conducted research discusses domestic or family violence instead of focusing on a specific behavior within this violence (e.g., physical or sexual abuse). Thus, it can be hard to determine how many women in Australia actually experience only one type of abusive behavior or whether these behaviors overlap, and how exactly these can be linked to homelessness. The published numbers also

* Brisbane is the capital city of Queensland, in Australia. In 2011, ABS (2011) counted 2,065,996 people living in the Greater Brisbane area.

misrepresent the actual picture of domestic or family violence in Australia, as a lot of abuse is not reported (Tually et al., 2008).

In the context of qualitative research on female homelessness, there are three studies that played an important role in understanding women's experiences of homelessness: Watson and Austerberry (1986) in the United Kingdom, Brown and Ziefert (1990) in the United States, and Casey (2002) in Australia. These qualitative studies undertook an exploration of gender within the field of homelessness and indicated the need for a gendered understanding of the homeless population to prevent women's homelessness and improve the lives of homeless women. In order to apply appropriate intervention mechanisms, we need to know exactly which kinds of behavior are the most threatening to women, how exactly these women experience such behaviors before becoming homeless, and how these behaviors lead to homelessness.

Present Study

This chapter presents part of the findings of a much larger exploratory study of female homelessness. Recent statistical information indicates that homelessness in Australia is increasing. Moreover, *female* homelessness has been rising in the past few years. A review of studies undertaken on homelessness demonstrated the lack of an in-depth understanding of female homelessness in Australia, indicating also that the existing literature tends to be gender-blind. Further review of the studies demonstrated a strong link between violence and homelessness, yet there is a lack of an in-depth understanding of these links, that is, the ways women experience violence and in what ways it contributes to homelessness. This chapter thus focuses on violence as a contributing factor to homelessness. It is important to note that violence is not the only contributing factor; however, it is considered a highly important one, especially since violence can have severe negative effects on the victims. Through the use of qualitative methods, women shared their stories of abuse and circumstances that led them, either directly or indirectly, to homelessness.

Methodology

We developed a research project* that aimed to give a "voice" to homeless women and make them visible. Based on the literature review, it was evident that there was a paucity of exploratory research, and thus we elected on such a design. In addition, a grounded theory approach was utilized. This is suggested when limited knowledge on the topic exists and when the research population is considered vulnerable (Brewer, 2000; Davies, 2008). Moreover, the nature of vulnerable populations (such as homeless women) also requires the methodological approach to be as flexible and unintrusive as possible (Liamputtong and Ezzy, 2005; Martin and Kunnen, 2008). As a result, an ethnography technique was employed.

A grounded theoretical approach with an ethnographic methodology enabled us to explore the experiences of homeless women in Brisbane. More specifically, participation

* The findings presented in this chapter show only one angle of the much larger research project (doctoral thesis), which was conducted by the primary author and supervised by the secondary author.

observation and in-depth interviewing allowed us to explore one of the three major research aims concerning the interaction between experiences of becoming homeless and the meanings attached to this. Over a period of 10 months, ethnographic fieldwork was undertaken in four major city locations by the primary author; numerous informal conversations and 10 recorded interviews were undertaken. In addition, all field observations were written in a fieldwork journal on a daily basis.

Stories of Violence

One of the aims of the larger research project was to explore the lives of homeless women; thus, their past, present, and especially their reasons for, and pathways into, homelessness seemed to be of crucial importance to understand their experiences. It became obvious that the way women embrace and react to the reasons for homelessness impacts their transition into homelessness. The literature suggests there are two types of causes for women's homelessness: structural and individual (Snow and Anderson, 1993; Main, 1998). Wright (2009) argues that structural components tend to be less common than individual ones. In most cases, the individual characteristics either contribute to or cause homelessness (Snow and Anderson, 1993). Yet, the scholarly literature predominantly focuses on structural understandings of homelessness.

This research found that for most women, the reasons for homelessness tended to be of an individualistic nature. Moreover, the majority of women revealed it was the violence at home that contributed to their homelessness. Violence in this context refers to physical, verbal, and sexual; a lot of times, these types of violence overlap. While some women choose to live with violence or seek help, the others have no other option than to transition into homelessness. To understand why some women endure the violence or why others become homeless, we have to examine their stories. Throughout the informal conversations and interviews, the women told stories of violence that led to their homelessness. In this instance, the women's stories demonstrate that violence either directly or indirectly led to their homelessness. While there were many similar stories of violence that different women spoke of, here we draw on Jade's experience of a direct impact of violence and Niki's* experience of an indirect impact of violence.

Direct Impact

Jade experienced sexual abuse in her adulthood; she referred to this as the direct reason for her homelessness. Jade is an aboriginal homeless woman in her early forties. Over an informal conversation, Jade revealed that in the past few years she had been experiencing domestic abuse (not only sexual, but also physical). Jade remembered the abuse:

> Once, my stepfather tied my mother to a chair ... then raped me in front of her ... he wanted her to watch. She never did anything because she was afraid ... that he would leave her. I never did anything 'cause he had, still does, legal custody of my son and threatened me that if I tell anyone I would never see him again.

* Both names (Jade and Niki) are pseudonyms.

Jade's stepfather was also continuously making inappropriate comments to her son: "He was always saying I'm a slut in front of my boy." With the use of derogatory connotations toward Jade, her stepfather discredited her as a mother and demonstrated his dominance. This eventually led to Jade's son's subsequent rejection of her as a mother. Jade explained: "He was becoming just like him … he started calling me all these nasty names."

Jade explained that when she left her mother's place, she got involved in a relationship that was similar to her situation at home. The man she became financially dependent on was also sexually abusing her. Jade remembered one situation: "He had me locked up, it was like a cage … and then he just had his way with me, whenever." Understandably, Jade did not want to go into graphic detail regarding her sexual abuse. She indicated that when she finally cultivated enough courage, she left her partner and escaped to the streets. For Jade, the transition into primary homelessness occurred rapidly when she left her abusive partner.

Indirect Impact

Niki, a woman in her early forties, discussed her journey into homelessness as being impacted by sexual abuse (which occurred during her childhood) and physical abuse (which occurred during her adulthood). When she was asked to state how her homelessness occurred, she said it all started with her parents winning the lotto. This enabled her mother to fly her grandfather from Scotland to Australia to stay with them. Niki's grandfather was actually the one who was sexually abusing her, and no one in the family knew about the abuse:

> He would be waiting for me and he'd molest me when I got home, but some days I could get away from him by being really … I learned how to be really quiet and stay on his blind side, and hide from him and he used to make me pretend that I was my dead grandmother who I was really close to, while he's doing his business. And I managed to keep it a secret from my brother, and my mother, and my father. And eventually he went back to Scotland to die and it all stopped. And I never told anybody and my parents were taking me to psychologists because they knew something was wrong, but I wouldn't say anything, and that was about when I was nine.

Niki was and still is keeping the abuse secret from her family. After her grandfather moved back to Scotland, she returned to normalcy, or as she said, "And then I went and lived this whole normal life." She was in a relationship and gave birth to her daughter. Yet, this relationship was not without obstacles. As Niki explains, "And yeah sure enough the beating started and he was a really big man, he was like 6 foot 3 and he was beating me up black and blue." Eventually the relationship broke down and she moved back in with her parents for additional support. However, it all came crashing down when in her late twenties she overheard her mother saying she was sexually abused by her father (Niki's grandfather). At that point, Niki left her parent's home as she felt betrayed. She remembered this crucial moment:

> And then my world came crashing down because my mother and my auntie were crying and consoling each other over the fact that they had been molested by their father. So I couldn't believe that my mother would bring him out to live with us and go to work every day and

> leave me with him, so I blamed her and then within four months I was smoking marijuana and then heroin, which I did solid for seven years and … so that's when it all came crashing down, until this day they don't know, they don't know still and …

As a coping mechanism, Niki said she started using drugs. She then became dependent on drugs, and to support her drug habit, she became involved in relationships that led to prostitution. During this time, she lost custody of her daughter and basically lived at different places or slept on the streets. These actions demonstrate the chaotic life she lived at that time. Niki's drug habit led her to one of the main drug dealers (John*) in Brisbane, for whom she also started dealing.

> With drugs comes prostitution…. Well it was a boyfriend that put me on the streets, first of all it was agency work [referring to sex work], and he had two kids and his wife to the two kids was a prostitute and a girlfriend he had before me was a prostitute. And then it was like well I'm not going out to do crime, the only way we are going to get money, is if you go and work … and at this stage I was living day to day you know, you know having first of all to work to pay for the hotel and then work to pay for drugs.
>
> And I remember the first time I scored for him for the day it [was] only a hundred dollars and I knew he lied to me and he said he threw a lot of money at me and said here, "You don't have to go out and do any errands or anything if you stay the night with me." And he didn't expect anything he just wanted to be with me because he had a little obsession going. So I continued dealing with him for only a short time.

As Niki said, "So then I'd started to get my stuff together and I ended up with a place in Hill End, a really nice house, not a really big [drug] habit even when I was working, my habit wasn't that big." At that time, she exited primary homelessness and regained control of her life; however, this did not last long. Niki spoke of being kidnapped a while later by the drug dealer she used to work with. After this, her life became particularly chaotic. From the day she was kidnapped onward, her drug habit became worse and she was in and out of homelessness:

> And they grabbed me and said, "Grab what's just the most important thing is to you." You know, I didn't know what was going on and then they tied me up and they put me in the back of the car. And so we are driving down Boundary Street in West End, John's rang them up and said, "How is everything going?" And I'm like screaming my head off. And he said, "I don't want her hurt, but shut her up," you know. And the next morning I'm like, "Oh well, I better get going now" and that. He said, "No you don't understand you live here now." I said, "What do you mean I live here?" He said, "You live here." So I proceeded for 19 days, just nothing but trying to escape. … And all the while you know as much drugs as I wanted. … But it was 19 days and then my habit had gone from $100 to $2000 a day in 19 days. And so I never forget that after 19 days, I couldn't escape because I couldn't support a habit like that.

While Niki's first contact with primary homelessness occurred rapidly, her second contact with primary homelessness occurred in a different way and lasted for about 11 years. She calculated her time in and out of homelessness by looking at the kidnapper's age: "He was 58 and he died at 69, so 11, 12 years ago." She explained that she slept on the streets every time she escaped; however, due to the drug habit and the attachment

* This is a pseudonym.

she developed, she tended to return to her kidnapper or he found her, as she says: "And it was just easier to stay with him and it wasn't really until he died a month ago that I really got away from him." For Niki, her actual transition into homelessness started in her mid-twenties when she started using drugs, which then led into prostitution; however, Niki considered her sexual abuse in her childhood as a contributing factor to her homelessness.

Discussion and Conclusion

For most women, the struggle before homelessness was more on an individual, than a structural, level. More specifically, their hardship was in most cases due to the childhood sexual or physical abuse or the abuse in their adulthood, which occurred within their home. Scholarly literature recognizes both individual and structural reasons for women's homelessness, yet recent research and responses focus predominantly on structural reasons. Moreover, the existing literature on homeless women lacks the in-depth understanding of the ways women experience these reasons for homelessness. In this research, the women's stories demonstrate the need for a better understanding of the individualistic causes that lead to homelessness, especially since for women in this research, the abuse took place in the "safety" of their home (Tually et al., 2008).

In addition to demonstrating the dominant abuse in these women's lives, their accounts also indicate that these individual reasons can be dormant for a long time before impacting their transition into homelessness. According to the women's stories, the hidden nature of these reasons tends to impact their behaviors and attitudes toward their relationships in their adulthood, where, in most cases, the women continued to endure abusive relationships. This establishes the vulnerability of these women within their home and before homelessness. Harden (2000) explains that women's vulnerability (being at risk or taking risk) is related to the experiences and perceptions of their own bodies in a particular given space. Consequently, the women's stories in this research demonstrate that this susceptibility at home made these women more prone to succumb to the additional personal struggles in their lives, which also impacted their transition into homelessness. In addition, the experience of the abuse in a domestic space impacted the women's perceptions of "home."

Grounded in women's stories, four typologies of the concept of home were developed. Within the context of women's reasons for homelessness, two of these categories were particularly relevant: (1) *past home based on negative experience* and (2) *ideal home*. First, when women reflected upon their negative experiences of the abuse, they constructed their idea of home. In this instance, women directly linked their experiences of the abuse they suffered to the notion of a domestic space. The lack of concepts such as *privacy* and *safety* demonstrate the women's idea of space. This is in agreement with Mallett's (2004) suggestion that the private sphere of home is described in terms of safety and security. Second, on the grounds of typology, the women's accounts point to the notion of an ideal home. In this instance, women identify home as the opposite to their experience of abuse. Moreover, the concepts of privacy and safety are identified as the key elements of such a home.

The literature on pathways into homelessness suggests that reasons for homelessness are directly linked to the pathway (Johnson et al., 2008), yet according to the women's stories, their transition tends to be more complex and individualistic. The women's accounts demonstrate that the reasons for homelessness are likely to impact their transition into homelessness directly or indirectly. This was established when women pointed to the abuse in their childhood as part of the reason. In addition to these direct or indirect links, the women's perception of homelessness impacted their awareness of their transition into homelessness.

According to the women who experienced childhood abuse, their pathways into homelessness occurred over time, and it was specific for each woman's idea of homelessness. Some of these women came in contact with homelessness during their teenage years, but never stayed homeless for long. Other women tended to move around a lot during their adulthood and spent time at their friends' places or even in boarding houses. According to the official definitions, this is considered secondary and tertiary homelessness (Chamberlain and MacKenzie, 2009), yet most of these women did not see themselves as homeless. Consequently, it can be concluded that women's pathways into homelessness vary on their perceptions of homelessness and personal circumstances, which are directly or indirectly related to their reasons.

Additionally, for women who experienced abuse in their adulthood, their transition into homelessness seemed to occur rapidly. These women experienced ongoing abuse with a specific incidence directly impacting their decision to leave their homes. According to the women's stories, this relates to the two key elements they considered when thinking about home: privacy and safety. Even though the street is a public space and there is a certain element of intrusion present, most of the women we spoke to still chose the street rather than to stay in an abusive home or go to a shelter. In this instance, the women's perception of a shelter service comes into play. According to the women's stories, these places did not offer enough privacy, which is integral to their idea of home.

In conclusion, women's stories demonstrate that the experiences of women's reasons for, and pathways into, homelessness tend to be complex, individualistic, and gendered. In this instance, the women discussed their ideas of home and homelessness grounded in their identity and relationships within the private sphere of the home. Due to their experiences of abuse, the women's stories suggest a male-dominated domestic environment. Moreover, the women's stories demonstrate that the impact of violence directly or indirectly leads to homelessness. The increase in numbers and the sensitivity of the contributing factors (such as domestic violence) for women indicate that women are more vulnerable than men. Consequently, this means that the general focus on homelessness and social policies needs to become more gender specific in an endeavor to decrease the numbers of homeless women and properly address the violence women experience in the domestic sphere.

References

Australian Bureau of Statistics (ABS). (2011). Census of population and housing: Estimating homelessness (no. 2049.0). Canberra: ABS.

Australian Institute of Health and Welfare (AIHW). (2008). Homeless people in SAAP: SAAP National Data Collection annual report. SAAP NDCA report series 12 (cat. no. HOU 185). Canberra: AIHW.

Australian Institute of Health and Welfare (AIHW). (2012). Specialist homelessness services 2011–12 (cat. no. HOU 267). Canberra: AIHW.

Bassuk, E. L., and Rosenberg, L. (1988). Why does family homelessness occur? A case-control study. *American Journal of Public Health*, 78(7): 783–788.

Bassuk, E. L., Rubin, L., and Lauriat, A. (1984). Is homelessness a mental health problem? *American Psychiatric Association*, 141, 1546–1550.

Bassuk, E. L., Rubin, L., and Lauriat, A. (1986). Characteristics of sheltered homeless families. *American Journal of Public Health*, 76(9), 1097–1101.

Breakey, W. R., Fischer, P. J., Kramer, M., Nestadt, G., Romanoski, A. J., Ross, A., Royall, R. M., and Stine, O. C. (1989). Health and mental health problems of homeless men and women in Baltimore. *JAMA*, 262(10), 1352–1357.

Brewer, D. (2000). *Ethnography*. Buckingham: Open University Press.

Brown, K. S., and Ziefert, M. (1990). A feminist approach to working with homeless women. *Affilia*, 5(1), 6–20.

Browne, A., and Bassuk, S. S. (1997). Intimate violence in the lives of homeless and poor housed women: Prevalence and patterns in an ethnically diverse sample. *American Journal of Orthopsychiatry*, 67(2), 261–278.

Burt, M. R., and Cohen, B. E. (1989). Differences among homeless single women, women with children, and single men. *Social Problems*, 36(5), 508–524.

Calsyn, R. J., and Morse, G. (1990). Homeless men and women: Commonalities and a service gender gap. *American Journal of Community Psychology*, 18(4), 597–608.

Casey, S. (2002). Snakes and ladders: Women's pathways into and out of homelessness. In T. Eardley and B. Bradbury (eds.), *Competing Visions: Refereed Proceedings of the National Social Policy Conference 2001* (pp. 75–90). SPRC Report 1/02. Sydney: Social Policy Research Centre, University of New South Wales.

Chamberlain, C., and Johnson, G. (2000). Early intervention: A research paper prepared for the Victorian Homelessness Strategy. Victoria: Department of Human Services.

Chamberlain, C., and Johnson, G. (2001). The debate about homelessness. *Australian Journal of Social Issues*, 36(1), 35–50.

Chamberlain, C., and Johnson, G. (2002). Homeless adults: Understanding early intervention. *Just Policy*, 26, 28–39.

Chamberlain, C., and MacKenzie, D. (1992). Understanding contemporary homelessness: Issues of definition and meaning. *Australian Journal of Social Issues*, 27(4), 274–297.

Chamberlain, C., and MacKenzie, D. (2009). Counting the homeless 2006: Queensland (cat. no. HOU 205). Canberra: Australian Institute of Health and Welfare.

Chung, D., Kennedy, R., O'Brien, B., and Wendt, S. (2000). Home safe home: The link between domestic and family violence and women's homelessness, [for the] Social Policy Research Group. Canberra: University of South Australia, Partnerships Against Domestic Violence.

Crystal, S. (1984). Homeless men and homeless women: The gender gap. *Urban and Social Change Review*, 17(2), 2–6.

Davies, C. A. (2008). *Reflexive Ethnography: A Guide to Researching Selves and Others* (2nd ed.). London: Routledge.

Department of Families, Housing, Community Services and Indigenous Affairs (FaHCSIA). (2008). *The Road Home: A National Approach to Reducing Homelessness*. Canberra: FaHCSIA.

Hagen, J. L. (1987). Gender and homelessness. *Social Work*, 32(4), 312–316.

Harden, J. (2000). There's no place like home: The public/private distinction in children's theorizing of risk and safety. *Childhood*, 7(1), 43–59.

Healy, J. (2002). *The Homeless*. Sydney: Spinney Press.

Johnson, G., Gronda, H., and Coutts, S. (2008). *On the Outside: Pathways In and Out of Homelessness*. Melbourne: Australian Scholarly Publishing.

Liamputtong, P., and Ezzy, D. (2005). *Qualitative Research Methods*. South Melbourne: Oxford University Press.

MacKenzie, D., and Chamberlain, C. (2008). Youth homelessness 2006. *Youth Studies Australia*, 27(1), 17–25.

Main, T. (1998). How to think about homelessness: Balancing structural and individual causes. *Journal of Social Distress and the Homeless*, 7(1), 41–54.

Mallett, S. (2004). Understanding home: A critical review of the literature. *Sociological Review*, 25(1), 62–89.

Martin, R. (2010). *Gender and Homelessness*. Perth: Curtin University of Technology.

Martin, R., and Kunnen, N. (2008). Reinterpreting the research path: Using qualitative methods in homelessness research. In P. J. Maginn, S. Thompson, and M. Tonts (eds.), *Qualitative Housing Analysis: An International Perspective*, vol. 10, *Studies in Qualitative Methodology* (pp. 61–89). Bingley: Emerald Group Publishing Limited.

Maurin, J. T., Russell, L., and Memmott, R. J. (1989). An exploration of gender differences among the homeless. *Research in Nursing & Health*, 12(5), 315–321.

Metraux, S., and Culhane, D. P. (1999). Family dynamics, housing, and recurring homelessness among women in New York City homeless shelters. *Journal of Family Issues*, *20*(3), 371–396.

Mina-Coull, A., and Tartinville, S. (2001). Homeless women in France. In B. Edgar and J. Doherty (eds.), *Women and Homelessness in Europe—Pathways, Services and Experiences* (pp. 141–151). Bristol: Policy Press.

Moss, K., and Singh, P. (2015). *Women Rough Sleepers in Europe: Homelessness and Victims of Domestic Abuse*. Bristol: Policy Press, University of Bristol.

Roll, C. N., Toro, P. A., and Ortola, G. L. (1999). Characteristics and experiences of homeless adults: A comparison of single men, single women, and women with children. *Journal of Community Psychology*, 27(2), 189–198.

Snow, D. A., and Anderson, L. (1993). *Down on Their Luck: A Study of Homeless Street People*. Berkley: University of California Press.

Tomas, A., and Dittmar, H. (1995). The experience of homeless women: An exploration of housing histories and the meaning of home. *Housing Studies*, 10(4), 493–516.

Toro, P. A., Bellavia, C. W., Daeschler, C. V., Owens, B. J., Wall, D. D., Passero, J. M., and Thomas, D. M. (1995). Distinguishing homelessness from poverty: A comparative study. *Journal of Consulting and Clinical Psychology*, 63(2), 280.

Tually, S., Faulkner, D., Cutler, C., and Slatter, M. (2008). Women, domestic and family violence and homelessness: A synthesis report. Canberra: Commonwealth of Australia.

Wardhaugh, J. (1999). The unaccommodated woman: Home, homelessness and identity. *Sociological Review*, 47(1), 91–109.

Watson, S., and Austerberry, H. (1986). *Housing and Homelessness*. London: Routledge and Kegan Paul.

Wright, J. D. (2009). *Address Unknown: The Homeless in America*. New Brunswick, NJ: Transaction Publishers.

Zugazaga, C. (2004). Stressful life event experiences of homeless adults: A comparison of single men, single women, and women with children. *Journal of Community Psychology*, 32(6), 643–654.

Market Women and Their Crime Reporting Practices in Oyo, Oyo State, Nigeria*

4

JOHNSON OLUWOLE AYODELE

Contents

Introduction

There are several difficulties that impinge on the collection of reliable statistics on criminal activity and victimization in Nigeria (Alemika, 2004). The inability of market women to play a significant role in Oyo's accusatory justice constitutes one of these difficulties. Being a multifaceted social challenge, crime has no easy fix, anywhere in the world. This explains why crime against market women in Nigeria is considered an enormous problem with far-reaching socioeconomic consequences. Also, it is an abuse of women's self-inclusion in income-generating investments. Nevertheless, crime reporting is one of the most effective responses by which members of civilized societies provide solutions to crime issues. The history of crime and its reporting by women in contemporary Nigeria has focused essentially on the interactions that occur among the offender, victim, and criminal justice system. In the quest to discover a great deal about how certain crimes are and are not reported, the network of social intervention, the gender structure of crime reporters,

* An earlier version of this chapter was published as "Crime-Reporting Practices among Market Women in Oyo, Nigeria" in SAGEOPEN under a Creative Commons Attribution 3.0 License: DOI: 10.1177/2158244015579940, published April 10, 2015.

and the twin spectacles of the apprehension and escape of offenders have stimulated this inquiry. It was almost invariably these individuals who decided whether a crime was to be prosecuted in the first instance, and it was their words that were recorded by magistrates during trials.

In spite of small businesses serving as major income earners and new employment providers for Oyo's teeming youth, overcoming business crimes that threaten the contribution of market women to the economic development of this ancient community is probably its most critical challenge. Though business and retail crimes are commonly assumed to include all crimes and disorder committed by or against businesses, the onslaught on them has lately become an issue of significant interest to individuals who monitor developments within the Nigerian economy with patriotic interest. Were up-to-date statistics that paint the exact picture of victimization of women within the economy available, these would have revealed how acutely deprived women traders have been in Nigeria.

Though some Nigerian laws exist to guarantee freedom of lawful competition, security of assets, and the protection of businesspeople's rights of ownership, conflict scholars present the theoretical argument that crimes serve as a sort of noninstitutionalized protest against existing social relationships, as well as a reaction to those relationships. Therefore, criminals who victimize market women respond to failures in social consciousness and in legislation intended to redistribute property and social status among various social groups (Tulyakov, 2004).

The commercial strength of market women has not attained the level at which they can, without being prodded, insure their wares for the purposes of risk management. It is high time these traders appreciated the broader context of doing businesses that must succeed. There is hardly a way the environment and its components, which sometimes have a counterproductive impact on business activities, will not, in some subtle ways, frustrate the crime reporting initiatives of market women. In reality, the boundaries between the business and public domains are far from discrete, and hence the effects of crime against businesses reverberate throughout society (Fisher, 1991; Cromie, 1993; Fisher and Looye, 2000). The organized and unorganized private sectors of the Nigerian economy, for example, contribute significantly to situations that threaten the well-being of businesses, even if they facilitate domestic capital investment, employment growth, and gross domestic product and economic well-being of the country in general. Therefore, any assault on the business sector is therefore an assault on the business strength, economic vigor, and social well-being of all Nigerians. It is this realization that makes an inquiry into crime reporting practices of Oyo market women irresistible, at this time.

On the whole, crime is a drain on the economy, inhibiting progress and damaging competitiveness. It imposes direct and indirect costs on the business, and it is often the impact of crime, rather than the direct cost, that is most devastating (Robson and Teague, 2005). The businesses of market women are usually done on a small scale. This makes their enterprises particularly vulnerable to collapse, since they lack a competitive market edge and hence experience greater difficulty in absorbing the costs of victimization (Snyder et al., 1989; Fisher and Looye, 2000). It is for these reasons that market women whose businesses fall victim to crime are often left to bear the cost alone or in conjunction with their friends and family members.

While substantial research has been conducted in relation to crimes against individuals, research into crimes against businesses has traditionally received less attention, although this gap has started to close in recent years (Mirrlees-Black and Ross, 1995a, 1995b; Walker,

1994; Felson and Clarke, 1997; Gill, 1998; Burrows et al., 1999; Hopkins, 2002; Tilley and Hopkins, 1998) in advanced countries perhaps, but not so appreciably in most developing countries of the world, particularly in Nigeria. Surprisingly, business crime has received relatively little attention by the UK government and criminologists, despite the fact that it can have a significant impact on businesses (FSB, 2005; Hopkins, 2002), in spite of the sophistication of British markets and public safety. Crime prevention efforts have similarly focused on households and individuals because they are the victims of a higher proportion of crimes than businesses (Burrows and Hopkins, 2005). While interest in business victimization has increased in recent years, research in this domain is still limited, and more work has been done in countries other than Australia (Fisher and Looye, 2000; Gill, 1998; Mirrlees-Black and Ross, 1995a; Tilley and Hopkins, 1998) and Nigeria. Studies conducted in the area of business crime provide support for the thesis that a substantial proportion of businesses suffer from crime. By virtue of their sizes and the income they bring about, small businesses lack the human and financial resources of larger businesses to implement crime prevention measures. Often, surveys report that approximately half of businesses surveyed had experienced a crime (Burrows et al., 1999; Gill, 1998; Perrone, 2000). Sometimes this figure can be even larger (up to 76%), as was found in another study (Wood et al., 1997).

In spite of the likelihood of women seeming too naturally scared about crime, it is alarming that studies have found that even businesses themselves are somewhat resigned to the experience of crime. A British Chamber of Commerce (1997) survey discovered that 85% of respondents were reconciled to accepting victimization as a fact of entrepreneurial life—a natural cost of doing business. Allegations of a "grudging acceptance [by retailers] that theft is a fact of [business] life" have also been noted in Australia (Hagopian, 1999–2000, p. 16). At this juncture, the consistent finding that commercial premises face a greater risk of criminal victimization and revictimization than their residential counterparts (Bamfield, 1994; van Dijk and Terlouw, 1996; Bowers et al., 1998; Naudé et al., 1999; Taylor, 1999) is of particular relevance, especially to small business enterprises, where multiple or chronic victimization is common (Hibberd and Shapland, 1993; Mirrlees-Black and Ross, 1995a, 1995b; British Chamber of Commerce, 1997; Tilley and Hopkins, 1998; Perrone, 2000). All these make the lack of interest in reporting business offenses by market women seem normative.

The limitations of official police recorded crime statistics are well known in that they only indicate the nature and level of crime that is reported to the police (Carcach and Makkai, 2002). It is even more difficult to accurately determine the true nature and extent of business crime because it is often left unreported (Taylor, 2002). It is against this backdrop that this study aims to contribute to the knowledge base of crimes against women's businesses through the involvement of the criminal justice system, in Oyo town, Nigeria, by providing answers to the following questions: (1) What is the nature of crime commonly committed against market women in Oyo town? (2) How do the women victims handle the reporting of crimes committed against their businesses? (3) How satisfied are these market women victims with the outcomes of the reports of their victimization?

Materials and Method

The study location was Oyo town in Oyo State. Oyo is mostly inhabited by the Yoruba people. The population for this study comprises residents, especially female traders aged 18 years and above, that is, young and old female traders who are resident in Oyo town where their experiences of crime incidents make them prone to reporting crimes that afflict their businesses. The study randomly selected 225 women traders at Akesan, Sabo, and Mosadoba markets in Oyo town, as respondents to copies of a questionnaire. The three markets from which the samples were drawn were randomly selected. The population of women traders in the three markets, the number of their customers, and the level of socioeconomic activities going on in these selected markets showed that they have the requirements to serve as representative samples of other markets.

In addition, these markets are located at different geographical and strategic areas of Oyo town with diversity in socioeconomic and cultural characteristics. These make selected respondents from the markets quite representative and therefore suitable for the study. Also, five focus group discussions were conducted to capture the underlying thoughts that inform market women's crime reporting practices, their sociodemographic characteristics, and suggestions for improving their crime reporting responses so as to guarantee safer commercial interactions and livelihoods in Oyo markets. This study adopted the probability and nonprobability sample procedures. Therefore, random sampling and purposive sampling methods were used in selecting study sites and respondents. Focus group discussion and in-depth and key informant interview respondents were selected through purposive sampling (opinion leaders such as market women leaders, police officers, customers, and members of civil rights fighters).

Theoretical Framework, Concepts, and Measurements

The social action theory of Max Weber was used as the theoretical framework of this study. His school of thought holds sociology as a comprehensive science of the subjective meanings of the understandable motives of human actors. These subjective meanings are attached to human actions in their mutual orientations within specific sociocultural contexts. Therefore, any behavior outside of this web, Weber insists, falls outside the purview of sociology. It is probably in this context that Secher (1962) credited Weber with the belief that an action is "social" if the acting individual takes account of the behavior of others and is thereby oriented in its course. In the context of crime against market women and their reporting practices, the emphasis of this theory is on how customs, values, and norms of their sociocultural environment encourage or frustrate individual action with respect to how or how not to respond to issues of business victimization. This theory tries to explain how actors and society interact in the aftermath of crime. Market women victims just do not base their crime reporting decision making on the contextual issues only; they often look beyond, especially at the broader interactional implications of their crime control initiatives for gainful future integration in the cultural milieu.

The dependent variable used for the study is whether market women reported crimes committed against their businesses prior to the survey. The independent variables are age, place of trading, marital status, educational level, occupation, religion, and volume of trade. For knowledge about crime prevention, respondents who mentioned more than three ways of preventing victimization were classified as having good or high knowledge about prevention. From the causes of crime against market women's businesses, only three of those options are correct; those who mentioned any of the options were regarded as having good knowledge about the causes, while others were categorized as having poor knowledge of the causes of victimization in this chapter.

Sampling Design and Selection

Furthermore, the three selected markets are heterogeneous enough to contain the diversity in sociocultural, political, and economic characteristics required for representativeness in the study. These make respondents quite suitable for the study. The sample size for this study was 225 female respondents (18 years and above) in Oyo town in order to study their crime reporting practices and the efficacy of such practices in containing business victimization in Oyo town. Also, five focus group discussions were conducted to provide complementary qualitative data. The sociodemographic characteristics of respondents make them appropriate for the provision of suggestions that could help strengthen security consciousness and make Oyo market women operate their businesses in a safer Oyo community. This study adopted the probability and nonprobability sample procedures. Therefore, random sampling and purposive sampling methods were used. In-depth and key informant interview respondents were selected through purposive sampling (opinion leaders such as market leaders and key community leaders such as the head of the vigilante group, a chief, and a police officer).

Data Collection

Both quantitative and qualitative methods were used for data gathering. While the questionnaire method was used to fetch quantitative data, focus group discussion and in-depth and key informant interviews provided qualitative data for the study. Five final-year students of the Sociology Department of Lagos State University, Nigeria, three men and two women, were engaged as assistants who conducted the in-depth and key informant interviews and focus group discussions and administered copies of the questionnaire with the author. These assistants were rigorously trained on the techniques of interviewing people in ways that will prevent respondents from holding any vital information back or injecting their personal biases. Preinterview practice sessions were held to avail the research assistants the skill to administer questionnaires, handle tape recorders, and transcribe their contents. These orientation exercises took five days.

Sample Selection

Quantitative

To make the sample size representative of the entire population of market traders in Oyo town in the study area, the three markets that were randomly picked from among the markets in the town provided quantitative data. From each of the three markets, 70 respondents were randomly selected to respond to copies of a questionnaire. In all, 210 copies of a questionnaire were correctly completed and analyzed for the study. From these responses, information about respondents' sociodemographic characteristics and crime reporting practices were captured.

Qualitative

Five focus group discussions were conducted to elicit information about the crime reporting responses of market women in Oyo town to capture the underlying thoughts that keep the observed crime reporting practices enduring in contemporary times. The focus group discussants were selected across different socioeconomic backgrounds within the study area. Each of the focus group discussions consisted of eight participants. In-depth and key informant interviews were also conducted. Consent forms were administered to all the participants before the discussions. Tapes, notes, and consent forms were safely kept by the researcher.

Data Analysis

Quantitative Data

Returned copies of the questionnaire were thoroughly edited. Being a precoded instrument, entry and analyses were facilitated. The quantitative data collected from this survey was subjected to two levels of analysis. The first level involves an examination of the distribution of the respondents according to selected characteristics. This is because the behavior of individuals in society is, to a large extent, determined by their personal characteristics, as well as those of the environment in which they live. For this reason, it is expected that crime reporting responses will be greatly determined by background characteristics such as education, age, marital status, and type of trade invested in. To this end, simple percentages were employed to describe these variables. The second level involves the examination of the pattern of relationship between the independent variable, that is, market women and other dependent variables, such as crime reporting practices.

Qualitative Data

The focus group discussions were transcribed and translated verbatim. Analysis involved developing a system of indexing the data into sets of categories or codes that provided structure to the data based on the research objectives and the topic included in the question guide. A qualitative ZY-index software package for ethnographic data was used for textual data analysis. Some striking expressions were used for verbatim reporting. Data from the qualitative survey have been extensively used in this chapter to validate quantitative analysis where and when desirable.

Results

Demographic Variables

Of the respondents who admitted having been victims of crime, 88.5% are between 26 and 40 years old, 37.8% hold a minimum of a West African school certificate, 36.7% hold a first school leaving certificate, 19.4% have a national certificate of education, and 6.1% have a first university degree. Of the market women victims of crime, 71.2% are married, 11.5% divorced, and 17.3% widowed. Also, of the respondents, 24%, who are Christians, admitted they have been victims of crime and 26.1% declined. However, 70%, who are Muslims, said they have been victims of crime, while 67.4% denied having ever been victims of crime.

Out of the respondents surveyed, 39.5% who admitted ever reporting a crime were between the ages of 36 and 40 years, 30.2% were between 31 and 35 years, and 19.0% were between 21 and 25 years. Of those respondents who conceded to having reported crimes to the police, only 9.5% were single, 52.4% were married, 19.0% were divorced, and 19.0% were widowed. A key informant interview respondent appeared to have explanations for more cases of reporting from the age brackets that notified the police:

> Market women who are between ages 31 and 40 and also those who are unmarried reported the most crimes because the cultural inhibitions they suffer is limited. Besides, the economy has become so biting that most of the cultural prescriptions that precluded women from giving expressions to their pains, especially in the context of victimization, appear to have been overcome by economic realities. Everyone, male or female, has a right to remain afloat economically. Therefore, if a market woman's items are stolen, she engages every legitimate avenue, including reporting the incident to the police, to ensure recovery.

Twenty-one percent of surveyed respondents who reported crime to the police hold a first leaving school certificate, 33.3% hold a West African school certificate, 24.6% have a national certificate of education, and 10.5% have a first university degree. And of those who admitted to having reported crimes to the police, 79.4% are Muslims, 11.1% Christians, and 9.5% other faiths.

On the nature of the crime and crime reporting, 71.1% of the respondents revealed that their victimization involved beating, 15.6% said it was offensive touching, and 13.3% noted that theirs was outright rape. The kind of offenses claimed to have taken place necessitated a question on the time of day in which these market women victims suffered their victimizations. In response, respondents indicated that the nature of crimes they suffered had an influence on their crime reporting practices: of the respondents who reported crimes to the police, 66.7% said that it occurred at night, 21.1% said the crime took place in the morning, and 12.3% could not precisely say when the crime occurred.

A female adult smoked fish seller who was an in-depth interview respondent noted

> Cases of abuse of market women are though disturbing, some of them derive from long-standing practices that we have been grudgingly tolerating for years. We have started to feel the impact of their onslaught more deeply, that informs our embrace of crime reporting in modern times.

But a key informant interview respondent who is a traditional ruler in the ancient city did not look at the question of market women's vulnerability and victimization from that seeming simplistic trend. He particularly decried the attitude of Yoruba women traders who seem to have forgotten their source by saying

> Christianity and Islamism have caused our market women to consign their traditional means of security to the background. This deliberate overzealousness about imported religions informs the tragedies which market women suffer in the contemporary times. Our forefathers did not need to remain awake throughout the night to ensure that their property remains secure. If our people could retrace their steps and embrace our tradition, the gods are competent at all times to secure their own people as well as their property. Our women, according to a Calabar proverb, cut the tree; that is why it has fallen on them.

Of the respondents, 60.6% said their victimization involved theft of money, 21.2% loss of food items, and 18.2% moveable economic items. However, 47.4% of the respondents said the offenders actually used weapons, 42.1% said no threat whatsoever was used, and 10.5% said offenders threatened persons they found on their premises.

After an exhaustive consideration of the probability that a market woman could be raped in the market, a focus group discussion concluded that any market woman who stays very late or comes very early to the market runs the risk of being a victim of personal crime. It is not impossible for women traders to be harassed or even raped in the market at such times, realizing the epileptic character of electricity in most parts of the country and the paucity of police surveillance in Nigeria. However, it is property crimes that market women are most commonly victims of.

A female cloth seller who was also an in-depth interview respondent added her own experience to provide practical evidence to the foregoing:

> When I experienced crime a few months earlier before the survey, I was extremely traumatized. I felt the urge to report, hoping I would recover some of the items stolen, but I feared the offender might seek revenge after he must have been arrested, prosecuted, punished, and released. For this consideration, I chickened out of reporting.

The availability of alternative conflict resolution structures in Oyo town also has its influence, no matter how subtle, on the crime reporting practices of market women. More importantly, the people in whom the respondents confided about the occurrence of crimes determined the structures to which they directed their crime reporting complaints: 60.8% of the respondents said that these individuals reported their victimizations to the police on their behalf, 27.5% said such individuals advised them, and 11.8% received support from those they told. Of the respondents who eventually reported their victimization, 65.8% did so to town associations, 18.4% to traditional rulers, and 15.8% to Oodua People's Congress (OPC). Nevertheless, 48.7% who reported to the police said the police believed their reported crime accounts, 35.9% said the police arrested the offenders, and 15.4% said the police ignored them and their complaints.

An in-depth interview respondent provided justification for her not having any iota of confidence in the police:

> I have no confidence in the police. Whenever they are alerted, they blow siren to alert the robbers of their arrival. In effect, the offenders would just leisurely walk away, undetected, suffer no apprehension, prosecution, and usually no punishment. What happened next? The police would begin to harass and arrest innocent citizens. This is really a humiliating tradition in the face of available best practices in crime control that characterize the twenty-first century world.

A chieftain of the OPC, a popular vigilante group in southwestern Nigeria, who is also a key informant interview respondent, expressed his dissatisfaction with the market women for abandoning their informal policing structure to make themselves unnecessarily vulnerable to all sorts of preventable victimization:

> The women wrongly believed that if they identified with us, their other colleagues will see them as fetish and this might affect their social profile is one key concern that drives the women's pretense about the potency of OPC to secure them and their markets. The women appeared to have forgotten that a doctor who invoked a storm on his people cannot prevent his house from destruction. The earlier these market women retraced their steps the safer they are and the more protected their wares become as well.

How satisfied are these market women victims with the process of their victimization? None of the respondents was very satisfied with the police handling of their complaints. While 65.8% of the respondents are dissatisfied with the police, 18.4% were satisfied and 15.8% found it extremely difficult to define their state of satisfaction with police services. The foregoing was corroborated by qualitative data volunteered by an in-depth interview respondent:

> Burglary of shops is the most common crime that market women face in Oyo town. We report them to market leaders who then notify the police. However, by conduct, the difference between the police and offenders is not clear. The police usually make reporters feel stupid as they request them to report at the station at odd times when the victims are supposed to be making efforts to overcome their losses through sustainable sales. At the end of the day, the offender may never get apprehended and losses too never recovered. This is double loss of some kind.

In spite of all the shortcomings of the police, market women suggested a way out of the commercial insecurity of women at Oyo markets. Fifty percent suggested that the government should invest in mass security education in the three main Nigerian ethnic languages and voters should elect good leaders for Nigeria in the future to ensure public safety. The image of the police is awful, but the respondents did not believe it had gone beyond redemption, as an in-depth interview respondent suggested. In addition, the foregoing quantitative recommendation still reposed confidence in the reformation of the police being able to cause a radical difference in the present outlook and expected profile:

> It is like the bad eggs outnumber the ethical ones in the Nigeria police. Government should overhaul the police totally and provide jobs for our teeming youths to reduce the threat of burglary to the economy of market women in Oyo town.

Not totally agreeing with the above, a focus group discussion concluded that the Nigeria police obviously need some form of intervention and argued that the only way to counter deep-seated traditional fears of Oyo women in terms of crime reporting of their abusers in the context of the lukewarm attitude of the police is to embark on aggressive crime reporting education that targets all the key stakeholders in public security. As if to align her thoughts with the focus group discussion's position, an embittered in-depth interview respondent observed

> The general air of discrimination against women on the basis of their sex has widely spawned a culture that rejects modern values which enjoin men to show consideration to women and their concerns. Except the police are desirably engendered, women traders are endangered as they go about their daily socioeconomic engagements.

It is significant to note that some respondents actually denied ever being victims because these denials have their roots in cultural orientation. The word for crime in Yoruba is *oran*, which is often interpreted as a tragedy. In typically cultural parlance, the criminal (*odaran*), his or her crime (*oran*), and the victims are symptoms of varying layers of misfortune to an average Yoruba person. Therefore, crime is often ascribed to cultural retribution of some kind. Unless a respondent has a deep sense of detachment from his or her natural entrapment in cultural indoctrination, to accept being a victim of crime in a deeply cultural environment such as Yoruba land is as clear as indicating that one is a cultural sinner. A concerned woman petty trader who was an in-depth interview respondent said,

> An old pepper seller respondent said such business abuses by offenders were part of a pattern of disturbing behaviour for years among young men in Oyo communities. Most of their sympathizers often attempted to reduce the effect of their misconduct by claiming that it was the bad economy that drove young men to violate the rights of market women in Oyo town. Beyond this, if all economy affected youth have to unleash their anger on market women, will their mothers still remain in most homes perpetuating motherhood expectations? Government should just provide employment for our youth to reduce the invasion of our markets.

A woman police officer who is a key informant respondent did not agree; she condemned the tragic assumption of market women about the whole essence of security consciousness when she said,

> Women traders take a lot of things for granted. They go to churches and their mosques to pray for the commitment of their businesses to the beings they believed controlled and sustained their worlds, forgetting that security is a tangible service that is provided not by the spirits but by persons trained in that business. These women are not proactive in their concern about victimization. They are mainly reactive. They do not think about security until they are victimized. It is high time market women embraced the culture of banking, insurance and patronage of the formal policing by reporting suspicious movements of strange faces around their markets.

Discussion

The absence of public trust in the police in Nigeria is not a new development. In the colonial epoch, the style and principles of policing were described as antipeople by several authors (Rotimi, 2001; Okafor, 2006; Alemika and Chukwuma, 2000; Ikuteyijo, 2009). This perspective appears not to have changed. It probably drives public lack of interest in the police. For the foregoing and other associated reasons, market women in Nigeria generally and those in Oyo town in particular are encouraged to develop the culture of business insurance. Unless their expectation of compensation in the aftermath of victimization is feasible, market women's crime reporting interest might not significantly improve.

Though the history of community police relations in Nigeria has been described as suspicious, as the idea of policing imposed on the country by the colonial masters was calculated to foster an antagonism between the policed and the police (Alemika and Chukwuma, 2000; Onoja, 2007; Tamuno, 1970), a lot could still be achieved in terms of public security, using the police as tools. The manner of inception of a formal justice system informs the mutual suspicion between the police and members of the public. The situation has become so daunting that the distrust emanating from the unhealthy relationship has assumed a mutual dimension.

The truth that most market women in Oyo town appear to ignore is that crimes against their businesses are usually crimes of opportunity. If they continue to make their markets easy for criminals to steal from them because of the absence of target-tightening barriers, chances are that even situational criminals who otherwise might not have taken to criminality will take advantage of their porous market situation. In the times past, the gum of solidarity that held society together was really adhesive. Everybody was the security of everybody. Now, the realities of modern life have imposed individuality on the community such that everybody now minds his or her business. For example, even the informal structures are no longer credited with a modicum of potency in security matters.

Conclusion

For a very long time to come, many crimes against market women may go unreported if the situation does not significantly change. Most women who were victims of business crimes were probably inhibited by cultural considerations to report their experiences. Or they were dissuaded by the attitudes of the police toward the recovery of stolen items through prompt apprehension of criminals. According to the highlights of social action theory, the theft from one market woman and not another has symbolic effects. The meaning attached to the idea of loss to theft in the context of market interaction of trading victims and rampaging offenders transcends common understanding of the effects of ordinary social disjunction. It extends to community members associating victimization to the consequences of retributive justice in some ways. Why is someone the victim and not another? If Nigerians decide to make good of a bad job, the police could be made to support the safety of market women by making crime against their businesses risky, costly, and unrewarding through proactive and protective measures.

Recommendations

Arising from the findings from this study, this chapter makes the following recommendations:

- Market women should overcome cultural limitations and begin to disclose crimes they have been traditionally disinclined to report.
- Public policy should simplify crime reporting procedures to further encourage women to report crimes involving them and their economic interests.
- In addition to imbibing the culture of crime reporting, market women should insure their business risks with insurance companies to have something concrete in terms of compensation to fall back on in times of inevitable victimization.
- Market women should save their money in banks, on a daily basis, to reduce their losses at each victimization episode.
- Market women should invest more in crime prevention strategies for less cost of business crime.
- The mindset that crimes against businesses are natural costs of doing business and therefore facts of business life should be changed because it is tolerant of crimes and criminals.
- Women should report crime against their businesses so that criminal data emanating from them could form critical components for the development of culturally based interventions.
- Market women in Oyo should deemphasize spiritual security of their economic wealth and invest in formal security channels.

References

Alemika, E. E. O. (2004). Crime statistics and information management in Nigerian justice and security systems. In E. E. O. Alemika and I. C. Chukwuma (eds.), *Crime and Policing in Nigeria: Challenges and Options*. Lagos: Network on Police Reform in Nigeria (NOPRIN).

Alemika, E. E., and Chukwuma, I. (2000). *Police-Community Violence in Nigeria*. Abuja, Nigeria: Centre for Law Enforcement Education and National Human Rights Commission.

Bamfield, J. (1994). National survey of retail theft and security, 1994. Northampton, UK: Nene College, School of Business.

Bowers, K. J., Hirschfield, A., and Johnson, S. D. (1998). Victimisation revisited: A case study of non-residential repeat burglary on Merseyside. *British Journal of Criminology*, 38(3), 429–452.

British Chamber of Commerce. (1997). Small firms survey on crime. London: British Chamber of Commerce.

Burrows, J., Anderson, S., Bamfield, J., Hopkins, M., and Ingram, D. (1999). Crimes against business in Scotland. Edinburgh: Scottish Business Crime Centre.

Burrows, J., and Hopkins, M. (2005). Business and crime. In N. Tilley (ed.), *Handbook of Crime Prevention and Community Safety*. Devon, UK: Willan Publishing.

Carcach, C., and Makkai, T. (2002). Review of Victoria police crime statistics. Research and Public Policy Series No. 45. Canberra: Australian Institute of Criminology.

Cromie, A. (1993). How retail crime pinches profits. *Business Review Weekly*, 4, 51–75.

Federation of Small Businesses (FSB). (2005). Cracking business crime. London: Federation of Small Businesses.

Felson, M., and Clarke, R. (eds.). (1997). *Business and Crime Prevention*. New York: Criminal Justice Press.

Fisher, B. (1991). A neighbourhood business area is hurting: Crime, fear of crime, and disorders take their toll. *Crime and Delinquency*, 37(3), 363–373.

Fisher, B., and Looye, J. W. (2000). Crime and small businesses in the Midwest: An examination of overlooked issues in the United States. *Security Journal*, 13(2), 45–72.

Gill, M. (1998). The victimisation of business: Indicators of risk and the direction of future research. *International Review of Victimology*, 6, 17–28.

Hagopian, A. (1999–2000). Industry losing battle against crime. *Security Australia*, December–January, 16–17.

Hibberd, M., and Shapland, J. (1993). *Violence in Small Shops*. London: Police Foundation.

Hopkins, M. (2002). Crime against Business: The Way Forward for Future Research. *British Journal of Criminology*, 42, 782–797.

Ikuteyijo, L. (2009). The challenges of community policing in Nigeria. *International Journal of Police Science and Management*, 11(3).

Mirrlees-Black, C., and Ross, A. (1995a). Crime against retail premises in 1993. Research Findings No. 26. London: Home Office Research and Statistics Department.

Mirrlees-Black, C., and Ross, A. (1995b). Crimes against manufacturing premises in 1993. Research Findings No. 27. London: Home Office Research and Statistics Department.

Naudé, C. M. B., Prinsloo, J. H., and Martins, J. H. (1999). *Crimes against the South African Business Sector*. Pretoria: University of South Africa.

Okafor, N. (2006). Relevance of African traditional jurisprudence on control, justice, and law: A critique of the Igbo experience. *African Journal of Criminology and Justice Studies*, 2(1).

Onoja, A. F. (2007). Sustaining a tradition of policing through alienation: An assessment of recruitment and training in the colonial and postcolonial Nigeria police. *Afrika Zamani*, 13/14, 137–151.

Perrone, S. (2000). Crimes against small business in Australia: A preliminary analysis. *Trends & Issues in Crime and Criminal Justice*, no. 184.

Robson, R., and Teague, A. (2005). *Cracking Business Crime.* London: Federation of Small Businesses.

Rotimi, K. (2001). *The Police in a Federal State: The Nigerian Experience.* Ibadan: College Press Limited.

Secher, H. P. (1962). *Basic Concepts in Sociology. Contributors: Max Weber.* New York: Citadel Press.

Snyder, N. H., Broome, O. W., and Zimmerman, K. (1989). Using internal controls to reduce employee theft in small businesses. *Journal of Small Business Management*, 27(3), 48–55.

Tamuno, T. N. (1970). *The Police in Modern Nigeria.* Ibadan: University of Ibadan Press.

Taylor, G. (1999). Using repeat victimisation to counter commercial burglary: The Leicester experience. *Security Journal*, 12(1), 41–52.

Taylor, N. (2002). Reporting of crime against small retail business. *Trends & Issues in Crime and Criminal Justice*, no. 242.

Tilley, N., and Hopkins, M. (1998). Business as usual: An evaluation of the small business and crime initiative. Police Research Series Paper No. 95. London: Policing and Reducing Crime Unit, Home Office.

Tulyakov, V. A. (2004). Victimization and organized crime. Nottingham, UK: Greater Nottingham Partnership, Business Crime Reduction Strategy for Greater Nottingham.

van Dijk, J. J. M., and Terlouw, G. J. (1996). An international perspective of the business community as victims of fraud and crime. *Security Journal*, 7, 157–167.

Walker, J. (1994). The first national survey of crimes against businesses. Canberra: Australian Institute of Criminology.

Wood, J., Wheelwright, G., and Burrows, J. (1997). *Crime against Small Business: Meeting the Challenges.* Swindon, UK: Crime Concern.

Discrimination and Victimization of Women at the Workplace in Serbia

Prevalence and Characteristics

5

VESNA NIKOLIĆ-RISTANOVIĆ,
SANJA ĆOPIĆ, AND BEJAN ŠAĆIRI

Contents

Introduction

Gender equality is one of the key preconditions for development of democracy, respect of human rights, achievement of peace and social justice, and the overall development of a society. One of the indicators of the achieved level of gender equality in a society is the position of women in the labor market, which also reflects the socioeconomic position of women in a country in general (Babović, 2007, p. 19). During the past several years, significant efforts were undertaken in Serbia toward the development of a legal and institutional framework for the promotion, affirmation, and achievement of gender equality in different fields of social relations (Nikolić-Ristanović et al., 2012). The legal framework for the protection from discrimination in the labor market in general, and of women in particular, has been significantly improved, particularly with the adoption of the labor law in 2005,* and later on with the passing of antidiscriminatory legislation,† particularly the law on gender equality in 2009,‡ and inclusion of antidiscriminatory clauses in other legal acts. In that way, the principle of gender equality, guaranteed by the Serbian Constitution from 2006, was further evolved. On the other hand, establishment of the gender equality mechanisms, as well as the establishment of the Commissioner for the Protection of Equality, contributed to the development of the institutional framework for the implementation of existing legal solutions in practice. These mechanisms are supposed to enable more efficient protection of women from all forms of discrimination in general, and in the labor market in particular. In addition, significant efforts were undertaken toward strengthening capacities of relevant state institutions§ for recognizing discrimination, and for the prompt reaction and protection of women who face discrimination in the labor market (Nikolić-Ristanović et al., 2012).

Notwithstanding these achievements, the position of women in the labor market in Serbia is still far from being satisfactory. Although not collected in a systematic way, the data of the relevant state institutions and independent state agencies,¶ as well at the results of the so far implemented researches in Serbia (Babović, 2007; UNDP, 2007; Kolin, 2009; Ignjatović et al., 2010), suggest that women do not have equal position and treatment as men in the labor market, and that they face different forms of discrimination and victimization in the field of labor and employment.

In 2011, the Victimology Society of Serbia conducted a nationwide victimization survey on discrimination and victimization of women in the labor market in Serbia. The survey was a part of a larger study of discrimination against women in the labor market in Serbia, which was conducted by the Victimology Society of Serbia from June 2011 to April 2012,** in cooperation with the United Nations Agency for Gender Equality and Empowerment of Women (UN Women), within the project "Mapping Out the Dimension and Characteristics of Gender Discrimination in the Labour Market in Serbia and Social Response to It."†† The aim of this chapter is to present survey findings on prevalence and characteristics of discrimination and victimization of women in the labor market in Serbia.

The chapter starts with enlisting crucial principles and standards foreseen in the main international documents that call for elimination of all forms of discrimination of women, including work-related violence. It proceeds with presenting the main findings on prevalence and characteristics of discrimination and victimization of women in the sphere of labor and employment. In the final part, based on the main survey findings, we give the conclusions and main recommendations that could contribute to changes of legislation

* Official Gazette of the Republic of Serbia, 24/2005, 61/2005, 54/2009.

† Such as the law on the prohibition of discrimination, Official Gazette of the Republic of Serbia, 22/2009, and the law on suppressing discrimination of persons with disabilities, Official Gazette of the Republic of Serbia, 33/2006.

‡ Official Gazette of the Republic of Serbia, 104/2009.

§ Such as the National Employment Service and the Labour Inspectorate.

¶ For example, Anketa o radnoj snazi, 2010 (Republički zavod za statistiku, 2011a), Republički zavod za statistiku (2011b), Nacionalna služba za zapošljavanje (2010), Redovan godišnji izveštaj Poverenika za zaštitu ravnopravnosti (Poverenik za zaštitu ravnopravnosti, 2011), and Izveštaj Pokrajinskog ombudsmana (Pokrajinski Ombudsman, 2010).

** More information about the whole research can be found in Nikolić-Ristanović et al. (2012).

†† This project constituted a part of the broader program of the United Nations Agency for Gender Equality and Empowerment of Women's (UN Women) "Advancing Women's Economic and Social Rights in Serbia and in Montenegro."

and practice in order to ensure proper reaction and protection of women against discrimination and other violations of their rights in the labor market in Serbia.

Discrimination and Victimization of Women at the Workplace: An Overview of Major International Documents

Since the mid-twentieth century, various documents brought on the level of international and regional organizations, such as the United Nations, European Union, Council of Europe, and International Labour Organization, have been calling for elimination of discrimination against women in the field of labor and employment in order to ensure the same rights to women as to men based on the principle of gender equality. Major international and European documents relevant for suppressing and combating discrimination against women in general and in the labor market in particular include the International Labour Organization's Equal Remuneration Convention (1951), Discrimination (Employment and Occupation) Convention (1958), Maternity Protection Convention (2000), and resolution concerning the promotion of gender equality, pay equity, and maternity protection (2004); the UN Convention on the Elimination of All Forms of Discrimination against Women (CEDAW) (1979); EU Directive 2002/73/EC—equal treatment (2002), amending Council Directive 76/207/EEC on the implementation of the principle of equal treatment for men and women with regard to access to employment, vocational training and promotion, and working conditions; and the Council of Europe Convention on Preventing and Combating Violence against Women and Domestic Violence (2011). Although not all of these documents are legally binding, they all foresee principles and standards that should guide national policies in developing legislation and practice that would enable gender equality in the field of work. Based on their analysis, we may classify all these principles and standards into three main groups: equal treatment of women and men with regard to access to employment, training, promotion, and working conditions; safeguarding of the function of reproduction and maternity protection; and protection of women from all forms of work-related violence.

Equal treatment of women and men with regard to access to employment, training, promotion, and working conditions relates to equal access to the labor market for men and women. This implies equal access to employment and equal employment opportunities; equal pay for work of equal value; equal rights to free choice of profession and employment, promotion, training, and job security; equal right to social security, particularly in cases of retirement, unemployment, sickness, invalidity, old age, or other incapacity to work; and equal right to paid leave, health protection, and a sound working environment and safe working conditions, including conditions governing dismissal.

The second group of principles relates to the protection of women with regard to reproductive rights, that is, pregnancy and maternity. Therefore, the states should undertake legal, administrative, and practical measures to prevent discrimination against women on the grounds of marriage, family status, or maternity. As foreseen in the UN Convention on the Elimination of All Forms of Discrimination against Women (CEDAW), for example, the states should prohibit and subject to sanctioning dismissal on the grounds of pregnancy, maternity leave, or marital status; introduce maternity leave with pay or with comparable social benefits without loss of former employment, seniority, or social allowances; encourage the development of supporting social services to enable parents to combine family obligations with work responsibilities; and provide special protection to women during pregnancy in types of work proved to be harmful to them. In the ILO Maternity Protection Convention, particular attention is given to the health protection of pregnant and breastfeeding women, who are not supposed to perform work that poses a risk to both their health and that of their child. The convention also guarantees women the right to maternity leave and leave in the case of illness or complication arising out of pregnancy or childbirth. Women should be protected from dismissal during pregnancy and their absence on leave, while they should be guaranteed the right to return to the same position or an equivalent position paid at the same rate at the end of the maternity leave. Finally, it is emphasized that the states should adopt appropriate measures to ensure that maternity does not constitute a source of discrimination in employment, including access to employment.

Finally, the third group of principles relates to the protection of women from work-related violence, particularly from sexual harassment. Violence against women presents a violation of human rights and a form of discrimination against women, whether occurring in public or private life. As stated in the preamble of the Council of Europe Convention on Preventing and Combating Violence against Women and Domestic Violence, violence against women is a manifestation of historically unequal power relations between women and men, resulting in domination over, and discrimination against, women by men, also being one of the crucial social mechanisms by which women are kept in a subordinated position compared with men. Therefore, the states shall take all necessary steps to eliminate all forms of violence against women, including work-related violence. In this respect, particular attention is paid to the prohibition of sexual harassment of women in the labor market. As provided for in EU Directive 2002/73/EC on equal treatment, sexual harassment is deemed to be discrimination on the grounds of sex, and is defined as a situation "where any form of unwanted verbal, non-verbal or physical conduct of a sexual nature occurs, with the purpose or effect of violating the dignity of a person, in particular when creating an intimidating, hostile, degrading, humiliating or offensive environment."

All these aspects of gender (in)equality in the labor market that may result in gender discrimination were taken into account while surveying the prevalence and characteristics of discrimination of women in the labor market in Serbia, which is going to be further elaborated.

Methodology

The subject of the survey conducted by the Victimology Society of Serbia was discrimination against women in the labor market in Serbia and the social response to it. For the purpose of the survey, discrimination against women in the labor market was defined as any unwarranted differentiation or unequal treatment, that is, omission (exclusion, limitation, or preferential treatment) with the purpose or effect of hindering, impairing, disabling, or nullifying a woman's recognition, enjoyment, or exercise of rights in the labor market, that is, in the sphere of labor and employment, on the grounds of her gender or other personal characteristics. The survey encompassed both discrimination against women in the process of access to employment and discrimination at the workplace. Special attention was paid to sexual and psychological violence against women at the workplace.

The survey covered a period of five years preceding the research. The data was collected in the period from August to October 2011. A combination of a victimization survey and feminist action research methods was used. The data was collected through *face-to-face* interviews. The study was conducted on a stratified random sample of 706 women aged 18–64 years, from six towns in Serbia. The data was analyzed by descriptive statistics, chi-square test, and Pearson correlations. In addition to a quantitative analysis, a qualitative analysis of respondents' answers to open-ended questions was performed.

The survey had an action character. Its goal was not only to collect the data on the subject, but also to work toward raising the level of women's knowledge and awareness about different forms of gender-based discrimination in the labor market, and providing them information about the Victimology Society of Serbia, which they could approach for assistance and support in the case of discrimination.* Finally, the survey was policy oriented, which means that its findings were used as a basis for developing recommendations for certain changes of both legislation and practice in the field of women's labor rights in order to enable the improvement of the overall position of women in the labor market and the protection of those women who were exposed to various forms of discrimination in this field.

Results

More than half of the respondents (431, or 61.0%) said that they were exposed to some form of discrimination in the labor market in the observed period. Of the total number of women who have faced discrimination in the labor market, 242 (56.1%) experienced discrimination in access to employment, while 342 (79.4%) experienced discrimination at the workplace. While some women were faced with discrimination only in access to employment or at the workplace, others were faced with both forms of discrimination. In addition, 72.2% (510) of respondents knew other women (a friend, relative, or a colleague) who experienced discrimination in the labor market: 464 (65.7%) women had indirect knowledge of other women being discriminated while accessing employment, and 372 (52.7%) had indirect knowledge on discrimination against other women at the workplace.

Discrimination of Women during the Process of Access to Employment

Of 452 women who were looking for a job in the observed time period, 242 (53.5%) experienced discrimination during the process of access to employment.

As suggested by the data in Table 5.1, the most common form of discrimination against women during the process of access to employment is questioning a woman about her private life during the job interview, which was experienced by almost half of the respondents who were looking for a job in the observed time period. Almost every other woman in the sample (217, or 48.0%) was asked during a job interview questions concerning her private life. In almost all of these cases, they were asked if they were married and whether they had children (200, or 92.2%). One hundred fifteen (53.0%) respondents were asked a question regarding their plans for marriage and child birth, 48 (22.1%) were questioned about other

* In 2003, a victim support service, VDS Info and Victim Support, was established within the Victimology Society of Serbia. It provides victims of crime, discrimination, and other forms of human rights violations emotional support, information, referrals to other relevant organizations and institutions, and support in the court. More information can be found at www.vds.org.rs.

Table 5.1 Forms of Discrimination during the Process of Access to Employment

Forms of Discrimination during the Process of Access to Employment	*N*	%
Questioning a woman about her private life during the job interview	217	48.0
Commenting upon physical appearance of a woman	44	9.7
Other forms of less favorable treatment in comparison to male candidates	30	6.6
Pregnancy and maternity as an obstacle to access to employment	23	5.1
Expectations regarding sexual intercourse with a supervisor or other person in the company as a condition for getting a job	3	0.7

private matters,* and in 30 (13.8%) cases, women were asked how often they used sick leave in a year prior to the job interview.

Quite expected, younger women (those below 35) were mainly exposed to questioning about family and marriage status, but even those who belong to the age category between 35 and 50 were not exempted from these questions. These questions were mainly posed to women who were cohabitating, who were not married, or who were divorced, which speaks in favor of the employer's fear that they will get married, give birth to a child, and use maternity leave, thus not being productive. This is also supported by the fact that women without children were more exposed to this kind of questioning than women who already had children. This kind of treatment by the employers presents not only discrimination of women on the grounds of sex, but also a violation of positive legislation that foresees that the employer is not allowed to look for data on the family and marriage status and child birth planning from the candidate in the process of employment.

The next most common form of discrimination during the process of access to employment was commenting upon physical appearance of a woman, which was experienced by 44 (9.7%) respondents. In most cases, comments came from men, that is, employers, business owners, directors, or other persons interviewing women. In two cases, the physical appearance of the respondents was commented upon by women that respondents had spoken to. Commenting upon physical appearance included comments about being good looking, physically or sexually attractive, and pretty, and looking younger than she was. These comments were unpleasant for the respondents due to the situation in which they were given, which can be illustrated by the words of some respondents. One respondent said, "The man I spoke to was eyeing on me and commenting that I was pretty. I felt uncomfortable, because I was wondering if he expected something from me." Another respondent stated that the potential employer said, "It's good to have such an attractive woman working in the boutique." In addition, in two cases respondents were told to lose weight, and in some cases, comments about their appearance were indirect, in terms of

* These questions could be classified into the following groups: questions about cohabitation or marriage and relationships with partners or husbands, questions about respondents' partners or husbands, and questions about family relations, housing opportunities, financial status, priorities, political orientation, and health status of the respondent. Thus, in most cases, questions related to whether the respondent had a boyfriend, was the relationship serious or long lasting, what was the relationship with her husband, where did her husband or boyfriend work and what did he do, did they have children and if not why, who was with the children when she was at work, where did her parents work, with whom did she live, what were the conditions in which she lived, was her priority family or career, where did she work prior to the interview, what was the reason for not working there anymore, what was her earning before, and so forth. In addition, respondents also noted that they were asked questions about their political orientation, and in one case the respondent stated that she was asked questions about her health status, namely, was she tested for sexually transmitted diseases and did she use protection during sexual relations.

turning women's attention to the fact that for the specific job, they should always be well and elegantly dressed, with makeup, or even that they have to be attractive and provocative, wearing a short and tight shirt with a deeper neckline, and so on.

Other forms of less favorable treatment in comparison to male candidates were reported by 30 (6.6%) respondents.* This was followed by pregnancy and maternity as an obstacle to access to employment (23, or 5.1%), and expectations regarding sexual intercourse with a supervisor or other person in the company as a condition for getting a job (3, or 0.7%). Pregnancy and maternity as an obstacle for access to employment were manifested through not hiring a woman that had a child under the age of 12 (13 cases), binding a woman not to give birth in a certain period of time (11 cases), binding a woman to sign a blanket dismissal that will be activated in case of pregnancy (7 cases), and not hiring a pregnant woman (5 cases).

Discrimination of Women at the Workplace

More than half of 596 women who worked at any moment within the period covered by the survey (342, or 57.7%) said that they had experienced some form of discrimination at the workplace. Generally speaking, women who work in the private sector (64.8%) were more exposed to discrimination at the workplace than those who work in the public sector (48.7%). The respondents who did not sign a contract with the employer have been increasingly discriminated against at work (70.4%) in comparison to women who were working under an employment contract or other types of contracts (54.3%). Finally, it was found that women who were employed part-time were to a greater extent subject to discrimination at the workplace (57%) than women who worked full-time (52.6%).

As the data in Table 5.2 suggest, female respondents were most often faced with discrimination in relation to working conditions (256 women [43%]). This was followed by sexual (132, or 22.1%) and psychological (131, or 22%) violence at the workplace. Discrimination against women at the workplace is also reflected in the lower wages of women compared to male counterparts for work of equal value and is an impediment of the promotion of women. In addition, 20 women experienced discrimination related to pregnancy and maternity, while 2 were discriminated against during job termination and payment of retirement benefits.

Discrimination Related to Working Conditions

The most frequent form of discrimination of women at the workplace is discrimination that is related to working conditions (256, or 43%). Particularly vulnerable from this form of discrimination are women working in tourism and catering services (70.6%), while the

* As reasons for unfavorable treatment of women, respondents generally stated that the male candidates were preferred because they are physically stronger, more militant, and "bite" more than women; they usually have a driver's license and are better drivers, which makes it easier to get a job; and it is normal in some professions to employ men. Also, they were preferred to avoid the admission of women, as there is a fear that women will go on sick leave or bear children, because they already had women similar to them in the office, or that women, especially younger ones, cannot be an authority for the population they should work with (such as students in high school). In addition, as reasons for less favorable treatment than men, respondents also noted that for men, there are no requirements in terms of dressing up, they are not forced to sign a blanket dismissal in the case of pregnancy, and in a job interview, they are not asked questions relating to child birth and family planning. In addition, although the number is small to draw general conclusions, it is necessary to point out that in almost half of the cases (14) in which women experienced less favorable treatment than men in finding employment, those women had a university degree.

Table 5.2 Forms of Discrimination at the Workplace

Forms of Discrimination at the Workplace;	*N*	%
Discrimination related to working conditions	256	43.0%
Sexual violence against women	132	22.1%
Psychological violence against women	131	22.0%
Discrimination related to wages	49	8.2%
Discrimination related to the promotion	48	8.1%
Discrimination related to pregnancy and maternity	20	3.4%
Discrimination related to termination and paying of retirement benefits	2	0.3%

least vulnerable are those working in education (14.5%). Women who work in the private sector (53.5%) are exposed to this form of discrimination almost twice as much as women working in the public sector (29.3%). Finally, women who did not sign a contract with the employer (60.9%) are significantly more exposed to this form of discrimination than women who work under the employment or other type of contract (38.7%).

Discrimination in relation to working conditions is manifested in the following ways: lack of premises separated from men's, where women can change their clothes; obliging a woman to do other duties outside of the job description, such as making coffee, cleaning, and courier and administration jobs; maladjustment of the machinery or other equipment for women; and exposure to other inconveniences on the grounds of sex or for some other reasons.

In 196 (32.9%) cases, respondents indicated that the organization or company in which they worked had no separate rooms in which the women could change their clothes, comprising more than a half of the cases in which the need for such premises existed (51.4%). One-third of employed respondents (189, or 31.7%) had to perform some other tasks not included in their job description. In this respect, women were obliged to perform jobs that are traditionally considered to be "female jobs," which is also tightly linked to the gender roles imposed by the society (e.g., making coffee, preparing meals, and cleaning). When it comes to the machinery and other equipment, the data shows that in 19 cases (3.2%), machinery and other equipment were not adapted for women.

Although almost 90% of the respondents (519, or 87.1%) said that they had not met with troubles at work on the grounds of sex, 43 (7.2%) thought that because of their sex, they were exposed to some other inconveniences, while 34 (5.7%) could not say that with certainty. Qualitative analysis of the respondents' answers to the question of what sort of inconvenience they experienced at the workplace based on their sex shows that it was primarily belittling of their abilities based on stereotypes and prejudices about gender roles. As stated by the respondents, women are treated as slaves, inferior beings, less worthy and capable, and their opinions are not valued or taken seriously into account, while men are known as better workers and better drivers, which is why they are provided with company vehicles, leading to gender inequality. In addition, women also faced sexual harassment, comments on their appearance and the way they dress, insults, yelling, and so on.

Finally, 34 (5.7%) women were exposed to inconveniences due to other reasons. Qualitative analysis of their answers suggests that in most cases, the reasons for such treatment were political in nature (political affiliation or noncommittal to any political option); this was followed by ethnic belonging and, in some cases, sexual orientation, different opinion, and a woman being a single parent or having a specific personal or health problem (e.g., tics or poor hearing). Therefore, multiple cases of discrimination of women at the workplace, that is, discrimination based on various grounds (personal characteristics), were found out; thus, in future studies this issue should be given special attention.

Sexual Violence

The second form of discrimination against women at the workplace by its frequency is sexual violence. In order to collect data about sexual violence (harassment and blackmail) against women at the workplace, respondents were asked about five groups of behavior through which this form of discrimination and violence against women at the workplace can be manifested. Questions covered both sexual blackmail (*quid pro quo*) and different behaviors that create a hostile working environment for women. Respondents were asked questions related to the following behaviors: conditioning promotion at the workplace and moving to a better paid job or getting a raise with entering into a sexual relationship with a supervisor or another person (sexual blackmail); coercion into sexual intercourse, that is, rape; exposure to unwanted physical contact of a sexual nature; exposure to sexual comments; and exposure to pornographic materials at the workplace.

The survey findings showed that 132 women (22.1%) who worked or used to work in the observed time period were exposed to at least one form of sexual violence at the workplace.

Forms of Sexual Violence at the Workplace

The most frequent form of sexual violence women were exposed to at the workplace was sexual harassment through sexual comments: it was experienced by more than three-quarters of respondents (105, or 79.5%). This was followed by unwanted physical contact (20, or 15.2%) and proposed sexual intercourse as a condition for promotion (sexual blackmailing) (11, or 8.3%). Four women (3.1%) were exposed to pornographic materials at the workplace, while three (2.8%) were coerced into sexual intercourse.

Victims of Sexual Violence at the Workplace

The most vulnerable to sexual violence at the workplace were divorced and separated women (43.9%), single women (25.6%), and widows (22.2%), while married women were among the least vulnerable (15.5%). Thus, the data suggests that there is a significant correlation between the marriage status of a woman and her exposure to sexual violence at the workplace ($\chi^2 = 24{,}918$, df = 4, $p < 0.01$). Women who did not sign a contract with the employer were significantly more exposed to sexual violence (33.9%) than those who did have a contract (19.3%) ($\chi^2 = 11{,}440$, df = 1, $p < 0.01$), as well as women who were employed part-time (22.5%) in comparison to those employed full-time (17.5%) ($\chi^2 = 15{,}189$, df = 2, $p < 0.01$).

Perpetrators of Sexual Violence

As expected, among perpetrators of sexual violence, the most dominant were managers and superiors, thus persons who were in a position of power in relation to women.

As the data in Table 5.3 suggests, managers were in general perpetrators in 18% of cases. Managers and superiors, independently or together with other employees, committed some form of sexual violence against 39.9% of respondents. In addition, in 24.8% of

Table 5.3 Perpetrators of Sexual Violence from the Point of View of Their Position in the Organization or Company

Who Was a Perpetrator of Sexual Violence?	*N*	%
Manager	12	9.1
Manager and superior	3	2.8
Manager and colleague/coworker	8	6.1
Superior	19	14.4
Superior and colleague/coworker	6	4.5
Superior and a client	4	3.0
Colleague/coworker	41	31.1
Colleague/coworker and a client	2	1.5
Subordinated person	4	3.0
Client/customer	20	15.1
No data	13	9.8
Total	132	100.0

cases, sexual violence was performed only by a person in a position of power, while in 15.1% of cases violence was committed by both persons in a position of power and other employees who were in a similar position as our respondents. Finally, perpetrators of sexual violence against women at the workplace were also colleagues and coworkers (31.1%), clients and customers (15.1%), subordinated men (3%), and colleagues and clients and customers together (1.5%).

If we look into the data on who were the perpetrators of some particular forms of sexual violence, we may see that, similarly to the survey findings in some other countries, women were exposed to sexual comments by persons in a position of power (48.6%) and colleagues and coworkers (48.5%) to the same extent (Crouch, 2001). However, in this survey we found something that was not identified in the surveys conducted in other countries: among those who victimized respondents by unwanted physical contact, clients and customers were dominant. In addition, the proportion of persons in the position of power and colleagues and coworkers who acted in the same manner was also rather high. As expected, sexual blackmailing originated primarily from the persons who were in the position of power in relation to the victim.

Psychological Violence

In order to obtain data about psychological violence against women at the workplace, respondents were asked if they were exposed to one or more of the following behaviors: threatened with violence; threatened with dismissal; not being given work; being given too much work; addressed with shouting, ignorance, or isolation; not being called to meetings; humiliated through derogatory words, gossip, or the spreading of lies about a woman; or having it made impossible to finish the given work.

The survey findings suggest that 131 women (22%) suffered from psychological violence at the workplace (mobbing). Psychological violence mostly consisted of giving women too much work, addressing them with shouting, and gossiping, which were followed by threatening with dismissal, spreading lies about a woman, and insults and humiliation through derogatory words. In most cases, psychological violence was perpetrated by the manager or immediately superior person (45%) (vertical mobbing), while horizontal mobbing was less present. One-quarter (25.2%) of respondents suffered from psychological violence from managers (directors) of their working organizations. In three cases, psychological violence from the subordinated person was recorded, while 6.9% of respondents were victims of both vertical and horizontal mobbing.

Discrimination Related to Wages

Taking as a departure point the fact that the average wage of women in Serbia is lower than that of men, we wanted to find out what was the experience of the respondents in this respect. Therefore, respondents were asked if they get the same salary as their male colleagues for work of equal value. In addition, they were asked if they consider it all right for men to get a higher wage for work of equal value than women.

In total, 49 (8.2%) respondents said that they had smaller wages than their male colleagues for work of equal value. On the other hand, 360 (60.4%) respondents answered that their wages are the same as those of their male colleagues. In addition, 72 (12.1%) respondents did not have male colleagues, so it was not possible to determine the existence of discrimination related to wages based on sex in this case. Finally, 86 (14.4%) respondents answered that they did not know if their wage was the same as that of their male colleagues. Wage gap is more present in the private (35, or 10.7%) than in the public (10, or 4.2%) sector.

On the other hand, as expected, most respondents (692, or 98.0%) answered that it would not be all right for men to get higher wages than women for work of equal value. Otherwise, according to their opinion, that would present discrimination, because women should be equal to men, gender should not be a criterion for deciding wages, and that would not be legal. Some respondents said that only in cases of hard physical work should men possibly be paid more, while there were also respondents who thought that women should have higher wages because they are more capable and better workers. However, some of the respondents (2, or 0.3%) said that it would be all right for men to be better paid than women if that is a decision of the employer, justifying this with the right of the employer to decide that on his own. In addition, eight respondents (1.1%) said that they were not sure about this issue, with one of them saying that maybe that is all right "because a man is the one who is a family breadwinner, while a child is a priority to a woman." This kind of attitude, as well as the answers of the respondents who were not explicitly against higher wages for men than for women, although rare, reminds us that patriarchal stereotypes related to the wages of men and women exist among women as well, and this fact should be kept in mind while creating measures to prevent discrimination of women at the workplace.

Discrimination Related to Promotion

Of the total number of respondents who worked at any moment in the observed time period, 48 (8.1%) answered that they could not be promoted because of their sex. Particularly vulnerable were young women (those below 30) whose direct superior was a man and who worked in organizations where men prevailed. This particular form of discrimination was especially faced by divorced or separated women. In 22 cases (45.8%), those were women with a university degree, while in 21 cases they had finished high school. In percentage, promotion was disabled almost to the same extent to women who worked in the private (8.9%) and the public (7.6%) sector. In addition, promotion was doubly disabled for those women who had male bosses (30, or 12.0%) than for those whose bosses were female (17, or 6.4%). Respondents who worked in primarily male organizations were faced with this form of discrimination (15, or 14.9%) more than those where there were more female employees (24, or 7.4%) or where there was almost the same number of employees of both sexes (7, or 6.5%).

Discrimination Related to Pregnancy and Maternity

The data showed that 20 (3.4%) women were discriminated against in relation to pregnancy and maternity, which makes 30.3% of all respondents who were pregnant at the time when they were employed and could have been exposed to this form of discrimination. All of the respondents who have had an experience of discrimination related to pregnancy and maternity were faced with the fact that after returning from maternity leave and leave for child care, they were not included in the training programs that were organized. In addition, 13 respondents could not return to their job after maternity leave and leave for child care, because they were moved to another, inadequate workplace, while 10 respondents indicated that material compensation had not been paid regularly during maternity leave and leave for child care. In seven cases, it was noted that the respondents were fired after maternity leave and leave for child care, two respondents were moved to another position during their pregnancy, two were dismissed during their pregnancy and two during maternity leave, and two respondents had to discontinue maternity leave and return to work; otherwise, they would have been dismissed.

Looking for Assistance and Support

Of 431 respondents who had experienced discrimination in the labor market, only 40 (9.3%) approached an institution, organization, or individual for assistance, support, or protection. In percentages, a slightly higher number of respondents who experienced discrimination at the workplace looked for assistance and support (10.5%) than those who were discriminated in the process of access to employment (7.8%). Of 40 women who looked for the assistance and support, 30 (75%) approached the manager (director) of the organization or company in which they worked, 7 approached individuals they felt could support them, 6 approached the labor inspectorate, 3 approached the trade union, 2 approached the court and the employment agency, and 1 respondent went to the municipal free legal aid service.

Generally speaking, respondents who approached someone for assistance and support were mainly dissatisfied with the reaction. The reasons for dissatisfaction were primarily nonreaction, misunderstanding, minimizing or denying the problem, inefficiency, and the lack of interest in solving the problem. This speaks in favor of the need for further awareness raising of both employers and institutions about discrimination of women and their capacity building for adequate treatment of women in such situations.

Respondents who did not ask for assistance and support were asked what the reasons for not approaching anyone for assistance were. As the key reasons for not approaching institutions, organizations, independent state agencies, or individuals, women pointed out the following: they were able to solve the problem on their own (136, or 34.8%), belief that no one could help them (135, or 34.5%), the problem was not serious (88, or 22.5%), fear of losing their job (49, or 12.5%), lack of knowledge about whom to address (45, or 11.5%), fear of not being able to get a job if they report discrimination (24, or 6.1%), lack of financial resources (16, or 4.1%), and lack of support from family and friends (3, or 0.8%).

Discussion and Conclusion

The data obtained through this survey show that discrimination against women in the labor market in Serbia is rather widespread, both in access to employment and at the workplace. Sexual victimization is most probably more widespread, but women are not ready to talk about it. In addition, it is not possible to compare the obtained data with the results of the surveys of discrimination in the labor market or sexual violence at the workplace conducted in other countries due to differences in the applied methodology (Schneider, 1993). Nevertheless, despite the lack of or incomparability with surveys in other countries, the results of the survey conducted in Serbia are similar to those in other countries of the region and worldwide (e.g., Croatia, Greece, Ireland, Ukraine, India, the United States, Canada, and Australia, and ILO global surveys) (Johnson, 1994; Human Rights Watch, 2003; Stamati, 2004; Galić and Nikodem, 2007; Russel et al., 2008; Women's Law Center, 2008; Dhar, 2010; International Labour Organization, 2011).

Discrimination against and victimization of women in the labor market in Serbia are very much based on gender stereotypes and expectations posed by society to women and men. Historically speaking, a woman's duty was to maintain the household and take care of children, which are considered to be her "natural jobs" (Stanković and Markov, 2011, p. 321), and remains up to the present. Therefore, on the basis of the above presented data, we may conclude that getting a job, and even keeping a job, as well as promotion or using other rights in the labor market, is rather hindered for women due to their reproductive function, that is, family duties and plans in regard to them (Ignjatović et al., 2010, p. 71).

As the research results suggest, when accessing employment, women are often questioned about their private life, that is, about marriage and family status and their plans to get married or have children. Particularly striking is considering a woman's body as an object, a thing, which is visible in cases of sexual violence at the workplace, but also in cases of commenting on a woman's appearance and sexually blackmailing her (*quid pro quo*) when accessing employment. It is important to point out that marriage in this case has a protective role: women who are married and belong to men are less exposed to sexual violence at the workplace and when accessing employment, as well as to other forms of discrimination, than those who are single, separated, or divorced.

In most cases in which women were ready to speak about sexual violence at the workplace, they spoke about sexual harassment that manifested in creating a hostile environment (sexual comments and unwanted sexual contacts) and less in using sexual relations as a means of blackmailing or hurting a woman by exposing her to pornographic materials. However, it is important to keep in mind the fact that each form of sexual violence at the workplace that comes from the person that is in a position of power is to some extent of instrumental character. Thus, even sexual comments and unwanted physical contacts could implicitly have a character of sexual blackmail if they originate from these persons; therefore, the real number of these forms of victimization could be even higher (Crouch, 2001).

At work, women are also faced with inadequate working conditions, particularly in terms of unconformity of the working place and the obligation to conduct additional duties out of the job description. In this respect, as suggested by the survey results, women are obliged to perform jobs that are traditionally considered to be "women jobs," which is also tightly linked to the gender roles imposed by the society. The data on gender wage gap and glass ceiling, that is, week vertical mobility of women in the labor market or the phenomenon of "vertical segregation of women in the lower ranked workplaces in the organisation" (Relja et al., 2009, p. 231), also speaks in favor of discrimination against women in the labor market in Serbia. If we link these data with the official statistics on the overall position of women in the labor market and the results of the research so far, we may argue that in Serbia, there is the so-called "gendering" of work, that is, a gender division in the labor market that is visible in all segments (horizontally, vertically, and by the profession and fields of education), similarly to the traditional division of gender roles in the family and household (Galić, 2011, p. 26).

The data also suggests that, generally, younger women are particularly exposed to discrimination. On the other hand, when speaking of discrimination in the workplace, it can be noticed that women are more exposed to discrimination in the private than in the public sector. Women who work part-time are more exposed to discrimination than those who have full-time employment. Therefore, we could conclude that women who are exposed to discrimination are actually those who work under uncertain circumstances (Galić, 2011, p. 28).

A very low number of women decided to approach some institution, organization, or individual in the case of discrimination. The key reasons for that were the women's endeavors to solve the problem on their own and their lack of trust in the institutions and individuals. Even if they decide to look for assistance, women mainly try to solve the problem on the level of the employer (organization or company), approaching the manager or director. When we link this data with the data on who are the women mainly exposed to discrimination, then we may conclude that fear from losing a job, rights, or privileges presents obstacles for women to look for assistance and support from the institutions, forcing them to try to find solutions on their own (Vuković, 2006, p. 3).

The survey results point out that women in the labor market in Serbia are faced with different forms of discrimination and victimization, which speaks in favor of the conclusion that in the field of work, gender equality de facto has not yet been achieved. In addition, the data also points out the violations of legislation by employers; therefore, there is a need for developing mechanisms for control and prevention of such treatment. The survey results point to the need for more intensive work on patriarchal stereotypes of both men and women, as well as to conducting research about them, because they significantly impact the positions of women in the labor market. In addition, we may argue that the application of international documents and standards, which call for the elimination of work-related discrimination, including gender discrimination and violence against women, is not appropriate, which requires further work on the improvement of both legislation and practice.

Recommendations

On the basis of the survey findings and the international documents, recommendations that should contribute to changes of legislation and practice in order to ensure proper reaction and protection of women against discrimination and other violations of their rights in the labor market in Serbia were drafted. These recommendations relate to the improvement of legislation, improvement of procedures and practices of relevant institutions and organizations in cases of discrimination and other forms of violation of women's rights in the labor market, support and protection of women against discrimination in the labor market, prevention, improvement of data recording, and research. Therefore, some of the main recommendations within these groups are as follows:

1. Improvement of legislation
    a. It is necessary to provide for the clear legal definition of sexual harassment and sexual blackmail (*quid pro quo*).
    b. It is necessary to provide for the full enforcement of the concluding comments of the UN Committee on the Elimination of Discrimination against Women.
2. Improvement of the procedures and practices of relevant institutions and organizations
    a. The establishment of mechanisms for better and more strict control of the practices of employers that lead to discrimination and other forms of violations of women's rights in the labor market should be considered.
    b. It is necessary to work toward informing state institutions about existing civil society organizations that can provide information to women about their rights and how to achieve them, as well as on the importance of support and empowerment of women victims of discrimination or other types of violations of their rights in the field of labor and employment that these organizations can provide.
    c. Establishment of a special, multifunctional body at the governmental level for monitoring and affirming women's employment should be considered.
    d. It is important to work toward further development of cooperation between relevant institutions and organizations and their networking in order to avoid fragmentation, lack of coordination, and unsystematic reaction in cases of discrimination against women in the labor market and, on the other hand, to ensure the effective protection of women against discrimination in the labor market.
3. Support and protection of women against discrimination in the labor market
    a. It is necessary to work toward raising awareness of women about discrimination and other forms of violation of their rights in the labor market in order to encourage them to seek protection (through informational materials, media campaigns, etc.).
    b. It is necessary to inform women about existing services and forms of assistance, support, and protection in case of discrimination and other violations of their rights in the sphere of labor and employment.
    c. It is necessary to work toward the development of a system of free legal aid for women who suffer from discrimination in the labor market.
4. Prevention
    a. Public awareness should be raised on discrimination and other forms of violations of women's rights in the sphere of labor and employment (through informational materials, media campaigns, and the like).
    b. Awareness should be raised and the capacity of employers strengthened in order to recognize cases of discrimination against women and properly respond to them.

c. It is necessary to intensify the work on patriarchal stereotypes of women and men at all levels of education and to conduct surveys concerning them because those stereotypes significantly influence the position of women in the labor market and their exposure to discrimination.
d. The transparency of actions should be ensured to prevent practices that lead to discrimination and other forms of violation of women's rights in the labor market, especially workplace abuse, including sexual harassment and *quid pro quo* (e.g., work in offices with open doors, transparent doors of offices, etc.).

5. Improvement of data recording
   a. It is necessary to keep gender-sensitive statistics in regard to the services provided by organizations and institutions that come into contact with cases of discrimination against women in the labor market and other forms of violation of women's rights in the sphere of labor and employment.
   b. Mechanisms for continuously and systematically recording data regarding cases of discrimination against women in the labor market and other forms of violation of women's rights in the sphere of labor and employment should be considered.
6. Research
   a. It is necessary to conduct regular surveys of discrimination against women in the labor market, that is, to collect data on the scope, structure, and characteristics of this phenomenon, with a focus on discrimination against women based on other personal characteristics, especially ethnicity and disability.

References

Babović, M. (2007). Položaj žene na tržištu rada [Position of women in the labor market]. Beograd: Program UN za razvoj.

Crouch, M. (2001). *Thinking about Sexual Harassment: A Guide for the Perplexed.* New York: Oxford University Press.

Dhar, A. (2010). India: 88% women victims of sexual harassment at workplace. *One World South.* Retrieved from http://southasia.oneworld.net/news/india-88-women-victims-of-sexual-harassment-at-workplace#.U7vHFUDN3Cs.

Galić B. (2011). Žene i rad u suvremenom društvu—značaj 'orodnjenog' rada [Women and work in the contemporary society—Importance of the "gendered" work]. *Sociologija i prostor,* 49(1), 25–48.

Galić, B., and Nikodem, K. (2007). *Istraživački izvještaj "Identifikacija standarda diskriminacije žena pri zapošljavanju"* [Research report "Identifying of standards of discrimination of women in access to employment"]. Zagreb: Vlada Republike Hrvatske, Ured za ravnopravnost spolova.

Human Rights Watch. (2003). *World Report 2003.* Retrieved from http://www.hrw.org/legacy/wr2k3.

Ignjatović, S., Pantić, D., Bošković, A., and Pavlović, Z. (2010). Građani i građanke Srbije o rodnoj ravnopravnosti—javno mnjenje Srbije o rodnoj ravnopravnosti [Citizens of Serbia about gender equality—Public opinion of Serbia on gender equality]. Beograd: Uprava za rodnu ravnopravnost Ministarstva rada i socijalne politike RS.

International Labour Organization. (2011). *Global Employment Trends 2011: The Challenge of Jobs Recovery.* Geneva: International Labour Organization.

Johnson, H. (1994). Work-related sexual harassment. *Perspectives on Labour and Income,* 6(4), 9–12.

Kolin, M. (ed.). (2009). Rodne nejednakosti na tržištu rada u Srbiji i podsticaji evropskih integracija [Gender inequalities in the labor market in Serbia and the impetus of the European integration]. Beograd: Evropski pokret u Srbiji.
Nacionalna služba za zapošljavanje. (2010). Mesečni statistički bilten, br. 100, decembar 2010–Nezaposlenost i zapošljavanje u Republici Srbiji [Monthly statistical bulletin, no. 100, December 2010—Unemployment and accessing to employment in the Republic of Serbia].
Nikolić-Ristanović, V., Ćopić, S., Nikolić, J., and Šaćiri, B. (2012). Diskriminacija žena na tržištu rada u Srbiji [Discrimination of women in the labor market in Serbia]. Beograd: Viktimološko društvo Srbije i Prometej.
Pokrajinski Ombudsman. (2010). Izveštaj Pokrajinskog ombudsmana za 2010. godinu [Report of the Provincial Ombudsman for 2010]. Retrieved May 12, 2011, from www.ombudsmanapv.org.
Poverenik za zaštitu ravnopravnosti. (2011). Redovan godišnji izveštaj Poverenika za zaštitu ravnopravnosti [Regular report of the Commissioner for the Protection of Equality]. Retrieved from www.ravnopravnost.gov.rs.
Relja, R., Galić, B., and Despotović, M. (2009). Položaj žena na tržištu rada grada Splita [Position of women in the labor market in the town of Split]. *Sociologija i prostor*, 47(3), 217–239.
Republički zavod za statistiku. (2011a). Anketa o radnoj snazi, 2010 [Manpower survey, 2010]. Beograd: Republički zavod za statistiku.
Republički zavod za statistiku. (2011b). Statistički kalendar Republike Srbije [Statistical calendar of the Republic of Serbia]. Beograd: Republički zavod za statistiku.
Russel, H., Quinn, E., O'Riain, R. K., and McGinnity, F. (2008). The experience of discrimination in Ireland: Analysis of the QNHS equality module. Project report. Dublin: Equality Authority Ireland.
Schneider, B. (1993). Put up and shut up: Workplace sexual assaults. In P. B. Bart and E. G. Moran (eds.), *Violence against Women: The Bloody Footprints* (pp. 57–72). London: Sage.
Stamati, A. (2004). First survey of sexual harassment in the workplace. European Industrial Relations Observatory On-line. Retrieved from http://www.eurofound.europa.eu/eiro/2004/07/feature/gr0407103f.htm.
Stanković, F., and Markov, S. (2011). Rod i ekonomija [Gender and economy]. In I. Milojević and S. Markov (eds.). *Uvod u rodne teorije* [Introduction into the Gender Theories] (pp. 321–335). Novi Sad: Mediterran Publishing.
United Nations Development Programme (UNDP). (2007). Preporuke mera za poboljšanje položaja žene na tržištu rada [Recommended measures for the improvement of the position of women in the labor market]. Beograd: Program UN za razvoj.
Vuković, D. (2006). Mobing na radnom mestu [Mobbing at the workplace]. *Temida*, 9(4), 3–10.
Women's Law Center. (2008). Sex discrimination in employment. Women's Law Center of Maryland. Retrieved from http://www.wlcmd.org/wp-content/uploads/2013/06/Sex-Discrimination-in-Employment-2008.pdf.

Fear of Crime among Women in Tiruchirappalli, India

A Spatial Examination of Transit Spaces

6

C. HANNAH, G. SUBBAIYAN, AND
T. SRINIVAS

Contents

Introduction

The issue of crime in today's world is one that is increasingly gaining attention and concern. It is very often the cause for death, injury, fear, damage, and inconvenience, as well as financial losses and expenditure. Being one of the primary forms of antisocial behavior, it is one of the important issues gaining attention from individuals, businesses, media, and society as a whole. Crime is characterized by a complex combination of economic, social, cultural, and environmental factors. The concept of *fear of crime* represents a person's anxiety about crime and felony. It represents an individual's diffuse sense of danger about being physically harmed by criminal violence, and is related to the concern about being alone and potentially vulnerable to personal harm. In recent times, fear of crime has been treated as a social problem in its own right (Doran and Burgess, 2012).

Researchers in crime studies have defined *crime* as an event caused by the concurrence of infringement of the law, an offender, a target, a place, and the lack of guardianship (Cohen and Felson, 1979). The offender, target, and guardian are the decision makers who control the territorial functioning and marking of places. The place or, in other words, the built environment, can dramatically impact or even reverse the choices and in turn the activities of these decision makers (Schweitzer et al., 1999). In spite of the passive role played by the built environment, it is a major factor determining the perception of fear of crime (more so with women), making it possible to design it out.

Women's vulnerability to crime is a result of several disparities when compared with men. Disparity in terms of physical capabilities is the key one, but this has no built environment remedy other than providing a guardian's support or "eyes on street" for immediate help, at the location, at all times of need. The right to use or experience a given space and the freedom to explore it depends on the volume of personal space around a person. Disparities in the definition and demarcation of personal and public space for women, which was once dependent on the division of societal responsibilities, are now undergoing changes with the increase in employment and empowerment of women. However, built spaces have not been redesigned or the effect of the physical environment and the built space on the behavior of women has not been studied and analyzed (McDowell, 1983). Since public spaces very often deprive a woman of the basic needs of safety and security, spatial avoidance is the most commonly adopted strategy to protect themselves from crime. This state deprives women of the right over any built space. Women still have to carry weapons, dress modestly, travel with escorts, and commute on motor vehicles to protect themselves from people with unpredictable demeanor. A woman's fear of crime thus has strong spatial influences. This chapter is a study on certain built environment features that affect the fear of crime of a woman.

Review of Literature

The feeling of safety in a physical environment that hosts different types of activities is influenced by a range of factors. It is difficult to separate the relative contributions of social, cognitive, territorial, and physical components to fear of crime. Studies have been made in the area of fear of crime for several decades, and it still attracts interest from social, economic, political, and research perspectives. Compositional studies examine potential offenders and victims based on sociodemographic characteristics like age, gender, financial background, social status, and the social mobility of inhabitants to identify their perception of vulnerability to crime. Ecological studies focus on the manipulation of physical and environmental characteristics for the mitigation of crime. The location and physical context of crime, specifically land use, visibility levels, access routes, and the built form, acquire significance in these ecological studies.

Environmental Backcloth for Crime

Studies on the physical characteristics of built settings show that though they are not the primary cause, certain physical attributes form the "environmental backcloth" for crime. These characteristics include block frontages, street widths, abandoned or occupied buildings, attached and detached buildings (Perkins et al., 1992), surrounding land use (Wuschke et al., 2009), intersections with alleys, midblock passages, multifamily housing, undesirable establishments like liquor shops, check cashing establishments, graffiti, vacant buildings (Loukaitou-Sideris et al., 2000), street segments that are highly accessible within the road network (Beavon et al., 1994), community identifiers, block signs, incivilities, maintenance (Perkins et al., 1992), building height, project size, materials, amenities, and distinctiveness of interior finish and furnishings (Newman, 1972). Studies on situational crime prevention find a relation between criminal activities and specific physical attributes of "hot spots" of crime (Clarke, 1992). They suggest environmental design as a tool for "designing out" crime. Redesign or transformation of certain characteristics of a space can lead to lower levels of crime (Liggett et al., n.d.).

The land use pattern, urban design, and transportation systems are the three primary components of any built environment. Land use pattern deals with the distribution of activities across spaces, location, and density. Urban design deals with the design of the city and the physical elements within it, including their arrangement and their appearance, along with the function and appeal of public spaces. Transportation systems comprise the physical infrastructure of roads, sidewalks, bike paths, railroad tracks, bridges, and so on, as well as the level of service provided as determined by traffic levels, bus frequencies, and the like (Handy et al., 2002). Research in the area of urban planning and transport systems development has examined and established relationships between urban form characteristics like density and intensity, land use mix, street connectivity, street scale, aesthetic qualities, regional structures, and travel patterns (Handy et al., 2002). Literature on criminology lists a range of factors that make people feel unsafe in various situations classified under three categories: neighborhood factors, situational factors, and demographic factors. The design of the built environment can affect crime through its effect on the degree of access, ease of entrance and exit, and surveillability (Greenberg and Rohe, 1984). Hence, the factors that contribute to fear of crime in general are not unique from those associated with crime itself in transit areas. Thus, the aspects of urban form like settlement size, mixing of land uses, local facilities, density of development, proximity to transport networks, road network type, and neighborhood type that affect the travel pattern will thus in turn affect the crime patterns happening along the routes and at the bus stops, thereby creating hot spots.

Crime and Transit Locations

Both crime and the fear of crime affect many aspects of everyday life. Citizens should have the freedom to be mobile, to walk from home or work to the bus stop, or to wait at bus stops without having the fear of being victimized. Bus stops are expected to provide a comfortable, safe, and secure environment. But due to the fact that they are crime hot spots, a feeling of fear and anxiety surrounds their usage. The fear for personal safety on public transport systems has a severe impact on the ridership by affecting travelers' choices of routes or stops (Tucker, 2003).

Age, race, class, cultural and educational background, sexual orientation, prior victimization experiences, and disability status are among the demographical factors that seem to play a role in a user's fear of public settings and transit environments (Loukaitou-Sideris, 2006). Empirical studies point to certain environmental factors like darkness, desolation, lack of opportunities for informal surveillance, lack of maintenance, and poor environmental quality as attractors of crime (Valentine, 1990).

Crimes at a bus stop are affected by a combination of social and physical variables at play at the bus stop and its immediate neighborhood. There exists a vast amount of literature that studies the relation between crime and the physical setting. Several environmental features have been identified and classified as explained here. Studies on the place as a setting for crime examine the spatial environment in the immediate vicinity of transit stops as a factor and study the impact of the physical environment on crime. The characteristics related to land use that seem to affect travel patterns can be classified as the strategic urban planning and include location with respect to its towns, cities, and infrastructure; size and shape of the structures; and the land use type. Though some aspects like clustering and concentration of development, density, and the level and scale of land use

Table 6.1 Environmental Indicators

Urban Form Characteristics	Factors Facilitating Escape	Alley, Midblock Connection, Number of Hiding Places (under Stairways, behind Pillars)
	Land use	Single-family residential, multifamily residential, small open commercial, small closed commercial, liquor shop, check cashing establishments, adult movie theater, adult book stores, surface parking lot, parking structure
	Condition	Vacant lots, vacant buildings, run-down establishments, graffiti, litter
Street characteristics		Street vehicle traffic, on-street parking
Bus stop characteristics		Visibility, lighting, public phones, bus shelters, visible guard, police substation, pedestrian presence

mix predominantly fall under the category of local urban design, they can also be classified under strategic design level. Issues related to the layout of development, movement, and network and neighborhood type fall under the immediate surrounding or the neighborhood design development and planning. Therefore, these physical characteristics of the immediate neighborhood where a bus stop or station is located can also affect people's perception of risk and fear. We can generalize and say that the overall physical environment of bus stop settings can be classified into surrounding built environment, street environment, and bus stop environment (Subbaiyan and Srinivas, 2012). Table 6.1 is a list of some of the environmental indicators that can be measured for a study on bus shelter safety.

Further, for classification purposes, crime falls under two groups: Type 1 crimes include criminal homicide, rape, robbery, aggravated assault, larceny theft, and burglary. Type 2 crimes include public nuisance crime against people and their property, like petty theft, disorderly conduct, verbal abuse, nonaggravated assault, public drinking, and vandalism (Liggett et al., n.d.). Type 2 crimes, although of a less serious nature, are very intimidating and particularly target the transit riders and street commuters. Different types of crimes occur under different environmental conditions. At bus stops, serious crimes are more isolated, while less critical crimes like pickpocketing, conning, and eve teasing are common due to frequent crowding. Violent (Type 1) crimes in particular, concentrated at locations of check cashing establishments, park-and-ride lots, or on station platforms near bus stops or alleys, had the strongest positive correlation with crime rates. However, Type 2 crimes, 90% of which were vandalism, were predominantly concentrated in the access routes to the platform from the parking lot or from the street, that is, stairs, elevators, or escalators (Liggett et al., n.d.).

Women and Fear of Crime

Recent modernization has changed the physical, sentimental, and cultural aspects of cities and resulted in a deepening sense of isolation, increasing vulnerability in sections of society. Factors such as gender, class, and age affect the vulnerability of a person, thereby negatively influencing access and mobility in streets and public spaces. This has had a severe impact on the crime rates in cities. Compositional studies in crime and fear of crime show that elders, women, urbanites, and people belonging to lower social and economic backgrounds are among the selective groups that have greater fear of crime than others (Hale, 1996). Across all research, women consistently seem to fear crime more than men, despite their risk of victimization being lower than that of men (Scott, 2003). Nuisance behaviors such as drunkenness, obscene language, verbal threats, and groping at bus stops prevents the women population from using them and makes them more frightened (Sideris, 2005).

Research points out that individuals worry about crime when they feel a lack of control over the situation as they appraise a threat and worry about the consequence of risk. Due to differences in physical capabilities and inability to control interaction with strangers, women feel more vulnerable and have a greater fear that they are most often the "targeted victim" (Jackson, 2009). Women's fear of crime is a consequence of being at the "sharp end" of patriarchy (Pain, 1997). Ferraro tries to explain women's worry about crime through his hypothesis about sexual assault. He notes that for any type of crime (theft, physical attack, or verbal abuse), the end result could be sexual assault, thus making women fear crime more than men, despite their lower victimization rates. Moreover, for women, rape and sexual assault rates are 10 times higher than those of men. This prominent risk of victimization makes women more likely to be fearful of rape or sexual assault (Ferraro, 1996; Stanko, 1994). Most women appear to go through at least one period in their lives during which much of their primary socialization has fear of sexual attack as a central concept (Warr, 1985). Women also take many more safety precautions than men do (Scott, 2003). Many women carry small weapons or instruments, dress modestly, travel in groups, and use motorized transport to protect themselves from people with an unpredictable nature. Concerns for safety prevent women from accessing some spaces and at certain times, thereby limiting their mobility and thus altering their choices or modes of transport. Women were found to make more daily trips but travel fewer miles (Taylor and Mauch, 1997): women chain trips (McGuckin and Nakamoto, 2004). Women try not to frequent places where the potential for sexual attack is perceived to be high (Valentine, 1992). Women express more fear and constrain their mobility, self-expression, and social experience or engage in behavioral fear to lower their chances of victimization (Sur, 2012). Women are more fearful of every event and judge every single event to be more harmful, and consistently rated their own probability to experience these events in the future as higher (Fetchenhauer and Buunk, 2005).

Results of the public perception survey conducted in Delhi as part of the multicity Gender Inclusive Cities (GIC) project, administered by Women in Cities International (WICI), supported by the UN Trust Fund, clearly describe the condition of women's safety in India. It found that only 19% of the surveyed feel the city is safe for women, and almost 90% feel that public transport is unsafe for women (Viswanath et al., 2009–2010). Indian women are not safe, and the threat of being the next victim is a persistent scenario among many, as women feel they can be easily victimized from any nook and corner of society (Mangoli and Tarase, 2009).

The absence of a responsible public culture and the domination of public spaces by men heighten a woman's sense of insecurity, restricting them from accessing different parts of the city with ease and comfort. When interviewed, women indicated the lack of visible guardians (49%), crowded bus stops (35%), and poor lighting (28%) to be among the factors that affect their fear of crime. Also, among a list of public places, roads (40%) and public transport (31%), followed by markets (17%) and spaces where women wait for public transport (10%), seem to be considered unsafe (Viswanath et al., 2009–2010). Women's access to and visibility in public spaces are determined by several factors, including time, place, and purpose. The lack of good lighting in many areas is a further hindrance to their mobility. In addition, pavement is often used as men's urinals, making access to these sidewalks extremely uncomfortable for women.

Transit Space and Gender Preferences

Public spaces are generally considered "gender neutral" by designers, officials, and users, and this is supported by an argument that spaces are experienced in the same way by women and men. As found in literature and discussed above, this is not so. Public spaces cannot be expected to be perceived the same way by everyone, everywhere. The character of a space actively contributes to how social relations evolve in that space; that is, the same space may be safe or unsafe for different people, depending on who uses it and in what manner (Khammar and Heydari, 2013). Specifically, spaces either promote or impede gender equality since gender plays a major role in how a place is experienced by different people.

In most cases, transportation is a system designed, built, and operated predominantly by men but used by both men and women. As a result, we tend to have transportation systems and pedestrian areas that women find unfriendly and vehicles designed with seats and seat belts that are not appropriate for a woman's body mass. Decisions involving planning of transportation do not reflect the different work–life balance that many women have and fare structures and job requirements that work against those who need to work flexibly or on a part-time basis (Frye, 2004). Urban transport planning and policy making all over the world remains strongly influenced by transport planning standards, procedures, and methodologies that were developed in the industrialized north over the course of the twentieth century and were biased in favor of individual journey-to-work trips that were increasingly assumed to be undertaken by private motorized means of transport (Peters, 2013). All these point toward the idea that although transit systems and environments are expected to be gender neutral, they are otherwise. The central idea of the transit systems is based on the traditional division of labor, that is, households consisting of a male breadwinner who travels to work and a female homemaker with the primary responsibilities of caretaking and bearing children. Significant changes have occurred to this model in this century, shuffling the household and family structure and changing the division of household responsibilities, thereby bringing more women to the streets. Women's increasing involvement in employment has thus altered the personal space of woman. Hence, in today's context, within most urban settings, women have inferior access to both private and public means of transport while at the same time assuming a significant share of their household's travel burden due to both professional and household responsibilities (Peters, 2013).

Personal space is defined as the physical space immediately around a person that when encroached makes him or her feel threatened or uncomfortable. It is known that women have larger personal spaces than men. This difference is also one of the key reasons why women perceive transit spaces differently than men. Current planning techniques do not take this into consideration, hence making public spaces relatively uninviting for women.

While traditional approaches to women's safety were based on restrictions, fear, and self-preservation, it is time to encourage a paradigm shift in urban design that considers a women's safety and gender inclusion, thereby making infrastructure, usage of space, and the nature of social institutions and policing more women-friendly and safe (Viswanath et al., 2009–2010). Planners and the community at large should work to make spaces accommodate the diverse realities of women's lives and socioeconomic roles and to challenge outdated sociocultural norms regarding gender roles (White, 1998). Public spaces should hence be planned to include features that support and encourage appropriate gender relations so that men and women can use those spaces safely together.

Compositional studies examine the environment and society and suggest changes in the system of policing and reformulation of the criminal justice and penal systems to address crime. As seen in the literature mentioned above, the design and layout of the physical environment can strongly affect crime, either by being conducive or by reducing opportunities for criminal activities. Some of the dimensions, like the physical characteristics of the built environment and the mix of land use, are outside the jurisdiction of both transportation authorities and criminal law. Crime at transit areas can thereby be curbed not only by dealing with social variables but also by dealing with architectural design, planning, and urban development (Liggett et al., n.d.). Since transit authorities cannot deal with these social variables that affect crime, building design and town planning policies will have to play a role in controlling the physical variables. Ecological studies indicate that manipulation of physical and environmental characteristics of a location will address the issue of crime. These studies further deduce a notion that the security of public transport users should extend from the bus stop to the public environment that surrounds the transit (Liggett et al., n.d.). Emphasis on policing, laws, rules, and regulations can be supplemented with crime prevention through environmental design (CPTED) (Monchuk, 2011). Land use policies and urban design policies can be used to promote more sustainable patterns of travel in neotraditional urbanism, compact cities, urban villages, and public transport-oriented development (Stead and Marshall, 2001).

The Present Study: Methodology

Transit crime is seen as a rather persistent but underreported trend that scares and intimidates riders—particularly women. The majority of incidents represent public nuisance crimes, and the majority of the victims are captive transit riders. It is observed that most research in this context was undertaken in countries like the United States and the United Kingdom, whereas not much research work is reported in developing countries like India.

This study investigates the influence of physical and nonphysical characteristics of bus shelters and their surrounding built environment on fear of crime of women waiting at the bus stops. The bus stops studied were selected in the city of Tiruchirappalli, the fourth largest city (corporation) in Tamil Nadu, India. Bus transport is the major form of public transportation, catering to an approximate population of 1 million in Tiruchirappalli. Approximately 100 bus stops are provided and maintained by the city corporation authorities. Fourteen bus stops were chosen for investigation based on the preliminary study of all bus stops on various aspects considered for the study.

The characteristic features of the built environment around bus stops and bus shelter characteristics of selected bus stops in Tiruchirappalli were recorded, and the people waiting at the bus stops were interviewed to assess their fear of crime. The features considered for this study include land use of surrounding areas (level of mix of uses and presence of negative uses), lighting in and around the bus stops (street lighting, surrounding premises lighting, and bus shelter lighting), and setbacks, compound walls or fences, visible openings, outdoor areas, and hiding elements of the surrounding buildings. A total of

248 women waiting at the bus stops were surveyed to ascertain their level of fear of crime and the association between the features of the surrounding built environment and their fear of crime at bus stops.

Results and Discussion

At all bus stops, most of the females expressed some level of fear of theft and fear of nuisance behavior. The mean fear level of females varied across bus stops from 1.63 to 3.04, on a 5-point scale. For the combined sample of all bus stops, it was noticed that fear of nuisance behavior ($M = 2.54$) was higher than fear of theft ($M = 2.39$). Women expressed the fear of chain and purse snatching, and harassment crimes such as eve teasing, other sexual harassment, and unruly behavior of drunks and youth gangs. In all bus stops, the fear level during night hours was higher than that during the daytime.

To investigate the relationship between fear of crime at bus stops and the features of the surrounding built environment, the selected 14 bus stops were grouped on each of the features of the surrounding built environment. Analysis of variance (ANOVA) revealed a significant variation in the total (combined day- and nighttime) fear of crime ($F_{(13,402)} = 10.174$, $p < 0.001$) among the 14 bus stops. It is evident that people experience different levels of fear of crime at different bus stops. ANOVA also revealed a significant difference in the total (combined day- and nighttime) mean fear of crime ($F_{(3412)} = 33.352$, $p < 0.001$) between the four bus stop groups based on the combination of the level of mix of land uses and the presence of negative uses. The *post hoc* analysis indicated that the mean fear of crime of people at bus stops with a good mix of land uses and without negative uses, and bus stops with a medium mix of land uses and without negative uses was significantly (at 0.05) lower than the mean fear of crime of people at bus stops with a medium mix of land uses and with negative uses, and bus stops with a low mix of land uses and with negative uses. It may be concluded that the mix of uses around the bus stops contributes more to the perception of safety of people waiting at the bus stops than the overall land use in which the bus stops are located. Diverse commercial activities and other uses that are open until late in the night and attract different sections of people were preferred in bus stop settings. Though the presence of diverse activities is preferred, the presence of certain negative uses, such as bars, wine shops, and vacant lots, increases the fear of crime of people.

There was a significant difference in the nighttime mean fear of crime among the seven bus stop groups ($F_{(6409)} = 17.966$, $p < 0.001$) based on the combination of street lighting, surrounding premises lighting, and shelter lighting. The *post hoc* analysis indicated that the mean fear of crime of people at bus stops with good street lighting and surrounding premises lighting, and in which bus shelter lighting is present, was significantly (at 0.05) lower than that of people at all other bus stops. The analysis revealed that the influence of street lighting on fear of crime was more evident than the influence of bus shelter lighting and surrounding premises lighting. It was noticed that surrounding premises lighting was the second influential factor, next to street lighting, whereas shelter lighting did not effectively influence the fear of crime, more particularly when the street lighting was good. On the overall lighting, the individual bus stops with bus shelter lighting and located in areas with good street lighting and surrounding premises lighting were rated as very safe. On other hand, the individual bus stops located in areas with poor street lighting, poor surrounding premises lighting, and poor bus shelter lighting were rated as either unsafe or very unsafe. On the whole, these findings confirm that uniform and adequate lighting needs to be provided over the bus stop environment, which includes bus stops and the surrounding street segment and built environment. As the findings indicate that uniform street lighting is crucial for the perception of personal security at bus stops, the location of the bus stops may be integrated with existing street lighting.

There was a significant difference in the level of total fear of crime of people between the six bus stop groups classified based on the site layout buildings ($F_{(5410)} = 19.149$, $p < 0.001$). The *post hoc* analysis indicated that the mean fear of crime of people is low at bus stops located in places where all or most buildings are attached and detached buildings with compound walls. The enhanced perceptions of personal security at bus stops with all attached buildings (without compound walls or fences) could be mainly due to the enhanced surveillance by occupants of buildings, the physical link between the street and ground floor of individual premises, and the elimination of concealment and escape routes for offenders. The enhanced perceptions of personal security at bus stops with mostly detached buildings with compound walls could be due to the elimination of concealment and escape routes for offenders, whereas increased fear of crime at bus stops with most buildings detached without compound walls may be due to the reason that setbacks provide concealment and easy escape for offenders.

The mean fear of crime of people at bus stops with fewer surrounding building openings and outdoor spaces visible from the bus stop ($M = 2.64$) was higher than that of people at bus stops with more surrounding building openings and outdoor spaces visible from the bus stop ($M = 2.00$), and the difference was statistically significant ($t_{(414)} = 8.988$, $p < 0.001$). The reason for an enhanced perception of personal security at bus stops with more visible openings and outdoor building elements could be due to increased surveillance of bus stops from surrounding buildings and the presence of people in outdoor spaces (Katyal, 2002; Desyllas et al., 2003). This study revealed that building elements such as openings and outdoor spaces of buildings enhance the surveillance opportunities and thereby reduce the fear of crime of people. In spite of the enhanced natural surveillance provided by the increased pedestrian presence on streets in Indian towns and cities, visible openings and outdoor spaces of surrounding buildings were found to be effective in providing surveillance and thereby provide confidence to people regarding their perceptions of personal security.

The mean fear of crime of people at bus stops with more building elements, such as niches, projections, and large columns that block prospects and offer concealment ($M = 2.68$), was higher than that of people at bus stops where these elements are either not present or fewer in number ($M = 2.05$), and the difference was statistically significant ($t_{(414)} = 8.883$, $p < 0.001$). The findings of this research confirm the earlier findings that features that block sight lines and offer concealment for offenders increase the fear of crime of people at bus stops (Vogel and Pettinari, 2002; Loukaitou-Sideris, 2009). The identified features that offer hiding places in this research include large columns, walls, deep niches or alcoves, deep projections, and open unused basements.

Multiple regression analysis was conducted to determine the best linear combination of independent variables (people's perception about contribution of land use, lighting, layout of buildings, visible openings, and hiding elements of buildings) in predicting the fear of crime of people waiting at the bus stops. Among the significant features of built environment, land use yielded the highest beta weight (−0.319), followed by hiding elements (−0.174), lighting (−0.168), and openings and outdoor spaces (−0.149). The adjusted R^2 was

0.378, which suggested that only 38% of the variance in fear of crime was explained by the independent variables in this model, whereas the remaining 62% of the variance in fear of crime of people might have been influenced by other variables not included in this study.

Conclusion

On viewing the transit environment behavior and preferences of the users, within the context of built environment factors, it was observed that the features of physical environment provide natural surveillance to the public and enhance the perceptions of personal security of people. Among the prominent features of the built environment, the land use mix seems more influential, followed by building features like visible openings and building setbacks. The influence of street lighting on fear of crime was more evident than the influence of bus shelter lighting and surrounding premises lighting. Thus, people's opinion about the contribution of these physical features of the built environment, on their perception of security, is significantly dependent on the specificity of the individual features.

This study thus points out the safety and security needs and desires of passengers due to gender differences. This gap that is identified in the transit environment should be bridged to serve the specific needs and particularities in travel behavior and patterns of its users. Currently, policies, support groups, and agencies to address the safety and security needs of women are sparsely available. The transit environment should be complementary and support accessibility and mobility of both genders. Further studies along this direction can help come up with assessment systems leading to the optimal use of resources and the inclusion of a gender design in urban design, planning, and governance.

References

Beavon, D. J. K., Brantingham, P. L., and Brantingham, P. (1994). The influence of street networks on the patterning of property offenses. *Crime Prevention Studies*, 2, 115–148.

Clarke, R. V. (1992). *Situational Crime Prevention: Successful Case Studies*. New York: Harrow and Heston.

Cohen, L. E., and Felson, M. (1979). Social change and crime rate trends: A routine activity approach. *American Sociological Review*, 588–608.

Desyllas, J., Connoly, P., and Hebbert, F. (2003). Modelling natural surveillance. *Environment and Planning B: Planning and Design*, 643–655.

Doran, B. J., and Burgess, M. B. (2012). Why is fear of crime a serious social problem? In B. J. Doran and M. B. Burgess, *Putting Fear of Crime on the Map: Investigating Perceptions of Crime Using Geographic Information Systems* (pp. 9–23). New York: Springer-Verlag.

Ferraro, K. (1996). Women's fear of victimization: Shadow of sexual assault. *Social Forces*, 75(2), 667–690.

Fetchenhauer, D., and Buunk, B. P. (2005). How to explain gender differences in fear of crime: Towards an evolutionary approach. *Sexualities, Evolution and Gender*, 7(2), 95–113.

Frye, A. (2004). *Research on Women's Issues* (pp. 15–16). Chicago: Transportation Research Board.

Greenberg, S., and Rohe, W. (1984). Neighborhood design and crime. *APA Journal*, 50(1), 48–61.

Hale, C. (1996). Fear of crime: A review of the literature. *International Review of Victimology*, 4(2), 79–150.

Handy, S., Boarnet, M. G., Ewing, R., and Killingsworth, R. E. (2002). How the built environment affects physical activity: Views from urban planning. *American Journal of Preventive Medicine*, 23(2), 64–73.

Jackson, J. (2009). A psychological perspective on vulnerability in the fear of crime. *Psychology, Crime & Law*, 15(4), 365–390.

Katyal, N. K. (2002). Architecture as crime control. *Yale Law Journal*, 111, 1039–1139.

Khammar, G. A., and Heydari, A. (2013). Immunization of urban spaces in Saqqez city, Iran. *American Journal of Engineering Research*, 2(11), 300–308.

Liggett, R., Sideris, A. L., and Iseki, H. (n.d.). Protecting against transit crime: The importance of the built environment. Retrieved from http://www.uctc.net/research/papers/725.pdf.

Loukaitou-Sideris, A. (2006). Is it safe to walk? Neighborhood safety and security considerations and their effects on walking. *Journal of Planning Literature*, 20(3), 219–232.

Loukaitou-Sideris, A. (2009). How to ease women's fear of transportation environments: Case studies and best practices (report 09-01). San Jose, CA: Mineta Transportation Institute.

Loukaitou-Sideris, A., Liggett, R. S., Iseki, H., and Thurlow, W. (2000). Measuring the effects of built environment on bus stop crime. Berkeley: University of California Transportation Center.

Mangoli, R., and Tarase, G. M. (2009). Crime against women in India: A statistical review. *International Journal of Criminology and Sociological Theory*, 2(2), 292–302.

McDowell, L. (1983). Towards an understanding of the gender division of urban space. *Environment and Planning D: Society and Space*, 1, 59–72.

McGuckin, N., and Nakamoto, Y. (2004). Differences in trip chaining by men and women. Presented at the Conference on Women's Travel Issues, Chicago, November 18–20.

Monchuk, L. (2011). The way forward in designing out crime? Greater Manchester police design for security consultancy. *Safer Communities*, 10, 31–40.

Newman, O. (1972). *Defensible Space—A New Physical Planning Tool for Urban Revitalization*. New York: Macmillan.

Pain, R. H. (1997). Social geographies of women's fear of crime. *Transactions of the Institute of British Geographers*, 22(2), 231–244.

Perkins, D. D., Wandersman, A., Rich, R. C., and Taylor, R. B. (1993). The physical environment of street crime: Defensible space, territoriality and incivilities. *Journal of Environmental Psychology*, 13(1), 29–49.

Peters, D. (2013). Gender and sustainable urban mobility. Nairobi: Global Report on Human Settlements.

Schweitzer, J. H., Kim, J. W., and Mackin, J. R. (1999). The impact of the built environment on crime and fear of crime in urban neighborhoods. *Journal of Urban Technology*, 6, 59–73.

Scott, H. (2003). Stranger danger: Explaining women's fear of crime. *Western Criminology Review*, 4(3), 203–214.

Sideris, A. L. (2005). Is it safe to walk here? Design and policy responses to women's fear of victimization in public places. In *Transportation Research Board Conference Proceedings*, Washington, DC, vol. 2, no. 35, pp. 102–112.

Stanko, E. A. (1994). *The Commercialisation of Women's Fear of Crime*. Canberra: Australian Institute of Criminology.

Stead, D., and Marshall, S. (2001). The relationships between urban form and travel patterns. An international review and evaluation. *European Journal of Transport and Infrastructure Research*, 1(2), 113–141.

Subbaiyan, G., and Srinivas, T. 2012. An investigation of the relationship between features of bus shelters and fear of crime at bus stops. *IUP Journal of Architecture*, IV(1), 54–63.

Sur, P. (2012). Fear of crime and victimization: Retracing women's risk perceptions in private spaces in the urban city of Kolkata. *Journal of International Women's Studies*, 13(1), 109–125. Retrieved December 15, 2015, from http://vc.bridgew.edu/jiws/vol13/iss1/7.

Taylor, B. D., and Mauch, M. (1997). Gender, race, and travel behavior: An analysis of household-serving travel and commuting in the San Francisco Bay Area. *Transportation Research Record: Journal of the Transportation Research Board*, 1607, 147–153.

Tucker, E. L. (2003). *Safer Stops for Vulnerable Customers*. Tallahassee, FL: National Center for Transit Research (NCTR).

Valentine, G. (1990). Women's fear and the design of public space. *Built Environment*, 16(4), 288–303.

Valentine, G. (1992). Images of danger: Women's sources of information about the spatial distribution of male violence. *Area*, 24(1), 22–29.

Viswanath, K., Gupta, M., and Ghosh., A. (2009–2010). *Understanding Women's Safety—Towards a Gender Inclusive City*. Delhi: Jagori.

Vogel, M., and Pettinari, J. (2002). Personal safety and transit: Paths, environments, stops and stations: Final report. Minneapolis: Centre for Transportation Studies.

Warr, M. (1985). Fear of rape among urban women. *Social Problems*, 32(3), 238–250.

White, J. (1998). *Plan It Safe*. North Melbourne, Australia: Pluto Press.

Wuschke, K., Brantingham, P., and Ginther, J. (2009). *Landscapes of Crime: Exploring Urban Crime and Land Use*. Vancouver, BC, GeoTEC Event 2009.

Interpersonal Crimes against Children and Youth

II

Restorative Practices for Juveniles in Hawai'i, United States

7

LORENN WALKER

Contents

Introduction

It was May 2000 and the end of the school year on the island of O'ahu in Hawai'i. My home telephone rang. It was my 13-year-old son's school vice principal, who was calling to tell me that our son "had been hit in the head by another student" (Walker, 2013). When I learned that the other student was a boy who had a history of fighting with our son, I became more worried and afraid of the possibility of further violence. I felt some relief and reassurance that the school took immediate action to protect our son and that there was a school rule against hitting, which was upheld and applied. My husband and I did not, however, agree with the school's rule that automatically expelled the boy from school for three days. I pleaded with the vice principal not to suspend the boy from school, but he said it was the rule and there was nothing we could do about it. We believed keeping the boy out of school was unhelpful for him, and that it would only exacerbate the problem and risked making him more resentful toward our son. It was also discouraging that we had no input into what the consequences for the boy would be. Additionally, it felt unfair that none of us, including our son, the boy, and his family, were consulted at all about what to do about the problem. It seemed clear that until the boy and our son worked out their differences, our son was at a risk of harm, and I would continue to worry about his safety.

Fortuitously, when our son was assaulted, I happened to be conducting a juvenile justice pilot project diverting arrested youth to restorative justice conferences (Walker, 2002). Also fortunate for us was having a facilitator for the pilot project who happened to live in our neighborhood, and who kindly agreed to arrange and conduct a restorative conference with the boy, his family, and our family at the boy's intermediate school.

The restorative conference was held two weeks after the assault. On the afternoon that the conference was scheduled, the vice principal and the principal from the intermediate school were suddenly unavailable to participate, and there was no one else at the school who could, so we could not have the conference there. Again luckily, the elementary school, which both boys had attended and each had younger siblings attending, was close by. The elementary school principal immediately changed her schedule to accommodate and participate in the restorative conference. This principal had known our son and the boy for years and was trained in restorative facilitation. She appreciated the value of the restorative conference and arranged to have the conference in her office after being asked only 15 minutes before.

During the conference, my son, my husband, the boy, his father, and I talked freely. Through open discussion, we came to see we were more alike than different. We also saw the kindheartedness in each other. We came into the restorative conference apprehensive and admittedly with some biases and misgivings about each other, but the conference gave us the opportunity to openly communicate our shared values. Our participation in the restorative conference helped us leave that day peacefully.

While restorative justice was needed when our son was hit, the rule against hitting others was just as necessary. The boy needed to know he could not assault others no matter how much he disagreed with them, and we all needed to know the rules would be fairly applied, including the boy and his family. At the same time, we also needed restorative justice and a way to address our harm caused by the violation of the rule.

Over the following six years that the boys attended school together, they never had another negative incident. My son even defended the boy one day when they were about 17 years old. I was driving him home after school had ended a few minutes earlier, and we saw the boy across town about 2 miles from the school. It was obvious that the boy had been truant. "Hmm, how'd he get over here so fast?" I asked out loud in the car. My son responded, "He walks fast, Mom." Ten years after we participated in the restorative conference, our son works with youth. He called me recently. "Mom, I need some restorative justice stuff. Some of the kids are fighting. One girl is picking on another kid. How do I do one of those circles?"

With deep sadness, however, I am very sorry to report that the boy who hit my son back in 2000 died shortly after he finished high school at the age of 19. Tragically, he was shot and killed by another teenager. His family and our community still grieve for his loss.

This chapter discusses the need for both the rule of law and restorative justice and describes how restorative justice has been applied and is evolving in Hawai'i for juveniles. Hawai'i's experiments providing restorative interventions for youth demonstrate how restorative justice strengthens individuals and communities, and is a necessary component to the juvenile justice system.

Defining the Rule of Law and Restorative Justice

"The rule of law is an ideal that relates to legality" (Tamanaha, 2012, p. 234). Rules and laws set boundaries for human behavior and establish group expectations for community members. The rule of law has been recognized as a vital component for societies since ancient times. In 350 BC, Aristotle said, "The rule of law is better than the rule of any individual" (Aristotle, *Politics*, Book 3:16, n.b.).

While most agree that the rule of law is necessary for stable communities, there is no universal consensus on its definition. How the rule of law is defined can be confusing even for scholars (Tamanaha, 2007). Brian Tamanaha, an American law professor, is a rule of law scholar who "distinguishes between formal and substantive definitions of the rule of law" (Moller and Skaaning, 2010, p. 5). The formal definition has also been called "thin" and the substantive definition "thick" by rule of law scholars.

The following is Tamanaha's definition of the formal or thin definition, which he believes can be applied to "a broad range of systems" (Tamanaha, 2007, p. 3):

> The rule of law, at its core, requires that government officials and citizens are bound by and act consistent with the law. This basic requirement entails a set of minimal characteristics: law must be set forth in advance (be prospective), be made public, be general, be clear, be stable and certain, and be applied to everyone according to its terms. In the absence of these characteristics, the rule of law cannot be satisfied.

The thick or substantive definition of the rule of law includes references "to fundamental rights, democracy, and/or criteria of justice or right" (Tamanaha, 2007, p. 3).

Like the rule of law, the definition of restorative justice also lacks universal agreement, but minimally its thin definition is that it is concerned with people's needs after they have been harmed by wrongdoing and social injustice, and how people affected by the harm might find healing (Zehr, 2013).

Restorative justice, like the rule of law, can also have a broader, or thicker, meaning. "Restorative justice is a broad term which encompasses a growing social movement to institutionalize peaceful approaches to harm, problem-solving and violations" (Suffolk University, 2012). Restorative justice is "victim-centered and looks at how 'victims,' very broadly defined, are affected and can be healed" (Boyes-Watson, 2003).

Restorative justice and restorative practices are different concepts. Restorative justice is a philosophy, while restorative practices represent the application of the philosophy to people involved in specific incidents of wrongdoing or social injustice. Ted Wachtel is the founder of the International Institute of Restorative Practices, which provides training and an accredited graduate school for the advanced study of restorative justice. Wachtel defines restorative practices as "a social science that studies how to build social capital and achieve social discipline through participatory learning and decision-making" (Wachtel, 2013, p. 1).

Restorative practices could be used in place of or in addition to detention and punishment. For adults, it is estimated that 97% of people convicted of felonies in the United States plead guilty to offenses (Givelber and Farrell, 2012). "Restorative justice emerged in the 1970s as an effort to correct some of the weaknesses of the western legal system while building on its strengths" (Zehr, 2013). Restorative justice is advocated for children and youth crime victims (Gal, 2011).

In our son's case, we desired a restorative approach that could resolve the problem and help everyone heal. Our family, the boy who hit our son, and his family were all affected from the assault, and all of us participated in the restorative conference. The elementary school principal participated too. She was there as a supporter for the boys, whom she had known for many years. She was also indirectly affected because both boys' siblings attended the school she administered.

In a restorative practice, each individual affected is respected and is offered equal participation opportunity, but no one is forced to participate. In my son's case, he was not initially interested in participating in a restorative encounter, and he did not want to meet with the boy and his family. When he came home from school the day he was hit, I told him, "We need a restorative conference." He rolled his eyes and adamantly said, "No way!" I explained to him, "I can't keep worrying about you getting hurt. We need to work this out. I need a conference." It was through motherly pressure that my son agreed to participate, and afterwards he was satisfied he had. "I'm glad we did it," he said later. Indeed, it was his participation in the restorative conference that resolved things between him and the boy. It was also because of his experience participating in the conference that he understood its value and was able to see the usefulness of restorative practices for the youth he works with 15 years later.

Application of the Rule of Law and Restorative Justice

The rule of law is necessary for establishing legal boundaries for human behavior and the legal mechanisms for dealing with violations of rules. Restorative justice is necessary for dealing with law violations that harm people to help them heal and rehabilitate. Both the rule of law and restorative practices are necessary for juvenile justice.

Archibald (2013) has discussed the rule of law for applying due process to restorative practices provided by community agencies. He suggests that administrative law principles be used to deal with any dissatisfaction in restorative outcomes. Other legal authors have discussed the interactions of restorative justice and the rule of law principles of legality and right to a fair trial.* There is compatibility between the rule of law and restorative justice.

To institutionalize restorative justice in the criminal justice system, and provide people with opportunities to engage in restorative practices, it may be necessary to adopt a thicker definition of the rule of law. Providing people harmed by crime and people who commit crimes with the opportunity to participate in restorative practices would become a rule of law beyond the formal or thin requirements that some scholars believe is minimally necessary (Tamanaha, 2007).

Hawai'i's Restorative Practices for Juveniles

A variety of restorative practices have been developed and benefited children and youth in Hawai'i for many years. Most of the projects have been evaluated and described in publications, including the following.

Child Welfare and Protection

Native Hawaiians have been using *ho'opnopono*, a restorative practice, for centuries to deal with interpersonal conflicts for families and children (Hosmanek, 2012). Modern restorative practices for Hawai'i's children and youth involved in child welfare and child protection have also been used since 1996 through the *'ohana conferencing* model for families (Walker, 2005).

* The right to a fair trial would be a thicker definition of the rule of law according to Tamanaha, as discussed above.

The 'ohana conferencing model is Hawai'i's version of *family group conferencing*, which is used all over the world today for child protection and family welfare (Asscher et al., 2014). 'Ohana conferencing outcomes have been studied and have been shown to be more helpful for children for several reasons. First, children, especially adolescents in foster custody, suffer increased risks for health problems, which increase with the frequency of foster placements (Gramkowski et al., 2009). Second, youth who are placed in foster care with relatives (kinship care) do better than those placed with unrelated families (Gramkowski et al., 2009). 'Ohana conferencing outcomes showed those children who had conferences stayed in the same placement and were not moved around as frequently as children who do not have a conference, and that children were more often placed with families than children who did not have 'ohana conferences (Walker, 2005).

Juvenile Justice Applications

Another restorative justice project in Hawai'i for juvenile offenders was shown to have better outcomes than traditional criminal justice processes (Walker, 2002). In 1999, this restorative pilot project was developed that diverted 102 juvenile offenders from the criminal justice system. Instead of sending youth to traditional diversion programs or to court, they were diverted to restorative conferences like the one our family participated in. A total of 405 people, including youth and adults, participated in the project, which used an experimental design to show it was more helpful for participant satisfaction (healing), obtaining restitution when it was requested by victims (only a small number requested restitution and most wanted only an apology), and youth who had conferences had a significantly lower rate of escalating to commit violent crimes. Additionally, the restorative conference intervention benefited even a harmed child and his family where the juvenile offender denied accountability for his wrongdoing (Walker, 2002).

Hawai'i's restorative juvenile justice study was reviewed as part of a meta-analysis of 28 experimentally designed diversion programs for youth, which looked at other interventions, including family therapy and youth or teen court (Schwalbe et al., 2012). "Results of this study recommend against implementation of programs limited to case management and highlight the promise of family interventions and restorative justice" (Schwalbe et al., 2011, p. 26). Other experimental research on teen or youth court has shown that intervention can increase youth criminality. Researchers in that study warn, "The results of this evaluation should signal practitioners and funders to use caution when implementing TC [teen court] programs and to make rigorous evaluation a priority" (Stickle et al., 2008, p. 154).

Hawai'i's restorative diversion project has been cited by the United Nations Children's Emergency Fund (UNICEF) organization as a resource for the restorative diversion of youth from the criminal justice system (UNICEF, 2010).

Foster Youth Emancipation and Transition Planning

In 2004, Hawai'i began applying a transition planning process for youth emancipating from state custody and foster care (Walker, 2005). Restorative justice scholar John Braithwaite wrote about the concept of youth making their own plans for emancipation and transition out of state custody (Braithwaite, 2004), and the idea was applied to develop a specific model for foster youth in Hawai'i using solution-focused (SF) brief therapy* (Walker, 2005).

* Described further in the section on "Application of Solution-Focused Methodology to Restorative Practices.".

In Hawai'i, youth who are in foster custody can begin having transition planning circles with their invited supporters and make plans for how they will become independent after exiting foster care, while they are still in state custody. The process is provided by the non-profit agency that provides 'ohana conferencing (EPIC 'Ohana, Inc., 2014). The youth circle model is strength based and goal oriented, and results in a neatly prepared written plan for the individual youth having the circle. Follow-up transition circles are also encouraged so youth can learn about planning and understand that goals may not be met as quickly as planned, or that their goals may change. Since the youth transition planning process was developed in 2004, more than 1000 transition circles have been held for foster youth in Hawai'i.

Homeless Youth

The *Waikiki youth circle* was developed and piloted for groups of homeless youth in Hawai'i who suffered serious social injustices and victimization, along with a few youthful offenders. The project also applied SF brief therapy and provided circles over a four-month period with an average of five youth participating in each circle. Forty-four percent of the youth who participated succeed in meeting goals that they set for themselves at the circles, including finding employment and housing (Walker, 2008).

Restorative Reentry Planning Processes for Incarcerated Youth

In Hawai'i, incarcerated youth and youth with incarcerated adult parents have also benefited from a reentry planning process. The *Huikahi reentry circle* has been provided for youth in correctional institutions and for youth whose parents are incarcerated (Walker and Greening, 2010). The process for adults is being replicated in other states, including New York and California.

The reentry circle planning process for youth and adults addresses reconciliation and other needs for a life desisting from crime and substance abuse (Walker, 2009). The circles also address victimization that the children and family members have suffered and have been evaluated to show healing can result (Walker et al., 2015).

Despite the massive incarceration rates in the United States, criminal justice generally fails at preventing wrongdoing and assisting victims. Additionally, without parental rehabilitation and reentry efforts, the children of incarcerated parents suffer (DHHS, 2007). Criminal justice experts commonly believe that the system provides a "criminal process [that] has become notorious for 'revictimization' or 'secondary victimization,' for many child victims" (Gal, 2011, citations omitted). The reentry circle model helps children and families heal from the shame of incarceration and also to make concrete plans for how to desist from crime and substance abuse (Walker and Greening, 2010).

Application of Solution-Focused Methodology to Restorative Practices

In 2002, *solution-focused* (SF) brief therapy methodology was first used and applied with a restorative intervention in Hawai'i for people harmed by crime,* where the person responsible for causing the crime does not participate in the process (Walker, 2004). Most criminal

* Efforts are made here to not refer to people who have been harmed or have harmed others with the labels *victims* or *offenders*, and in the event the labels are used, it is only for expediency purposes.

cases go without anyone ever being identified or arrested in the United States. Only about 21% of all reported crimes result in an arrest or with anyone identified sufficiently for an arrest as the person responsible for causing the crime (U.S. Department of Justice, 2014).

SF brief therapy cofounder, the late Insoo Kim Berg, assisted me in developing SF applications to our restorative processes in Hawai'i, including the youth circle transition planning model for foster youth described above, and our reentry process for people in prison (Walker, 2005, 2013).

Following Ms. Berg's assistance, we have also applied the SF model of optimism and goal orientation in a 12-week cognitive course for people in prison (Walker and Sakai, 2013). Many people in prison do not know who they hurt, for example, burglaries and thefts. The 12-week training helps imprisoned people find ways to make reparations and amends for their harmful behavior to their unknown victims without requiring personal contact with them. To date, more than 400 imprisoned adults have participated in this SF restorative justice training program. There is also an effort to apply aspects of the adult cognitive program to incarcerated youth in Hawai'i (Walker, 2014).

In addition to successfully applying the SF approach to restorative justice programs, it is used frequently by *therapeutic jurisprudence* courts (King, 2009). "Therapeutic jurisprudence is the study of the role of the law as a therapeutic agent" (Wexler, 1993, p. 280).

Hawai'i's Juvenile Justice Law Reform

In 2013, the hawai'i Legislature amended its juvenile justice law to provide for the "informal adjustment" of juvenile law violators to include "restorative justice programs" (Hawai'i Revised Statutes, 2013).

Later in 2013, the state analyzed the almost $200,000 it spends in 12 months to incarcerate one juvenile (Hawai'i Juvenile Justice Working Group, 2013). It was determined that this cost was unjustified because imprisonment, and the expenditure of these funds, did not prevent 75% of the youth imprisoned from repeating crime after their release (Hawai'i Juvenile Justice Working Group, 2013). Also, juveniles who committed minor offenses, nonviolent offenses, and status offenses were being incarcerated at an alarmingly high rate when imprisonment itself can lead to criminality (U.S. Department of Justice, 2014). These concerns led to a working group being convened in August 2013, of which I was a member. We met with the help of the PEW Foundation, a nonprofit "global research and public policy organization" (PEW Charitable Trusts, 2014).

"The Working Group was charged with analyzing Hawai'i's data, policies, and practices; reviewing research on evidence-based principles and national best practices; and recommending policies that will move Hawai'i toward a more effective, equitable and efficient juvenile justice system" (Hawai'i Juvenile Justice Working Group, 2014, p. 2). The working groups efforts resulted in a new juvenile justice law in Hawai'i reflecting "justice reinvestment" (Hipp, 2014, p. 1).

The policies contained in H.B. [house bill] 2490 advance priorities in three areas:

1. *Reduce the use of secure confinement and protect public safety.* Limiting space in expensive secure facilities to the most serious juvenile offenders will help Hawai'i produce the greatest public safety benefit from the juvenile justice system. In addition, providing certain youth adjudicated for low-level crimes with the

opportunity from early interventions will ensure that they are held accountable and that resources are put to their best use.

2. *Strengthen community supervision and probation practices.* Effective community supervision will allow Hawai'i to maximize the public safety return on taxpayer investments in juvenile justice. By grounding probation practices in data and research, the state can better hold lower-risk youth accountable while reducing recidivism.
3. *Sustain effective practices and cultivate stakeholder collaboration.* Regular collection and analysis of data and outcomes is necessary to continue improving and maximizing public safety returns. By increasing avenues for collaboration across agencies, H.B. 2490 allows for efficient system management and case planning, enhancing decision making and resource allocation (Hipp, 2014, pp. 1–2).

The new law prevents juvenile incarceration for status offenses unless the juvenile is on probation for a felony (something that I argued against). The new law also provides for more community-based services. It does not specifically mention restorative justice, but during the working group meetings, we discussed restorative justice, and the state Office of Youth Services is promoting it with community service providers.

Conclusion

Restorative practices have been shown to be more healing for people than current punitive practices that focus mainly on offenders. Restorative practices can help juveniles harmed, and juveniles who did the harming too, to develop resiliency. Unfortunate things happen to people, including being assaulted at school as our son was. Engaging in harmful behavior is also unfortunate, but it is not unexpected behavior for youth who are in the process of developing maturity and learning. The opportunity to look at these events and outcomes in terms of how they might strengthen a person, compared to how they can diminish a person, has been shown to be a successful educational strategy (Hollister, 1967). Further, restorative processes as a whole help promote resiliency (Walker, 2000). It is my hope that further advancements will be made in Hawai'i to inform people about restorative practices, and to provide them for all people harmed by crime, for juveniles in the justice system, and for the community.

References

Archibald, B. (2013). Restorative justice and the rule of law: Rethinking due process through a relational theory of rights. Retrieved August 28, 2014, from http://dx.doi.org/10.2139/ssrn.2395224.

Asscher, J., Dijkstra, S., Stams, G., Dekovic, M., and Creemers, H. (2014). Family group conferencing in youth care: Characteristics of the decision making model, implementation and effectiveness of the Family Group (FG) plans. *BMC Public Health.* Retrieved September 13, 2014, from http://www.biomedcentral.com/1471-2458/14/154.

Boyes-Watson, C. (2003). Refining justice: An interview with Carolyn Boyes-Watson. Ikeda Center for Peace, Learning, and Dialogue. Retrieved September 20, 2012, from http://www.ikedacenter.org/thinkers/boyeswatson_int.htm.

Braithwaite, J. (2004). Building institutions of hope: Emancipation and hope. *Annals of the American Academy of Political and Social Science*, 592, 79–98.

EPIC 'Ohana, Inc. (2014). Building partnerships for Hawai'i's at-risk families, children and youth. Retrieved August 16, 2014, from http://www.epicohana.net/services.aspx.

Gal, T. (2011). *Child Victims and Restorative Justice: A Needs-Rights Model.* New York: Oxford University Press.

Givelber, D., and Farrell, A. (2012). *Not Guilty: Are the Acquitted Innocent?* New York: New York University Press.

Gramkowski, B., Kools, S., Paul, S., Boyer, C., Monasterio, E., and Robbins, N. (2009). Health Risk behavior in foster youth. *Journal of Child Adolescent Psychiatric Nursing*, 22(2), 77–85. Retrieved September 2, 2014, from http://www.ncbi.nlm.nih.gov/pmc/articles/PMC3436904/pdf/nihms239956.pdf.

Hawai'i Juvenile Justice Working Group. (2013). Final report. Retrieved September 5, 2014, from http://www.pewtrusts.org/~/media/legacy/uploadedfiles/jjriworkinggroupfinalreportfinalpdf.pdf.

Hawai'i Revised Statutes. (2013). Section 571-31.4 (b) (11): Informal adjustment, law violators. Retrieved September 10, 2014, from http://www.capitol.hawaii.gov/hrscurrent/Vol12_Ch0501-0588/HRS0571/HRS_0571-0031_0004.htm.

Hipp, D. (2014). *Justice Reinvestment.* Office of Youth Services. Retrieved September 14, 2014, from http://humanservices.hawaii.gov/wp-content/uploads/2014/08/HB-2490-Summary-Article-Aug-14..pdf.

Hollister, W. G. (1967). The concept of strengths in education: A challenge to curriculum development. In E. M. Bower and W. G. Hollister (eds.), *Behavioral Science Frontiers in Education.* New York: John Wiley & Sons.

Hosmanek, A. (2012). Cutting the cord: Ho'oponopono and Hawaiian restorative justice in the criminal law context. *Pepperdine Dispute Resolution Law Journal*, 5(2), 6. Retrieved September 20, 2012, from http://digitalcommons.pepperdine.edu/drlj/vol5/iss2/6.

King, M. (2009). *Solution-Focused Bench Book.* Melbourne: Australasian Institute of Judicial Administration Incorporated. Retrieved August 28, 2014, from http://www.aija.org.au/Solution%20Focused%20BB/SFJ%20BB.pdf.

PEW Charitable Trusts. (2014). Mission & values. Retrieved September 14, 2014, from http://www.pewtrusts.org/en/about/mission-and-values.

Schwalbe, C. S, Gearing, R. E., MacKenzie, M. J., Brewer, K. B., Ibrahim, R. (2012). A meta-analysis of experimental studies of diversion programs for juvenile offenders. *Clinical Psychology Review*, 32(1), 26–33. doi: 10.1016/j.cpr.2011.10.002.

Skaaning, S.-K., and Moller, J. (2010). Systematizing thin and thick conceptions of the rule of law. Presented at APSA 2010 Annual Meeting. Retrieved September 2, 2014, from http://ssrn.com/abstract=1643367.

Stickle, W., Connell, N., Wilson, D., and Gottfredson, D. (2008). An experimental evaluation of teen courts. *Journal of Experimental Criminology*, 4, 137–163.

Suffolk University. (2014). Restorative Center for Restorative Justice, College of Arts & Sciences. Retrieved September 19, 2014, from http://www.suffolk.edu/college/centers/15970.php.

Tamanaha, B. (2007). A concise guide to the rule of law. In N. Walker and G. Palombella (eds.), *Florence Workshop on the Rule of Law.* Oxford: Hart Publishing Company. Retrieved August 30, 2014, from http://ssrn.com/abstract=1012051.

Tamanaha, B. (2012). The history and elements of the rule of law. *Singapore Journal of Legal Studies*, 232–247. Retrieved August 30, 2014, from http://dx.doi.org/10.2139/ssrn.2012845.

UNICEF. (2010). Toolkit on diversion and alternatives to detention. Retrieved September 18, 2012, from http://www.unicef.org/tdad/index_56513.html.

U.S. Department of Health and Human Services (DHHS), Assistant Secretary for Planning and Evaluation Research and Practice. (2007). Symposium on marriage and incarceration: A meeting summary. Retrieved September 19, 2012, from http://aspe.hhs.gov/hsp/07/marr-incar/report.pdf.

U.S. Department of Justice. (2014). Five things about deterrence. Washington, DC: U.S. Department of Justice, National Institute of Justice. Retrieved July 23, 2014, from https://ncjrs.gov/pdffiles1/nij/247350.pdf.

Wachtel, T. (2013). Defining restorative. p. 1. Bethlehem, PA: International Institute for Restorative Practices, Graduate School. Retrieved on November 15, 2014, from http://www.iirp.edu/pdf/Defining-Restorative.pdf.

Walker, L. (2000). Conferencing: A group process that promotes resiliency publication. Presented at Second International Conference on Conferencing and Circles: Restorative Practice in Action, Toronto, Ontario. Retrieved September 19, 2012, from http://www.iirp.edu/article_detail.php?article_id=NDc5.

Walker, L. (2002). Conferencing: A new approach for juvenile justice in Honolulu. *Federal Probation Journal*, 66(1).

Walker, L. (2004). Restorative justice without offender participation: A pilot program for victims. International Institute for Restorative Practices. Retrieved September 18, 2012, from http://www.iirp.edu/library/lwalker04.html.

Walker, L. (2005). A cohort study of 'ohana conferencing in child abuse and neglect cases. *Protecting Children*, 19(4), 36–46.

Walker, L. (2008). Waikiki youth circles: Homeless youth learn goal setting skills. *Journal of Family Psychotherapy*, 19(1). Retrieved September 18, 2012, from http://www.lorennwalker.com/articles/Waikiki%20Youth%20Circles.pdf.

Walker, L. (2009). Modified restorative circles: A reintegration group planning process that promotes desistance. *Contemporary Justice Review*, 12(4), 419–431. Retrieved September 14, 2014, from http://www.lorennwalker.com/articles/Modifiedrestorativecircles12-2009.pdf.

Walker, L. (2013). Solution-focused reentry and transition planning for imprisoned people. In P. De Jong and I. K. Berg (eds.), *Interviewing for Solutions* (pp. 318–328). Belmont, CA: Brooks/Cole.

Walker, L. (2014). Correspondence with US District Court Judge Leslie Kobayashi. August 21.

Walker, L., and Greening, R. (2010). Huikahi restorative circles: A public health approach for reentry planning. *Federal Probation Journal*, 74(1). Retrieved September 20, 2012, from http://www.uscourts.gov/statistics-reports/publications/federal-probation-journal/federal-probation-journal-june-2010.

Walker, L., and Sakai, T. (2013). Restorative justice skills building for incarcerated people. In K. S. van Wormer and L. Walker (eds.), *Restorative Justice Today: Practical Applications* (pp. 163–174). Thousand Oaks, CA: Sage.

Walker, L., Tarutani, C., and McKibben, D. (2015). Benefits of restorative reentry circles for children of incarcerated parents in Hawai'I. In T. Gal and B. F. Duramy (eds.), *Promoting the Participation of Children across the Globe: From Social Exclusion to Child-Inclusive Policies* (pp. 333–357). London: Oxford University Press.

Wexler, D. (1993). Therapeutic jurisprudence and the criminal courts. *William & Mary Law Review*, 35(1), 279–299. Retrieved September 8, 2014, from http://scholarship.law.wm.edu/cgi/viewcontent.cgi?article=1781&context=wmlr.

Zehr, H. (2013). Restorative justice? What's that? In K. S. van Wormer and L. Walker (eds.), *Restorative Justice Today: Practical Applications* (p. 7). Thousand Oaks, CA: Sage.

Prevention of Interpersonal Crimes and Violence among Children and Youth through Virtue Education

A Roadmap

8

JOHN CHRISTOPHER AND
JOHAN DE TAVERNIER

Contents

Introduction

Many people view the contemporary world as verging on moral bankruptcy and view our institutions as failing to inculcate good character (Kotva, 1996, p. 6). But it is not a new phenomenon, since moral panics have occurred throughout recorded history. The immediate query would be whether our human nature as such is more prone to narcissism and brutality than altruism and benevolence, or whether our society is interested more in pessimism than in positive human qualities and optimistic behavioral interventions. This envisages an essential question of our interest: What measures are to be implemented to ensure human behavior or prevent crimes and victimization among children?

One of the aims of virtue education is to find a solution to social problems that have been caused by people's materialistic and individualistic attitudes (Sanderse, 2012, p. 20). Unfortunately, the contemporary educational system focuses more on preparing students to become smart and generate employment opportunity. In other words, it is reasonably successful in proffering an "education for knowing" with an emphasis on communicating facts and figures that help children to analyze, synthesize, and manipulate them, along with practical skills and techniques. But the importance of character development and inculcation of virtues has been totally abandoned.

This chapter primarily focuses on the kind of basic virtue education that should be given in schools to minimize the risk of interpersonal crime among children and youth. First, we analyze the contribution virtue ethics, in particular a virtue approach to virtue education as a theoretical perspective, can deliver to preclude violence in schools. Second, we aim to propose three unique orientations that are attached to this perspective: education that outshines from knowing to doing and to being, an education that transcends from information to formation and transformation, and finally, an education that transforms from curriculum centered and teacher centered to person centered.

Does Education Have a Role in Crime Prevention?

Indisputably, education has been proven to be a great catalyst for "change"; yet this change has had both positive and negative effects. Positive, since there has been remarkable growth in literacy, health care, knowledge of economic matters, scientific and technological development, and so forth; also negative, however, since despite all our efforts to eradicate violence and criminality from our lives, crime still exists around the world and is even a growing phenomenon. There has been a colossal increase in crimes and violence, in fact, and this poses a grave threat to humanity. Human rights violations, corruption, human trafficking, rapes, and especially crimes against children and juvenile delinquency against peers, school staff, and property have increased sufficiently. Of course, violence and crime are a matter of concern everywhere. Mostly, they are considered to be taboo and a last resort to exercise. Yet under certain circumstances, they are even used as a mechanism of social control. In fact, there is a paradox about violence. Many people think that they are safe and secure only by repelling violence with violence; at the same time, they deprecate and condemn it (Turpin and Lester, 1997, pp. 1–2). They also recognize that "violence is caused not simply by individual psychological factors, biological impulses, or social-structural factors alone but by a web of casual connections between personal-level and global-level structures, processes, and behaviors" (Kurtz and Turpin, 1997, p. 208).

Against this backdrop, the observation of Kofi Annan, the former Secretary General of the United Nations (UN), makes sense: "Violence cuts short the lives of millions of people across the world each year, and damages the lives of millions more. It knows no boundaries of geography, race, age or income. It strikes at children, young people, women and the elderly. It finds its way into homes, schools and the workplace. Men and women everywhere have the right to live their lives and raise their children free from the fear of violence. We must help them enjoy that right by making it clearly understood that violence is preventable, and by working together to identify and address its underlying causes" (Krug, 2002).

In this precarious scenario, we situate a *taken for granted* context, namely, *school*, which has enormous potentiality as a *locus* for crime prevention. School is an abode where both criminality and victimization are simultaneously demonstrated. There are students with criminal temperaments, and there are children who are very often scapegoats to victimization in the same classroom. Of course, children are the most vulnerable and potentially defenseless members of an increasingly globalized society (Gearon, 2001, p. 143). However, Marta Santos Pais, Special Representative of the UN Secretary General on Violence against Children, articulates, "Education has a unique potential to generate an environment where attitudes condoning violence can be changed and non-violent behavior can be learned. From children's early years, schools are well placed to break patterns of violence and provide skills to communicate, to negotiate and support peaceful solutions to conflicts" (WHO, 1998, p. 3). Obviously, schools cannot control many factors that contribute to violence. Yet, they can address a broad range of behaviors, skills, communication patterns, and attitudes that support and perpetuate violence. The most effective medium to accomplish this purpose is virtue education. In other words, educating children with character and virtues contributes to minimize interpersonal violence among children.

Virtue Ethics and Virtue Approach to Education

The concept of virtue has a long tradition in ethical theory. Virtue ethics is a theoretical perspective in ethics that holds that judgments about the inner lives of individuals (traits, motives, dispositions, and character) are more important than judgments about the rightness or wrongness of external acts or the consequence of acts (Louden, 1998, p. 498). According to Livino Melina (2001, p. 39), it is an "ethics of the first person" that is rooted within the perspective of the subject, who in his or her acting is called upon to realize acts that are excellent. This directs him or her to a concern with his or her own fulfillment and not "an ethics of the third person," which is situated within the perspective of the observer, who evaluates the external act according to its conformity to a rule. Jan Steutel and David Carr (1999, p. 5) define virtue ethics "as a systematic and coherent account of virtues." Their primary concern is to identify certain traits as desirable, or not, by analyzing and classifying them with the exposition of their moral significance. In this way, they aim to justify those traits as virtues. Concisely, virtue ethicists are not primarily interested in particular actions but in persons. Their primary focus is not so much on what he or she does or how he or she acts, but who should he or she become (Keenan, 1998, p. 84).

The pertinent question, which is of great importance with regard to virtue education, is the following: How can virtues be inculcated through education? Aristotle believes that the inculcation of a virtuous character is first acquired by exercising them through vigorous practice: "We become builders by building and lyre-players by playing the lyre. So too we become just by doing just actions, temperate by temperate actions, and courageous by courageous action" (Aristotle, 2000, *Nicomachean Ethics* [NE], 1103b). In the process, role models often play a significant part. Developing a virtuous character is often the fruit of imitating a virtuous person (Vanlaere and Gastmans, 2007, p. 761). Therefore, it is equally true that a virtuous character does not occur and flourish in a vacuum.

Aristotle's account of *phronesis*, which translates as *prudentia* in Latin and *prudence* or *practical wisdom* in English, begins with the assertion that virtue, in the strict sense, cannot exist without practical wisdom (NE, 1144b17, 1144b20–21). This claim becomes effective when people possess the kind of moral knowledge required to exercise virtues in their concrete everyday life situation. In this context, of course, practical wisdom is an understanding of what makes an act virtuous. It is a single virtue with several manifestations (Smith, 2001, p. 213). Obviously, as Curzer (2012, p. 12) argues, "virtuous people already know which acts are virtuous; what they learn in order to become properly virtuous is why virtuous acts are virtuous." Moreover, we can technically stipulate virtue as practical wisdom; its existence implies the existence of practical wisdom (Dahl, 1984, p. 13).

Concisely, practical wisdom is a virtue by which one deliberates or reasons well in a practical way (NE, 1140a24–28). It is not a deductive science to make right choices from moral axioms. And it is also not a *technê* that will always guarantee a precise outcome. But essentially, practical wisdom demands for a special focus on the actual life situations impinging upon individuals (Fitterer, 2008, p. 32). This reciprocal interdependence of practical wisdom and virtue is overtly accepted at NE 1144b30–32, where

Aristotle says, "It is clear then from what has been said, that it is not possible to be good in the strict sense without practical wisdom, nor practically wise without moral virtue" (Dahl, 1984, p. 63).

One of the inexorable conclusions to be drawn is the fact that the school is one of the contexts where virtues can be trained and developed. As the school could be a community of persons, the teamwork or collaboration among all those who involved—the interaction of students with teachers and the whole school environment—is of utmost importance. The school as a community is the abode where character, virtues, attitudes, dispositions, and personality traits of students are developed through practice. And these practices are generally understood as virtues leading to the goal of achieving the goods of society (Langston, 2001, p. 141).

In this process, teachers could become the agents of transformation. They discharge not only their professional duties, but also their personal character. In fact, the professional goodness of a teacher is not simply a question of acting according to the professional standards. A good teacher is the one who, through practice and hard work, has learned to put both heart and soul into the job, and to do as a matter of course what is expected of a good teacher: to be concerned about the well-being of the students, and to be expert, honest, fair, cordial, reliable, and more, and all at the right time, toward the right person, and so forth (Gastmans, 2002, p. 499). Thus, teachers become game changers. They help children to inculcate virtues through constant practice, with rational knowledge, critical thinking, and practical wisdom. Moreover, the mutual and intimate relationship between teacher and student, which is always a dialogue rather than monologue, heals those children who are victimized and retrieves those children who engage in violent and aggressive activities. As Mar Ivanios (2006, p. 70) rightly exhorts, "virtues flow only from the virtuous." "If you want to know what virtue is, then you simply watch to see what a virtuous person does" (Selling, 1998, p. 5). Teachers should be the role model. They must never forget that students need a companion and a guide during their period of growth. Good teachers can mold good citizens.

Educating the Whole Person

Once virtue ethics is placed as the theoretical base for the conception of education and virtue education in particular, the purpose of education also becomes similar to that of virtue ethics, namely, the development of certain traits, along with the promotion of some understanding of their moral value or significance through justification (Steutel and Carr, 1999, pp. 6–7). This necessitates the understanding of the characterization of virtues in different contexts. George Sher (1992, p. 92) distinguishes three ways of understanding virtues. In agreement with the Aristotelian tradition, he articulates that "virtues are traits that are conducive to their possessor's flourishing, or to a person's living a life that is in his or her best interest." The fundamental question is whether those virtues are traits conducive to the flourishing of their possessors (self-regarding) or others (other-regarding). Meanwhile, on the other hand, the deontological tradition seeks virtues as traits conducive to right action. The crucial question here is not whether a trait contributes to anyone's well-being, but whether it leads its possessor to fulfill his or her moral duties. Similarly, in the perfectionist approach, a trait is a virtue whenever it, or its possession, has intrinsic value or worth. This position explains virtue in terms of moral good rather than right, and equates virtues not with character traits that are good for their possessors, but rather with traits that are good in themselves. At this point, Sher (1992, p. 92) exposes the presence of profound differences among the three approaches, but for him, the crucial question is not what is meant by the term *virtue*, though he identifies virtue as "character trait that is for some reason desirable or worth having." On the contrary, his primary interest is to know if there are any character traits that can be known to be objectively valuable. In brief, his conclusion brings about the possibility of making a clear distinction between two categories: there are human values that are not counted as virtues since they do not belong to the class of character traits; conversely, there are character traits that are not treated as virtues since they are not seen as worthwhile or desirable.

With regard to the idea of the good life, one can distinguish between the good life that one has "led" and the good life one has "had." According to Frankena (1970, p. 17), when we say that one "led a good life," it implies that he or she led a morally good life, and this does not necessarily mean that he or she was a happy or had a good life. Again, when we say that one had a good life, we mean that one's life was happy or desirable; we do not necessarily mean that one was a morally good person. Therefore, we must distinguish the moral or morally good life from the happy or nonmorally good life. In virtue ethics theory, these two kinds of good life are normally called a "virtuous life" and a "flourishing life" (Steutel, 1998, p. 129). In relation to education, Frankena (1970, pp. 18–19) distinguishes between two kinds or parts of education: moral education, or "educating the good wo/man" [for virtuous life], and nonmoral education, or "educating for the good life" [flourishing life]. So, there could be moral education in view of virtuous living on the one hand, and nonmoral education in view of a flourishing life on the other. If leading a virtuous life is sufficient for a flourishing life, then educators will concentrate only on preparing children for virtuous living, and the flourishing life will automatically follow. Conversely, if leading a virtuous life is necessary for a flourishing life, then no one can flourish without leading a virtuous life either. Put succinctly, cultivating virtues is indispensable to preparing children for a flourishing life (Steutel, 1998, pp. 129–130). Indeed, this is a defining characteristic of an ethics of virtue and one of the criteria that distinguishes the virtue approach to education from other leading approaches, such as values clarification theory, Kohlberg's cognitive developmental theory, and care ethics.

On the issue of human flourishing, Carr (1991, p. 226) refers not only to the welfare of the community or society, but also to the well-being of a virtuous agent as such: "a sensible wo/man regards it as in her/his own interest and therefore wants to be wise, courageous, just and temperate." In this respect, Steutel (1998, p. 141) observes that most virtue ethicists regard living virtuously not only as conducive to a flourishing life but also constitutive of such a life. In substance, "education for the morally virtuous life will be an indispensable part of education for the good life as such."

Education from Knowing and Doing to Being

In the previous section, we sought to reaffirm virtues and the virtue approach to education as the cornerstone to minimizing the attitude of violence among children, especially when they are in conflict with rules and regulations. In the "Education from Information over Formation to Transformation" section, we propose three fundamental features or remedial strategies that could prevent crimes and violence among children. First, we need a rebalancing of education toward doing and being to reduce the knowing–doing gap (Dater et al., 2011, p. 16).

It may be clear now that the present educational system, however, is much less effective at an "education for being." It is said that the education for being is a nebulous concept, beneficial for facilitating children to feel good about themselves. Sometimes it is even accused of creating no impacts on others or holding any practical use. But the undeniable fact is that education for being is "designed to help children to do such things as understand and respect themselves, empathize with others, appreciate the wonders of creation, show a concern for the environment, express feelings in personally authentic but socially acceptable ways, give and receive love, identify worthwhile life goals and the means towards their attainment, and develop and articulate a mature philosophy of life" (Fontana, 1997, p. 339). This may be very difficult to quantify, but it is very essential to our sense of being human. Unfortunately, the focus of education today is more on imparting knowledge and acquiring information. The quantity of knowledge is periodically evaluated through test and examination. In addition, knowledge is obtained to get a better job, and education has been prioritized to generate good professionals who can perform and act well.

According to Lickona (1992, p. 6), "good character consists of knowing the good, desiring the good, and doing the good. Schools must help children *understand* the core values, *adopt* or commit to them, and then *act upon* them in their own lives," which lead them to transformation. And the educational goals are the holistic development of the students, proper orientation of their lives, and cultivation of virtuous attitudes and character or excellence in their activities (Gastmans, 2002, p. 501). Of course, knowing, doing, and being should go hand in hand while educating our children. At the same time, an education for being would certainly enhance the effectiveness of an education for knowing and doing (Fontana, 1997, p. 343). This significant shift in educational system emphasizing education for being against education for doing will contribute to minimizing the moral decline leading to vandalism, violence, crimes, and bigotry.

The American ethicist Gula (1989, pp. 6–7) explicates morality in terms of "the sort of persons we ought to be" and "the sorts of actions we ought to perform." The sort of person one is depends to a great extent on the sorts of decisions and actions one has taken, and conversely, the sort of decisions and actions that one has taken depend in part on the sort of person one is. As a result, "both being and doing or character and action, constitute independent concerns and must be taken together." The point of his contention is that "moral goodness depends upon the quality of person that which is constituted not by rule-keeping behavior alone, but by cultivating certain virtues, attitudes, and outlooks" (Gula, 1989, p. 7). Subsequently, his emphasis is on what is happening to the person performing actions, rather than on the actions the person performs. In the light of such points, the role of virtues becomes prominent since virtues are those personal qualities that stimulate us to act in certain ways in a particular situation. The right action comes from a good person. Our interiority, dispositions, habits, intentions, virtues, and character get expressed in our external behavior. It is similar to the biblical saying that the good tree bears good fruits and the bad tree bears bad fruits (Mathew 7:17–18). "An 'ethics of being' focuses on the good person; an 'ethics of doing' focuses on right actions" (Gula, 1989, p. 8). What sort of actions we should perform is the primary concern of an ethics of doing. Our actions are the signs that express our interiority (intention). The distinction between the ethics of being and the ethics of doing also helps us understand the distinction between "right" action (or judgment of moral rightness) and "good" action (or judgment of moral goodness). The term *right* answers "What should I do?" by pointing to actions, and the term *good* answers the same question by pointing to what falls under the notion of virtue—such as motives, dispositions, and intentions. Morality in the strict sense pertains to the person, to character. Actions are moral only in a derived or secondary sense because the person expresses himself or herself in actions. Strictly speaking, *good* and *bad* properly refer to the person; *right* and *wrong* refer to the action (Gula, 1989, pp. 6–8).

In the context of increased violence among children, our educational system has to (re)focus more on training their being, character, dispositions, and integrity, and unfolding their potentialities. Education for being is the same as the views of Gula on ethics of being. The more the students are prepared to be good and virtuous, the better the fruits of their being will be. The emphasis on children's training in obligations or the imposition of prohibitions has to be reoriented toward the internalization of virtuous character traits and positive internal motivation.

To achieve this virtue approach perspective, the educational process has to become a coordinated teamwork (teachers, parents, managements, government agencies, etc.) where teachers play a pivotal role. They must fulfill a number of necessary positive conditions like attentiveness to the genuine needs of the children, discharging responsibilities to achieve their goals, and the competency to be acquired to accomplish the needs (Vanlaere and Gastmans, 2007, p. 162). By this way, the relationship between the teacher and the student is weighed. Moreover, the fact is that children take shape or given formation or even inculcate virtues only in and through relationship with other persons. This is not merely a process of transmitting information, but a meticulous insistence on character formation for transformation.

Education from Information over Formation to Transformation

In addition to focusing on knowing, doing, and being, education should help people to become smart and good. As we have seen in the "Education from Knowing and Doing to Being" section, the integral development of children involves their whole character, though the importance of this has been neglected in the present educational scenario. In that scenario, the focus has shifted from character formation to professional and job-oriented education, where acquiring information or knowledge has become primary and even the sole objective. Yet, this acquired knowledge has been neither assimilated nor converted in such a way as to promote personal development and human flourishing. As a result, the passive, violent, and cruel temperaments of children are not transformed, and they are not enabled to become self-motivated members of an oriented, proactive, and meaningful school community. In fact, cultivating the good conduct of citizens and preparing well-cultured, educated persons with esteemed character are the major aims of this transformative education. On this backdrop, the role of virtue education becomes significant.

The very use of the term *transformation* calls for a change in substance or function. At least in the rhetorical sense, it stands for change and implementation of certain goals and objectives (Ginsburg et al., 2010, p. 453). The *Oxford Dictionary* identifies this change as a metamorphosis. The fact is that both persons and things are capable of undergoing transformation (Wade, 1998, p. 713). Yet the word *transformation* has been popularized as a buzzword, even made to refer in one place to the "change of mindset that will allow the [U.S.] military to harness the technological advances of the information age to gain a qualitative advantage over any political foe" (Ahmed, 2010, p. 511). But personal transformation is something quite different from this. When it occurs, it conveys the individual to an advanced level of being and charges him or her with a new passion for life and a greater sense of power and freedom. Generally, it is defined as the "state of being conscious of one's consciousness." In the words of Gail Holland Wade (1998, p. 716), "it is a dynamic, uniquely individualized process of expanding consciousness whereby individuals become critically aware of old and new self-views and choose to integrate these views into a new self-definition."

Education in a broader sense is indeed synonymous with transformation or transformative learning (Ahmed, 2010, p. 511). It entails a process of dialogue inquiry that enables children to explore self-discoveries and enter into an inner dialogue. Transformation, from an educational viewpoint, is thus seen as an interactive process (Wade, 1998, p. 714) focused on a change in consciousness (De Souza, 2008, p. 27) where the human potential is opened wide and human dignity and rights are cherished. The role of the teacher in this context is very significant, for those teachers who undergo personal transformation are better equipped to empower their students to discover new avenues through their experiences. Moreover, such teachers engage in mentoring and nurturing activities to encourage self-knowledge and permit students to realize their potentials. In the process, both the teacher and the student grow to be mutually committed to unearthing their potentials for the betterment of themselves and others. Students are capable of transformation. The capability theory of Nobel Laureate Amartya Sen could be applied not only in the effort to conceptualize and evaluate the ideas of social justice and individual well-being, but also in order to better understand educational and individual transformation. Sen looks upon education as the means to expand human capabilities, freedom, choice, and agency (Ahmed, 2010, pp. 512–516).

It is fair to say that, up to today, the present educational system has failed to affirm the human person as an at once rational, emotional, and spiritual being, one who thinks, feels, and intuits. When the complementarities of these three dimensions are integrated into the learning process, education itself becomes a catalyst of formation and transformation (De Souza, 2008, p. 34). According to Buchanan and Hyde (2008, p. 311), "students in schools not only achieve the cognitive competencies that comprise any given curriculum area, but engage in the type of learning experiences which have the power to be transformative," and for learning to go "beyond the surface and touch the soul of the students." Clearly, effective education presupposes inner transformation; it is not merely an effort to convey factual knowledge through indoctrination, but rather requires students to engage in a critical analysis, to withstand an emotional crisis, and to construct meaning from their experiences (Taplin, 2014, p. 6). This approach does not focus on the attainment of knowledge and skills, but on character development and virtue inculcation.

Education from Curriculum Centered to Teacher Centered and Person Centered

Education can be defined as an ethical practice based on the ethical imperative to promote the well-being of the student by caring for him or her in a personal relationship. The teacher–student relationship is the heart of education, and this is the goal-oriented character of education. Thus, education, especially in early childhood, may be regarded as equivalent to the nursing care discharged to patients.

Generally, the goal of education is described as the promotion of students' well-being by providing good care in the wider meaning of the word (i.e., on the physical as well as psychological, relational, social, moral, and spiritual levels). Sometimes this is called holistic education, because it cannot be reduced to any single technique. It is the art of cultivating meaningful human relationships; it is the dialectic between teachers and learners within a caring community (Bosacki, 2001, p. 163).

Teaching is an ethical practice. As an ethical practice, it is made concrete through personal relationship between the teacher and student. The quality of teaching must always be assessed in the light of this relationship between a unique teacher and a unique student. The student must not be considered a passive object to which an educational technology is to be applied. On the contrary, educational activities presuppose a reciprocal interaction between human persons who enter into relationships with each other based on their uniqueness (Gastmans, 2002, p. 496). By indulging in teaching, and developing the attitude and skills associated with this activity, the teacher enters as a person into a relationship with the student. The fundamental reciprocity of a relationship of understanding and respect can be found in the dynamic interaction between these two. Such an environment enables children to inculcate virtues in addition to academic learning. They are given not only intellectual formation, but also emotional training. Indeed, every educational endeavor is both overtly and covertly oriented toward the inculcation of virtues and formation of character. It is a display of both the personal traits and exercising professional calibers of a teacher to educate children in character and the virtues.

Therefore, in a person-centered education, the customary educational vocabulary has to be broadened. In addition to often-used rationalistic concepts like principles, judgments, methods of analysis, and intellectual endeavors, the language of virtues, character, intuition, vision, spirituality, personality, emotion, moral perception, and moral sensitivity must be incorporated prominently in any educational program and curriculum design (Gastmans, 2002, p. 502). Education should thus never be compartmentalized, but rather oriented toward both intellectual and emotional development of students. Such an emphasis on a person-centered education brings to view new horizons in the life of the children: a sense of direction and meaning, positive and durable dispositions, optimistic and constructive attitudes, emotional and poignant maturity, practical and intellectual wisdom, and prudence. On the whole, each student is prepared to face the complex and challenging realities of life with a face that is both virtuous and brave (Ginsburg et al., 2010, p. 451).

It is widely acknowledged today that the curriculum-centered one-size-fits-all approach to education has not produced the desired educational result or accomplished the wishes of students within a globalized world (Hope, 2013, pp. 2–3). Terms such as *student centered*, *learner centered*, *child centered*, and *person centered* are often used in distinction from more traditional approaches that are said to have been teacher centered, teacher directed, and curriculum centered (Schooley, 2012, pp. 3–4; Catalano and Catalano, 1999, pp. 538–539). One solution proposed was a person-centered education emerging from the teacher–student relationship. Educators create an environment of freedom, trust, and respect in the classroom, making trust, individual autonomy, and freedom its cornerstone, that is, trusting students, building credible relationships, and showing the trustworthiness of facilitators (Hope, 2013, pp. 7–8). Students are permitted to study, experiment, and try to find their own solutions, and in this, it is apt that this approach has been said to promote a democratic classroom (Ugaste and Oun, 2007, pp. 54–55).

However, it is important to note that the terms *child centered*, *student centered*, and *learner centered* are used in very different ways by various schools, colleges, universities, and informal education providers. Although any institution might exhibit a person-centered approach, in reality the meaning of these terms in different contexts is not consistent. For instance, sometimes these terms mean that certain institutions are committed to the student's opinion, or otherwise, that students are given an opportunity to make their own decisions about learning, designing their own curriculum and even creating their own discipline. The fact is that the language of a person-centered approach used by some educational organizations in their policies or promotional materials is often little more than a catchphrase. Surely, these expressions can be opaque, and on various occasions can be used as a mask to conceal organizational practices that are opposed to a person-centered approach (Hope, 2013, p. 11); therefore, we must first consider the alternatives, commonly known as teacher-centered and system-centered approaches.

The very idea of a teacher-centered approach implicitly assumes that teachers are the experts. Since the times of ancient Greece and of *gurukul* education, this approach has occupied a prominent position among the classical forms of educational method. Of course, education as an operational process is hardly possible without some sort of dialogue between teachers and students (Kozyrev, 2006, p. 215). Nevertheless, within a school community, teachers generally consider themselves to be the most creditable people and the ones most able to take decisions about curriculum, teaching styles, evaluation methods, content of sessions, and behavior expectations. Students who fail to achieve their expectations are either said to have failed or labeled as "unteachable." This is not a participatory, developmental style of teaching (Hermans, 2003, p. 282). In the case of their relationship with students within the classroom, teachers sometimes even exercise their power over students quite arbitrarily (Hope, 2013, p. 11).

Before proceeding, we should note that the educational reforms in the recent past have been mostly focused on students. We live in a time when education is "all about kids." Hardly any attention has been paid to the work of the teacher, who plays such a critical role in education. It is sometimes observed that if we create the schools our teachers deserve, we will have created the schools our children deserve. For instance, the distinct ideals, ethos, and charisms of a particular school are largely exhibited through teachers, who converse, represent, and transmit them (Cohen, 2002, pp. 533–534). Unfortunately, recent educational reforms lay emphasis only on what should be taught, how, when, and with what materials. Teachers, to some extent, are treated as a part of the curriculum. Yet, "affect, attitude, and persona have a much more powerful impact on classes than do the books they use or the pedagogical techniques they employ" (Cohen, 2002, p. 534). Today, we need "better schools for students and greater professional status for teachers" (McGhan, 2002, p. 538).

The system-centered approach, on the other hand, emphasizes the "system as a whole." Individuals must adapt themselves to the demands of the system. If something goes wrong, it is the system that is to be blamed, not vice versa. In other words, the system controls and regulates every educational enterprise. Teachers are not given sufficient freedom; they are required to use standard lesson plans and formal examination procedures. Students who come up with new ideas are not encouraged to display their creativity, innovation, and imagination; rather, they are asked to assume their places in the established system.

Consequently, teachers and the supporting staff are reluctant to make decisions that might go against the established procedure. In sum, although this approach maintains that it is more student centered, in fact, one finds little consistency in its claims and practice. "Quite often, conversely, it adheres to the policies and procedures of the system even at the cost of human causalities within this" (Hope, 2013, p. 12).

Yet the significance of a person-centered education should not be underrated. For, first of all, it regards children as ends, not means. Second, it provides a peaceful environment in which children can grow and flourish and never imposes a way of being on them. Third, it respects children's autonomy and passion and understands things from their point of view. Admittedly, an understanding of children's perspectives and of inner life helps teachers to help children by leading them to discover their own way of life (Grant and Piechowski, 1999, p. 8). Fourth, it integrates the psychological, social, and spiritual aspects of human growth and evaluates children in their totality. Thus, getting to know the persons or students is essential (Steenbergen, 2013, p. 35).

Above all, a final point to be addressed here is the possibility of developing a person-centered educational organization. In the present scenario, many individuals earnestly strive to be person centered within the organizations to which they belong. Nonetheless, Hope (2013, p. 3) calls for a paradigm shift "whereby person-centered educators are working within the person-centered systems." He argues that these person-centered schools' *way of being* is greatly consistent with a person-centered approach both inside and outside of classrooms. Educators receive a peaceful environment and unconditional support to work within the system, and students develop a sense of belonging to the school as a whole, as well as of being individuals. Eventually, a strong interpersonal relationship is developed not only between teachers and students, but also between peers (Hope, 2013, pp. 4–6).

As a summary, we want to stress that a person-centered organization presupposes the following five characteristics: (1) they are established on the principle that individuals can be trusted, (2) mutual respect and an excellent relationship between students and teachers lead to successful learning, (3) decision making is mostly done by those who are affected by decisions and must develop structures and processes that support this, (4) it questions and challenges the customary hierarchical power structures, and (5) it promotes transparency and honesty, and endeavors to expand organizational congruence (Hope, 2013, p. 14).

Conclusion

The primary objective of this chapter was to explore and investigate strategies to reduce violence among children. On the outset, we situated school and education as catalysts for change. Realizing the unique characteristics of virtue education, first, we presented virtue ethics, virtue approach, and virtue education as a theoretical perspective to preclude violence in schools. Second, we proposed a person-centered education, focusing on being rather than on doing and transcending education from the level of information to the level of transformation as possible remedial solutions to not only minimize violence, but also use as a preventive measure. The efforts and energy put into education are not an expense, but an investment. It is an investment in our children, young people, and the future of our nation. Undoubtedly, we can counter violence with virtue.

References

Ahmed, M. (2010). Education as transformation: Education for transformation. *Development*, 53(4), 511–517.

Aristotle. (2000). *Nicomachean Ethics*, ed. R. Crisp. Cambridge: Cambridge University Press.

Bosacki, S. L. (2001). "Theory of mind" or "theory of the soul?" The role of spirituality in children's understanding of minds and emotions. In J. Erricker, C. Ota, and C. Erricker (eds.), *Spiritual Education: Cultural, Religious and Social Differences: New Perspectives for the 21st Century* (pp. 156–169). Brighton, OR: Sussex Academic Press.

Buchanan, M. T., and Hyde, B. (2008). Learning beyond the surface: Engaging the cognitive, affective and spiritual dimensions within the curriculum. *International Journal of Children's Spirituality*, 13(4), 309–320.

Carr, D. (1991). *Educating the Virtues: An Essay on the Philosophical Psychology of Moral Development and Education*. London: Routledge.

Catalano, G. D., and Catalano, K. (1999). Transformation: From teacher-centered to student-centered engineering education. *Journal of Engineering Education*, 88(1), 59–64.

Cohen, R. M. (2002). Schools our teachers deserve: A proposal for teacher-centered reform. *Phi Delta Kappan*, 83(7), 532–537.

Curzer, H. J. (2012). *Aristotle and the Virtues*. Oxford: Oxford University Press.

Dahl, N. O. (1984). *Practical Reason, Aristotle, and Weakness of the Will*. Minneapolis: University of Minnesota Press.

Dater, S. M., Garvin, D. A., and Cullen, P. G. (2011). Rethinking the MBA: Business education at a crossroads. *Strategic Direction*, 29(3), 15–18.

De Souza, M. (2008). Education for transformation: Meeting student's need in changing contemporary contexts. *International Journal of Children's Spirituality*, 13(1), 27–37.

Fitterer, R. J. (2008). *Love and Objectivity in Virtue Ethics: Aristotle, Lonergan, and Nussbaum on Emotions and Moral Insight*. Toronto: University of Toronto Press.

Fontana, D. (1997). Symposium commentary: Steps towards an education for being. *British Journal of Educational Psychology*, 67(1), 339–343.

Frankena, W. K. (1970). Educating for the good life. In H. E. Kiefer and M. K. Munitz (eds.), *Perspectives in Education, Religion and the Arts* (pp. 17–42). New York: State University of New York Press.

Gastmans, C. (2002). A fundamental ethical approach to nursing: Some proposals for ethics education. *Nursing Ethics*, 9(5), 494–507.

Gearon, L. (2001). The corruption of innocence and the spirituality of dissent: Postcolonial perspectives on spirituality in a world of violence. In J. Erricker, C. Ota, and C. Erricker (eds.), *Spiritual Education: Cultural, Religious and Social Differences: New Perspectives for the 21st Century* (pp. 143–155). Brighton, OR: Sussex Academic Press.

Ginsburg, M., Moseley, S. F., and Pigozzi, M. J. (2010). Introduction: Reforming education for transformation: Opportunities and challenges. *Development*, 53(4), 451–456.

Grant, B. A., and Piechowski, M. M. (1999). Theories and the good: Toward child-centered gifted education. *Gifted Child Quarterly*, 43(1), 4–12.

Gula, R. M. (1989). *Reason Informed by Faith: Foundations of Catholic Morality*. New York: Paulist Press.

Hermans, C. A. M. (2003). *Participatory Learning: Religious Education in a Globalizing Society*. Leiden, Holland: Brill.

Hope, M. A. (2013). Conceptions of person-centered education in the 21st century: Developing a position statement for ways of being in educational organization. Retrieved April 8, 2014, from http://www.tandfonline.com/doi/abs/10.1080/14779757.2013.811610?journalCode=rpcp20.

Ivanios, M. (2006). *Girideepam*, vol. 1: *The Complete Works of Archbishop Mar Ivanios*, translated by Sr. Rehmas, edited by A. Valiyavilayil. Trivandrum, India: Cause of Canonization of Mar Ivanios.

Keenan, J. F. (1998). Virtue Ethics. In Bernard Hoose (ed.), *Christian Ethics* (pp. 84–94). London: Cassell.
Kotva, J. K., Jr. (1996). *The Christian Case for Virtue Ethics*. Washington, DC: Georgetown University Press.
Kozyrev, F. (2006). The roles of dialogue in religious education: A Russian perspective. In D. Bates, G. Durka, and F. Schweitzer (eds.) *Education, Religion and Society: Essays in Honour of John M. Hull* (pp. 214–227). London: Routledge.
Krug, E. G. (2002). World Report on Violence and Health, Volume 1. Geneva: World Health Organization.
Kurtz, L. R., and Turpin, J. (1997). Conclusion: Untangling the web of violence. In J. Turpin and L. R. Kurtz (eds.), *The Web of Violence: From Interpersonal to Global* (pp. 207–232). Urbana: University of Illinois Press.
Langston, D. C. (2001). *Conscience and Other Virtues*. University Park: Pennsylvania State University.
Lickona, T. (1992). *Educating for Character: How Schools Can Teach Respect and Responsibility*. New York: Bantam Books.
Louden, R. B. (1998). Virtue ethics. In R. Chadwick (ed.), *Encyclopedia of Applied Ethics* (pp. 498–500). New York: Academic Press.
McGhan, B. (2002). A fundamental educational reform: Teacher-led schools. *Phi Delta Kappan*, 83(7), 538–540.
Melina, L. (2001). *Sharing in Christ's Virtue: For a Renewal of Moral Theology in Light of Veritatis Splendor*, translated by W. E. May. Washington, DC: Catholic University of America Press.
Sanderse, W. (2012). *Character Education: A Neo-Aristotelian Approach to the Philosophy, Psychology and Education of Virtue*. Delft, Netherlands: Eburon Academic Publishers.
Schooley, H. (2012). *Student-Centered Learning in the Elementary Classroom*. University Park: Pennsylvania State University.
Selling, J. A. (1998). Introduction. In J. A. Selling (ed.), *Personalist Morals: Essays in Honor of Professor Louis Janssens* (pp. 1–8). Leuven, Belgium: Peeters.
Sher, G. (1992). Knowing about virtue. In J. W. Chapman and W. A. Galston (eds.), *Nomos XXXIV: Virtue* (pp. 91–116). New York: New York University Press.
Smith, T. W. (2001). *Revaluing Ethics: Aristotle's Dialectical Pedagogy*. New York: State University of New York Press.
Steenbergen, E. E. (2013). Perspectives of person-centered care. *Nursing Standard*, 27(48), 35–41.
Steutel, J. (1998). Virtues and human flourishing: A teleological justification. In D. Carr (ed.), *Knowledge, Truth and Education: Beyond the Postmodern Impass* (pp. 129–142). London: Routledge.
Steutel, J., and D. Carr. (1999). Virtue ethics and the virtue approach to moral education. In D. Carr and J. Steutel (eds.), *Virtue Ethics and Moral Education* (pp. 3–18). London: Routledge.
Taplin, M. (2014). A model for integrating spiritual education into secular curricula. *International Journal of Children's Spirituality*, 19(1), 4–16.
Turpin, J., and Lester, R. K. (1997). Introduction: Violence—The micro/macro link. In J. Turpin and L. R. Kurtz (eds.), *The Web of Violence: From Interpersonal to Global* (pp. 1–27). Urbana: University of Illinois Press.
Ugaste, A., and Oun, T. (2007). Teachers' experience in child-centered education in Estonia. *Young Children*, 62(6), 54–56.
Vanlaere, L., and Gastmans, C. (2007). Ethics in nursing education: Learning to reflect on care practices. *Nursing Ethics*, 14(6), 758–766.
Wade, G. H. (1998). A concept analysis of personal transformation. *Journal of Advanced Nursing*, 28(4), 713–719.
World Health Organization (WHO). (1998). *Violence Prevention: An Important Element of a Health Promoting School*. Geneva: WHO.

Underage Commercial Sex and Criminal Prosecutions in Singapore

Who Are the Real Victims?

9

S. CHANDRA MOHAN

Contents

Introduction

In 2007, the Singapore Penal Code was amended to create a new offense of obtaining for consideration the sexual services of a person under the age of 18 years. The new Section 376B of the Singapore Penal Code, which came into effect in January 2008, reads,

> Any person who obtains for consideration the sexual services of a person, who is under 18 years of age, shall be punished with imprisonment for a term which may extend to 7 years, or with fine, or with both.

This is a novel provision, considering that the legal age of consent for sexual intercourse is 16 and that prostitution itself is not an offense in Singapore. Section 376B reads with Section 377D, which prohibits the defense of mistake as to the age of the victim, except for a person below 21 years of age who has not been previously charged with this or a similar sexual offense, creating what the law regards as an absolute liability offense. Other defenses under the penal code, with perhaps the defense of insanity, are unlikely to be relevant in relation to the offense of having paid sex with a person below 18 years of age under Section 376B of the penal code.

The creation of an absolute liability offense of having paid sex with a minor below 18 years in Singapore has resulted in many successful prosecutions and convictions of even persons defrauded into having paid sex with a female under the age of 18.

Rationale for the New Offense

It is quite apparent that the new law was introduced in response to the U.S. Trafficking in Persons (TIP) Reports since 2001, in which Singapore was described as a "destination country for women and girls trafficked for the purpose of commercial sexual exploitation." The TIP Report allows the U.S. government to engage with foreign governments having concerns with human trafficking and to propose reforms. In the TIP Report, each country is placed on one of three tiers, based on the extent of its government's efforts to comply with the "minimum standards for the elimination of trafficking" found in Section 108 of the U.S. Victims of Trafficking and Violence Protection Act (2000), which has since been renewed in subsequent years.* Tier 1 countries are those that fully comply with the act's minimum standards, while Tier 3 countries are those that are regarded as not complying with the minimum standards and not making significant efforts to do so. The classification is based on the extent of a country's efforts to tackle trafficking, rather than the extent of the problem in the country.

Beyond just an adverse perception of the country, a Tier 3 status can also mean less funding from the U.S. government for trade or humanitarian aid and worse, an even bigger financial implication from direct intervention or opposition from the United States when it comes to Tier 3 countries seeking development aid from international financial institutions, like the World Bank or the International Monetary Fund.†

In the TIP Report 2004, Singapore was classified under Tier 2, indicating that Singapore had not been fully compliant with minimum standards stipulated under the U.S. Trafficking Victims Protection Act (2003). Countries listed in Tier 2 are considered not fully complying with the act's minimum standards, but making significant efforts to bring themselves into compliance with those standards. The 2004 report had consequently recommended that the Singapore government "should consider changing its law to enhance penalties against persons who facilitate prostitution by 16 and 17 year olds and enact and publicize laws against customers involved in commercial sex acts with prostitutes of these ages."

TIP 2004 included a recommendation to the Singapore Parliament to approve proposed amendments to the penal code that would criminalize soliciting or receiving commercial sexual services from minors under the age of 18, extend extraterritorial jurisdiction over Singapore citizens and permanent residents who receive or solicit sexual services from a minor under the age of 18, and criminalize the organization and promotion of child sex tours. Amendments to the penal code that represented these recommendations were eventually passed in Parliament as Section 376B (commercial sex with minor below 18), Section 376C (similar offense committed outside Singapore), and Section 376D (organizing commercial sex tours with minors outside Singapore) by the Penal Code (Amendment) Act 51 (2007). These amendments to the penal code came into law in 2008, by which year

* Prosecutorial Remedies and Other Tools to End the Exploitation of Children Today (PROTECT) Act (2003) and the Trafficking Victims Protection Reauthorization Act.

† TIP Report 2006.

the U.S. Trafficking Victims Protection Act required countries to also furnish statistics of prosecutions for human trafficking offenses for publication in the TIP Report each year.

Rationale for the New Provision as Declared in Parliament

During the second reading of the Penal Code (Amendment) Bill, which introduced the new offenses, the main rationale for including Section 376B in the penal code was, however, stated in Parliament to be the protection of "immature" minors. Senior Minister of State for Home Affairs Ho Peng Kee told Parliament,

> Young persons, because they are immature and vulnerable and can be exploited and, therefore, should be protected from providing sexual services. Although there is no evidence to suggest that we have a problem with 16- and 17-year-olds engaging in commercial sex in Singapore, we decided to set the age of protection at 18 years so as to protect a higher proportion of minors.*

A government backbencher, member of Parliament Teo Ho Pin added,

> As for commercial sex against minors under 18, I fully support that we should send a clear message to curb the demand for child prostitution both in and outside Singapore. Sections 376B, C and D will enhance the protection of child's rights, and hopefully, reduce child trafficking or abduction for sexual services. As reported in today's Straits Times, the child sex industry is thriving in South-East Asia, despite some high profile prosecution of child sex abuse cases. The key failures are due to home grown demand for child sex and the lack of co-operation among governments.†

Going by the statements in Parliament, Section 376B, which prohibits underage commercial sex, was meant to protect "immature" minors from exploitation through prostitution, in order to curb the demand for child prostitution in Singapore.

What then is the *wrong* of commercial sex with an underaged person under the new law? Not the sex act, which is consensual;‡ not the nature of the transaction for profit, as prostitution per se is not an offense; and not even the having of a sexual relationship with a much younger person, as that is the very nature of the activity. It is solely that the prostitute has not yet reached 18 years and hence is not considered mature enough to engage in commercial sex and ought not to be encouraged to offer such services. As it is lawful to engage in consensual sex with a person above 16 years, it is only the fact that the offender is *paying* for the sexual services that make it an offense.

Since Section 376B is ostensibly meant to provide strong protection for the welfare of impressionable minors, the penal code prescribes a range of heavy penalties to offenders liable under Section 376B, namely, imprisonment up to seven years, a fine, or both. Interestingly, for such a strongly worded provision, Section 377D, which denies the defense of mistake as to the age of the person in prostitution, only received a single mention

* Singapore Parliamentary Debates, Official Report (October 22, 2007), vol. 83 at cols. 2175–2242.

† Singapore Parliamentary Debates, Official Report (October 22, 2007), vol. 83 at cols. 2175–2242 (Teo Ho Pin, member of Parliament).

‡ Section 375(1)(b) of the penal code (Cap. 224) only declares that a person who has sex with a female below 14 years of age, *with or without her consent*, is guilty of rape.

during the second reading of the Penal Code (Amendment) Bill, touching on the fact that individuals below 21 years of age are entitled to the defense.*

Issues with Section 376B (Commercial Sex with a Person below 18 Years)

While the declared purpose of the new offense is laudable, the imposition of absolute liability, the removal of the defense of mistake as to the age of the minor for adults, and the setting of a higher age limit for commercial sex have raised many concerns.

Stipulated Age of Maturity for Commercial Sex

Setting the age of maturity for commercial sex at 18 is at odds with the legal age for consensual sex at 16 under Singapore law. Is a minor who consents to recreational sex at 16 more mature than one who consents to it for "consideration"? An Australian parliamentary paper on the age of consent (New South Wales, 1997) discussed the issue in depth and concluded that there is no objective method for determining whether a young person is able to properly consent to sex. If any age of consent were to be set, it would necessarily be one set for the "average" individual. This would not take into account the individual's personal level of maturity. For the need for legal certainty in the law, an age of consent is often set, although setting the exact age of consent may be an arbitrary decision.

However, where the child is the offender, Section 83 of the Singapore Penal Code requires the court to be satisfied that a child between 7 and 12 years of age has attained sufficient maturity of understanding "to judge of the nature and consequence of his conduct" for him to be held criminally responsible. The law appears to recognize that there could be differences in the degree of maturity between different children of the same age. The lack of a universal age of consent is significant in cases where an underaged minor has freely decided to enter into what he or she regards as a commercial transaction. In such cases, is the person necessarily the victim of sexual exploitation?

An attempt was made to explain why the difference in the age of consent for commercial sex was set higher at 18 years during the second reading of the amendment bill by Senior Minister of State Ho Peng Kee:

> Although there is no evidence to suggest that we have a problem with 16- and 17-year-olds engaging in commercial sex in Singapore, we decided to set the age of protection at 18 years so as to protect a higher proportion of minors.†

On this reasoning, why was the age not set at 21, the age of majority under Singaporean law? And minors of age 16 or 17 could also be vulnerable to being exploited for consensual sex. Should all prostitutes below 18 years be considered immature and hence victims, and do they need the absolute protection of the law?

* Singapore Parliamentary Debates, Official Report (October 22, 2007), vol. 83 at cols. 2175–2242 (Ho Peng Kee, Senior Minister of State for Home Affairs).

† Singapore Parliamentary Debates, Official Report (October 22, 2007), vol. 83 at cols. 2175–2242 (Ho Peng Kee, Senior Minister of State for Home Affairs).

An argument may be made that minors are more likely to be exploited by the lure of material gains through commercial sex. However, this must be balanced with the absolute liability nature of the offense. The provision needlessly penalizes all customers of the underage sex worker, whether they knowingly or unknowingly seek the sexual services of a minor, and even those who are deceived into believing, both by false representations and conduct that the minor is above 18 years of age.

The age of 18 appears to have been set to bring Singapore in line with the provisions in countries such as the United Kingdom and Australia, and in accordance with the United Nations [UN] Convention on the Rights of the Child (1989) and the Stockholm Declaration and Agenda for Action (1996). The UN Convention on the Rights of the Child is a human rights treaty that sets out the civil, political, economic, social, health, and cultural rights of children. Article 1 of the convention defines a child as "every human being below the age of eighteen years, unless under the law applicable to the child majority is attained earlier." The Stockholm Declaration and Agenda for Action, which was released at the First World Congress against Commercial Sexual Exploitation of Children in Stockholm in August 1996, affirmed the commitment of governments "to a global partnership against the commercial sexual exploitation of children."

Absolute Liability

Sexual offenses with minors are the only absolute liability offenses under Singapore law. In such offenses, there is at least one objective element of the offense that does not require a corresponding *mens rea* for conviction (Chan, 2013). A mistaken belief, however reasonable, as to the age of the sex partner is no defense to an accused person above 21 years of age. Other defenses under the Singapore Penal Code too, with the exception of insanity, are not applicable to such offenses, although in a 2014 case the high court, rather innovatively, suggested that the defense of accident could apply.

The High Court of Australia has hence held in *He Kaw Teh v. The Queen* (1985) that "the requirement of mens rea is … a humane protection for persons who unwittingly engage in prohibited conduct." Similarly, the House of Lords in *B v. Director of Public Prosecutions* (2000) has observed that "the more serious the offence, the greater is the weight to be attached to the presumption [of mens rea], because the more severe is the punishment and the graver the stigma which accompany a conviction."

Comparison with Other Jurisdictions

While the United Kingdom and Australia were held up in the Singapore Parliament as examples of countries having similarly criminalized commercial sex with persons under the age of 18, what needs to be emphasized is that in both these countries, a defense of reasonable mistake as to the age of the person in prostitution is available to every accused person.

For example, under the 1992 Prostitution Act in the Australian Capital Territory, there is absolute liability only in cases where the child is below the age of 12. In the case of children 12 years or older, Section 22 provides a defense if the accused (1) took reasonable steps to ascertain the age of the child concerned and (2) believed on reasonable grounds that the child had attained 18 years of age.

The legislation in the United Kingdom is similar to that of the Australian Capital Territory. Liability for commercial sex is absolute only if the child is under 13 years old

(Sexual Offences Act 2003). If the child is between 13 and 18, the accused is liable only if he "does not reasonably believe" that the child is 18 years or older (Section 47(1)(c)). It is for the prosecution to prove beyond a reasonable doubt that the accused could not have had such a reasonable belief in all the circumstances of the case (Rook and Ward, 2010).

The current UK legislation against underage commercial sex was introduced in 2003. Initially, the government had been in favor of designating all underage commercial sex acts as strict liability offenses in a review of sexual crime laws in early 2000 (UK Home Office Consultation Paper, 2000). However, in *R v. K* (2001), a case of sexual assault, the House of Lords held that the prosecution had to prove that the accused had not honestly believed that the victim was above the statutory protected age for a sexual offense conviction to be upheld. The overarching reason given was the presumption of *mens rea* for a criminal offense. The House of Lords was reluctant to support the conviction of accused persons who were honestly mistaken about the age of the minor.

Eventually, when the UK Sexual Offences Act (2003) was passed, whether underage commercial sex was an absolute liability offense depended on whether the minor was below 13 years old. Only if the minor was below 13 years old would liability be absolute and a defense of a mistake of fact as to the age not permitted. Thus, absolute liability is confined to instances where the accused has deliberately sought to have sex with a child below 13 years.

In Canada, the Federal Tackling Violent Crime Act (2008) amended the Criminal Code (1985) by raising the age at which youths can consent to nonexploitative sexual activity from 14 to 16 years, while maintaining the existing age of 18 years for exploitative sexual activity, such as child prostitution. However, an honest and reasonable belief as to the age of the child following due diligence or taking all reasonable steps to ascertain the age of the person in prostitution remains a defense (*R v. Hess*, 1990).

Thus, those who seek out persons in prostitution of legal age responsibly, ensuring that they are not intentionally engaging in paid underage sex, are not caught by the law in many jurisdictions. This strikes a fair balance between providing protection for minors from underage commercial sex and being fair to customers who may make genuine mistakes in judging the age of sex workers, even in cases where there is no willful misrepresentation as to the age of the minor. Singapore's law with respect to underage commercial sex is thus harsh and may therefore lead to very unfair outcomes, as the case discussed below illustrates. In creating the offense of underage commercial sex under the penal code, Parliament has made no effort to balance the need to protect the underaged person in prostitution and fairness to adults who may unwittingly be involved in commercial sex with persons below 18 years of age.

The Prosecution Blitz and the Case of "Chantelle," the 17-Year-Old Prostitute

Background

While there had been occasional prosecutions under the new law (*Tan Chye Hin v. PP*, 2009), matters came to a head in December 2011. In that month, 51 men aged between 20 and 70 years were produced in court and charged under the new Section 376B in a massive prosecution exercise. They were charged with obtaining paid sexual services from a 17-year-old girl who went by the name Chantelle. A pimp had, according to one trial judge (*PP v. Tang Boon Thiew*, 2013), "persistently represented" her age as 18 years on a website that advertised the escort and sexual services of Chantelle, among other girls. The pimp had further told Chantelle not to reveal her real age or show her identification card to customers. Indeed, in some cases, customers had tried to verify her age, but her pimp had brushed them off.

As of October 2014, following extensive media publicity, 45 of the 51 men had been convicted and jailed (Chong, 2014). Their prison sentences have ranged from 8 to 16 weeks, with 12 weeks being the benchmark. In many of these cases, the accused persons were not seeking to engage in exploitative sex with an underaged girl, support the trafficking of minors, or even to intentionally break the law. However, a criminal record will follow them throughout their lives.

Court's Treatment of Section 376B (Underage Commercial Sex)

In interpreting Section 376B, the courts seem to have proceeded solely on the basis that Parliament's intention in enacting the provision was to protect minors from being exploited through commercial sex, and that consequently, any inquiry as to their conduct in the offense is irrelevant. Despite viewing Section 376B as an absolute liability offense, the courts have not exercised their discretion in sentencing to reduce the harshness of the provision in deserving cases.

Even though Chantelle and her pimp had worked together to lie about her age, the Singapore courts have ruled that the responsibility to determine the actual age of the person in prostitution lies always with the customer. In *PP v. Shaw Chai Li Howard* (2012), the court accepted that customers "believed from the bare representation on the website" that Chantelle was 18. However, the court held that reliance on such a "bare representation" was insufficient even as a mitigating factor during sentencing. It was for the customer to have "exercised caution and [to have] made the necessary enquiries and not be guided solely by his belief" since he had deliberately sought out an 18-year-old. In another case (*PP v. Ng Guan Mean*, 2013), the trial court stated that

> if the escorts are indeed underage, it would reasonably be expected that there would be some form of misrepresentation of their true age so as to avoid the notice of law enforcement officers who may be trawling the internet. It would also be reasonable to expect a minor to lie about her true age if the client were to casually ask for her age.

In both the above-mentioned cases, the court found that the accused did not actively or intentionally seek commercial sex with an underage sex worker. Yet, this was insufficient to constitute even as a mitigating factor for sentencing. The trial judge in the district court held that since both customers took the advertised age of Chantelle at face value and had made no effort to verify her age separately (with no indication as to why or how that was to be done), he "did not see any mitigating force in the argument that the accused was deceived by the conduct of the minor" (*PP v. Shaw Chai Li Howard*, 2012), and that the customer failed in "mitigat[ing] the seriousness of the offence" (*PP v. Ng Guan Mean*, 2013).

In an earlier unrelated case (*Tan Chye Hin v. PP*, 2009), the high court had considered due diligence in this regard as at least mitigating:

> At the least blameworthy end of the spectrum would be an accused who unwittingly and unintentionally engages the sexual services of a person who is just below the age of 18 years but whose appearance and demeanour do not suggest that he or she is below 18 years of age.

> The accused checked the age of the minor but was given a good forgery of an identity document that showed that he or she was over 18 years old. In those circumstances, a fine could be appropriate in the absence of other aggravating factors.

However, this principle does not seem to have been followed in the cases involving Chantelle. In *Buergin Juerg v. PP* (2013), the high court found that Chantelle had showed the appellant her older sister's identification card, for which reason the customer did not know she was Chantelle or that she was short of 18 years. However, this fact was ignored by the trial court and by the high court, which upheld the conviction, holding the defense of reasonable mistake was precluded by Section 377D. Unfortunately, the high court judge did not also see the need to reduce the sentence of imprisonment of 4 months and 3 weeks, a longer sentence than that of the others because *Buergin* had contested the charge at trial without pleading guilty. Chantelle, meanwhile, is not liable for prosecution for aiding and abetting a sex offense, as the courts have held that where the purpose of the law is to protect certain persons, these persons cannot be prosecuted for aiding and abetting the offense.*

Furthermore, the trial courts have been unnecessarily judgmental, speaking in tones of moral culpability and almost disapproving of prostitution and the conduct of the accused in seeking commercial sex, even though prostitution is not an offense in Singapore. For example, in *PP v. Shaw Chai Li Howard* (2012), the court observed,

> The defense described this as a 'classic case of entrapment, deceit, and trickery perpetrated on the accused'. The uncontroverted fact, however, is that it was the accused who had gone online in the first place and initiated contact with 'B' through her pimp to procure her sexual services. Focusing on 'B's' behaviour to mitigate punishment effectively means that 'B' rather than the accused is being judged, and her conduct as a minor, rather than the conduct of the accused, is being scrutinised and tested for blameworthiness.

In *Sim Choon Wee Kenny v. PP* (2013), only the second of the 40 Chantelle cases to have reached the high court after *Buergin Juerg*, the high court was rather dismissive of submissions made on behalf of the accused, that Chantelle was almost 18 years of age at the time of the offense and that there was a deliberate misrepresentation of her real age, with the observation that "people who skate on thin ice cannot complain should they fall through the ice." In the subsequent case of *Leu Xing-Long v. PP* (2014), the high court further opined that if an adult had been deceived into believing erroneously that the minor was above 18 years of age, the deception afforded him no defense to the charge. The fact that his belief might have been "honestly or reasonably held was also irrelevant for the purpose of determining guilt." Further, the court, rather surprisingly, reasoned that "the fact that he took proper care and caution and had made careful investigations of the age of the minor was again irrelevant."

Sentences of the Court

The sentences of imprisonment imposed by the courts on 42 of the 43 offenders, with the remaining 20-year-old receiving a probation sentence, have been heavily influenced by the first case, in which a prison sentence was imposed without much regard to individual

* *R v. Tyrell*, [1894] 1 QB 710; *R v. Whitehouse*, [1977] 3 All ER 737.

circumstances of the offense or the offender. In *PP v. Lee Lip Hong* (2012), one of the earlier cases in this series, the offender was sentenced to nine weeks imprisonment, although he did not seek out an underage person in prostitution and accepted the bare representation on the website and by Chantelle's pimp that she was 18 years old. Later cases have all followed this sentencing precedent without questioning why it is necessary to impose a custodial sentence in the first place on all the offenders. What is more strange is that in two other prosecutions, involving Vietnamese and Chinese prostitutes who were younger and who had been trafficked for purposes of prostitution, the sentences of the courts to the offenders, whose culpability was much higher, were not much different, ranging from 9 weeks to 12 weeks imprisonment.

In *Shaw Howard*, the court stated that custodial sentences were necessary for offenders of Section 376B unless there were "exceptional mitigating circumstances." However, in only one of the 39 cases dealt with, which involved a 20-year-old who was granted probation, was a sentence of imprisonment not imposed. While deterrence is a dominant sentencing principle in Singapore, courts must not lose sight of the principle of proportionality. Besides, this is not keeping with the direction of the chief justice in *Yang Suan Piau Steven v. PP* (2013), that "a custodial sentence should not be lightly or readily imposed as a norm or a default punishment unless the nature of the offence justifies its imposition retributively or as a general or specific deterrent, where deterrence is called for."

The court further added that even though deterrence is a relevant consideration, it should not be "crushing" to the offender. Other levels and forms of punishments other than a custodial sentence might also be more suitable and appropriate for certain crimes.

Should imprisonment, which Parliament has not considered mandatory, be imposed in all such cases, including those where the accused have not sought out a minor but found themselves in breach of the law due to want of due diligence, inadvertence, or deception by the prostitute herself or her agent? Should the courts impose prison terms on luckless victims or those who are morally innocent? And should they disregard the many unintended victims of the prosecution with respect to even one-off acts of indiscretion?

There has been a gag order to prevent the press from identifying the true identity of Chantelle, but the 48 persons who have been charged have all been named and shamed in the local media. At the time they were charged, the media was given a list of all their names, ages, and occupations, which were duly published (Asiaone, 2012). The accused persons come from varied but respectable backgrounds and include a banker, teachers, a school principal, a legal officer, a navy officer, a senior police officer, an engineer, and businessmen. Initial reports suggest that following the prosecutions and convictions, there has been considerable disruption in the lives of many of the offenders and their families. The publicity given to the cases in a small state such as Singapore; the loss of reputations, jobs, and careers following the arrest and conviction; the disruption to family life due to separations and divorces; and the effect on children appear not to have been taken into account by the sentencing courts nor by the high court in the two appeals (*Buergin Juerg* and *Sim Choon Wee Kenny*) that were heard by the court. As has been pointed out by Ferguson (2014 p. 99), conviction, sentence, and imprisonment (not to mention arrest and the pre-trial process) "represent official punishment and each segment has its own independent punishment for the offender." With an overemphasis on the rights of victims in all cases, without considering the degree of blameworthiness of all players concerned, the courts may well be in danger of exaggerating the nature and effect of the crime to the detriment of the offender.

Who Is the Real Victim? The Statutory Offender or the Statutory Victim?

The 1985 UN Declaration of Basic Principles of Justice for Victims of Crime and Abuse of Power provides a wide definition of the word *victim*. Article 1 of the UN Declaration defines victims as "persons who, individually or collectively, have suffered harm, including physical or mental injury, emotional suffering, economic loss or substantial impairment of their fundamental rights." Sometimes, the real victim might be the statutory offender himself. This has been noted by Prittwitz (1999), who opined that "[it is a] naïve idea that it is sufficient to look only at the offender … in order to understand criminal acts. Victimology discovered crime as an interaction. Indeed, sometimes it is not even clear who is the offender and who is the victim." While those who engage in exploitative sex with minors deserve punishment, it is important for prosecutors and the courts to ensure that Section 376B is not used to create victims out of morally blameless or luckless victims. Punishment must be on the basis of what the offenders intended to do and not just what they did. In the Chantelle cases, the commercial sex acts of the 17-year-old were more opportunistic on her part than exploitive of her.

Criminal punishment is typically harsher when victims are vulnerable or innocent and less harsh when victims are powerful or culpable (Kleinfield, 2012). However, in the Chantelle cases, the courts have punished all offenders harshly and needlessly in prison without considering their actual blameworthiness. Concurrently, the conduct of Chantelle, who obtained high rewards for her sexual services, chose expensive hotels for the sexual encounters, and induced the offenders by deceit, was ill considered by the courts. By ignoring the role of the statutory victim in the crime in this case, and by even making excuses for her behavior, the offenders have been victimized by both the law and the statutory victim herself.

The imposition of absolute liability also requires individuals to exercise "extreme, and not merely reasonable, care" (New South Wales, 2006). This would require that before one engages in commercial sex, he or she must positively verify the age of the sex worker, for example, with identification documents. However, it is common for sex workers to deny such requests with no legal consequences. Sex workers who look older than their age also pose a risk to customers who might not be alerted to the fact that they have contracted with an underage sex worker. Without a legal requirement for sex workers to produce identification when requested, the law might catch unsuspecting customers who inadvertently hire an underage sex worker. Such customers become victims of the law.

It has been suggested that if a minor, whether for commercial reasons or not, deceives an adult into having sex by impersonating an older person of legal age to have sex, this would amount to rape of the adult (Christopher and Christopher, 2007). Consent is vitiated through the fraud. A minor who deliberately misrepresents his or her age and conducts her affairs as if she were an adult (e.g., by demanding expensive hotels, charging high fees, and communicating with clients through short messaging service on the telephone, as Chantelle did) defrauds the adult, vitiating the consent given, thereby leading to a sexual assault on the adult. Alternatively, it may be argued that the customer who is so deceived lacks the requisite *actus reus* for the offense, as it has not been a voluntary consensual act because of the deception. The adult then becomes a victim, consequently suffering the harm brought about by severe punishment and its consequences to his life.

Comparatively, 17-year-old Chantelle does not fit the profile of a minor who is immature, vulnerable, and exploitable, whom Parliament is trying to protect under Section 376B of the penal code. Together with her pimp, she willfully misrepresented her age to many customers for commercial gain. It is difficult to say that she was too immature to decide on her actions when she actively took precautionary steps to ensure that she would be able to entice customers and not invoke their suspicions or those of the authorities, made demands of her clients, and communicated directly with them.

Conclusion

As the 51 prosecutions demonstrate, labeling victims as innocent and offenders as always bad and evil can at times be a rather simplistic classification. Where the innocence of the "victim" is questionable, sympathy for her and even for justice could diminish (Meloy and Miller, 2011). The arrest, prosecution, and imprisonment of 42 of the 51 offenders to date, in all circumstances of these cases, under the new law prohibiting underage commercial sex, may not necessarily represent just desserts for perpetrators of sexual exploitation of minors. On the other hand, this may be an example of the overreach of a harsh law, resulting in unnecessary incarceration and the destruction of reputations, careers, and families, thus creating perhaps multiple victims of the law.

References

Asiaone. (2012). Names of 48 persons charged for sex with underage prostitute. April 17, 2012. Retrieved from http://news.asiaone.com/News/Latest+News/Singapore/Story/A1Story20120417-340294.html.

B (a minor) v. Director of Public Prosecutions. [2000] 2 AC 428.

Buergin Juerg v. PP. [2013] 4 SLR 87.

Chan, W. C. (2013). No punishment without fault: Kindling a moral discourse in Singapore criminal law. *Singapore Academy of Law Journal*, 25, 801.

Chong, E. (2014). Man convicted of paid sex appeals. *My Paper*, October 28.

Christopher, R. L., and Christopher, K. H. (2007). Adult impersonation: Rape by fraud as a defense to statutory rape. *Northwestern University Law Review*, 101, 1.

Ferguson, R. A. (2014). *Inferno: an Anatomy of American Punishment.* Harvard: Harvard University Press.

He Kaw Teh v. The Queen. [1985] 157 CLR 523.

Home Office. (2000). Consultation paper on the review of Part 1 of the Sex Offenders Act 1997. London: Home Office.

Kleinfield, J. (2012). A theory of criminal victimization. *Stanford Law Review*, 65, 1087.

Leu Xing-Long v. PP. [2014] 4 SLR 1024.

Meloy, M. L., and Miller, S. L. (2011). *The Victimization of Women: Law, Policies, and Politics.* New York: Oxford University Press.

New South Wales (NSW). (1997). The age of consent. Parliamentary Briefing Paper No. 21/97. Sydney: NSW.

New South Wales (NSW). (2006). Strict and absolute liability: Discussion paper. Legislation Review Committee. Sydney: NSW.

PP v. Lee Lip Hong. [2012] SGDC 231.

PP v. Ng Guan Mean. [2013] SGDC 212.

PP v. Shaw Chai Li Howard. [2012] SGDC 319.
PP v. Tang Boon Thiew. [2013] SGDC 52.
Prittwitz, C. (1999). The resurrection of the victim in penal theory. *Buffalo Criminal Law Review*, 3, 112.
Prostitution Act 1992. (ACT) s 20(1).
R v. Hess. [1990] 2 SCR 906.
R v. K. [2001] 3 WLR 471.
Rook, P., and Ward, R. (2010). *Rook & Ward on Sexual Offences: Law & Practice*, 4th ed. London: Sweet & Maxwell.
Sexual Offences Act 2003. (c 42) (UK) s 47(1).
Sim Choon Wee Kenny v. PP. [2013] SGHC 182.
Stockholm Declaration and Agenda for Action (1996).
Tan Chye Hin v. PP. [2009] 3 SLR(R) 873.
Trafficking Victims Protection Act 2003. 22 USC Chapter 78.
United Nations Convention on the Rights of the Child. (1989).
United Nations Declaration of Basic Principles of Justice for Victims of Crime and Abuse of Power. (1985).
Victims of Trafficking and Violence Protection Act 2000. 114 STAT. 1464.
Yang Suan Piau Steven v Public Prosecutor 2012. SGHC 224. High Court of Singapore. Suit No: Magistrate's Appeal No 119 of 2012, Decision Date: 2 November 2012. Retrieved from http://www.singaporelaw.sg/sglaw/laws-of-singapore/case-law/free-law/high-court-judgments/15059-yang-suan-piau-steven-v-public-prosecutor-2012-sghc-224.

III

Culture Conflict and Victimization of Groups

Policing Domestic Violence in South Africa

10

DORAVAL GOVENDER

Contents

Introduction

Violence against women and children is still the most widespread human rights abuse in the world. Everyday, women are murdered, physically and sexually assaulted, threatened, and humiliated by their partners within their own homes and communities (Heyzer, 1995, p. 26). Victims of domestic violence may be anyone. There is no color, creed, or culture when it comes to victims of domestic violence.

In South Africa, domestic violence is prevalent because of its deep-seated patriarchal system. In patriarchal households, domestic violence is committed predominantly by men against women and children (Tyska and Fennely, 1999; Manamela et al., 2010; Chibba, 2012).

There are many causes and contributing factors for domestic violence (Klopper et al., 2002; Manamela et al., 2010). The victims are subjected to various forms of violence and abuse by their partners, which include physical, economic, emotional, and sexual abuse (Chibba, 2012).

Before 1994, democratic dispensation in South Africa, little attention was paid to the rights of domestic violence victims in the South African criminal justice system. Like many other things, the post-1994 transition brought about a restructuring of the criminal justice system and a new approach to the criminal justice process. The National Crime Prevention Strategy (NCPS), a policy document developed in 1996, provided for the criminal justice system to focus on victims of crime (Simpson and Rauch, 1999). In response to the patriarchal system in households and our deep-seated atrocious past, South Africa introduced the Bill of Human Rights in the South African Constitution of 1996 and the Domestic Violence Act (DVA) 116 of 1998 (Independent Police Investigative Directorate, 2010, p. 2).

The DVA 116 of 1998 was implemented in South Africa during 1998 to provide protective measures for victims of domestic violence. The DVA is the result of reforms to the Prevention of Family Violence Act 133 of 1993 (South Africa, 1993, 1998). The DVA is supported by the South African Police Service (SAPS) National Instruction 7 of 1999 (SAPS, 1999). The DVA requires dedicated members to be appointed at police stations to attend to complaints of domestic violence and to investigate cases of domestic violence. Needs-directed training is to be provided to police officers appointed to attend to complaints of domestic violence and those investigating cases of domestic violence. Specific incident reports (SAP508a) and a domestic violence register (SAP508b) are kept by each police station to maintain statistics (SAPS, 2011, p. 2). Section 18 of the DVA 116 of 1998 makes it a contravention of the law if a member of SAPS fails to comply with the act. National Instruction 7 of 1999 sets out in detail the responsibilities and duties of a station commander (station commissioner) and all members attending to domestic violence cases.

All domestic violence crimes reported in South Africa are registered by the police as statutory and common law crimes. The National Instruction requires the completion of an incident report (SAP508a) for all complaints of domestic violence and also requires that all domestic violence incidents be recorded in the incident register (SAP508b). Police officers attending to domestic violence cases are compelled to inform victims of their rights, including the right to apply for a protection order from our courts. Some police stations also provide victim-friendly rooms to victims of domestic violence. A referral list of service providers is made available at the community service center, at the victim-friendly, rooms and in police vehicles (SAPS, 1999, 2011). This chapter makes recommendations for innovations in policing domestic violence.

Review of Literature

Causes and Contributing Factors of Domestic Violence

Geldenhuys (2012, p. 25) divides the causes of domestic violence into three categories: alcohol abuse, psychological disorders, and unrealistic expectations and demands by spouses. Persons may also become victims of domestic violence by

- Calling names and throwing insults
- Stopping one from seeing family or friends

- Attempting to control how money is spent
- Attempting to control how a person dresses and where he or she goes
- Preventing a person from going to work
- Acting jealously or possessively
- Threatening him or her with violence or a weapon
- Hitting, kicking, shoving, slapping, choking, or otherwise hurting the person or his or her children or pets
- Assaulting the person while sleeping
- Forcing a person to have sex or engage in sexual acts against his or her will

A human rights activist in South Africa lodged a complaint with the South African Human Rights Commission about a version of the Muslim holy book written by the late Abdulla Yusuf Ali, an Indian author. He took issue with Ali's interpretation of the quote "As to those women on whose part you fear disloyalty and ill conduct, admonish them (first), (next), refuse to share their beds, (and last) beat them (lightly)." "The interpretation gave a license to every Muslim man to beat his wife and claim his religious right or duty to do so. Literally this religious right may be seen as contributing to Domestic Violence" (Legalbrief, 2012b).

It is generally accepted that culture plays a role in social behavior patterns. Not only are there significant differences from one society to the next, but the various groups within that society will, for instance, also have different views on the respective roles of the members of a family. The South African society consists of communities and groups with conflicting cultural concepts. Cultural differences can introduce complexities of a special nature and give rise to conflicts between individuals and groups (Fourie, 2001, p. 219).

Women are assaulted and in some instances murdered by their husbands for failing to bring sufficient *dowry* (gifts; usually jewelry given to the bride at the time of her marriage providing her with some financial security) to the marriage (Richard et al., 2008, p. 207). In South African communities, it is customary to pay *lobola* or *bogadi* (gifts; usually cattle and cash). The effect of this is that customary payment of *lobola* gives the husband the right of ownership over his wife, and he feels that that this gives him the right to abuse his wife and to do whatever pleases him (Ludsin and Vetten, 2005, p. 24). Customary law in some communities gives the husband the right to inflict punishment on his wife. If this is exceeded, the wife is entitled to permanently leave her marital home and return to her family home (Bekker and Coetzee, 1982, p. 140).

Female genital mutilation (FGM) is also a cultural requirement carried out by some communities in Africa, the Middle East, and the United Kingdom. Men in some of these communities do not marry a woman who is not subjected to FGM, while others believe that FGM will prevent the women engaging in extramarital affairs (Richard et al., 2008, p. 209). Cross-cultural relationships also give rise to domestic violence. This is prevalent in communities where a person is married to someone of a different culture and whose practices are contrary to the other's beliefs and value system. Many factors may be cited as causes of domestic violence (Klopper et al., 2002, p. 37).

Types of Abuse Experienced by Domestic Violence Victims

According to research conducted during 2009, in Kwa Zulu Natal, South Africa, with victims of domestic violence, it was found that a large majority of cases involved physical violence, followed by verbal or emotional abuse (Hargovan, 2009, p. 32). Physical violence is used by almost all perpetrators of domestic violence, irrespective of their positions in society. It was reported in the *Natal Mercury* that a Pretoria prosecutor punched, kicked, and throttled his girlfriend, trampled on her face, and, thinking that she was dead, tried to stuff her into the freezer; when he could not, he pulled a plastic bag over her head before throwing her into a dustbin. A postmortem report revealed that she died of suffocation (Legalbrief, 2012c). In another reported incident, a director general from a government department slapped his wife when she refused to cook for him (Malefane, 2009).

Women who abuse men don't differ much from their abusive male counterparts. These women kick, punch, push, or bite their victims. Weapons such as knives, firearms, or any object that can be used to strike, such as pans, bottles, vases, and cake rollers, are also sometimes used in domestic violence cases. Although physical abuse is considered the most obvious form of domestic abuse, emotional abuse (insults and intimidation) is sometimes more devastating than physical abuse because it is difficult to prove and therefore hard to stop. Husbands are mainly subjected to emotional abuse rather than physical abuse, as the latter is less likely to be rewarding for the abuser due to the physical abilities of the women (Geldenhuys, 2012, p. 25).

According to Cambell (2010), two in every five victims of domestic violence in the United Kingdom are male. In the United States, it is reported that 3.2 million males a year are victims of domestic violence (Kennard, 2007). Hargovan (2009, p. 32) found in her research in Kwa Zulu Natal, South Africa, that the majority of domestic violence cases are perpetrated by husbands (males), boyfriends (males), parents, and children on parents; a small proportion of victims of domestic violence are male.

Economic abuse takes place when spouses are forced into employment to provide for the needs of their partners. Women are found to be the main victims in this regard. They are forced into menial work by their unemployed spouses. This causes tension between partners. In other instances, the perpetrator forcefully takes the money earned by the spouse. Wives are sometimes physically abused when they ask for money to buy food and clothing for their children and themselves (Mafuya and Ramalepe, 2008, p. 51).

Emotional abuse takes place when the perpetrator of the domestic violence abuses the victim by constantly belittling the victim in public and picking on the victim's ideas, perceptions, and personality characteristics, for example, by locking a spouse out of the house and humiliating him or her in public (Barkhuizen and Ovens, 2012, p. 21). According to Richards et al. (2008, p. 204), forced marriage is an abuse of human rights and a form of physical pressure (threatened to be physically hurt) and emotional pressure (accused of bringing shame to the family).

According to Wilson (1977, p.239), sexual abuse or assault is said have taken place if a woman is forced to do things against her will or when her physical body parts are violated or when she is treated as a sex object.

Response by the South African Police to Domestic Violence Complaints

The DVA 116 of 1998, which has a bearing on victims of crime, can be said to have the effect of placing them at the center of criminal justice processes. Through a range of sections, it obliges the police to render assistance to victims of domestic violence at the scene of the crime or during the process of taking down the complaint (South Africa, 1998, Sections 2, 4, 7(1), and 8).

The National Instruction requires the completion of incident reports (SAP508a) for all complaints of domestic violence and the recording of domestic violence incidents in the incident register (SAP508b). As soon as the victim of domestic violence is attended to, an incident report SAP508 (a) is completed. Corresponding entries are made in the SAP508 (b), the occurrence book (SAP10), and the police officers' pocket book (SAP206). The occurrence book (SAP10), SAP508b register, and SAP508a are kept at the police station community service center (charge office). SAPS has provided special capacity at bigger police stations to solely handle domestic violence cases and complaints. The proper implementation of the DVA is monitored by senior managers from national, provincial, cluster, and police station levels. The registers and reports are regularly inspected by senior officers.

There is a standardized procedure followed in relation to domestic violence incidents involving firearms. The procedure requires that the police officially seize the firearm involved and enter it into the exhibit register (SAP13), so that it is kept as an exhibit until the conclusion of a fitness inquiry in terms of Section 102 of the Firearms Control Act 60 of 2000. According to Minnaar and Mistry (2003, p. 31), this inquiry is conducted to determine the fitness of the licensee to possess the firearm. A person may be declared unfit to possess a firearm if, on the grounds of information under oath or affirmation, it appears that

- A final protection order had been issued against such a person in terms of the DVA.
- That person had expressed the intention to kill or injure himself or herself or any other person by using a firearm or other dangerous weapon.
- Because of the person's mental condition, inclination to violence, or dependence on any intoxicating or narcotic substance, it would not be in the interests of that person that a firearm be in his possession.

In terms of the Firearm Control Act, a police officer may, without a warrant, enter into and search a place or person and seize any arm or ammunition that may have been used or is intended to be used on a victim of domestic violence.

National Instruction 7 of 1999 compels police officers attending to domestic violence cases to inform the victims of their rights, including the right to apply for a protection order from our courts. Nongovernmental organizations (NGOs) also assist victims with information and the process to obtain protection orders from the courts. Most police stations also provide victim-friendly rooms to victims of domestic violence. Referral lists of service providers are available at the community service center and at the victim-friendly rooms. If the victim requires medical treatment, the police official should assist the victim by making arrangements for the victim to receive immediate medical attention. In the case of a criminal charge, a medical report (J88) is completed by the medical practitioner. The visible injuries shown by the victim are also recorded in the occurrence book and in the police officers' pocket book. Police officers should also assist victims in retrieving their personal property where necessary. The purpose of accompanying the victim is to ensure his or her safety. The police officer will not become involved in any dispute about the ownership of the property. The police should also assist the victim in finding a suitable shelter. Details of any organization in the area that may be able to provide suitable shelter and relevant support or counseling services should be provided to the victim. The victim is to be assisted in contacting the organization and obtaining transport.

The police officer who attends to the complaint should take all reasonable steps to secure the scene of the crime. The DVA and Criminal Procedure Act 55 of 1977 provides for powers of arrest, as well as policing powers to enter premises for the policing of domestic violence. The failure by police officers to follow the DVA and the National Instruction will give rise to an internal disciplinary inquiry (SAPS, 2011, p. 2).

The Independent Police Investigative Directorate conducts audits at police stations on the implementation of the DVA and the National Instruction. The 2010 audit report by the Independent Police Investigative Directorate showed that 309 police stations were audited for compliance of the DVA. Only 26 police stations were 80%–99% compliant. They found that there was noncompliance in the following:

- There was widespread failure to apply for exemptions for complaints.
- There was a general lack of understanding of the obligations of the DVA.
- Record keeping and form filling were incomplete.
- DVA and the National instruction were not readily available.
- Lists of service providers were not available or updated.
- Copies of protection orders and warrants of arrest were not filed properly.

According to Vetten (2011), local police stations often do not have space or facilities suitable to interview victims. Victims are often interviewed in communal offices, where they can be overheard by others. Poorer victims are often denied access to counseling services because detectives cannot readily transport them to social workers, including when this is required for court assessments. Since the restructuring of the SAPS in 2006, the crucial network of relationships between NGOs, social workers, doctors and nurses, teachers, and prosecutors that is so essential to the provision of comprehensive and integrated services has not been easy to access.

Altbeker (2005) found in the course of his research that the police who attend to DVA complaints often rate them as domestic disturbances. The police officers would hear both the parties and offer advice about talking to their parents or their priest, getting a protection order, or finding ways of learning to live with each other. The police would then leave the scene and report to radio control that no crime was committed, and no further action was required. Altbeker attributes the lack of enthusiasm for positively investigating complaints of domestic violence to heavy workloads, not having enough time to take down statements in petty cases of domestic violence, and the perception that most DVA cases are petty and that they will be withdrawn before the case goes to court, resulting in a waste of time, energy, and resources.

Police officers also frequently failed to inform victims about accessing a protection order or laying a criminal charge. Numerous incidents were reported citing the appalling attitude of police officials, who often subject victims to secondary abuse. There are concerns regarding protection orders, specifically as to whether they ensure the safety of persons requesting protection orders, and the reluctance and often refusal of police officers to serve the orders, or to arrest a perpetrator who has violated a protection order (Abrahams et al., 2010).

Of particular concern is the fact that there is no publicly available national record of cases of domestic violence reported to the police. Such a record would be useful in determining whether cases recorded as assault or assault with the intention to cause grievous bodily harm are in fact taking place within the context of domestic violence (Gould et al., 2012).

Magistrates who review applications for protection orders find great discrepancies between the applications for protection orders and the affidavits of the victims, especially regarding the violence, abusive action, and weapons involved. When police investigation is sloppy and witness statements are poor, missing, or illegible, cases are withdrawn by the courts (Artz, 2004).

Conceptual Definitions

Domestic Violence

To get a better understanding of the meaning of *domestic violence* in South Africa, it is good to know the legal definition of *domestic violence* in South Africa. According to Section 1(a) of the DVA 116 of 1998, it is the

> physical abuse, sexual abuse, emotional abuse, verbal and psychological abuse, intimidation, harassment, stalking, damage to property, entry into complainants' residence without consent where the parties do not share the same residence, any other controlling or abusive behaviour towards a complainant which may cause or is intended to cause harm to the safety, health or well being of the complainant.

Although the DVA is mainly applicable to families living together under one roof, the Supreme Court of Appeal (SCA) in South Africa ruled that the DVA applies to brothers, although they do not share a common house (Legalbrief, 2012a).

Berns (2001, p. 65) defines domestic violence as the physical, sexual, or psychological abuse that occurs between two adults in an intimate relationship regardless of marital status or sexual orientation. Barkhuizen and Ovens (2012, p.18) are of the view that this definition includes abuse within same-sex relationships.

Policing

Policing can be defined as that form of coercive action, within the structure of formal social control, that is directed at the maintenance of internal order in conformity with the principles of legal jurisdiction and the constitutional rights of the individual (Van Heerden, 1982, p. 18).

According to a sociological perspective, the police have the job of identifying and arresting offenders, discovering breaches of the law, and maintaining public order (Smith and Natalier, 2005, p. 83).

Methodology

A qualitative case study design was used to evaluate the policing of domestic violence. Literature study, interviews, documentary study (record review), and the experience of the author as a former assistant commissioner in SAPS was used in this study.

During September 2006, the Marico area in the North West Province was demarcated for this study based on the nature and extent of domestic violence in the Marico area. The author, who was then the area commissioner of the Marico area, personally conducted the evaluation.

The study identified the causes that gave rise to the domestic violence, the type of violence and abuse used by the perpetrator(s), and the way in which the police responded to their complaints. Interviews and documentary study (record review) were used for this purpose.

The respondents and the case dockets were chosen using the incident reports (SAP508a) and the incident report register (SAP508b). The random sampling technique (lottery technique) was used to sample the respondents and the case dockets for this study. Two hundred victims, consisting of men and women, rural and urban residents, employed and unemployed persons, were sampled from 36 police station precincts to conduct interviews. The purpose of the interview was explained to them. All 200 victims accepted to be interviewed. The participants supported the study by voluntarily taking part in it under anonymity. They were assured of their privacy and confidentiality. They could withdraw from the interview at any time, if they so wished. None of the participants withdrew from the study. A documentary study (record review) of the incident register (SAP508b), incident reports (SAP508a), and criminal case dockets opened by the victims was conducted. Documentary study was carried out on 200 domestic violence cases reported by these victims.

An interview guide was formulated to guide the semistructured interviews and the documentary study. The study was conducted over a period of three months. The interviews and the documentary study (record review) focused on three main questions, followed by probing to clarify the answer, with follow-up questions to pursue the implications of the answer to the main question. The respondents were asked the following main questions relating to their domestic violence complaint:

- What was the cause of the domestic violence?
- Can you describe the type of violence and abuse you experienced during the domestic violence incident?
- Can you explain how the police responded to your complaint of domestic violence?

The data analysis spiral was used to analyze the collected data to make findings and recommendations (Leedy and Omrod, 2001).

Main Findings: Based on Questions

What Was the Cause of the Domestic Violence?

- Twenty-eight percent of the respondents indicated the causes of domestic violence to be related to patriarchy (power struggle in families).
- Twenty-five percent of the respondents indicated alcohol and substance abuse as a contributing factor to domestic violence.
- Fifteen percent of the respondents had provoked abuse through nagging or making unreasonable demands to their partners.
- Fourteen percent of the respondents indicated unemployment as a contributing factor to domestic violence.
- Twelve percent of the respondents indicated poverty as a contributing factor to domestic violence.
- Four percent of the respondents indicated culture as a contributing factor to domestic violence.

- Two percent of the respondents indicated religion as a contributing factor to domestic violence (license to beat wife and claim religious right or duty to do so).

Can You Describe the Type of Violence and Abuse You Experienced during the Domestic Violence Incident?

- **Physical abuse:** Sixty-five percent of the respondents experienced physical abuse, which included hitting with fists, kicking, and slapping.
- **Economic abuse:** Twenty-three percent of the respondents indicated that money caused strained relationships between partners. In most cases, wives were made to work and hand their earnings over to their partners.
- **Emotional abuse:** Ten percent of the respondents indicated that they suffered emotional abuse, which included being lied to, being cheated on, and their partner having affairs with girlfriends.
- **Sexual abuse:** Two percent of the respondents suffered sexual abuse by being raped, sexually assaulted, or forced to commit indecent acts.

Can You Explain How the Police Responded to Your Complaint of Domestic Violence?

- Eighty-three percent of the respondents are not satisfied with the way in which the police enforce the DVA.
- Seventy-five percent of the respondents feel that victims of domestic violence are not all treated in a consistent manner.
- Sixty-seven percent of the respondents have experienced bad attitudes by the police.
- Fifty-four percent of the respondents believed that the police do not effectively implement the DVA in their areas.
- Fifty-two percent of the respondents consider female police officials to be just as bad as their male counterparts.

Author's Personal Assessment of the Management of Domestic Violence by Police

During the assessment of the police stations, I found that many incident reports (SAP508a) were not completed for incidents recorded in the incident register (SAP508b) or occurrence book (SAP10). In some instances, only an occurrence book (SAP10) or pocket book (SAP206) entry was made regarding the domestic violence complaint, which was recorded as a domestic disturbance or a domestic dispute and referred to the patrol van driver for attendance. Criminal case dockets were not opened for investigation in every reported incident of domestic violence.

Many of the criminal allegations of domestic violence were dismissed by the police as a domestic dispute or disturbance, without any documentation or criminal investigation. The inconsistent documentation implies that the police do not record domestic violence crimes consistently; neither do they record all domestic violence complaints attended by them. These complaints are not treated as domestic violence crimes with the seriousness they deserve. Criminal case dockets arising from complaints of domestic violence are not effectively investigated along with other supporting evidence. As a result of poor recording of domestic violence statistics, no performance indicators are accurately determined to proactively reduce and combat domestic violence.

I found that very few criminal investigations were effectively undertaken by the investigating officers. Most of the criminal case dockets related to assaults, with a small proportion of malicious damage to property and other crimes, such as *crimen injuria* and attempted murder. In the absence of accurate crime statistics with respect to domestic violence, it was difficult to identify which case docket was domestic violence related, as one had to be guided by the incident reports and the incident register. Many case dockets only included the victim's statement, which was incomplete without the elements of a report on the criminal conduct or a certificate by a commissioner of oaths. In many instances, no supporting statements, documentary evidence, explanation by the suspects, or exhibits were collected.

SAPS is unable to give a statistical indication of what proportion of violent crimes is made up of domestic violence crimes. This is because it only records reported crimes of domestic violence as incident reports (SAP508a) in an incident register (SAP508b). Criminal cases of domestic violence are registered on the crime administration system (CAS) as statutory and common law crimes, such as assault and rape. This makes it difficult for the police to conduct content analysis of domestic violence case dockets per se to measure the contribution of domestic violence to violent crime.

Although there has been ongoing training on the application of the DVA and the National Instruction, the training does not focus on the innovations used by modern policing agencies to police domestic violence.

Recommendations

To successfully police domestic violence, policing agencies need to change their philosophy of how they police it (Edwards, 2011). The Minister of Police in South Africa, Nathi Mthethwa, also highlighted the need to change the attitudes of police officials as a key priority in handling domestic violence cases (Geldenhuys, 2012, p. 27). Innovations should be built around preventing, combating, and effectively investigating domestic violence. The starting point should be the accurate recording by SAPS of the number of cases of domestic violence reported by gender, cluster, and province, so that the police can keep track of trends. Accurate statistics on domestic violence cases will only be possible if domestic violence cases are disaggregated from assault, murder, and other interpersonal crime statistics, such as violence against women (Gould et al., 2012).

The following are some of the innovations recommended for the policing of domestic violence in South Africa.

Putting Domestic Violence into Context

For many years, the police response to allegations of domestic violence has been insensitive, ineffective, and unprofessional, because the police have never recognized and understood the concept of domestic violence. Police see domestic violence as arguments and disagreements that take place inside homes. Domestic violence is considered as just another domestic dispute that needs a "domestic dispute intervention" (Richards et al., 2008). Domestic violence has to be put into its proper context as a violent crime.

Changing the Policing of Domestic Violence

Researchers on domestic violence in the United States found that by not arresting the perpetrator and by referring the victim to other services, the police have made a significant contribution to the continuation of domestic violence. The claim on all sides is that police should stop, or at least reduce, the number of domestic violence crimes instead of referring victims to outside agencies for intervention. More operational policing of domestic violence is needed than is presently being provided by the police. There is a need to improve the policing of domestic violence by providing alternative ways of policing domestic violence (Sheptycki, 1993).

In order to investigate the causes of the domestic violence and the actions of the alleged perpetrator, social workers, psychologists, and other health care professionals need to consider the broader context in which the behavior has occurred, as well as examining alternative explanations for the behavior (Bandura, 1977). According to Barkhuizen and Ovens (2012, p. 17), a victim-centered approach should be followed to police the causes of domestic violence. According to Sheptycki (1993), domestic violence units established in London to police domestic violence proved very successful. These units provided consistent service to victims of domestic violence. There was an increased involvement of police officials and other social services. The "victim protection–offender arrest" model used by the London Metropolitan Police is recommended for implementation.

Content Analysis of Case Dockets Regarding Domestic Violence

According to Tilley (2009, p. 123), crime pattern theory is important for policing domestic violence, as it will help describe and explain the geographical distribution of domestic violence–related crimes. From the author's own experience, content analysis of case dockets is very important in directing prevention and combating strategies. The content analysis information will also help investigators in the investigation process, by increasing apprehensions and the clearance of cases. Crime pattern analysis is a product derived from the content analysis that looks at links between domestic violence crimes and other incidents to reveal similarities and differences. It will help investigators in identifying patterns of criminal conduct, the geographic concentration of acts of domestic violence, and recidivism of perpetrators (Ratcliffe, 2009; Sheptycki, 1993).

Resituating the Discourse

Scientific studies show that traditional policing does not always produce the desired results. Social scientists of today regard policing as a professional practice that is based on police effectiveness. Studies conducted in the United States indicated that arrests were the only answer for women who suffered at the hands of violent perpetrators, and also for the police who had suffered negative publicity. Other social responses considered in the research were counseling programs for men who batter their wives, the provision of shelters for female victims and their children, and other types of victim-based strategies (Sheptycki, 1993).

Intelligence-Led Policing Approach

Intelligence-led policing had its origins in the United Kingdom and was later introduced in Australia, driven by a number of police commissioners. The National Intelligence Model (NIM) that has been adopted in the United Kingdom uses four elements as its tactical tasking in the implementation of intelligence-led policing. A specific model was designed to address domestic violence. The focus is on targeting the criminal and not the crime. This is because research has shown that a small percentage of repeat offenders (recidivists) commit a large number of domestic violence crimes (NCIS, 2000).

Intelligence-led policing will assist police in identifying and targeting the most dangerous perpetrators and the most vulnerable victims. In the United Kingdom, NIM is being promoted as a tool for improving the collection and use of intelligence in domestic violence cases. Analysis of the statistics is crucial in intelligence-led policing of domestic violence (Richards et al., 2008).

Effective Investigation

In theory, domestic violence should be one of the easiest crimes to investigate, as both the victim and the offender are known to each other and the scene of the crime is easily identifiable. However, this is not the case in practice. Lack of successful prosecutions is due to poor investigation at the scene and too much reliance on the sole evidence of the victim to secure a prosecution, only to learn at a later stage that the victim has withdrawn the charges at court or is reluctant to assist in finalizing the investigation. This may lead to prosecutors' withdrawing charges against the perpetrators because there is insufficient evidence to prosecute (Richards et al., 2008).

Criminal investigation involves locating, gathering, and using information to bring an offender to justice, or to achieve one of the other objectives laid down by the police service, such as victim support, information and intelligence gathering, or managing risks. Understanding investigative practice requires an understanding of the phenomenon of domestic violence. Arrest will be necessary to allow the investigation to be completed without interference and prevent further abuse. The perpetrator should be interviewed and his or her statement should be obtained under caution (Stelfox, 2009).

Risk Identification, Assessment, and Management

The risk management cycle (RMC) begins with the identification of the person(s) to be protected. The risk factors associated with the person(s) prone to violence are prioritized according to certain vulnerability developmental factors (Ireland et al., 2009, p. 180). This is followed by the analysis or assessment of the effects of the risks according to probability, frequency, and impact. This analysis results in the identification of alternative actions to manage the risks (Clark, 2010; Rogers, 2008). Risk management in domestic violence cases should include a multiagency approach that is based on appropriate information sharing and the development and implementation of interventions and plans of action to manage the risks.

Three stages of risk should be considered for the purposes of policing domestic violence: risk identification, risk assessment, and risk management (Richards et al., 2008).

Preventing violence and abuse is desirable in terms of averting physical and emotional harm. In order for the risk of violence and abuse to be reduced, the factors that generate risks for violence and abuse should be prevented. If violence and abuse risk assessments are conducted, such assessments will have the potential to evaluate and manage risk of future violence and abuse, and thus can play a critical role in preventing violence and abuse in society (Ireland et al., 2009, p. 3).

Information Sharing

Domestic violence will always need a multiagency approach. It is this approach that makes the sharing of information even more necessary (Richards et al., 2008). According to Ratcliffe (2009), information sharing is not intelligence-led policing, and police departments that do share information are not necessarily practicing intelligence-led policing. The safety of the victims of domestic violence and their children should come first, and therefore we must work with the widest possible range of information available. We cannot hide behind data protection and human rights issues as an excuse for our failure to share information. To hold offenders accountable, identify and manage risks, and protect victims and their families, the police will have to gather and share information within the service, with other agencies, and with the general public (Richards et al., 2008).

Conclusion

The police are trying hard to comply with the prescriptions of the DVA and the National Instruction. From the reports presented to the Parliamentary Portfolio Committee by the police and the Independent Police Investigative Directorate (IPID), it appears that the policing of domestic violence has not improved. The police should move toward addressing the perpetrators of domestic violence. This will only be possible if crime statistics on domestic violence are accurately captured for measurement. It is therefore crucial for the police to look at innovative ways to police domestic violence in South Africa. Since only victims of domestic violence were sampled for interviews, the findings may be generalized to similar victims.

References

Abrahams, K., Levendale, C. Rhoda, G., and Watson, J. (2010). *Strategic report on public hearings on implementation of Domestic Violence Act for Portfolio Committee on Women, Youth, Children and Persons with Disabilities*. Research Unit, Parliament of South Africa.

Altbeker, A. (2005). Policing domestic violence: The enthusiasm gap. *South African Crime Quarterly*, 12, 13–18.

Artz, L. (2004). Better safe than sorry, magistrates' views on the Domestic Violence Act. *South African Crime Quarterly*, 7, 1–7.

Bandura, A. (1977). *Social Learning Theory*. Englewood Cliffs, NJ: Prentice Hall.

Barkhuizen, M., and Ovens, M. (2012). A conceptualisation of the South African male victim of domestic violence within a heterosexual marriage or cohabitating relationship. *Acta Criminolgica*, 25(1), 16–28.

Bekker, J. C., and Coetzee, J. J. J. (1982). *Seymour's Customary Law in Southern Africa*. Johannesburg: Juta and Co.

Berns, N. (2001). Degendering the problem and gendering the blame: Political discourse on women and violence. *Gender and Society*, 15(2), 262–281.

Cambell, D. (2010). More than 40% of domestic violence victims are male, report reveals. *Observer.* Retrieved September 4, 2012, from http://www.theguardian.com/society/2010/sep/05/men-victims-domestic-violence.

Chibba, S. (2012). Police part of domestic violence problem. Masimanyane. Retrieved from http://www.masimanyane.org.za/?q=content/police-part-domestic-violence-problem.

Clark, R. (2010). *Intelligence Analysis. A Target Centric Approach.* 3rd ed. Washington, DC: CQ Press.

Edwards, C. (2011). *Changing Policing Theories for 21st Century Societies.* 3rd ed. Salisbury, UK: Griffin.

Fourie, M. (2001). Managing diversity. In F. Reynecke and M. Fourie (eds.), *Police Management: Beyond 2000* (pp. 28–44). Landsdowne, South Africa: Juta.

Geldenhuys, K. (2012). Male victims of domestic violence. *Servamus*, 105(11), 24–27.

Gould, C., Burger, J. and Newham, G. (2012). The SAPS crime statistics: What they tell us and what they don't. *South African Crime Quarterly*, 42, 3–12.

Hargovan, H. (2009). Doing justice differently: Is restorative justice appropriate for domestic violence? *Acta Criminolgica*, 2, 25–41.

Heyzer, N. (1995). *A Woman's Development Agenda for the 21st Century.* New York: United Nations Development Fund for Women.

Independent Police Investigative Directorate. (2010). Domestic violence report. Retrieved September 11, 2012, from https://pmg.org.za/committee-meeting/14578/

Ireland, J. L., Ireland, C., and Birch, P. (eds.). (2009). *Violent and Sexual Offenders: Assessment, Treatment and Management.* Portland, OR: Willan Publishing.

Kennard, J. (2007). Intimate partner violence against men. Retrieved from https://www.verywell.com/intimate-partner-violence-against-men-2329040.

Klopper, H. C., Fourie, A. E., Roets, S. J. J., and Van Deemter, E. (2002). *Domestic Violence: Study Guide.* Pretoria: Ubuntu.

Leedy, P. D., and Omrod, J. E. (2001). *Practical Research: Planning and Research.* 7th ed. Upper Saddle River, NJ: Prentice Hall.

Legalbrief. (2012a). Domestic Violence Act applies to brothers.

Legalbrief. (2012b). Koran wife beating passage.

Legalbrief. (2012c). Judge ups murderer's plea bargain sentence.

Ludsin, H., and Vetten, L. (2005). Spiral of Entrapment: Abused Women in Conflict with the Law. Johannesburg: Jacana Media.

Mafuya, N. P., and Ramalepe, M. (2008). Experience of abuse among women in a rural subdistrict of Limpopo Province, South Africa. An assessment. *Acta Criminolgica*, 2, 46–55.

Malefane, M. (2009). Intelligence boss's shock admission: 'I beat my wife because she would not cook'. *Sunday Times*, September 20, p. 1.

Manamela, M., Smit, J., and Ngantweni, G. (2010). Policing domestic violence effectively at Rietgat police station: An assessment. *Acta Criminolgica*, 2, 99–113.

Minnaar, A., and Mistry, D. (2003). Declared unfit to own a firearm. Are the courts playing their role? *Crime Quarterly*, 6, December.

National Criminal Intelligence Service (NCIS). (2000). The National Intelligence Model. London: Home Office, NCIS.

Ratcliffe, J. 2009. *Intelligence Led Policing.* Cullompton, UK: Willan Publishing.

Richards, L., Letchford, S., and Stratton, S. (2008). *Policing Domestic Violence.* Oxford: Oxford University Press.

Rogers, C. (2008). A security risk management approach to the measurement of crime in a private security context. *Acta Criminologica: Southern African Journal of Criminology, Crimsa 2008 Conference Special Edition (3)*, 2008, 150–156.

Sheptycki, J. W. E. (1993). *Innovations in Policing Domestic Violence.* Aldershot: Avebury.

Simpson, G., and Rauch, J. (1999). Reflections on the National Crime Prevention Strategy. In A. Maharaj (ed.), *Between Unity and Diversity: Essays on Nation-Building in Post-Apartheid South Africa* (pp. 295–314). Cape Town: David Philip.

Smith, P., and Natalier, K. (2005). *Understanding Criminal Justice: Sociological Perspectives.* Wiltshire, UK: Cromwell Press.

South Africa (Republic). (1993). Prevention of Family Violence Act 133 of 1993. Pretoria: Government Printer.

South Africa (Republic). (1996). Constitution of the Republic of South Africa. Pretoria: Government Printer.

South Africa (Republic). (1996). National Crime Prevention Strategy. Pretoria: Government Printer.

South Africa (Republic). (1998). Domestic Violence Act, No. 116 of 1998. Pretoria: Government Printer.

South African Police Service (SAPS). (1999). South African Police Service National Instruction 7/1999. Pretoria: National Commissioner of the SAPS.

South African Police Service (SAPS). (2011). Department of policing briefing, Domestic Violence Act implementation. Retrieved September 11, 2012, from https://pmg.org.za/committee-meeting/13827/.

Stelfox, P. (2009). *Criminal Investigations: An Introduction to Principles and Practice.* Cullompton: Willan.

Tilley, N. (2009). *Crime Prevention.* Cornwall, UK: Willan.

Tyska, L. A., and Fennely, L. J. (1999). *Investigations: 150 Things You Should Know.* Waltham, MA: Butterworth-Heinemann.

Van Heerden, T. J. (1982). *Introduction to Policing.* Pretoria: University of South Africa.

Vetten, L. (2011). Finally, some real police intelligence. Centre for the Study of Violence and Reconciliation. Retrieved April 22, 2013, from http://www.csvr.org.za/index.php? option=com_content&view=article&id=2462:finally-some-real-police-intelligence-030411&catid=139:media-articles&Itemid=37.

Wilson, G. T. (1977). Alcohol and human sexual behavior. *Behavior Research and Therapy,* 15, 239-252.

Domestic Violence Legislation and Its Application in Serbia

The Impact of Gender of the Offender and Other Factors

11

VESNA NIKOLIĆ-RISTANOVIĆ
AND LJILJANA STEVKOVIĆ

Contents

Introduction

Civil society advocacy has significantly contributed to the changes in Serbian legislation on violence against women (VAW) that have occurred in recent years. As a consequence, the legislation on VAW in Serbia is currently very different than in the period prior to 2000. Changes in the law started in March 2002, when a new criminal offense was introduced, domestic violence, and it was further developed in the 2005 Criminal Code. In this criminal code, domestic violence is prescribed as a criminal offense in Article 194, which was amended in 2009, introducing more severe sanctions. Domestic violence is therefore a separate criminal offense, prosecuted *ex officio*, and includes punishment for the emotional and physical abuse of a family member. There are five forms of domestic violence for which different penalties are prescribed.* The punishment is proportional to its consequences on the victim; the most severe form of violence is that resulting in the death of the victim, and the least severe form consists of breaching protection orders. According to the 2005 Family Code, a range of protection orders can be issued in civil procedure, while their violation is punishable as the most lenient form of the criminal offense of domestic violence. The amendments to Serbian legislation to date have rendered it highly compliant with the requirements of the most important international documents. However, there are still significant gaps in the legislation, but much more in the implementation of laws and other practical solutions.

Despite the gaps in the application of laws and clearly increasing trend† in the prosecution and conviction of women, to date, surveys have not explored the influence of the offender's gender on the application of domestic violence laws in Serbia, nor developed reliable methodology and indicators for comprehensive, sustainable, and comparable monitoring.

Bearing that in mind, the aim of this chapter is to analyze the impact of gender and related factors on the application of domestic violence (criminal) laws to both men and women, based on findings of the research carried out in Serbia on the sample of court files of 219 male and female offenders. The focus of the survey was the implementation of legal provisions that regulate domestic violence as a criminal offense in cases where both the man and the woman are prosecuted, including dual conviction cases, that is, where the man and the woman are both the victim and the perpetrator.

* (1) Whoever by use of violence, threat of attacks against life or body, insolent or ruthless behavior endangers the tranquillity, physical integrity or mental condition of a member of his family, shall be punished with imprisonment from three months to three years.
(2) If in committing the offence specified in paragraph 1 of this Article weapons, dangerous implements or other means suitable to inflict serious injury to body or seriously impair health are used, the offender shall be punished with imprisonment from six months to five years.
(3) If the offence specified in paragraphs 1 and 2 of this Article results in grievous bodily harm or serious health impairment, or if committed against a minor, the offender shall be punished with imprisonment from two to ten years.
(4) If the offence specified in paragraphs 1, 2 and 3 of this Article results in the death of a family member, the offender shall be punished with imprisonment from three to fifteen years.
(5) Whoever violates a protection order for domestic violence that was imposed on them by the court in accordance with the law shall be punished with imprisonment from three months to three years and fine.

† Statistical data for Serbia, which were used as a starting point for the survey, that findings of which are presented in this chapter, suggest that the number of women convicted for domestic violence in 2009 (111) is almost two times higher than that in 2007 (58), while in the same period, the number of convicted men also increased, but to a much smaller extent (27%).

The main focus of research was on how courts deal with domestic violence cases, although some data were also collected on the application of laws by the police and prosecutors. The survey was conducted using both quantitative and qualitative methods. The quantitative part included the collection of data from court files and their analyses using descriptive statistics and the Pearson chi-square test. Before the presentation of Serbian survey findings, an overview of worldwide research findings is presented.

Overview of Research Findings on Factors That Influence the Application of Domestic Violence (Criminal) Laws to Both Men and Women

Since the 1990s, many studies on domestic violence have focused on factors that influence the official response in these cases. Two groups of studies can be identified within rich empirical material: studies on reasons for prosecution and factors that influence the decision to prosecute, and studies on factors affecting court decisions in domestic violence cases. Although women also appear as perpetrators of domestic violence, and are also prosecuted and convicted for it, there are so many studies that assess the official response to domestic violence committed by men and so few studies that assess the official response to domestic violence committed by women. The various factors identified in these studies can be grouped into two large groups: legal factors (e.g., prior arrest) and nonlegal factors (e.g., gender of offender and victim and relationship between offender and victim). More precisely, factors that may influence the prosecutorial and court decision making in domestic violence cases include characteristics of the offender and victim, the nature of the offense, and the availability of evidence (Henning and Feder, 2005).

When it comes to gender, many surveys showed that it is a significant predictor of the decisions made by prosecutors and judges. The surveys carried out worldwide suggest that, compared to women, men are more likely to be charged or cautioned, convicted, and sentenced to imprisonment (Kingsnorth and MacIntosh, 2007; Garner and Maxwell, 2009). Also, compared to males, female offenders are less likely to be charged with felony, and more likely to receive charges reduced to a misdemeanor or a violation of probation (Kingsnorth and MacIntosh, 2007). When they are charged, females are more likely than males to have a pretrial release and have their charges dropped by prosecutors. They are also more likely to receive a nonguilty verdict, and if and when convicted, they receive lighter penalties (Belknap and Graham, 2000; Cramer, 1999, Davis et al., 2003; Dawson and Dinovitzer, 2001; Henning and Feder, 2005; Russell et al., 2009). On the other hand, male offenders are more likely than females to be charged and sentenced to imprisonment (Henning and Feder, 2005; Kingsnorth and MacIntosh, 2007). It is interesting that these differences persisted even once other legal and extralegal variables were controlled (Henning and Feder, 2005). In some countries, judges overlook the history of violence, power, and control in relationships, and fail to understand the distinctive nature of domestic violence (Busch and Robertson, 1993).

In some surveys, the relationship between the offender and the victim of domestic violence has also been identified as a significant factor that affects decisions throughout the adjudication process. An ongoing emotional relationship, cohabitation, and coparenthood reduce the likelihood of prosecution, while a marital relationship has the opposite, unpredicted effect (Kingsnorth and MacIntosh, 2007).

In terms of offender characteristics, prior criminal history, particularly earlier convictions for domestic violence and protective orders, and use of drugs or alcohol are positively correlated with the likelihood of arrest, placement under pretrial detention, or sentence to imprisonment (Henning and Feder, 2005; Worrall et al., 2006). Similarly, some factors of offense severity have the same influence. Namely, offenders are arrested or placed under pretrial detention or sentenced to prison more often if they had seriously injured the victim physically or used a weapon during the violent attack (Henning and Feder, 2005; Hirschel and Hutchison, 2001; Eigenberg et al., 1996; Ferraro, 1989; Schmidt and Steury, 1989; Worrall et al., 2006). On the other hand, use of alcohol or drugs by the victim decreases the likelihood of prosecuting a domestic violence case, while victim support for prosecution increases it (Hirschel and Hutchison, 2001; Kingsnorth and MacIntosh, 2007).

Mutual violence leads to less probability of prosecution, due to difficulties in determining the primary aggressor (Miller, 2001; Worrall et al., 2006). Mutual violence more likely results in dual arrest (Martin, 1997). Dual arrest is significantly related to prosecution efforts, court dispositions, and the sentences imposed. Those dually arrested are more likely to be charged with misdemeanors than felonies and less likely to be convicted than singly arrested, but once the decision to prosecute has been made, dually arrested offenders are more likely than singly arrested to be convicted (Henning and Feder, 2005). However, a higher proportion of dually arrested women are prosecuted and convicted than dually arrested men (Martin, 1997), although the majority of women that used violence were acting in self-defense or fighting back (Martin, 1997; DeKeseredy et al., 1999).

Survey on the Application of Domestic Violence Laws in Serbia

The survey was carried out in 2010–2011. The main aim was to collect data on the impact of gender on decisions on indictment, convictions, penalties, and the overall treatment of offenders in criminal procedures in domestic violence cases in Serbia. The aim was also to identify other factors that may influence the application of laws in domestic violence cases and to compare their impact to that of gender. Also, the survey intended to identify cases where women were convicted, although they were the primary victim, as well as cases of dual arrest or conviction, and to analyze the application of laws in these cases.*

Accordingly, three main research questions were raised:

1. What impact does gender have on the processing of domestic violence cases?
2. What other factors, in addition to gender, have an impact on the processing of domestic violence cases?
3. Is there an impact of dual or single arrests on the processing of domestic violence cases?

* In this survey, the authors piloted the use of some of the indicators for measuring the effectiveness of legislation on VAW that were suggested during a regional meeting held by United Nations Development Fund for Women (UNIFEM) (now UN Women) (Sarajevo, November 23–24, 2009). These indicators were further developed and implemented by an international consultant, Lori Sudderth (2010), and adjusted to the focus of the study by one of authors of this chapter, Vesna Nikolić-Ristanović, who was the local consultant for UN Women.

Methodology

The survey was conducted using both quantitative and qualitative methods. The quantitative part included the collection of data from court files and their analyses using descriptive statistics and the Pearson chi-square test. The main dependent variables included the types of domestic violence according to Article 194 of the criminal code, arrest or pretrial detention, duration of criminal procedure, court decisions, and criminal sanctions (indicators of the application of laws by courts). The main independent variable was gender, whereas data on the offender, the victim, the criminal offense, protection orders, victim support for prosecution,* the identification of the primary aggressor,† and so forth, were examined as control variables (indicators of potential other factors that influence the application of laws and decision making of prosecutors and judges).

Qualitative analysis was primarily used in analyzing answers to open-ended questions and other qualitative information obtained from court files, in particular those related to the cases of dual arrest or prosecution and the prosecution of victims as secondary aggressors.

Data were collected using the semistructured questionnaire, completed for each offender. Accordingly, in the cases with several offenders, a separate questionnaire was filled out for every offender. Also, in the cases of dual conviction, separate questionnaires were filled out for both offenders involved in the mutual violence; in cases where there was more than one victim, data on all of the victims were included in the questionnaire on the offender who abused them.

After the data collection, most of the open-ended questions were answered, while some were left open and used only for qualitative analyses. Also, the questionnaire needed several adjustments during data collection, since either some unexpected data emerged or some missing data created problems in completing the questionnaire.

Problems emerged in particular in dual prosecution cases and in cases with several perpetrators and victims. Dual prosecution cases were especially complicated. Since both sides were at the same time both victim and perpetrator, it was methodologically challenging to decide on how to address this in the questionnaire. Thus, as mentioned above, it was decided to collect data for each perpetrator separately. In cases of mutual violence and dual prosecution, for each offender and his or her victim, it was necessary to identify the primary aggressor, as well as the primary victim, and then how they were treated by the criminal justice system. Since quantitative analyses used in the survey thus showed limitations in the analyses of these cases, it was necessary to supplement them with qualitative analyses, which were extremely useful for developing the monitoring methodology. This methodology was mostly developed throughout the data collection and coding, and was finalized on the bases of overall survey findings and experiences with data collection.

Survey Sample

The sample included all available court files on women sentenced for the criminal offense of domestic violence (Article 194 of the Serbian Criminal Court) from selected basic

* Although not required by law, it is a widespread practice that prosecutors and judges ask victims whether they support prosecution.

† "[The] primary aggressor is better described as the dominant or most significant aggressor at the scene of a domestic violence crime when both parties have committed some sort of violence toward the other" (California Alliance against Domestic Violence, 2000).

courts,* that is, former municipality courts,† as well as a relatively random sample of available court files where offenders of the same offense were men. Data obtained from the Serbian Statistics Bureau served as the basis for determining the sample.

Since the authors were largely dependent on the court administration and the availability of court files, it was not possible to create a random sample of male offenders according to the planned criteria by selecting every four male cases. Thus, the sample of male offenders was generally created by randomly choosing from available cases while ensuring that all forms of domestic violence were included.

Bearing in mind the small number of cases of convicted women and that these cases are extremely dispersed, the sample included eight courts with the highest percentage of convicted women, covering the Belgrade suburb (Lazarevac and Obrenovac), and the following courts from central and south Serbia: Niš, Kruševac, Leskovac, Valjevo, Veliko Gradište, and Aleksinac.

Thus, a stratified random sample of men and women who were convicted during 2007, 2008, and 2009 (for a total of 1317, of which 79 were women) was created, including a total of 219. The sample consists of 166 men (75.8%) and 53 women (24.2%). The geographical structure was as follows: Niš (18.3%), Kruševac (15.5%), Leskovac (6.4%), Valjevo (12.8%), Veliko Gradište (10.5%), Obrenovac (14.2%), Lazarevac (8.7%), and Aleksinac (13.6%).

The men–women ratio in the sample is around 3:1, whereas according to Statistics Bureau data, this ratio is around 16:1 within the total number of convicted persons in Serbia. An oversampling of women was necessary in order to obtain enough relevant information on the application of laws to women as perpetrators of domestic violence, as well as to ensure that cases where women were convicted, although they were the secondary aggressors, are included. It should also be noted that the sample included 67% of all women convicted in Serbia in the 2007–2009 period according to official statistics.

Accordingly, the findings obtained are highly representative of the application of domestic violence law to women in Serbia, excluding Vojvodina and central Belgrade. Although the percentage of convicted men included in the survey is much lower, it was adequate for collecting and comparing the necessary data to answer research questions.

Also, it is important to bear in mind that for this pilot survey, which is the first of its kind in Serbia, the representation of women is of central importance, since it has allowed testing and developing a survey instrument and a general methodology that can be later used in similar surveys. Moreover, it allowed us to identify cases of mutual violence and analyze the application of law in these cases, including, in particular, the differentiation between primary and secondary victims and abusers or aggressors.

Additionally, it is important to mention that the sample consists of both partner and nonpartner violence, including child abuse. As will be seen from the findings, this is

* The only court that was unwilling to provide court files was the First Basic Court, which covers the central Belgrade municipalities. Although the author planned to include at least 50 cases from this court, and up until the very end of the data collection had tried various ways to obtain its permission, including requesting the commissionaire for free access to public information and the protection of personal data, she had to finally exclude that part of the sample.

† The cases included in the sample were processed by the municipality courts, which in 2010 were incorporated into the basic courts. According to the recently adopted law on the organization of the courts (2008), "Judicial power in the Republic of Serbia is vested in courts of general and special jurisdiction. Courts of general jurisdiction are basic courts, higher courts, appellate courts and the Supreme Court of Cassation" (Article 11).

important for the overall assessment of the application of domestic violence law, as well as for the comparison of its application in cases of partner and nonpartner abuse.

Main Problems Encountered during Data Collection

The main problems encountered during data collection were related to access to court files and the lack of relevant information in court files, that is, poor record keeping. Access to court files was a particular problem: some courts prohibited access, while others allowed for access but with long delays. Also, since the authors were not provided with all the required files, they could not create a random sample of convicted males.

It is important to note here that the survey was carried out just after a major reform of the court system, which required that the archives be moved, changes in the court administration and data recording methods, and so forth. In addition, at that time, electronic data recording was just being implemented in most Serbian courts. Due to the court system reform and other reasons, some of the court files were not in the court archives at the time of data collection, which was the reason all the requested files were not available.

Access to court files is based on the law on access to information of public interest. However, notwithstanding this law and the request to the commissionaire for free access to information of public interest and personal data protection sent by the Victimology Society of Serbia, the First Basic Court in Belgrade refused access to court files. Moreover, the only justification provided by the commissionaire was that they were overburdened with requests but would respond to the request soon. However, since the finalization of this study, no further decision was received.

Problems concerning lack of information were mainly related to the following: often incomplete information about the victims and the lack of information about prior violent behavior of the abuser or about protection orders.

Information on victims is mostly found in police files, that is, in victim crime reports, or in records of the hearings of victims during investigations or trials. This information usually includes, although inconsistently, names, as well as data on age, occupation, and nationality. However, very often, some of the mentioned data are missing. Moreover, it is not obligatory to provide data on the victim in the verdict; however, the name and other information are available in the verdict if the victim was also an offender in the case or if the information (e.g., age) is relevant for the application of the law.

It was particularly difficult to obtain information on prior abuse by the victim, prior or current reports, prosecutions and ongoing trials against the victim who was also the abuser, and convictions and protection orders issued against the victim who was also the primary aggressor. This information could only be found when the victim was also convicted, that is, in cases of double convictions. In addition, the court files of the cases that qualified for a simplified procedure lacked even more basic information, since they do not need to have justification for indictment and verdict.

Main Survey Findings

The main survey findings are grouped in three main sections according to different factors that impact the application of domestic violence law: findings on the impact of gender on the application of the law, findings on the impact of other factors, and findings on the impact of mutual violence on the processing of domestic violence cases.

Impact of Gender on Processing of Domestic Violence Cases in Serbia

Gender of the Perpetrator and the Applicable Paragraph of Article 194 of the Criminal Code (Form of Domestic Violence)

As mentioned above, there are five forms of domestic violence for which different penalties are prescribed in different paragraphs.

Most of the convicted perpetrators in the sample were sentenced under paragraph 1 (50.2%) and paragraph 2 (28.8%), while a smaller percentage were sentenced under paragraph 3 (15.5%); 4.6% were sentenced under both paragraphs 2 and 3, 0.5% under paragraphs 1 and 2, and 0.5% for paragraphs 1–3. The author did not come across any case of sentence under paragraphs 4 and 5 (with a lethal consequence and an offense that consists of the violation of a protection order, respectively). This is most probably because cases with lethal consequences are processed by the district courts, and convictions for violations of protection orders are rare.*

There is no significant impact of gender in this regard, and the distribution of sentences regarding the type of offense (i.e., the legal qualification of certain violent behavior) is similar for both genders. Most commonly, both genders are sentenced under paragraph 1, then under paragraph 2, and least commonly under paragraph 3. However, legal qualification is more evenly distributed among female offenders, and the percentage of women sentenced under paragraph 3 (mostly for child abuse) is much higher than that of men sentenced for the offense qualified in the same way.

Gender and Domestic Violence as a Continuous or Isolated Event

Information on continuous or isolated events was obtained on the basis of detailed research of court files, including police and social welfare records, as well as trial transcripts. Thus, the data on continuous or isolated events are the result of the researcher's estimation on the basis of all available data, including victim statements in various phases of the criminal procedure, and regardless of the court's judgment. For example, if the victim and sometimes offender or other witnesses stated that the violence had continued for a longer period or that he or she had reported it many times, the author considered that there was a continuous pattern of violent behavior. This indicates that there was a high risk of more serious violence and injuries, and it was expected that the entire criminal justice system would react accordingly. Thus, it was of interest to learn how the court treated individual offenses—as part of continuous violence or as an isolated event—and what kind of consequences they had in terms of court decisions, such as pretrial detention and criminal sanctions.

The largest percentages of patterns of domestic violence (72.3%) were continual domestic violence offenses committed by men. Since male violence was predominantly partner violence (73.5%), it can be assumed that most long-lasting violence committed by men is VAW. Women were more often convicted for domestic violence as an isolated offense than as continuous abuse. However, although much less often than men, women were

* For example, the number of persons convicted for this form of domestic violence was as follows: 1 in 2007, 12 in 2008, and 9 in 2009.

also sentenced for continuous violent behavior against the same victim (43.4%). However, unlike men, in these cases, their victims were either children or female in-laws. In exceptional cases, victims were also their partners. More precisely, there was only one case of a woman who continuously abused her male partner and was also victimized by him. She abused her former husband, who was granted custody of their child; however, from the court files, it was not possible to identify who the primary aggressor was.

In 21% of the cases, the courts correctly treated violent events as part of continuous abuse, while in almost a half of cases (44.3%), the court regarded the offense as an isolated event, although it was evident that the abuse was continuous. In 34.7% of the cases, the court correctly treated the violence as an isolated event.

There is a significant correlation between gender and the court's treatment of the offense. Women prevail among those whose violence is correctly treated as an isolated event, while men are those whose violence is much more often treated as an isolated offense although there was continuity. In the majority of cases where it was clear that there was continuous abuse (97 out of 143, or 67.8%), domestic violence was treated as an isolated event. In most of such cases (79, or 81.4%), the men were the abusers; therefore, these findings have clear gendered consequences. However, there was also a considerable percentage of cases of female offenders where abuse was present, but was incorrectly not considered continuous. It seems that it is the judges' lack of knowledge about the nature of domestic violence in general, and about male partner abuse in particular, rather than gender, that affects the court's inappropriate judgment of the type of abuse. Thus, the majority of judges do not take into consideration the wider context of violence, but only the specific event.

By contrast, the violence committed by 41 men (34.2%) and 5 women (21.7%) whose violent behavior seems to be continuous was treated as such. This suggests that some judges looked at the larger context in which violence occurred, which is clearly an example of good practice.

It is especially important to stress the consequences of a correct or incorrect judgment of continuous violence; the judgment of continuous violence affected court decisions on pretrial detention and sanctions, and consequently the protection of victims. The findings show that judges tended to impose prison sentences more often in cases where they treated the offense of domestic violence as continuous abuse, that is, as part a broader context of long-term violence. This finding seems to suggest that judges who were capable of identifying a history of abuse tended to treat these cases as more dangerous. This highlights the need to educate judges on correctly identifying cases of continuous abuse. However, the seriousness of the abuse was not reflected in the length of the prison sentences. Therefore, as can be seen from the analyses of the impact of other factors, some of the latter can have a greater influence on court decisions with respect to the length of the prison penalty.

Arrest or Pretrial Detention and Gender

Both men and women are rarely arrested by the police or placed under pretrial detention for domestic violence. Only two women from the sample were arrested and detained by the police, and only one was put in pretrial detention. Also, only one woman stayed in pretrial detention until her verdict became final. Men were more often than women arrested by the police (10.2%) or placed under pretrial detention (10.2%). Also, when men were placed under pretrial detention, it was mostly for a very short time (up to 5 months in 12 cases, or 70.5%), while only in 3 cases, or 17.6%, were they held in pretrial detention for between 5 and 12 months. In addition, seven men, or almost one half of those who were placed under pretrial detention, but only 4.2% of those sentenced, were held in pretrial detention until the verdict became final. The only woman who was held under a pretrial detention was subject to a prolonged pretrial detention until the verdict became final.

Duration of Criminal Procedure and Gender

In general, criminal procedures are quite lengthy in Serbia, including in domestic violence cases (Konstantinović-Vilić and Petrušić, 2007). This was also confirmed by our survey. In almost half of the cases, the procedure* lasted between one and three years. Most procedures (36.5%) lasted between 1 and 2 years; only 10.5% of the procedures lasted up to 5 months, 24.2% lasted between 5 and 9 months, and 14.2% lasted between 9 and 12 months. In four cases (1.8%), the procedure lasted more than three years.

It was of interest to determine which phase of the criminal procedure takes the longest time and which is the most efficient. The shortest phases seem to be the trial and the period between reporting to the police and the police referring the case to the prosecutor. Notably, 51.6% of the trials lasted for only one day, while 17% of the trials lasted between two days and one month; 24.2% lasted between one and six months; and only 6.9% lasted between six months and two years.

In addition, 49.8% of the cases were referred to a prosecutor within less than five days. In 30% of the cases, it took between 5 and 30 days, whereas more than 2 months was required for 6.8% of the cases. However, there are four cases in which this period lasted more than five months, including one case that lasted more than a year. It has been observed that the longest period is between the indictment and the beginning of trial, and between the referral of the case to the prosecutor by the police and the indictment.

Data obtained in this survey showed no significant correlation between gender and the duration of the criminal procedure. As expected, the duration of the criminal procedure is influenced by other factors.

Sentencing and Gender

In the entire sample, the most often imposed sanction was the conditional sentence (72.5%), with only 1.8% including as a condition certain obligations for the offender. Imprisonment was imposed considerably less often, in 14.6% of the perpetrators, while 8.7% were sentenced to fines. Although more men than women were sentenced to imprisonment, the sample showed that there was no significant correlation between gender and imprisonment or conditional sentences.

However, there is a significant correlation between gender and the sentencing of a fine. It is interesting to note that no woman from the sample was sentenced to a fine. It is difficult to provide an explanation for this finding, but it may be that the judge assumed that women were not breadwinners and therefore unable to pay.

Taking into consideration sociodemographic data of the sample that highlights the difficult economic situation of both male and female offenders, it may be suggested that either judges believed in some cases that the men could afford to pay or other factors also influenced their decisions. In several cases, a fine was replaced by imprisonment since the

* The duration of the procedure was examined more in terms of a factual duration than in strictly legal terms; that is, the duration of the procedure was measured starting from the time of submission of the report by the victim or another person up to the time when the verdict became final. This included first instance courts and, in the case of an appeal, second instance courts as well.

offender was not able to pay, which may suggest that the decision to sentence a fine is not based on a realistic assessment of the offender's economic capacity to pay.

Security measures, such as obligatory medical treatment for alcohol or drug addiction, obligatory psychiatric treatment, or the removal of objects used in committing a crime, were imposed on 6.8% of the offenders. Although only three women were subject to security measures, there is no significant correlation between gender and security measures.

In addition, in a few cases, the offender received a judicial warning or was released from charges. The only person who received a judicial warning was a man, while a similar number of men and women (three and four, respectively) were released from charges.

The second-degree courts mostly confirmed the sanction imposed by the first degree court (59.5%). The decision on sanctions was changed for only 18 offenders (24.3%). More severe sanctions were imposed more often (66.6%) than lighter ones (33.4%), but bearing in mind the small number of cases, it is difficult to arrive at any significant conclusion. Also, sentences were rarely revoked and the trial was repeated (in 12 cases, or 16.2%). In these cases, the sanctions were mostly confirmed or were less severe, while in one case only, the sanction imposed in the new trial was more severe. No gender impact is observed in this regard, but bearing in mind the small number of changed sanctions or revoked sentences, it is difficult to draw a reliable conclusion.

Impact of Other Factors on the Processing of Domestic Violence Cases in Serbia

In order to better understand and compare the main factors that influence the application of domestic violence law, the relationships between several independent variables other than gender were explored. These include legal qualification of the offense; type of violence, partner or nonpartner violence; the use of weapons or other objects that can seriously harm the victim; alcoholism of the offender (when there is evidence in the case file that the perpetrator is an alcoholic); the number and ages of victims; recidivism; mutual violence and dual or single prosecutions; and victim support for prosecution and protection orders.

Impact of Legal Qualification on Arrest, Pretrial Detention, and Sanctions

As can be expected, the arrest or pretrial detention and prison sentence are in correlation with the legal qualification of the offense under the specific paragraph of Article 194. Arrest and pretrial detention most often occur in cases qualified under Article 194(3).

Similarly, the cases involving prison sentences are in correlation with the legal qualification of the offense and the punishment prescribed. However, there is no significant correlation between the legal qualification of the offense and a conditional sentence, which is, regardless of the seriousness of the offense, the prevailing sanction for domestic violence in Serbia. Also, fines were usually imposed on the perpetrators of the most lenient form of domestic violence. This, as well as the overall small number of perpetrators who received a prison sentence, suggests that legal qualification, although it has some impact, is not decisive when it comes to pretrial detention and type of sanction.

In addition, the number of offenses for which the perpetrator is convicted is not a strong predictor of either arrest or pretrial detention or of the prison sentence. Findings suggest an unusual trend that arrest or pretrial detention occurs most often, and pretrial detention lasts longer when the perpetrator is charged for only one offense. More important is the correlation with the prison sentence, which has a higher chance of being imposed if the perpetrator is charged with more than one offense.

Impact of the Type of Violence on Arrest, Pretrial Detention, and Sanctions

Survey findings show a significant connection between the type of violence and decisions on arrest or pretrial detention and sanction. The chances that a perpetrator is arrested or placed under pretrial detention and sentenced to prison increase with the increase in the severity of the violence. Thus, the following combinations of different types of violence are more likely to lead to arrest or pretrial detention and imprisonment, and less likely to a conditional sentence: threats and physical violence; threats and psychological and physical violence; and threats and psychological, physical, and sexual violence. Moreover, in cases where the second-degree court changed the decision on the penalty, when these combinations of different types of violence existed, it usually replaced the penalty imposed by the first degree court with a more severe one.

There is a close correlation between the type of violence and the consequences it has on the victim. Thus, it was interesting to observe whether there was any correlation between the type of violence and the consequences, on the one hand, and the responses of the criminal justice system, on the other. It was determined that there was no significant connection between these variables. However, findings suggest that offenders are arrested or placed under pretrial detention or sentenced to prison more often if they had seriously injured the victim physically, which is in line with similar findings in some other countries, such as New Zealand (Busch and Robertson, 1994).

Partner and Nonpartner Violence

Research findings show a significant difference in the application of the law in cases of partner, nonpartner, and a combination of partner and nonpartner violence. It should be noted that the chances that the offender is arrested, placed under pretrial detention, or imprisoned are highest if the violence is committed against both the partner and other members of the family (including children, parents, and parents-in-law).

Offenders were arrested or placed under pretrial detention approximately three times more often when, in addition to the partner, the victims were also other family members. The same significant difference is shown with respect to the duration of the pretrial detention, which indicates that these are also the offenders who spent the longest time in pretrial detention.

Although there is no significant correlation between partner or nonpartner violence and imprisonment, this sanction was more often imposed on those who abused both other family members and the partner (26.9%) than on those who only abused their partner (14.2%).

There is no significant connection between the type of violence (partner, nonpartner, or both) and the frequency of the conditional sentence. However, there is a significant difference with respect to the fine: those who only abused their partners were sentenced to fines more often than those whose victims were not their partners, but also more often than those whose victims were both their partners and nonpartners.

The existence of a significant correlation between gender and partner or nonpartner violence suggests that the background of the above findings is gender related. Thus, men are most often sentenced for partner violence, and women for nonpartner violence. However, men also constitute the majority of those who commit the combination of partner and nonpartner violence.

It can be assumed that if, in addition to the partner, the male abuser abused other family members (only one woman from the entire sample was under pretrial detention for having abused her mother), this has a high impact on the assessment of risk. This may also indicate that for the judges to perceive a danger that the male abuser may commit an even more serious abuse, it is not enough that the partner alone is endangered.

Also, it is noteworthy that findings show a significant relationship between the age of the victim and criminal justice responses, but this does not suggest a trend toward a more rigorous application of laws in cases where only minors are the victims. However, and in accordance with the above findings on partner or nonpartner violence, decisions on arrest or pretrial detention and imprisonment are more likely to be made in cases in which there are both adults and minors; also, a conditional sentence is less likely to be imposed in these cases.

Also, by examining the relationship between the gender of the victims and the partner–nonpartner variable, it can be seen that the combination of partner and nonpartner violence is most often committed against both male and female victims, whereas partner violence is committed predominantly against women, and much less often against men. This is in line with data on the gender of the perpetrator. Nonpartner violence is also predominantly committed against female victims and less often against male victims, and only rarely against both male and female victims. Women are most often sentenced for abusing in-laws (26.4%) and children (24.6%), but less often for abusing their partners (22.7%). No woman was sentenced for abusing both her partner and her children, compared to 6% of the men.

Thus, on the basis of all of the data presented in this section, it can be concluded that since judges tend to use more severe sanctions and pretrial detention primarily in cases with a combination of partner and nonpartner violence, the most severe criminal justice response against domestic violence is not related to the most widespread partner VAW, but to cases where victims include both adult men and women, as well as children (i.e., minors). It seems that judges in Serbia consider domestic violence a criminal offense against the family, rather than as VAW. This may be directly linked to the fact that the criminal offense of domestic violence is prescribed within the criminal code chapter "Criminal Offenses against Marriage and the Family," and consequently, it is broadly interpreted in this sense.

Use of Weapons or Other Objects That Can Seriously Harm the Victim, and Arrest, Pretrial Detention, and Sanctions

In only six cases were weapons used; however, in 91 cases, other objects were used that could seriously harm the victim. There is no significant correlation between the use of weapons and arrest, pretrial detention, and sanctions. However, due to the small number of cases where a weapon was used, this finding needs to be taken with reservation. Also, there is no significant correlation between the use of other objects that can seriously harm the victim and arrest, pretrial detention, and sanctions. The only possible impact noted with respect to the prison sentence is where offenders who used these objects were sentenced more often than those who did not (19.6% compared to 10.7%); however, this correlation is not significant. Also, it is interesting that, in these cases, the courts tended to impose conditional sentences more often than when these objects were not used. Only in one case where a weapon or other object that can seriously harm the victim had been used for committing the offense was a security measure applied, namely, seizure of the weapon.

Does the Number of Victims Have a Significant Impact on Decisions on Arrest, Pretrial Detention, and Sanctions?

The research findings suggest that it does not. In cases with more than three victims, imprisonment is less often imposed than in cases with three victims, but more often than in cases with one or two victims. Also, a conditional sentence was more often imposed when there were more than three victims.

Does an Offender's Alcoholism Have an Impact on Decisions on Arrest, Pretrial Detention, and Sanctions?

Research findings suggest that alcoholism has a significant impact on the police decision on arrest and the court's decision on pretrial detention, but not on the decision on the penalty or conditional sentences. However, as mentioned above, in these cases, the courts imposed the security measure of medical treatment on those who committed crimes under the influence of alcohol. Yet, out of 49 perpetrators who committed a crime under the influence of alcohol, the court imposed the security measure of obligatory addiction treatment or psychiatric treatment on only 10 offenders (20.4%).

These findings tend to suggest a better response of the criminal justice system immediately after reporting than in later stages; however, this also needs to be taken with caution since, as mentioned above, the number of offenders arrested and placed under pretrial detention is quite small. In general, it seems that there is no appropriate response in these cases that are predominantly of long-term partner abuse against women and children, and sometimes other family members as well.

Impact of Recidivism on Arrest, Pretrial Detention, and Sanctions

It is particularly interesting to examine the impact of recidivism on arrest, pretrial detention, and sanctions imposed on domestic violence offenders. Thus, the author analyzed both the impact of earlier sentences for domestic violence and other violent and nonviolent crimes, and the impact of whether there were earlier reports of domestic violence to the police and of charges for domestic violence regardless of the respective decision.

Earlier convictions for domestic violence seem to have a significant impact on the decisions of judges to place the abuser under pretrial detention (for similar findings, see Busch and Robertson, 1994). Also, earlier convictions for domestic violence are significantly correlated to the duration of pretrial detention. The offenders who were already convicted for domestic violence have a greater chance of being held longer under pretrial detention.

Offenders with a history of domestic violence convictions also have a greater chance of being sentenced to imprisonment. Most often, the offender committed violence against the same victim, but this correlation is also significant in cases when an earlier conviction relates to domestic violence against another victim. Research findings also show a significant correlation between earlier convictions for domestic violence and the length of the prison sentence. Offenders who were already convicted for domestic violence more often receive longer prison sentences than those convicted for the first time.

The findings on the significant correlation between earlier convictions for domestic violence and conditional sentences are in line with the above-mentioned findings: offenders who were sentenced previously for domestic violence have a lower chance of receiving a conditional sentence. However, there is no significant correlation between earlier domestic violence convictions and fines.

In addition to the correlation of pretrial detention and sanctions with earlier convictions for domestic violence, there is also a significant correlation between them and earlier convictions for other violent offenses. There is a significant positive correlation between earlier convictions for other violent offenses and arrest or pretrial detention, and duration of pretrial detention and prison sentences, as well as a negative correlation with conditional sentences.

The research did not discover any significant connection between previous convictions for nonviolent crimes and decisions about pretrial detention and sanctions. However, survey findings suggest that, in addition to legal recidivism, there is an impact of earlier reports of domestic violence to the police, regardless of whether they resulted in convictions. It seems that the decisions on both imprisonment and the conditional sentence were significantly dependent on the existence of earlier reports to the police, although courts lack guidance in this regard (Konstantinović-Vilić and Petrušić, 2004, 2007).

Earlier reports also have an impact on the decision on pretrial detention and fines, but this correlation is less significant.

Overall, survey findings on recidivism suggest that both earlier convictions and reports of domestic violence are strong predictors that an offender will be placed under pretrial detention and be sentenced to imprisonment or a fine, while they also decrease his or her chances of receiving a conditional sentence. Offenders with prior convictions also have a greater chance of being sentenced to longer imprisonment. These findings may suggest that the courts tend to react more harshly when the first conviction (almost always a conditional sentence) was not effective or did not stop further violence, but also in the cases where earlier reports did not lead to prosecution. However, this also suggests that they base their decisions on legal recidivism, since, as analyzed above in the section on continuity or isolated events, they do not take into consideration the overall context of victimization repeated over time, regardless of whether it was previously addressed by the criminal justice system. In this way, as observed in the early application of domestic violence laws in some other countries (Busch and Robertson, 1994), judges overlook the history of violence, power, and control in relationships, and thus fail to understand the distinctive nature of domestic violence in comparison to other violent crimes that occur as isolated events.

It is important to stress that the findings on recidivism concern a small number of those previously convicted (21)* and reported (47) for having committed domestic violence, and that the majority of those who were convicted or reported earlier are male offenders. Moreover, 78.7% of the men and 21.3% of the women from the sample were previously reported to the police for having committed domestic violence. Also, men constitute the majority of those convicted previously for having committed both domestic violence (85.7%) and other violent crimes (95%). Indeed, only three women were convicted earlier for domestic violence. Unlike men, who are sometimes convicted several times, all three of these women were convicted only once.

It is important to also mention that in the majority of cases (133, or 60.7%), there was no information available on previous domestic violence reports. In addition, it should be stressed that violent male partners sometimes falsely reported their female partners for domestic violence, which was one of the control tactics used as part of their abuse. The authors identified examples of good practice in that regard, in which some courts released

* Convictions included domestic violence as both a criminal offense and a misdemeanour.

the woman from charges in such cases and justified the decision by the lack of evidence that a criminal offense was committed.

Impact of Mutual Violence on the Application of Law in Domestic Violence Cases

Mutual violence between victims and offenders occurred in 38 cases (17.4%) included in the survey, while in the remaining cases, only one side was violent. Mutual violence occurred in 52.6% of partner violence cases and in 39.5% of cases of nonpartner violence. Less often, it occurred in cases with a combination of partner and nonpartner violence (7.9%). In cases of mutual violence, both sides are both offenders and victims, but their contribution may vary. There could be mutual violence in which both parties are equally or similarly responsible for the violence, or mutual violence in which one person is the primary aggressor and the secondary victim, and the other is the primary victim and the secondary abuser. This latter usually acts in self-defense or is provoked by the violence of the former.

In roughly more than one-third of all mutual violence cases, violence was committed as a defense from the attack of the other side (39.4%). Violence is committed in defense in a similar proportion in cases of partner (53.3%) and nonpartner (46.7%) abuse.

In 23 out of 38 cases of mutual violence, both sides were convicted* (60.5%). Thus, in the remaining cases (39.5%), only one of the perpetrators involved in the mutual violence was convicted, but he or she was not always the primary aggressor.

Also, women commit domestic violence more often in defense, that is, as a reaction to the other side's violence. The ratios between partner and nonpartner violence in these cases are similar (53.3% and 46.7%, respectively). In 19 cases, the primary aggressor or secondary victim was identified by research, which constitutes half (50%) of all offenders involved in mutual violence, and 8.6% of the sample.

The primary aggressors or secondary victims were convicted in 57.9% of cases of mutual violence. However, among those convicted were also those who were primarily victims or secondary aggressors. They were convicted in more than half (52.6%) of the cases of mutual violence, which is similar to the percentage of convicted primary aggressors.

There is a high correlation between the gender of the convicted perpetrator and cases where the victim was the primary aggressor. Secondary victims or primary aggressors were mostly observed in cases of convicted females; women were convicted twice as often as men despite being the primary victim.

There were convictions of primary victims in both partner (52.6%) and nonpartner (47.4%) violence cases. In these cases, the court considered domestic violence an isolated event, even when these events occurred one after the other and in a causal relationship, without properly considering, if at all, the continuous abuse or the fact that the primary victim or secondary aggressor acted in self-defense. These cases were mostly those of partner violence, but there were also cases of nonpartner violence (e.g., mutual violence between son and father). It seems that in cases of mutual violence, ignorance about the nature of both gender and other imbalanced power relations plays a role in the inappropriate application of the law.

* In some cases, there were several individuals on each side.

In these cases, the court's general attitude toward the abusive behavior of the primary aggressor or secondary victim was not to take into consideration the primary aggressor's responsibility, including his or her long-term violence and numerous reports to the police against him or her. In cases where one side (usually the male partner) had been abusive for a long time, and then assaulted the victim (usually the female partner) as part of the criminal offense for which they both were sentenced, and the victim reacted in self-defense, the court treated both equally.

Self-defense in these cases is not considered to be the grounds for legal self-defense. In Serbia, self-defense is defined as the defense that is necessary for the victim to repel a concurrent illegal assault (Article 19 of the code). Thus, it is assumed here that the interpretation of these cases as not having the appropriate grounds for being considered a concurrent reaction to an assault is decisive. Moreover, the courts did not consider these cases to have exceeded the limits of self-defense due to extreme provocation or fear caused by an assault. The author believes that, in at least several cases, the court could have treated the cases of women's violence as having exceeded the limits of self-defense, which would have very important legal consequences. Punishment of a perpetrator who has exceeded the limits of self-defense may be mitigated, while a perpetrator who exceeds the limit of self-defense due to extreme provocation or fear caused by assault may be acquitted. Moreover, in most of these cases, there was no mention in the verdict of previous abuse, that is, of otherwise a greater contribution of the primary aggressor, which led to both sides being sentenced either equally or very similarly. Only in one case was the primary victim or secondary aggressor (female) exempt from the charges.

It emerged that in domestic violence cases, there are fewer possibilities for the mitigation of the penalty than in cases of similar violent offenses committed against other persons. For example, a less severe punishment is prescribed for murder or bodily injury, but not for domestic violence, if it is committed in a state of extreme provocation or fear caused by the behavior or abuse of a victim. This is probably another consequence of this offense being considered an offense against the family, rather than against the person. Also, the excuse of self-defense is applied in a traditional manner, and there is no guidance for its application that takes into consideration the specific context of control and fear in domestic violence cases.

These findings clearly suggest that judges are not aware of the difference between primary and secondary aggressors, and that their interpretations in this regard are not appropriate and have negative consequences for the primary victims. The distinction between primary and secondary aggressor seems to be completely irrelevant in the application of laws on domestic violence in Serbia. Survey findings suggest the lack of correlation between the existence of secondary victim or primary aggressor and decisions on arrest or pretrial detention and criminal sanctions, that is, sentences. The results of quantitative analyses are supported by a qualitative analysis of court files, which do not contain any sign of identifying and giving importance to the difference between the primary and secondary aggressor.

Victim Support for Prosecution and Penalty

The survey findings suggest a significant correlation between the victim's support for prosecution and decisions about penalties (imprisonment and fines), as well as a negative correlation with conditional sentences.

The obtained findings seem to confirm earlier findings in this regard (Konstantinović-Vilić and Petrušić, 2007) and provide additional proof that court decisions greatly depend on victim support of prosecution.

However, most victims do not support prosecution, and those who do not support it are predominantly women. This has very important gender implications since women victims of long-term violence are often afraid to support prosecution or do not support it because they want their partners to change or receive medical treatment rather than be punished. These findings may suggest the importance of support that women receive during the criminal procedure, which may also encourage them to support prosecution: "Women who receive support from specialized advocacy services are more likely to give evidence and more satisfied with the legal proceedings" (Council of Europe, 2006).

Aggravating and Mitigating Circumstances Taken into Consideration in Sentencing

Qualitative analyses of mitigating and aggravating circumstances taken into consideration in sentencing for domestic violence showed that the courts usually only redraft legal text, stating that all mitigating and aggravating circumstances are taken into consideration without listing them or, just as for any other criminal offense, list several such circumstances, such as whether the offender has a family or children, the age of the offender (too young or too old), whether the offender was convicted previously, whether the offender had confessed or repented, whether the victim supported prosecution, or whether the victim had claimed compensation. These circumstances are often only formally enlisted, and often make little sense when related to a man who has been abusive against his wife and children for years (see Konstantinović-Vilić and Petrušić, 2004, 2007; Jovanović, 2010). For example, the age of the offender was mentioned without explaining the reason for which it was considered a mitigating circumstance.

Earlier convictions are among the most often mentioned aggravating circumstances; however, verdicts rarely specify the criminal offenses underlying the convictions. It was mentioned only in a few cases that earlier convictions were for domestic violence or other violent offenses. Only rarely was factual recidivism, that is, continuity of violence, mentioned as an aggravating circumstance. Sometimes, facts such as there were several victims and the victim was pregnant were also considered aggravating circumstances.

In addition, in several cases, the fact that the offender was under the influence of alcohol was considered a mitigating circumstance. Also, in two cases, the victim's contribution to the violence was considered a mitigating circumstance. However, in both cases, there were female victims or secondary aggressors who reacted to long-term abuse of the predominant aggressor. On the other hand, the long-term primary abuse was usually not taken into consideration as an aggravating circumstance. In addition, in one case of mutual violence, the court mentioned as an aggravating circumstance the degree to which the object of protection, that is, the family, was endangered by the mutual violence of both partners, without making any distinction between the primary and secondary aggressor. This example clearly shows what is implicitly recognizable from other data, that is, that judges consider domestic violence a crime against the family rather than against the person.

Discussion and Conclusion

Similarly as in other countries, findings of the survey carried out in Serbia suggest that there is an impact of both gender and other factors on the application of law on domestic violence by the criminal courts in Serbia.

It is obvious that men are more often arrested and placed under pretrial detention, as well as sentenced to imprisonment and fine, which is consistent with results of Kingsnorth and MacIntosh's (2007) and Garner and Maxwell's (2009) research. However, unlike some research (Henning and Feder, 2005; Kingsnorth and MacIntosh, 2007), where the results indicate that gender is a significant predictor of imprisonment in domestic violence cases, findings of the survey carried out in Serbia suggest that there is no significant correlation between gender and imprisonment. These findings suggest that other factors, such as the seriousness of the violence, established continuity of violence, and recidivism, have a more decisive influence on these decisions. This is confirmed by data on the influence of other factors. Courts imposed prison sentences more often in cases where they treated the offense of domestic violence as part of a wider context of long-term violence. Survey findings show a significant correlation between the type of violence and decisions on arrest or pretrial detention and sanction. Also, the chances that the perpetrator is arrested or placed under pretrial detention and sentenced to prison increase with the increase in the severity of the violence, which is in line with similar findings of Henning and Feder (2005), Hirschel and Hutchison (2001), Ferraro (1989), and Worrall et al. (2006). Moreover, the fact that other members of the family were abused (both adults and minors) in addition to the partner has a strong impact on decisions on arrest or custody and sanctions. Research findings also suggest that alcoholism has a significant impact on the police decision on arrest and the court's decision on pretrial detention, but not on decisions on penalties or conditional sentences. Security measures aimed to provide medical treatment for the perpetrator are not imposed on all those who committed violence in connection with alcoholism. In contrast to the above-mentioned findings are findings that suggest the lack of a significant connection between the use of weapons and arrest, pretrial detention, and sanctions. These findings are in contrast to those of Henning and Feder (2005) and Worrall et al. (2006), which found that offenders are more often arrested, placed under pretrial detention, or sentenced to prison if they used a weapon during the violent attack.

Earlier convictions and reports of domestic violence have the strongest impact on decisions on arrest or pretrial detention and sentence. This may indicate that the police and the judges believed that this constituted proof that the domestic violence had a longer history, that is, that it was more dangerous. Also, the impact of earlier convictions for other violent crimes is identified. However, survey findings suggest that the court mostly took into consideration legal recidivism of the offender.

The survey discovered some examples of good practice, particularly in taking into consideration the history of violence and the nonconviction of women who were reported by their abusers. These examples may be used for training the police, prosecutors, and judges; the judges who applied these good practices can be involved in this training.

Moreover, this survey shows important gender implications in the application of domestic violence law in Serbia, rather than direct discrimination against women. These implications are generally related to the inappropriate treatment of cases where there is continuous violence (usually male VAW), as well as cases of mutual violence where the victim (usually male) is the primary aggressor, yet the woman is convicted, although the primary victim. It is clear that the police, prosecutors, and judges do not understand the history of violence, power, and control in male–female relationships, which has serious negative consequences on how they apply domestic violence laws (Busch and Robertson, 1994).

The survey also exposed the lack of some highly important information in the court files, but also in the public prosecutors' and police files, and how this may have negative consequences for monitoring the application of domestic violence laws. This is partly explained by the lack of or underdeveloped intersector cooperation and exchange of information, particularly between the civil and criminal courts, and partly due the fact that the police, public prosecutors, and judges are not obliged to keep records of important information.

Missing information includes, in particular, the following: detailed information about the victim, including any previous abuse by the offender (if the primary aggressor) and the impact that the domestic violence had on the victim; information on the protection order; information on related parental right or child custody procedures initiated or measures taken, as well as other child protection measures taken; and information on the presence of a representative of a victim support organization. Also, information about victim or witness protection measures initiated or applied was available only in several court files and mostly related to the protection of minor victims. However, since the courts are not obliged to keep records of this important information, it is difficult to assess whether these measures failed to be applied or whether the information was missing. Since in Serbia it is not obligatory to notify the victim about the release of the perpetrator, it is not unusual that this information was unavailable in the court files.

The identification of information missing is very important for future (court) monitoring activities. It is particularly important as the basis for advocacy for the advancement of a Serbian criminal justice data recording system in general and in relation to domestic violence in particular.

References

Belknap, J., and Graham, D. (2000). Factors related to domestic violence court dispositions in a large urban area: The role of victim/witness reluctance and other variables—Final report. Washington, DC: National Institute of Justice.

Busch, R., and Robertson, N. (1993). "What's love got to do with it?": An analysis of an intervention approach to domestic violence. *Waikato Law Review*, 1, 109–140.

Busch, R., and Robertson, N. (1994). Ain't no mountain high enough (to keep me from getting to you): An analysis of the Hamilton Abuse Intervention Pilot Project. In J. Stubbs (ed.), *Women, Male Violence and the Law* (pp. 34–63). Sydney: Institute of Criminology, Sydney University Law School.

California Alliance against Domestic Violence. (2000). *Domestic Violence Arrests: Beyond the Obvious. Improving Strategies in the New Millennium*. Sacramento: California Alliance against Domestic Violence.

Council of Europe. (2006). Combating violence against women—Stocktaking study on the measures and actions taken in Council of Europe member states. Retrieved from http://www.coe.int/t/dghl/standardsetting/equality/03themes/violence-against-women/CDEG(2006)3_en.pdf.

Cramer, E. (1999). Variables that predict verdicts in domestic violence cases. *Journal of Interpersonal Violence*, 14(11), 1137–1150.

Davis, R., Smith, B., and Taylor, B. (2003). Increasing the proportion of domestic violence arrests that are prosecuted: A natural experiment in Milwaukee. *Criminology & Public Policy*, 2(2), 263–282.

Dawson, M., and Dinovitzer, R. (2001). Victim cooperation and the prosecution of domestic violence in a specialized court. *Justice Quarterly*, 18(3), 593–622.

DeKeseredy, W. S., Alvi, S., Schwartz, M. D., and Perry, B. (1999). Violence against and the harassment of women in Canadian public housing. *Canadian Review of Sociology and Anthropology*, 36, 499–516.

Eigenberg, H., Scarborough, K., and Kappeler, V. (1996). Contributory factors affecting arrest in domestic and non-domestic assaults. *American Journal of Police*, 15(4), 27–54.

Ferraro, K. (1989). Policing woman battering. *Social Problems*, 36(1), 61–74.

Garner, J. H., and Maxwell, C. D. (2009). Prosecution and conviction rates for intimate partner violence. *Criminal Justice Review*, 34(1), 44–79.

Henning, K., and Feder, L. (2005). Criminal prosecution of domestic violence offenses: An investigation of factors predictive of court outcomes. *Criminal Justice and Behavior*, 32(6), 612–642.

Hirschel, D., and Hutchison, I. (2001). The relative effects of offence, offender, and victim variables on decision to prosecute domestic violence cases. *Violence against Women*, 7(1), 46–59.

Jovanović, S. (2010). *Pravna zaštita od nasilja u porodici* [Legal Protection from Domestic Violence]. Belgrade: Institut za kriminološka i sociološka istraživanja.

Kingsnorth, R. F., and MacIntosh, R. C. (2007). Intimate partner violence: The role of suspect gender in prosecutorial decision making. *Justice Quarterly*, 24(3), 460–497.

Konstantinović-Vilić, S., and Petrušić, N. (2004). *Krivično delo nasilja u porodici: pravna praksa u Republici Srbiji* [Criminal Offense Domestic Violence: Legal Practice in Republic of Serbia]. Niš: Ženski istraživački centar za edukaciju i komunikaciju.

Konstantinović-Vilić, S., and Petrušić, N. (2007). *Krivično delo nasilja u porodici—aktuelna pravosudna praksa u Beogradu i Nišu* [Criminal Offense of Domestic Violence—Actual Legal Practice in Belgrade and Nis]. Belgrade: Autonomni ženski centar and Ženski istraživački centar za edukaciju i komunikaciju Niš.

Martin, M. E. (1997). Double your trouble: Dual arrest in family violence. *Journal of Family Violence*, 12(2), 139–157.

Miller, S. (2001). The paradox of women arrested for domestic violence: Criminal justice professionals and service providers respond. *Violence against Women*, 7(12), 1339–1376.

Russell, B., Ragatz, L. L., and Kraus, S. W. (2009). Does ambivalent sexism influence verdicts for heterosexual and homosexual domestic violence in self-defense cases? *Journal of Family Violence*, 24(3), 145–147.

Schmidt, J., and Steury, E. (1989). Prosecutorial discretion in filling charges in domestic violence cases, *Criminology*, 27(3), 487–510.

Sudderth, L. (2010). Improving data collection on violence against women in South East Europe. UNIFEM. Retrieved from http://www.unifem.sk/uploads/doc/ImprovingDataCollectionOnVAW.pdf.

Worrall, J., Ross, J., and McCord, E. (2006). Modeling prosecutors' charging decisions in domestic violence cases. *Crime & Delinquency*, 53(2), 472–503.

Labeling of Denotified Tribes
Revisiting the Ramoshis in Maharashtra, India

12

DATTATREYA BHANDALKAR

Contents

Introduction

Labeling theory is one of the most important theories in criminology. It is one of the important theories that focuses on the criminalization process and highlights social responses to crime and deviance. It also emphasizes the criminalization process as the cause of crime and how labeled persons behave after labeling. Very importantly, it suggests that crime may be heightened by criminal sanctions stigmatizing them and leading to other severe consequences. In 1938, Tannenbaum proposed that individuals who were identified, stigmatized, or labeled in any special way would eventually behave as the label suggested. Tannenbaum called this process the "dramatization of evil." Lemert (1951) developed this idea further with the distinction between primary deviance, which is the initial act leading to the label, and secondary deviance, which occurs after an individual accepts the label and acts on it. Lemert's ideas are now known as societal reaction theory, and other theorists, such as Becker (1963), Erikson (1966), Schur (1971), and Hartjen (1974), have contributed to the theory.

Braithwaite (1989) proposed that shaming is utilized by society—specifically, the criminal justice system—as a form of social control. Shaming can be reintegrative or disintegrative. Reintegrative shaming occurs temporarily while the offender is being punished, but once punishment is complete, the offender is welcomed back into society (Katz, 2002). Such an approach allows the offender to once more become a fully contributing member of society. Disintegrative shaming occurs when an offender is not welcomed back into society upon completion of a sentence and is instead shunned and stigmatized. According to Braithwaite, such treatment creates a group of social outcasts who become increasingly entrenched in the criminal lifestyle. Disintegrative shaming is also considered permanently detrimental to one's self-esteem (Katz, 2002). At the core of labeling theory is the assumption that the label *deviant* can be both the cause and the effect of criminal behavior (Akers, 2000). Today, labeling theorists focus more on the process of how the label is applied and what its social context is (Akers, 2000). Braithwaite (1989) distinguishes between reintegrative shaming and disintegrative shaming, the latter of which occurs when an offender is prevented from reintegrating and reconnecting to society and may in response commit subsequent offenses.

As Becker (1963) argues, social groups create rules in society whose violation constitutes deviance. These are rules of sanctions put by dominant others in society on particular groups. Labeling theory highlights social responses to crime and deviance. It emphasizes what happens to criminals after they are labeled, and suggests that crime may be heightened by criminal sanctions stigmatizing them and leading to other severe consequences. A label can be applied formally or informally. Formal labeling would come from institutions such as the police, courts, and corrections. Informal labeling would come from parents, peers, and so forth. Application of a formal label through sanctioning magnifies the effect of labeling (Adler and Laufer, 1993).

Labeling theory arose from the study of deviance in the late 1950s and early 1960s. Tannenbaum was among the early labeling theorists. His main concept was the dramatization of evil. He argued that

> the process of tagging, defining, identifying, segregating, describing, and emphasizing any individual out for special treatment becomes a way of stimulating, suggesting, and evoking the very traits that are complained of. A person becomes the thing they are described as being. (Tannenbaum, 1938, p. 19–20)

Labeling theory or social reaction theory focuses on the linguistic tendency of majorities to negatively label minorities or those seen as deviant from norms. Labeling theory or social reaction theory is concerned with how the self-identity and behavior of individuals may be determined or influenced by the terms used to describe or classify them, and is associated with the concept of a self-fulfilling prophecy and stereotyping.

Lemert was the founder of the *societal reaction* approach. Briefly, this approach distinguishes between primary deviance (where individuals do not see themselves a deviant) and secondary deviance (which involves acceptance of a deviant status). Primary deviance arises for a wide variety of reasons, biological, psychological, or sociological. Secondary or intensified deviance becomes a means of defense, attack, or adaptation to the problems caused by societal reaction to primary deviation. Societal reaction theorists claim that the process of defining and suppressing deviance is important to social solidarity. Approaches to deviance assumed that deviance could be understood as consisting of behavior that violates social norms. Deviance is therefore something objective: it is a particular form of behavior. Labeling theory rejected this approach and claimed that deviance is not a way of behaving, but is a name put on something as a label. Law is culturally and historically variable: what is crime today is not necessarily crime yesterday or tomorrow.

Individuals who were arrested, prosecuted, and punished may be labeled as criminals. Others view these people as criminals, and this increases the likelihood of subsequent crime for several reasons. Labeled individuals generally have trouble obtaining legitimate employment, which increases their level of strain and reduces their stake in conformity. Labeled individuals also find that conventional people are reluctant to associate with them, and they may associate with other criminals as a result. This reduces their bond with conventional others and fosters the social learning of crime. Labeled individuals may eventually come to view themselves as criminals and act in accord with this self-concept.

Labeling and reacting to offenders as "criminals" has its negative consequences, aggravating the criminal behavior and making the crime problem worse. Being a criminal becomes a person's master status. It controls the way they are identified in public. People who are labeled deviant tend to lose contact with their conformist friends and start associating with similarly labeled deviants.

Denotified tribes in India are a unique example of how a group of people can be labeled as criminal by birth and segregated from the mainstream population. People belonging to such groups are prone to discrimination and victimization. Time has changed, but the label attached to their community haunts them even today. Culture conflicts arising out of caste, religion, class, and ethnicity are among the significant fault lines that hinder development and result in victimization of vulnerable and marginalized groups. A significant number of marginalized tribal communities in India, once classified and declared as criminals with the declaration of the Criminal Tribes Act (CTA) in 1871, were registered and notified as criminals. They continue to live with stigma, discrimination, and exclusion, deprived and denied of many of their basic rights even today. They are victimized not only in the hands of polity, society, and state machinery, but also in the hands of other dominant sections of the society. They are still referred to as "born criminals" by many in our modern-day society. The label attached to them continues over generations. This chapter makes an attempt to understand the views and experiences of Ramoshi tribes and how they are labeled in society by using the conceptual tool of labeling theory. It also emphasizes issues like the origin of the process of construction of labeling, the process of continued labeling over years, and the effects on the community.

Denotified Tribes in India

The term *denotified tribes* includes all those communities who were notified under the several versions of CTAs enforced during the British rule between 1871 and 1947 throughout the Indian territory and were "denotified" by the repeal of these acts after the independence of India. In India, denotified tribes are also known as *Vimuktajaatis*, or the Ex-criminal tribes, because they were branded as criminals by birth under the CTA of 1871, enacted by the British government. In spite of the repeal of the act in 1952, they are still being treated as criminals by birth and subjected to harassment and persecution at the hands of the police and the state machinery. The denotified and nomadic tribes (DNTs) are an integral part of the Indian society. The DNTs are not just a neglected section, but a complex one as well. Their problems are not only grounded in contemporary reality, but also deeply rooted in history. They have suffered injustices at the hands of both polity and society, but their issues are not sufficiently redressed (Bokil, 2002).

The nomadic and denotified tribes constitute about 6 million people in Maharashtra and about 60 million all over India (Rathod, 2000). A majority of these tribes still exhibit their primitive and ethnic traits. Many of them still live in tribal groups, wander from one place to another in search of livelihood, and do not have any permanent shelter of their own. They are still a wandering community with no specific occupation, poor education, and no employment, wandering in search of livelihood. They have specific rituals, beliefs, and religious practices of their own, and those are unique to themselves. Neither globalization, liberalization, nor open market economy could improve their situations to a significant extent. Although the "criminal tribes" were decriminalized with the repeal of the CTA of 1871 postindependence by the government of India, it made no special provisions to improve their situations. The denotified communities were not categorized under any special constitutional schedules like the scheduled caste and scheduled tribes. Hence, no special provisions were designed to address the problems of the denotified communities. In a few states, some of the DNTs have been included in the respective state lists of either scheduled castes or scheduled tribes. However, there is no uniformity in the status of these tribes across the country. With the declaration of the CTA of 1871 and through its several versions, the police were given arbitrary powers to not only have control over the tribes by restricting their movements and supervising their actions, but also kill tribesmen. Being declared criminals by the British government, the tribe was perceived differently as "others" in society. They were not accepted and allowed to mingle with the mainstream population.

Postindependence after the repeal of the act in 1952, although the population was decriminalized, no efforts were made to reintegrate the tribes with mainstream society. They continued to be viewed differently by other dominant sections in society. The atrocities with these tribes continued over ages, and no provisions are being made to protect the rights of these tribes. The human rights violations against the denotified tribes are not protected by legislation, such as the Scheduled Castes and Scheduled Tribes (Prevention of Atrocities) Act (1989). Being primarily nomadic in nature even today, most of these tribes remain excluded from enumeration in the census. In most cases, they do not have any proof of identification, like the voter ID or ration card, and remain denied of their citizenship rights.

The Ramoshis in Maharashtra, India

The Ramoshis, once declared the criminal tribe in Bombay Presidency, were involved in uprisings against the British. The Ramoshis, often referred to as a "warrior tribe," are primarily a wandering population; their traditional occupations are as hunters, gatherers, and guardsmen. The tribe used to reside primarily in the districts of Maharashtra and the northwest districts of Karnataka. They were also based in some parts of Andhra Pradesh. The Ramoshis in Karnataka and Andhra Pradesh were referred to as *Berad* and *Boya*. The Ramoshis were primarily concentrated in areas of the Kolhapur, Satara, Sangli, Solapur, and Pune districts of Maharashtra. They had served the Marathas as a fighting force. The Ramoshis had served the great king for Maharashtra, *Chhatrapati Shivaji Maharaj*, for a very long period. The tribe was actively involved in protection of the boundaries of the kingdom. In the early nineteenth century, the British National Forest Policy and the conflicts it created over forest use forced many of these tribes, who were dependent on the forests for their livelihood, to draw on their traditions of force of arms, into criminal livelihoods. Consequently, along with other tribal groups that forcibly opted for thefts, plundering, or similar activities in order to earn their livelihood with the change in the forest policy, the Ramoshis were declared a criminal tribe under the CTA of 1871. The tribe had organized themselves and revolted against the British. The rising protest against the British alarmed them, and eventually with the declaration of CTA, the Ramoshis were notified. Although postindependence the tribes were decriminalized, they were further classified and notified as "habitual offenders" with the declaration of the Habitual Offenders Act of 1959 and later notified further as denotified tribes.

The Ramoshis were the first among many of these wandering tribal communities who started settling down in villages, postindependence. They usually resided outside the main village community. Some of them continued staying in the settlements, and others continued their nomadic nature. Being primarily a nomadic population, they were unsettled and had no lands for cultivation. In crisis of earning their livelihood, they continued wandering from one place to the other. The situations of the Ramoshis have not significantly changed over the years; they continue to be labeled in society and the stigma persists.

Methodology of the Study

This study is an empirical research undertaken with a qualitative research paradigm in order to explore the reality of the denotified tribes. The journey of this research began with exploring various literatures about the denotified population, helping to understand various contexts pertaining to the social reality of the subject of the study. The literature review helped to develop an in-depth understanding of the denotified tribes at large and identify the areas still unexplored and untold about the tribes that demanded further inquiry. The qualitative research paradigm provided a platform to understand the social reality pertaining to a context and allowed the research process to be nonlinear, iterative, and responsive to the field situation and remain context specific. The research followed an exploratory research design with a case study methodology. The study was an empirical inquiry that investigated a phenomenon within its real-life context. This qualitative study had adopted an interpretive paradigm (Burrell and Morgan, 1979). The research was conducted with the Ramoshi tribe residing in Phaltantaluka of the Satara district in Maharashtra.

The research participants were individuals from both within and outside the Ramoshi community, belonging to different age groups. Apart from individuals within the community, the participants included individuals from other dominant castes, police personnel from the local police station, and a school teacher residing in the village. The researcher reached out to the local community-based organizations working with issues related to the tribesmen specifically, identified and reached out to the key village leaders, attended village meetings initially, and then started residing in the village, among the tribesmen, to observe them in a nonparticipant manner. The participants were identified using a purposive sampling technique and postfield observations, such that in-depth and relevant data could be captured from the participants. The researcher conducted in-depth interviews with individual participants and also focus group discussions with youth and other tribesmen.

The researcher used multiple research techniques in order to ensure and increase the reliability and validity of the findings of the study. The triangulation method (Mason, 1996, p. 25) was deployed using in-depth unstructured interviews, focus group discussion, and nonparticipant observation methods for the purpose of data collection. The responses of participants were recorded and translated in English, and verbatim transcripts were developed, followed by case narratives. Case narrations were developed from the transcripts and analyzed individually. A cross-case analysis method was also used to analyze the cases. A group of common themes emerged from it, which were discussed and confirmed with the participants. The researcher captured the theme or pattern prominent across cases based on the subject of the study. The unique themes or patterns arising were further analyzed using a case study method. A theoretical sampling technique was used during the process of data collection.

Reflections from the Field: The Voices Unheard

This section elaborates upon the history of the community, the situation of the Ramoshi tribe, and their experiences of being denotified in society, and also discusses the reasons identified by the researcher as primary causes resulting in stigma and discrimination. It uncovers the historical situation that impacts the lives of the Ramoshis in Maharashtra. Further, it aims to explain how the historical background of the community has impacted the lives of the Ramoshis leading to the origin of labeling among the tribe.

Ramoshis are one among many such tribes in India who were declared a criminal tribe with the declaration of the CTA of 1871 by the British. The tribe predominantly belongs to the state of Maharashtra; however, the responses of the participants also mention the history of the Ramoshi population residing in the states of Andhra Pradesh and Karnataka and migrating to Maharashtra. This was predominantly because of the wandering nature of the tribe, and they were primarily involved in the occupations of hunting, gathering, and wandering in search of their livelihood. The responses of the participants also mention the tribe being actively involved with Chhatrapati Shivaji Maharaj, one of the greatest kings in Maharashtra. The Ramoshis used to work as guardsmen and protectors for of all the king's forts. This helped the tribe get recognition among other people in society. They were referred to as the warrior tribe. Only a few Ramoshis are actively involved in the occupation of protection; a significant section are still hunters, gatherers, and wanderers and did not have any fixed occupation within the community. The caste-based classification of occupation had fixed jobs for almost all communities in society. The Ramoshis, like a few other then-declared denotified tribes, were in contrast to this scenario. They were wanderers, moving from one place to another in search of livelihood, and had no fixed occupation. The responses of the participants from within the tribe primarily emphasize that the declaration of the CTA of 1871 in British India changed the scenario of the Ramoshis in society. The tribe was suddenly perceived as criminals in society.

One of the community members shared that according to the CTA of 1871 in British India, the Ramoshis were declared criminals. The British referred their leader, Umaji Naik, who organized the Ramoshis to fight against the British, as a traitor. The community mainly used to work for the police *Patil*, village *Patil*, and moneylenders (*Sahukars*). These people used to exploit Ramoshis for their personal purposes and criminal activities. An elderly person of the community shared about the nomadic nature of Ramoshis. He said,

> Ramoshi community had a Nomadic culture; they were not supposed to stay at one village for more than three days. Even our rites during funeral do not happen on the tenth day but on the third day. This too signifies our nomadic nature. The upper caste people used Ramoshis as personal guards or in other activities like kidnapping, blackmailing, etc. At times the Ramoshis were forced by upper castes to involve themselves in murders, loots, etc.

The response of the elderly participant clearly indicates not only the nomadic nature of the community, but also the caste hierarchy existing, and how the tribe was often utilized by the other dominant sections for their personal purposes.

He further added,

> In 1959 after the enactment of the Habitual Offenders Act, Ramoshis started getting settled at villages and they received lands under 16B regulation of the act. Only some of them could

> start agriculture farming in the lands. The lands were mostly in hilly areas and were barren and infertile in nature.

The Ramoshis were primarily landless, and hence did not have any agricultural activity to generate income for the family. If they were settled in a particular village, they used to work as manual laborers in the lands of other dominant castes in the village at a very meager wage. In some cases, they used to provide labor in exchange for grains. In cases where the Ramoshis received land under the regulations, it was primarily in hilly areas, and hence was barren and infertile in nature. This hindered their agricultural activity, affecting their income.

A youth member of the community, when asked about the history of the community, mentioned the origin of the tribe. He said that Ramoshi means *Ram-vanshi*, descendent of Hindu lord Ram. He added that this tribe had its origin in the southern part of India. They were guards and warriors in various kingdoms in South India and Maharashtra. As ages passed and kingdoms disappeared, Ramoshis started working at the village *Patil* leader's house. The main work pattern of Ramoshis was guarding their houses, farms, and whatever the *Patils* said they should do. In exchange for this work, they were given grain and money, as well as clothes on a yearly basis. At some villages, the system of *Balutedari** is still prevalent.

Another young member of the community mentioned,

> According to Balutedari (Jajmani system) there were fixed jobs for each community but not for Ramoshis. So they started stealing for upper caste communities, providing them security, guard them from other powerful people in society, etc. In British era the Ramoshis used to work for Sahukar (moneylenders), rich people of the village. They used to plunder rich travelers, rich people of other villages and they used to offer the entire wealth to the Sahukar. The Sahukars in return used to give grains and other groceries for their family.

The responses of the participants within the community primarily highlight the prevalence of the occupational crisis among the tribe. Due to the prevalence of caste-based occupations among people in Hindu society, every individual has a specific occupation based on the caste in which he or she is born. But the Ramoshis were primarily a nomadic population, unsettled in nature, depending on the forests for their livelihood. They were hunters, gatherers, and guardsmen. With the change in the British National Forest Policy, their means of earning a livelihood was threatened. They were forced into alternate means of earning a living. Some of the dominant castes took advantage of this situation and used these tribes for their personal purposes. This indulged their involvement in crime and other illegal activities.

When asked about involvement in crime and illegal activities, a member of the community added that initially crime was a source of their livelihood, but now involvement in crime is much less. He added that in some illegal activities, like wine and liquor production and the threatening of villagers, the Ramoshis are involved. Because of their involvement with politicians and also illegal means of liquor production, the police notice the

* *Balutedars* were the hereditary village servants, who were classified based on the caste they belonged to. Their roles and responsibilities in the villages were defined based on the occupation-based caste classification. The concept of *Balutedars* stratified all the individuals, based on their castes, into specific subgroups.

Ramoshis. But now, mostly people work as casual laborers in agricultural lands, as daily wage earners, although a part of the population is still involved in criminal activities. He aggressively remarked, "But as far as caste is concerned Ramoshis are labeled and seen still as criminals."

Because of the occupation, the Ramoshis were identified with dacoits and referred to as criminals in society. According to one community member, who is also a leader in the village among the Ramoshis,

> This criminal label was attached with this community since then as they were involved in plundering the upper castes and all sorts of criminal activities in society. They were also involved in liquor production and other addictive activities. Since there was no fixed occupation attached to this caste, they became habitual to stealing, plundering and they started enjoying the fear in other people's eyes. The people in upper caste were using them for their purpose and they only stigmatized them in society. Some people but not all in the community were once involved in crime, but the whole community still today is labeled as criminal.

An elderly person said that initially crime was a source of livelihood for Ramoshis, but now involvement in crime is much less. He added that at the village level, if a Ramoshi goes to another's field, then people think that he came to steal vegetables. At times, Ramoshi people were involved in agricultural stealing, so villagers still look at them suspiciously. He reflects that the tribe is not involved in serious crimes now. They are mostly involved in liquor selling, sandalwood smuggling, and petty theft. There were such groups who used to be dangerous dacoits in the past. Ramoshis were primarily involved in plundering and theft. But later, even though they were not involved in any such activity, police officials would arrest them without any reason. They had no basis for the arrest, but because they belonged to this community, they were arrested. However, the frequency of such incidences is gradually decreasing.

One of the community members commented that Ramoshis stay out of the village or at the entrance of the village, but separate from others. Although the villagers do not directly refer to them as criminals, they make it evident that they still consider them as such by their behavior. Their children are also affected by such discriminating behavior. Because of their involvement in the illegal liquor business and drinking, police officials frequently arrest the Ramoshis and beat them in front of family members. Ramoshis have started searching other profitable business. Some groups are becoming involved in sandalwood smuggling or illegal smuggling of river sand to small contractors of the construction industry. The location of the houses of these tribes also indicates that they are treated differently from the rest of the villagers. Due to the location of the houses, their involvement in village activities is also limited. Because these villages are geographically backward or located in dry areas, Ramoshis are searching for new means of earning their livelihoods. The community member emphasized, "According to me because of their situation they are forced to do crime. They are forced to do it for their survival." Another Ramoshi added, "Our village is also known as *Chorachegaon* [thieves' village]. As compared to other community, if any crime occurs police first verify the crime and then, they arrest but in our cases, this does not happen. Police first arrests us and then they verify. It is only because of our image as criminal in past, innocent people even today face problems."

These responses highlight that involvement in crime and other illegal activities is primarily because of their occupation crisis and no means of earning a livelihood. The responses also show that the Ramoshis are still perceived as criminals. The location of their houses, their village being named *Chorachegaon*, indicates clearly that the tribe is stigmatized and discriminated against. Due to poor economic conditions, they are forced to participate in illegal activities, and their addiction to liquor also impacts their situations. Due to their involvement in crime, the local police officials often arrest them. The ill treatment by local police officials, the perception of others in the village, the location of their houses, and their poor involvement in village activities imply that the tribe is still subject to stigma and discrimination.

The responses of the participants from both within and outside the Ramoshi community elaborate upon the incidences and experiences of stigma and discrimination among the tribe. One of the community members shared that according to the British government, Ramoshis were declared to be criminal tribes, but in 1952 this act was demolished by the Indian government; however, the impact of that act continues to affect the community. The Ramoshis were again notified as habitual offenders, those habituated to commit offenses. He adds that this tribe is not discriminated against noticeably, but people's perception of Ramoshis should change. They still believe that Ramoshis are associated with crime. Although people do not directly accuse Ramoshis, if there is a crime in a nearby village, like theft or an agriculture crime, the villagers doubt them.

A youth member from the community shared his experiences. He said,

> In my school life I faced so much discrimination being a Ramoshi. We used to have separate seats from other students in school and even if we stood first in our school then also our identity will be Ramoshi or if stood last then also we remain the same. People used to say that Ramoshis are not supposed to get educated.

At the village level during celebrations, Ramoshis have to sit on the other side during lunch or dinner. However, this does not happen very frequently and distinctly. Although situations have changed, people's perception of the Ramoshis has not changed over the years. Even in Marathi cinemas, Ramoshis play the role of villains. The projection of Ramoshi men in Marathi cinemas has also been primarily that of a villain, a negative role involved in plundering, thefts, kidnapping, and other criminal activities. This projection as a negative character adds to creating stigma for the community. The viewers still identify Ramoshis as criminal tribes. This underlying categorization is always experienced and felt.

An elderly member of the community added,

> Even today Ramoshis do not have appropriate reservation facility in Maharashtra. I feel we were ignored, deprived and discriminated by the government due to political reasons and also sometimes due to personal rivalry. There are different Committees formed for the welfare of the OBCs [other backward classes], but they are not functioning properly. The reservation policy fails to cover OBCs to their extent of need. There are not much appropriate schemes available for VJNT [*Vimuktajaties* and nomadic tribes] communities. Over the years our people have started developing on their own, we cannot rely on the government.

A youth from the community added that in the village, they are treated differently and have a negative image. People see them differently. People think that Ramoshis were dacoits and still are. He mentioned that the criminal involvement of Ramoshis has reduced over the years, but they are still perceived differently by others. He said, "We always get secondary status in society."

There are many cases registered where Ramoshis were arrested without any involvement in crime or any evidence of being accused. The tribe has had to fight against this *harassment by local police* for years. The tribesmen in villages wrote letters to ministries to address the mistreatment of police officials toward Ramoshis. The responses of a few Ramoshi youth mention that there are many false cases registered against the Ramoshis. Based on the false cases, the local police still exploit Ramoshis, and if they go to register any case against the upper caste, the police officials refuse to register the same. They do not follow any procedure for arrest. Because of their historical background, the community police officials refuse to listen to the Ramoshis.

An elderly community member shared an incident in his village. He added that Ramoshis used to do crime, but mostly they used to get harassed due to the suspicious nature of the police. Many times, police come to the village to arrest the Ramoshis. He added,

> Some days before, in the nearby village there was a case of theft and police started investigation. After one day police directly came to our village and arrested four males from our community and they took their fingerprints, measured their footprints and held them in lock ups for two days. After two days they allowed them to go home. Like this many incidents still happen; only on the basis of suspicion police arrest our community people and they do not even register that they arrested such person. The harassments and exploitation of our community happens simply because our community was known as the community of criminals.

A member of the community added, "Initially local police used to arrest our people for any petty reason and they used to beat them and force them to accept the fact that this crime is done by him. There were too many harassment cases which happened due to suspicious identity of Ramoshis." An outsider of the community said, "If police van comes to our village you will see the picture that these people start running to hide themselves." The reason behind such reactions of Ramoshis toward the police van is due to pending cases. If the police arrest them, then their family members have to continue the business. Many times, they pay some money to be released from lockup. This business is also negatively impacting their children.

The responses highlight that the local police officials are a major threat to the tribe. On the one hand, where the local police are supposed to be the law bearers and protectors from atrocities for these tribes, the Ramoshis are harassed and ill treated by them. The historical background of the community plays a crucial role here. The Ramoshis being labeled as a criminal tribe has created a negative image in society. In spite of the repeal of the CTA in 1952 and the community being decriminalized long before, this negative image has prevailed in the eyes of the society over the years. The CTA gave arbitrary powers to the police to control the tribes. Even though the act has been abolished, the image has remained and the police continue to utilize the power. Unfortunately, the protectors have become the primary threats to the Ramoshis in these villages. The process of being labeled as criminals, though, started with the declaration of the CTA in 1871, and has continued over the years and impacted the community immensely.

Being Labeled as Criminals: The Origin and Process of Labeling

The responses regarding the historical background of the community across the 10 case studies suggest that the CTA of 1871 played a significant role in the lives of the Ramoshis. It was a turning point in the history of the Ramoshis, since the British legally declared them to be criminals in society. This action imposed the label of *criminal* upon the Ramoshis. This labeling began in history with the declaration of the act and continued over the years. The responses of the Ramoshis also highlight the impact on the community for being labeled as criminals. It also throws light on the present situation of the tribe and how several factors have affected the community.

According to one of its members, the community is still struggling for settlement of social and economic conditions. Due to their poor socioeconomic background, Ramoshis are forced to commit crime. There are several cases registered on many in the village. They are not even told the charges the police register against them. There are many crimes registered because of the liquor selling business. Police arrest female members as well. This affects the children. The community member added that education is little in the community. Youths are mostly engaged in daily wage earning; wage earning is the only big source of income for these people. They do not have their own land, and they have to work as laborers on other people's lands. They are not appropriately paid, and the male ends up spending the entire day's wage on liquor. Additionally, there are associated problems because of criminal history. He further added, "Even today also our people face discrimination based on their castes in their own villages. People treat them differently. If any theft or robbery happens at neighborhood or in the village then police first arrests Ramoshis." For livelihood purposes, Ramoshis started plundering and their actions were identified as crime by society. Situations compelled them to continue this, and after a time, stealing became a habit of Ramoshis. The upper caste people started using them for their selfish purposes, and Ramoshis became professionals after a period. Criminalization affects their day-to-day life. In villages, Ramoshis are involved in the liquor making and selling business. This is not legal, and thus these people are arrested by the local police and exploited.

According to the labeling theory, as defined by Tannenbaum, the process of tagging, defining, segregating, and describing a person for a specific treatment is a way of stimulating and evoking the same traits in him. The theory suggests that the likelihood of committing crime increases in individuals who are involved in crime and thereby arrested, prosecuted, and punished and labeled as criminals. This is because others label them as criminals, and henceforth they are perceived as the same. A similar response was received through the case studies about the behavior of the Ramoshis post enactment of the CTA of 1871. The tribe was primarily nomadic in nature, and postdeclaration, they were imprisoned in settlements where they had hardly any freedom. The tribe soon ran away from the settlements. They did not have any specific skill, and according to the *Balutedari* system prevalent during that period, all castes had specific jobs to earn their livelihood. Once labeled, it was difficult for the Ramoshis to get employment, and they started working for upper caste communities, who used them for personal purposes. Powerful individuals from other communities then utilized the Ramoshis, and they got involved in criminal activities like theft, plundering, kidnapping, and blackmailing; thereby, other people in the villages started to perceive them as criminals, and due to the absence of any specific skills and occupation, they continued their involvement in crime. Thus, the origin of labeling started with the community with enactment of the CTA of 1871.

The theory also explains that the labeled individuals find that other people in society are reluctant to associate with them and accept them as equals. This leads to formation of a self-concept as criminals, and they tend to lose association with other individuals in society. The case studies depict that the involvement in crime among Ramoshis continued primarily due to the absence of specific skills and a stable source of income. However, the perception of other people in society also played a major role in the lives of the Ramoshis. The police *Patils* and village *Patils* continued oppressing them and forced them to commit crime to serve their selfish purposes. They used to offer grain and crops in exchange for criminal activities. Thus, in order to feed their family, the Ramoshis continued their involvement in crime. A self-concept as criminals was formed, and they enjoyed the fear in other people. Thus, the occupational pattern and oppression by upper castes played a major role in the process of continued labeling. The general perception of people from other communities also played a significant role. The responses show that sometimes even though the tribe was not involved in agricultural theft, other communities observed them suspiciously. Even policemen used to arrest them without any formal procedure, but on prior assumptions based on their historical background and caste.

The majority of the respondents in the study shared that problems of discrimination arise because of their historical background. Ramoshis are primarily discriminated against because of their historical involvement in crime. This background led to discrimination at the village level. This labeling, which is attached to this tribe, is ancestral. It started from their ancestors and continues to the present generation. On the other hand, their behavior or habits were also responsible for their labeling. The majority of the respondents shared that they have faced discrimination at the individual, family, and village level too. Ramoshis were forcefully arrested in many cases, although they were not involved in the crime. The criminal labeling of the community also affects their children and their family. It is evident from the responses that in some cases, Ramoshis were involved in petty crime, but the entire community suffers due to historical criminalization.

The process of formal labeling started with the declaration of the CTA of 1871 and continued over the years. The enactment of the Habitual Offenders Act of 1959 did not succeed in changing the situation in the country. Ramoshis were formally labeled as habitual offenders. The process of formal labeling continues as a result of the mistreatment by police officials, the correctional administration, and the legal system of the country. The Ramoshis are arrested without procedure, based only on suspicion of the policemen, as Ramoshis were once declared a criminal tribe. No special provision has been made for addressing the various issues of the Ramoshis. In later years, some efforts were made on the part of the government, but they were not effective enough to address the issues of the Ramoshis. However, the perception of people in the neighborhood, peer groups, and school officials did not change toward the tribe. They do not evidently mark them as criminals, but their behavior does. This process of informal labeling affects the social, economic, political, and psychological aspects of the lives of Ramoshis. Thus, several collective factors play a very significant role in the criminalization of the Ramoshi tribe. They were declared and discriminated as criminals in British India, but this discrimination continues even today. They are still treated as criminals in society. The tribe suffers in the hands of the state, polity, and other dominant sections in society. It is evident from the responses of the participants of this study that the process of formal as well as informal labeling still continues. The state, society, and polity have a distinct role to play. They were labeled as criminals in British India and habitual offenders in independent India, and now are labeled as ex-criminal or denotified in "shining" India.

Conclusion

The study aimed at understanding the origin of labeling among a specific group of tribal population in India, the denotified tribes. The chapter not only elaborates on how the process of labeling originated with the tribal group, but also discusses how labeling got integrated into the life cycle of Ramoshis, a tribal subgroup with the denotified population, and how it is experienced by the Ramoshis in their everyday lives. Labeling theory has been used as a critical conceptual tool in this research. The study being exploratory in nature, based on a qualitative paradigm, the researcher did not have a predefined theoretical framework before starting the data collection process. The field experiences and participant responses led to emergence of a reality that was analyzed using labeling theory as a conceptual tool. The research explores various reasons for labeling that affected the Ramoshi tribes over the years, and it is evident from the responses of the community members that ancestral labeling has a significant role in the continued labeling process of the tribe. The process of formal and informal labeling and the roles of social and political institutions have been discussed critically in the study and throw light on how these roles and their functions affect the overall conditions of the tribe. These tribes still remain deprived of their basic rights and opportunities and continue living a life with stigma and discrimination even today. This chapter is a sincere endeavor to understand the process of construction of labeling among denotified tribes, with special reference to the Ramoshi tribe of Maharashtra. The chapter brings to the forefront the voices and experiences of the Ramoshi tribesmen about being denotified in society.

References

Adler, F., and Laufer, W. S. (1993). *Advances in Criminological Theory*, Volume 4. Rutgers University in Piscataway, New Jersey: Transaction Publishers.

Akers, R. L. (2000). Social learning theory. *In Criminological Theories: Introduction, Evaluation, and Application*. (pp. 71–97). Los Angeles: Roxbury Publishing Company.

Becker, H. S. (1963). *Outsiders: Studies in the Sociology of Deviance*. New York: Free. Press of Glencoe.

Bokil, M. (2002). De-notified and nomadic tribes: A perspective. *Economic and Political Weekly*, 37(2), 148–154.

Braithwaite, J. (1989). *Crime, Shame and Reintegration*. Cambridge: Cambridge University Press.

Burrell, G., and Morgan, G. (1979). *Sociological Paradigms and Organizational Analysis*. London: Heinemann.

Erikson, K.T. (1966). *Wayward Puritans: A Study in the Sociology of Deviance*. Boston: Allyn and Bacon.

Hartjen, C. A. (1974). *Crime and Criminalization*. New York: Praeger.

Katz, S. R. (2002). *Re-examining the integrative social capital theory of crime*. Western Criminology Review, 4(1), 30–54.

Lemert, E. M., (1951). *Social Pathology: A Systematic Approach to the Theory of Sociopathic Behaviour*. New York: McGraw-Hill.

Mason, J. (1996). *Qualitative Researching*. London: Sage.
Mehta, B. H. (1955). Ex-criminal groups in India. *Indian Journal of Social Work*, 16(1), 10–18.
Rathod, M. (2000). De-notified and nomadic tribes in Maharashtra. *Denotified and Nomadic Tribes Rights Action Group Newsletter.*
Schur, E. M. (1971). *Labeling deviant behavior: Its sociological implications.* New York: Harper & Row.
Tannenbaum, F. (1938). *Crime and the Community.* Boston: Ginn & Company.

Sex Trafficking in Gujarat, India

Case Studies of Women Victims Turned Offenders*

13

PAVITHRAN NAMBIAR AND
SUHAS P. NAMBIAR

Contents

Introduction

Trafficking in females is one of the threats faced by the society wherein women have a significant role in committing crimes against other women. A large number of females are involved in trafficking women and children, and a major chunk of the female offenders were victims of trafficking in the past. By assuming the new role as perpetrators, they escape from their own victimization and are enabled to acquire more wealth and power. These perpetrators target their victims after analyzing the latter's economic condition, vulnerability, and possibility of success in their attempts. They make false promises,

* The names of the offenders and victims in the chapter have been changed to conceal their identities.

tell fabricated success stories, assure a better financial condition and bright future to the would-be victims, and lure them. The victims fall in this trap and ultimately end up in brothels or in coerced conditions. The rationale behind this chapter is to analyze the role of women in perpetrating female trafficking in Gujarat. While human trafficking can be for a variety of purposes, this chapter focus on cases in which women are involved in crimes against other women by deceiving and trafficking them and pushing them into flesh trade. Moreover, instances in which women persuaded other women to practice prostitution were also examined.

Methodology

This chapter is based on a study carried out in Gujarat in 2010. The study is basically qualitative in nature; it tries to find the modus operandi of women in enticing other women and girls with job opportunities and a better future, how they were trafficked and pushed into the flesh trade. Similar cases that happened in 2011, 2012, and 2013 have also been incorporated in this chapter. Secondary data was collected from police records. Statements of the women offenders were recorded. Similarly, minor girls who were trafficked from other states to Gujarat were interviewed. With an aim to prove crime by women against other women, details of only a few felonies have been enumerated in this chapter. All the cases could not be explained due to shortage of space. Nevertheless, it was found that the modi operandi adopted by women traffickers were similar with minor variations, and the crimes they committed on other females were also somewhat the same. While the study deals with trafficking of women and minor girls from other states to Gujarat, a case relating to an attempt to traffic minor girls from Gujarat to Maharashtra is also dealt with. The major part of this chapter is prepared from the firsthand experience of the lead author with women traffickers and victims of trafficking.

Human Trafficking in Gujarat: Role of Women Offenders

A large number of trafficking cases have been registered in Gujarat. The number of trafficking cases reported in this state during the last 10 years is shown in Table 13.1.

The majority of these cases involve trafficking of women and children from other states to Gujarat and pushing them into prostitution. Similarly, there were also many incidents in which women from Gujarat were coerced to be a part of the flesh trade. A distinctive factor in all these incidents was that it was the women who played a crucial role in trafficking and forcing other women and girls into this menace, making it a crime by women against other women and girls. To illustrate this, let us examine some of the trafficking cases registered in 2010, 2011, 2012, and 2013. It needs to be mentioned here that in all cases, women had committed crime against other women.

Table 13.1 Human Trafficking Cases in Gujarat State for 10 Years

Year	2004	2005	2006	2007	2008	2009	2010	2011	2012	2013
No. of cases	30	41	82	40	46	30	31	27	35	80

Source: Interview with the Criminal Investigation Department (CID), Gujarat Police, 2014.

Women Brothel Owners

A series of raids carried out at different brothels in Ahmedabad, Gujarat, in 2010 resulted in the arrest of 49 agents or pimps and 57 prostitutes. The agents or pimps included 28 women who were brothel owners. These women trafficked women and girls (including minor girls) not only from different places of Gujarat, but also from other states like Maharashtra, West Bengal, Jharkhand, and Orissa for running their brothels. These women and girls were given false promises and assured jobs in Ahmedabad, and once they reached here, they were forced to engage in the flesh trade. If anybody objected to it, they were locked in rooms, tortured mentally and physically, and denied food and freedom to move around. These women brothel owners belong to different states and were in different age groups (Tables 13.2 and 13.3).

Since the principal theme of this chapter is to highlight the role of women in committing crimes against other women, the statements of a few of the women brothel owners, in their own words, are given below to illustrate their modus operandi and role in trafficking women and girls and running brothels.

Woman Offender: Case Study 1

Rakhiben Rabari, widow, age 45 years, occupation—brothel owner, resident of Odhav, Ahmedabad city, native of Patan district, Gujarat

> I am the second wife of my husband who died in 2003 due to heart attack and I live with one of my sons, who is a divorcee. Another son is married and stays separately. My three daughters are married and they stay at their in-laws' house. I own a house which has 23 rooms and these rooms are used for flesh trade. We bring women and girls from different parts of Gujarat and from other states too. One Magan, his wife Mita and their daughter are one

Table 13.2 Native State of Women Brothel Owners

Native State of Women Brothel Owners	Number
Gujarat	3
Maharashtra	1
West Bengal	20
Jharkhand	1
Orissa	3
Total	28

Table 13.3 Age of Women Brothel Owners

Age of Women Brothel Owners (Years)	Number
18–23	9
23–28	11
28–33	5
33–38	1
38–45	2
Total	28

of my tenants and they use to supply girls for sex work, who come from Bombay and other states. Some time back, Magan and his friend Raju had brought two girls named Leela and Rani from Bombay. In one of my rented rooms one Ashrafkhan and his wife Sita are staying and involved in sex trade. They brought Pooja and Khadija from Bombay and Hyderabad, so as to supply in hotels here. Kishan and Preeti are staying in another room, who also do flesh trade in their room and supply girls in hotels. My son Chhaganbhai is also involved with these people in flesh trade. Customers either come to our house or these girls are supplied at different places by these pimps. Income from the prostitution was shared by me, agents and the girls. My woman tenants used to bring women and girls from their native states.

Woman Offender: Case Study 2

Jyoti, wife of Abdul, age 22 years, occupation—prostitution, resident of Chandlodia, Ahmedabad city, native of Barasat, West Bengal

I live with my husband and daughter Shabana at Pooja. Earlier I was staying with my father, mother and an elder sister at my native place. My elder sister is married. My father was a carpenter and mother has been working as laborer. I am illiterate. As my father has got heart problem, responsibility of our house was on my mother and my shoulder. I had been making packings for noodles in a factory. I met Sanjay there and we fell in love. He told me that he was a Hindu and his name was Sanjay. However, on marriage day he took me to a masjid in our village and we got married. On inquiry, he told me that he was a Muslim and a native of Bangladesh. He also told that he already got married, but his wife could not conceive and hence he married me. Three months after the marriage, we went to Bombay (Meera road area) and stayed there with his friends for around two years. There he worked as a mason. His first wife, Bilkish has been staying in the same area in a separate house. Meanwhile, I gave birth to a girl child.

While doing white wash on a building, Sanjay fell and got seriously injured on his vertebra. We spent lot of money for his treatment and incurred huge debt. Then his friend Kalia told that I could earn money as a bar dancer. Hence, Sanjay sent me with Kalia to a beer bar situated on the Meera road, where I earned Rs. 100–150 daily. However, as this money was not enough to clear our debt, Sanjay forced me to take up prostitution. Though I objected, he sent me to "Sheela Maasi" who was running brothel in Thane area. There I used to get Rs. 200 from a customer. As there was pressure on Bangladeshi nationals by police, I could not run my business properly.

One Khan was staying near our house on Meera road in Bombay. His wife, Pinaki was staying in Ahmedabad and running brothel. Relation of Khan and his wife Pinaki was strained and hence they were living separately. One Kasam at Raju was staying with Pinaki and helping her in her flesh trade. Thus, after collecting address from Khan, Sanjay and I came to Ahmedabad and stayed with Pinaki who lived in Naroda area. We had left our daughter Shabana at Pooja with Sanjay's first wife Bilkish in Bombay.

From Pinaki's house, I was sent to a guest house at Naroda Patiya, where I had to satisfy two to three customers daily. After staying there for five days, as per directions of Pinaki, Kasam took me to Surat, where I stayed in a brothel of Bhavik and his wife Poonam. Earlier, Poonam worked as a prostitute, but after marrying Bhavik she left this trade. However, they brought girls from outside and ran their business. They use to keep a girl for 15 days and after this the girl is changed and another is brought. Thus, they brought two girls in a month. My work started from eight in the morning and it went on till one in the night. During this time I had to satisfy five or six ustomers. After 15 days, Kasam took me back to Ahmedabad.

In Ahmedabad, Pinaki rented out a room for us and I started to run my brothel. After 35 days I handed over my savings to my husband Sanjay and asked him to bring my daughter

Shabana from Bombay. Hence, he went to Bombay and brought our daughter. After coming back he told that he would shift our daughter Shabana to his mother's place in Bangladesh, and planned to go to Bangalore along with five girls.

In 2007, Vijay received a call from his elder sister in Bangladesh that his younger sister was sick. Hence, Sanjay and daughter Shabana went to Bangladesh where they stayed for a month and thereafter went to my parents' house in Calcutta. He stayed in Calcutta for a few days and during this time he came in contact with one Kishor. Thereafter he returned to Ahmedabad.

In July 2007, Kishor and his wife Ganga came to our house with Seetarani. I paid Rs. 3000 to Kishor and they left the place, leaving Seetarani at our house. Though I took Seetarani to hotel for prostitution, she did not agree. Hence, after 10 days, as per my call Kishor came with another girl named Reena (belongs to Calcutta). He left Reena with us and took Seetarani to Viratnagar, where she was kept for three days. Reena stayed with us and worked as a prostitute. Later on Sanjay took Seetarani to Mehsana. After eight days, he brought her back to Ahmedabad and raped her. Later on, she ran away from our house. But when I and Sanjay located her near Chandlodia lake, we tried to bring her back. But she screamed due to which mob gathered from nearby area. Seeing the mob, we fled the scene.

Woman Offender: Case Study 3

Runa, wife of Kishan, age 32 years, occupation—brothel owner, resident of Tharsali, Vadodara, Gujarat

I live with my two kids and husband Kasim at Kishan. I was born in Baroda and I have four brothers. My father had been working in a mill and he died in 1995 due to sickness. Our economic condition was very poor. My mother had been working as a domestic servant. My husband worked as a laborer and was a drunkard. I worked as a domestic servant and earned a meager amount. We were in debt and hence we had to sell our house. My husband spent money in drinking and physically tortured me. As I was fed up, we got separated. There was a beauty parlor on the ground floor of the building where I worked as domestic servant. There I learned the work of beauty parlor. Thus, I worked as a maid as well as in the beauty parlor. Later on, I left this and started to work in the Gujarat Industrial Development Corporation, where I came in contact with a girl named Dipa. She was a prostitute and asked me to join her so as to earn more money. On agreeing, Dipa took me to a guest house near railway station, Baroda. That day I got Rs. 200 from a customer. Thereafter, I started to work as a commercial sex worker. If I go to a customer through any tout, I have to pay commission to him also. Generally I use to go with two or three customers and earn Rs. 300–400 daily. I am in this occupation from the beginning of 2006.

During this period, I came in contact with Kamluddin, who started to stay with me. With the help of Kamluddin I started brothel. I have women at my disposal, who are brought from other parts of Gujarat and other states. Customers use to come to my brothel, or sometimes my women are sent to hotel or other place as per demand of customers.

Woman Offender: Case Study 4

Sangita, wife of Sagar, age 25 years, occupation—brothel keeper, resident of the house of Bhikhabhai, Chandlodia, Ahmedabad, native of Medinipur district, West Bengal

I stay at rented house with my husband Sagar, friend Jivan and Priya. My son and daughter are living with my parents at our native in West Bengal. I run a brothel, and my husband and Jivan brought customers. Recently we brought Priya from my native. Customers use to come to our brothel and also sent Priya to different places for flesh trade. A part of the money which

> we got from customers was given to Priya and the rest was used by us. As we are getting easy money we are running the brothel. I, my husband and our friend Jivan brought girls from West Bengal for prostitution. The girls whom I brought from my native were known to me earlier, and their economic condition was very bad. I promised them job and better future and brought here.

Woman Offender: Case Study 5

Mona, age 30 years, occupation—brothel owner, resident of Nirnaynagar, Ahmedabad, native of Baleshwar district, Orissa

> I came to Ahmedabad from Orissa with my husband Kartik. After staying there for three months I returned to Orissa and met parents of Shanta and Sheela. Looking to their condition I said that I could get some work for their daughters in Ahmedabad. As they were known to me and very poor, they agreed to send their daughters with me. I paid Rs. 2000 to their parents to buy new clothes and other needy items for coming to Ahmedabad. I contacted some more friends, who were poor and have daughters. I convinced them that I could get work for these girls. I took the names of other girls who were to come with me. This helped me to get their consent to send their wards with me. Thus, I came to Ahmedabad with (1) Shanta, (2) Sheela, (3) Shobhana, (4) Priya, (5) Ronak, (6) Babu, and (7) Basu. We all stayed in a rented house of Kokilaben, which we got through Basanti.
>
> Here I am running a brothel with these girls. Shanta was sent with Basanti for prostitution, but she refused to do it, and hence, she was not given food and locked in a room. However, later on she agreed to do this work, and hence she was given freedom to move around. One day she was asked to go out and throw the waste, but she did not return. Later on police came to our rented house and arrested us.

As mentioned earlier, 28 female brothel owners were arrested. However, case studies of only a few brothel owners are described here. The purpose is to show their modus operandi in enticing women and girls, and the way in which they deceive other females and commit crimes. Case studies of other woman brothel owners are similar to those mentioned above. An analysis of cases of woman brothel owners shows that all worked as prostitutes earlier. Gradually, they found it profitable to run a brothel by bringing girls from different parts of India. As the demand is high, they used all kinds of tricks to lure women and girls and to bring them to Ahmedabad. Pimps and agents helped them not only to procure females, but also to keep an eye on them so that they wouldn't escape from their clutches. Thus, it can be seen that the act of woman brothel owners is certainly a crime against other women and girls. It is not that these women brothel owners were involved in bringing adult women and persuading them into prostitution. These are only some of the examples of adult women committing felonies against other women; there have also been cases in which women trafficked minor girls from other states to Gujarat with false promises and pushed them into the flesh trade.

Trafficking Minor Girls: Role of Women

Some of the sensational cases of trafficking minor girls from other states to Gujarat and pushing them into the flesh trade, as well as attempts made to traffic minor girls from Gujarat to other states, are mentioned below to illustrate the role of women in these crimes and their modus operandi.

Woman Offender: Case Study 1

Janki of Pune

The Ahmedabad police, while on patrol, arrested a lady, Janki of Pune, along with two girls aged 10 and 11 years on March 18, 2009. It was while these girls were kidnapped and being taken to Pune that they fell in the net of police. The aforesaid accused, on questioning, revealed that there was a systematic network that operated in different parts of India, which kidnaps minor girls, who are used for making pornography. Thereafter, these girls are either sold in Pune or any other place or sent to Arab countries with the help of middlemen. The above accused further admitted that she, along with her accomplices, had kidnapped many girls from South India.

Janki at Khama mortgaged her ornaments with Kamla and borrowed a huge amount. When Janki's husband came to know about it, there was big quarrel and he asked her to get the ornaments back. As she did not have the money to do so, Kamla told her that she could earn huge money if she could get small girls and sell them. To this, Janki agreed. Janki was born and brought up in Sardarnagar, Ahmedabad, and was married off in Pune. Thus, keeping this idea in mind, she came to Ahmedabad.

On the particular day, Janki went to Saibaba Temple, Shahibaug. Near the temple, there was a Dabeli stall, where she saw three girls who had come to buy Dabeli. She went to them and told that she had organized a religious function at her house in which small children are given food, and asked them whether they would go with her to have food. One girl declined this invitation, whereas the remaining two agreed. Of these two, Dhara was 10 years old and Kiran 11 years old. As the two girls agreed, Janki took them to a nearby vehicle and forced them into it, driving it toward Indira bridge. On the way, she left the vehicle and telephoned somebody. While proceeding further, their vehicle was stopped by the police, who were on patrol. As they were not able to properly answer the questions, the police arrested them.

Janki, on interrogation, revealed the entire episode to police. Janki is 49 years old, studied up to the seventh standard, and lives in Pune. She is married and her husband is running a big sweet shop in Pune. His income is around Rs. 5000 daily. Her elder son, Pratap, is 28 years old and owns a big footwear showroom, and the younger son, Punit, 24 years old, is engaged in the sweet business with his father. They have a big building in which the sweet shop, the footwear shop, a godown, and their house are situated. According to her, she got Rs. 50,000 on selling a girl, and she did this business with the help of her friend Kamla. As per disclosures made by Janki, police arrested the other lady, Kamla, from Pune and Basappa from Chennai.

Woman Offender: Case Study 2

Kamla of Pune

Kamla is 65 years old and lives in Pune. She has three sons aged 37, 33, and 30 years old, and all three own separate electric shops, and their father helped them in this business. Kamla works as a tailor. According to Kamla, she kidnapped a girl from any place, depending on the suitability, and took her to Mumbai by train. During the journey, if the girl cried, she was given her preferred eatables and made quiet. If the girl was still adamant, she was forcefully administered medicine and made unconscious. On reaching Mumbai, they boarded a bus to Pune, where Kamla and the girl passed the daytime in a garden. Meanwhile, Kamla would have contacted her agent. Accordingly, the agent came at night and took the girl away. The next day, the agent made a payment to Kamla.

Kamla used her occupation to lure, kidnap, and traffic girls. Being a ladies tailor, women used to come to her, along with their daughter. During conversation with them, she was able to identify girls who could be kidnapped. She inquired about their family, girl's study and school, and so forth, which helped her to decide the mode and place from where the girl could be picked up. Accordingly, she plotted the kidnapping with the help of her gang members.

Woman Victim: Case Study 1

Seetarani, age 13 years, occupation—domestic work, resident of Varasan North, Pargana, West Bengal

Seetarani had been staying at the above-mentioned address with her mother, Meena, two sisters, Itani and Onisha, and brother Michel. While the victim was studying in the sixth standard in Loreto Entally School in 2006, her father left them and married another woman. When he left, her mother was pregnant, and after a few months, a boy was born to her, whom she named Michel. Per the direction of her mother, Seetarani discontinued her studies to look after her brother. She took care of her brother and did domestic chores. Her mother was the only breadwinner, working as a daily wager and earning around Rs. 1000 per month, leading a poverty-ridden life.

One day, the trafficker Gita and her male accomplice Kishan, in the guise of her husband, went to Meena's house. Being a friend of Meena, Gita started to show pity for the former's poverty-ridden situation. She also showed her willingness to get work for Seetarani in Gujarat. She assured Meena that Seetarani would be able to send money every month, and they would take care of her daughter as their own. Hence, the mother showed willingness to send her. When Seetarani inquired about the nature of work she would have to do, Gita told her that there were many other girls also her age in Gujarat who were earning money by performing dance at various functions, and she could also dance with them and earn money. At that time, Gita gave Rs. 4000 to her mother (Meena), and thus Seetarani got ready to come to Gujarat.

After a few days, Seetarani started her journey with Gita and her husband in a train bound to Gujarat from Howra railway station. On the way, she heard Kishan talking to somebody on his mobile: "We are coming with a girl, do arrangements for accommodation." They reached Ahmedabad railway station in the evening, after 2½ days, where a lady (Setthani) around 45 years old had come to pick them up with a Tata sumo and its driver. They all reached a flat (ground floor) in the Viratnagar area. There were around five or six rooms adjacent to it. There was one girl, named Rani from Kolkata, about 20 years of age, and two other Muslim girls (names not known) staying there. The lady called customers using her mobile, and they were asked to work as prostitutes. There Seetarani stayed for two or three days. Thereafter, Kishan and Gita took her to Chandlodia, to Sanjaybhai and Reena. There Sanjaybhai gave Rs. 30,000 to Gita in the presence of Seetarani. Kishan was happy and said, "She will earn a lot for you." Sanjaybhai was about 30 years, tall, and spoke Hindi and Gujarati. His wife, Reena, was about 25–27 years old, fat, and of medium height; they had a three-year-old daughter. Thenceforth, Seetarani was sold and bought by different people, raped, and forced to work as a commercial sexual worker. She was taken to different places, like Baroda and Mehsana. Later on, she was brought back to Ahmedabad and handed over to Sanjaybhai. Unable to continue suffering rapes and atrocities, one day, around 8:30 p.m., when Sanjaybhai had gone out and Reena was cooking food in the kitchen, Seetarani escaped from the house, ran through the main road, and reached near

Chandlodia lake. By this time, Sanjay and Reena reached there and started to beat her, trying to take her back to their house. However, as people gathered, Sanjay and Reena had to flee.

A person from the gathered crowd took Seetarani to a voluntary organization. With the help of this organization, Seetarani was able to register a complaint with the police for her confinement at different places, being forcefully sold and bought, threats and rape, and being pushed into prostitution against her wishes. Based on this complaint, police conducted raids at various places in Ahmedabad.

Woman Victim: Case Study 2

Nabisa at Parvana, daughter of Abdulkhan, age 13 years, occupation—domestic work, resident of Vasai, East Mumbai, Maharashtra

Nabisa had been staying with her mother, Nabisa, who was working as a maid. The victim has two younger brothers, Parvez, studying in the first standard, and Subaid, in kindergarten in Vasai. She has three married sisters. Her father died due to TB in 2006. Nabisa studied up to the second standard in Dagdi school. Thereafter, she started to work as a maid, like her mother. Her other relatives are staying at Manor and Santoli, Mumbai; relations with them are strained due to allegations that the victim's mother did not give proper medical treatment to her father, and hence he died. However, the fact is that her father had owned a garage, which her mother sold and spent the money for his treatment.

Saina at Sugra, her husband Salman, son Salim, and daughter Khatija were staying near the house of Nabisa. Nabisa used to work as a maid at their house. One day, Saina told Nabisa's mother that she could arrange a better job for Nabisa in Baroda. After getting her permission, Saina and Salman took Nabisa and another girl, Riya, and left for Baroda by train. On reaching the Baroda railway station, they hired an auto rickshaw and reached near a petrol pump. From there, they rang up somebody and after some time, a lady came in her Indica car. At the same time, another man reached there on his motorcycle. Saina said that their names were Amita and Manoj. Saina and Amita took the girls, Nabisa and Riya, to a double-storied house, which was five minutes running distance from the petrol pump. By that time, Salman and Manoj also reached there on the motorcycle. Amita gave Rs. 5000 to Saina. Thereafter, Salman, Saina, and Amita left the house. When Nabisa started to cry, Manoj said that her money was given to Saina and threatened her to keep quiet. After this, he left the house, locking the door from outside. After some time, Amita and Manoj returned with food. At night, they asked the two girls to have food, locked the house, and left. Then Riya said that she had been there earlier also and earned Rs. 20,000 in a week and returned to Mumbai.

The next day, Amita came and took Nabisa to a hotel, where the owner raped her. Later on, another customer who came there said that she was too young and he was interested in a grown-up girl. Hence, Amita took her back to the house. In the afternoon, Manoj came with a man, who gave Rs. 500 to Manoj. Nabisa was sent to the room, where she was forcefully raped by that man. After some time, Manoj brought another person, from whom he received Rs. 500. When Nabisa objected, as she was having severe pain in her private parts, she was pushed in the room and raped by that person. At night, when Nabisa told Manoj that she did not want to do prostitution and wanted to return to her house, he threatened her, saying that she was sold to him and would be beaten up if she did not obey. The next day, she had to satisfy three customers.

Then on another day, Amita took Nabisa and Riya to a new apartment, where five or six people were having liquor. After some time, Nabisa and Riya were sent to a room, where a middle-aged person was present. When Nabisa objected, she was threatened by him that he was a police officer. He then enjoyed sex with the two girls. After some time, they came out of the room. He gave Rs. 500 to Amita. Around 10 p.m., Amita took both the girls back to the house. After some time, Manoj went out with Riya.

The next morning, when Nabisa inquired about Riya, Manoj replied that she had left for Mumbai. Then Nabisa pleaded with him to also send her to Mumbai, to which Manoj said that she could go the next night. She was also ordered to satisfy the customers for two days. In the afternoon, Manoj brought a man, who raped her. In the evening, Amita took her to the apartment where she was taken the day before. There, she was raped by two persons, who gave Rs. 1000 to Amita. Nabisa was then taken back to the house. At night, Manoj came with a person and asked Nabisa to go with him. When Nabisa opposed, she was beaten up and forced to go with him. He dropped her back in the late night. He gave Rs. 1500 to Manoj.

On another morning, while Nabisa was doing her packing, Manoj told her that she had to go to Mumbai by bus that night. During the daytime, she was raped by four persons, who gave Rs. 500 each to Manoj. In the evening, Manoj also raped her. Later on, Manoj took her to another house and gave her food. Thereafter, a man was sent to the room where Nabisa was present. Seeing that man, she started to cry. When asked, she told him that she was forcefully confined by Amita and Manoj and compelled to work as a prostitute. He told her that he was a police person and asked her to keep silent; within a few minutes, police reached there and arrested Amita and Manoj.

Woman Victim: Case Study 3

Sharmila, age 13 years, and Parul, age 16 years, both daughters of Shibusingh, occupation—domestic work, resident of Khadakpur, Baleshwar district, Orissa

Sharmila and her sister Parul had been living with their mother, father, two sisters, and a brother. Their sisters were ages 10 and 8, and their brother was 6. Parul studied up to the fifth standard, but could not study further due to poverty. The girls' mother worked as a laborer at building construction sites, and their father worked as a daily wager. Sharmila and Parul's mother was known to Basanti, and the latter was fully aware of the former's poor economic condition. One day, Basanti and her friend Mala went to Sharmila's house, met her parents, and while talking, mentioned that they could arrange jobs for Sharmila and Parul in a jeans factory in Ahmedabad. Thus, following their assurance, their parents got ready to send them to Ahmedabad with Basanti. The parents told their daughters that if they faced any problem, they should go to the nearby police station and thus return to the native.

After a few days, Sharmila and Parul left Orissa with Basanti and Mala and reached Ahmedabad by train. On reaching here, they were taken to Basanti's house in Nirnaynagar, which was a rented one. Other girls, named Shobhita, Pinki, and Dhiren, and Basanti's daughter Tina also stayed in that house. On the third day, Basanti told Sharmila that her skin was black and she had to stay in house for a few days so that she would become somewhat attractive. But Sharmila could not understand what she said. Thereafter, Basanti asked Parul to get ready, and she was taken to a place, where she was introduced to some other girls. Parul was told that she had to do the same work the other girls did, that is, satisfy her customers. But Parul refused to do this work. Hence, she was threatened by Basanti and brought back to her house. Here, Parul told Sharmila what happened. At the house, Basanti told Parul the next day that she must go for work and return with Rs. 150. If she did not bring the money, she would not be given food. Parul was also beaten up by Basanti. When Parul told her that she would telephone her parents and inform them of all the happenings, her diary and purse were snatched away. She was abused by Basanti and Mala and was locked in a room. The next day, Shobhita and Pinki tried to convince Parul, saying that Basanti Didi would treat her well if she agreed to do what Didi said. So, Parul said that her health was not good and once she got well, she would do what other girls did.

A day later, Mala gave waste to Parul and asked her to throw it out. As there was no other person there, she quietly went down the house. Thereafter, as she did not return for a long time. Basanti Didi went in search of her but she could not trace Parul. The next day, police raided the house, based on a complaint lodged by Parul at the Mahila police station. Basanti and Mala were engaged in prostitution, and they brought girls from outside. They were being helped in this business by the son of the owner of the house.

Woman Victim: Case Study 4

Sarita, 13 years, belonging to Jharkhand

The victim is from a very poor family. Her parents came in contact with a placement agency in Delhi and requested them to find any work for their daughter. One Tejsing and his wife residing in Rajkot, in need of a servant who could take care of their five-year-old daughter and their house, contacted the placement agency. This agency provided Sarita to Tejsing.

In April 2009, an unidentified caller informed the Social Security Squad, Police Commissioner Office, Rajkot city, that a girl was forcefully being confined and tortured in the house of Tejsing. On the basis of this telephonic message, police reached the place and brought the girl, Tejsing, and his wife to the police station. The girl was confined in the house, forced to work for long hours, and was not allowed to move out. However, the girl did not give any complaint against Tejsing and showed her willingness to go back to her parents. As she was sent to Rajkot by the placement agency of Delhi, she was restored to this agency, with a direction to send her back to her parents.

Findings

- Women played a crucial role in running brothels. They lured women and girls and, if needed, forced them to engage in flesh trade.
- Women have a significant role in selecting girls and trafficking them to Gujarat.
- Women traffickers were known to all the victims' families.
- They took advantage of the poverty of the victim's families.
- They lured victims' families through false promises that they could get work for their wards in Gujarat.
- After the girls were brought to Gujarat, they were forced to engage in the flesh trade. Those who did not budge were locked in rooms, threatened, beaten, and not given food.
- Economically well-off women also indulged in girl's trafficking.
- Crime by women against women is rampant in human trafficking.

Discussion and Conclusion

What Do These Case Studies Show?

The role of women is prominent in trafficking these minor girls from different states to Gujarat, taking them to different places, and forcing them into commercial sex. In all these cases, women traffickers were the friends of the parents of the victims, and they played a crucial role in convincing victims' parents to send their daughters with them. The women traffickers took their male counterparts with them posing as their husbands, with an aim to win over the confidence of the parents of victims. They knew the poor economic condition of the victims' families and fully misused their friendship and took advantage of their poverty. They target their victims after studying their economic condition and vulnerability and the possibility of success in their attempts. They adopted a variety of tactics to lure the parents and make them agree to send their daughters with them (traffickers). This also shows the extent to which these women criminals go to fulfill their greed for money by crucifying minor girls.

What Makes Women Fall Prey to the Ploy of Other Women?

Women who are in trouble would be looking for a solution for their problems. When the "solution" is offered by another woman, they are more tempted to accept it. In the same way, when the woman offering help is a known person, the victims do not think twice, and simply believe what the former says. Here, in almost all cases, the woman traffickers were known to the victims or their families. By the time they understood their folly, it was too late.

Recommendations

- There is an urgent need to sensitize police about the menace of human trafficking. Human trafficking could be for exploitative labor or sexual exploitation. Hence, this subject has to be incorporated into the syllabus of their training.
- The mindset of police toward victims of human trafficking has to be so as to encourage them (victims) to file a case.
- Intelligence collection on human trafficking at the police station level should be augmented.
- Meetings need to be periodically organized between officials of police stations, nongovernmental organizations (NGOs), and the general public, so that police can learn their problems, help improve the police–public relationship, and enable easy collection of information on human trafficking.
- Police have to be in close coordination with NGOs working with women and children, so that they can inform police about victims of trafficking.
- Source, destination, and transit points like railway stations, bus stations, border check posts, and so forth, need to be identified, and police personnel, especially those at the lower levels, should be made aware of their importance in human trafficking.

- Districts having international borders must identify centers of immoral trafficking of women and children, prepare notes on such vulnerable places of villages, and ensure that vigil is maintained permanently and stringent action is taken under the Immoral Traffic Prohibition (ITP) Act.
- Community policing and the Mohalla Committee system need to be revitalized so as to enhance cooperation between citizens and police. Sensitized and conscious citizens are good sources who could pass on vital information regarding suspicious and trafficking activities in their neighborhood.
- Programs should be devised to sensitize students to human trafficking at school and the college level, so that they are cautioned about this menace and can also become sources to the police.

How Can Victimology Become Positive?

14

NATTI RONEL

Contents

Introduction

In the coming pages, I present a relatively new concept—positive victimology—and describe some aspects of its application. Following my earlier definition of *positive criminology* as a new concept in criminology (for a description of its development, see Ronel, 2015)—different than *positivistic criminology* (Gottfredson and Hirschi, 1987)—it was initially all but natural to expand it to the field of victimology. However, the process of defining this concept was not an immediate one. I found myself hesitating more than once. To clarify it, I initialized several discussions with colleague victimologists; we also presented such a group discussion at the 14th International Symposium of the World Society of Victimology (Ronel et al., 2012). I was invited to present this topic at several international conferences and courses (Ronel, 2012, 2013b, 2014), including the Second International Conference of the South Asian Society of Criminology and Victimology (SASCV), Kanyakumari (2013), which serves as the basis for this book. Notwithstanding the warm acceptance of this concept, I still had my reservations: victimology, to my understanding, ought to always be positive. Therefore, positive victimology might be a redundancy (Toren, 2015). There is no need to add a new concept that adds nothing. Actually, an anonymous reviewer of one of our positive victimology papers claims the same, adding that according to the rule of parsimony, there is no need for positive victimology. In a way, I do agree with this straightforward reviewer, but I also do not. My purpose here is to show how positive victimology, as a concept and as a topic of research, theory, and practice, can contribute to theoretical and applied victimology.

The Need for Positive Victimology

Somehow to continue my above reservation, one may justly claim that in an ideal world, there is no need for positive victimology. Any step in victimology, in theory, research, or practice, should be positive, in a general, everyday understanding of the meaning of having a positive attitude. Victimology should be victim oriented, listen to victims and know their wishes and needs, act for the benefit of victims, and theorize and teach accordingly. This is my ideal concept of victimology, which victimology actually follows, more often than not. But wait a minute—in an ideal world there is no need at all for victimology. Surely people will not abuse their power against others, and there is no need to study it or provide assistance. And to continue this line of wishing for an ideal world—as I was several times asked by my clients during sessions of clinical criminology (and victimology) practice—why does God allow evil and harm? Why does he let them exist? And this painful cry of victims is our painful inspiration for an ideal or perfect world where there is no harm and no need for victimology or positive victimology. Reality, however, is different. Individuals, groups, and societies do abuse the power they may have over others and do cause harm and bring about suffering. And here enters victimology, with its attempt to study, understand, explain, and offer a helpful hand. Nevertheless, victim blaming does exist in society, and even among some professionals and law enforcement employees. It may also influence research and theories, which are not always victim oriented only, and sometimes do represent various motives. Secondary victimizations are known phenomena (Groenhuijsen and Letschert, 2014), and like any other profession, even victimologists may fall under these as well. Therefore, there is a special need within victimology to put an extra emphasis on the positive aspect of victimological practice and study and to make this attitude a leading one. Here comes positive victimology, as a subfield within victimology, that on the basis of a positive perspective will attempt to offer theories, plan studies, and provide practices and principles for intervention.

What Is Positive Victimology About?

Victimology is a growing discipline that involves constructing knowledge by research, theory, and experience and applying it by various interventions for victims (e.g., Fattah, 2014). Correspondingly, positive victimology stands for existing models of intervention, approaches, and theories in victimology. However, these models and theories were not yet connected by a comprehensive concept, and this is suggested by the term *positive victimology* (Ronel and Toren, 2012).

Victimology deals with victimization. Victimization is usually perceived as forced negative and traumatic experience for direct and indirect victims at any level (Herman, 1992; Ronel, 2008a). The reaction to this event or chain of events might cover a wide range of possibilities (Lindgren and Nikolić-Ristanović, 2011). Within this range of different reactions, positive victimology continues both positive psychology (Seligman and Csikszentmihalyi, 2000; Sheldon and King, 2001) and positive criminology (Ronel and Elisha, 2011; Ronel and Toren, 2012), by emphasizing the need for a positively experienced social reaction to victimization. Positive victimology also resumes the approach defined by Ben-David (2000) as "victims' victimology," to emphasize the focus on victims' needs, wishes, and well-being, from the standpoint of victims themselves.

Positive victimology covers different models and theories about change processes and the reaction to victimization that share common perspectives:

- They indicate a *positively experienced reaction*. As I said above, we commonly aspire to bring justice to victims at any level and stage and to promote their well-being as much as possible. Although this approach is shared by most victimologists, unfortunately it is not yet shared by many others whom victims might meet

(Levy and Ben-David, 2008; van Dijk, 2006), whom we may call "victimologists by practice"—for example, members of the criminal justice system, who are many times major figures that encounter victims and may sometimes cause "second victimization" (Groenhuijsen and Letschert, 2014; Hulsmann, 2006). Therefore, the positive approach has to be emphasized time and again—victims deserve social (and scientific) reactions that attempt to provide them with positive experiences as much as possible under circumstances, such as acceptance and acknowledgment of the injustice they suffered, providing them with unconditional support, keeping their rights, assisting and supporting their struggle for survival, and the like. The underlying assumption is that positive experiences can be as influential on individuals, families, and the community as negative ones, and at times the "good" can overcome the "bad" (Fredrickson, 2001; Ronel, 2006, 2013a; Ward et al., 2007). While the idea of positive reaction is directly related to any intervention and victim assistance endeavor, it can also be connected to research and theory, for example, generating a positively experienced participatory action research that might empower the participants (Kemmis and McTaggart, 2000).

- Since a positively experienced reaction is a subjective definition, it might be that for some individuals, a positive experience may be harmful. For example, survivors of past victimization may find themselves abusing substances or falling into substance addiction (Ben-David and Goldberg, 2008). From the standpoint of these individuals, at least at the earlier stages of their substance abuse, it is a positive experience that might calm their inner chaos. Many times, I confronted this during my clinical work—drug abuse, albeit having negative consequences, was positively experienced by survivors. Is it a positive victimology practice to assist these individuals to maintain their abuse? Or to assist a young woman in cutting herself whenever she confronts stress, to get some relief beyond the physical pain? Positive victimology, as I understand it, is by no means neutral to such issues. Therefore, the positively experienced reactions should be limited to those interpersonal or personal reactions to the victimization that have *healing potential* for direct and indirect victims. That is, positive victimology is aimed toward healing the wounds caused by the victimization event (or events) at any level (Ronel, 2008a): individual, family, or community. It also aimed toward a process of recovery that might continue beyond healing the direct wounds of victimization (Brende and McDonald, 1989; Brende, 1993). Although unfortunately some wounds of victimization cannot be wholly healed, the direction of healing can improve existing circumstances and might initiate a journey of recovery. Positive victimology emphasizes healing as a basic right of victims and a social duty of any reaction, as well as indicating recovery as an enduring possibility (Herman, 1992). In addition, positive victimology targets healing as a research topic and attempts to provide theories of change, growth, and healing, for example, theories on forgiveness and its role and limitations (Hart and Shapiro, 2002) or theories on mourning processes that include possibilities of growth (Balk, 1999; Marrone, 1999) or theories on the growing field of posttraumatic growth (Ronel and Elisha, 2011).
- The positively experienced, healing-aimed reaction attempts to *increase the experience of integration* at any stage after victimization (Ronel et al., 2013). A common experience of most victims is a sense of separation, even to the degree of feeling isolated. This sense of separation may be experienced during the victimizing

> event, or by a nonaccepting social reaction, as well as by the victim's tendency to keep the victimization in secret. Victim blaming (Levy and Ben-David, 2008) or nonaccepting reactions of law enforcement agents may increase this sense of separation (Luria et al., 2014). Therefore, a major part of the victim's identity is formed around this sense of separation (Ronel, 2008a). Consequently, the integration reaction is a necessary attempt to heal the separating and isolating nature of victimization. It is the direction of recovery. Research in positive victimology might target integration initiatives and their various components as a sound topic for studies, to generate a theory on the integration of recovering victims.

Following the experience of positive criminology (Elisha et al., 2012), positive victimology suggests three levels of integration (Ronel and Toren, 2012)—interpersonal, intrapersonal, and spiritual. On the interpersonal level, positive victimology calls for social actions of inclusion that can prevent or decrease a sense of isolation. While a certain degree of interpersonal separation experience is sometimes inevitable following victimization, as, for example, is manifested in victim blaming (Levy and Ben-David, 2008), a well-planned social reaction might minimize such an experience. Inappropriately, more often than not, interpersonal reactions after victimization increase the experience of separation, and by doing, so they further increase the suffering of direct and indirect victims (Dancig-Rosenberg, 2008; Lindgren and Nikolić-Ristanović, 2011). Positive victimology attempts to increase the awareness of the high need for interpersonal inclusion following victimization, to develop means of such an inclusion, and to establish theoretical, research-based, and practical knowledge of interpersonal inclusion.

On the intrapersonal level, positive victimology calls for knowledge and practice aimed at integration of the victimized self. Unfortunately, the experience of being victimized many times creates a typical process of formation of a victim identity that includes a certain experience of powerlessness (Ronel, 2008a). Also within this identity, there is an experience of a chaotic self (Batson, 2013). This chaotic self might be reorganized in a struggle that attempts to avoid future victimization by minimizing any perceived risk. Consequently, the individual might become self-centered in a self-protective, unhealthy manner. A process of reintegration of the self is needed as an integral part of the recovery process, as suggested by positive victimology.

In addition, positive victimology carries a spiritual vision of a process directed toward exploration and unification with a power greater than oneself (Brende, 1993). Previous research confirms positive victimology assertion that traumatic events and negative experiences can lead to positive changes, despite the inevitable pain involved. Such a change is associated with positive psychological adaptation, and may lead to a spiritual transformation (Balk, 1999; Marrone, 1999). It is a process of growth beyond the boundaries of the everyday struggle of recovery into new possibilities for the self. Many times, recovering victims that experience powerlessness are facing an existential crisis; such a crisis may open new directions, including among the spiritual development. An experience of greater spiritual unification provides individuals with new meaning and vision, sometimes never experienced before (Ronel, 2008a). Positive victimology indicates this vision as a potential opportunity.

Different models of practice hold the perspective defined as positive victimology. In the field of criminal justice, positive victimology calls for a victim-oriented system. Such a system, for example, may expand the concept of due process, traditionally directed toward offenders only, to include victims as well, that is, a due process for victims during any criminal justice intervention and in court (Luria, 2012). In addition, positive victimology embraces victim-oriented law enforcement procedures that might enhance positive experiences for recovering victims, such as an appropriate restitution (Aharoni-Goldenberg and Wilchek-Aviad, 2008), a victim empowering procedure (Bitton, 2008), or a therapeutic jurisprudence model (Dancig-Rosenberg, 2008; Wexler, 2013). A protruding example is the practice of different restorative justice methods (Braithwaite et al., 2006; Shachaf-Friedman and Timor, 2008; Timor, 2008). Restorative justice is aimed at providing a positive healing experience of social integration that may lead to integration of self and also has the potential to bring a spiritual transformation; thus, it represents all aspects of positive victimology. Support groups for recovering victims (Brende, 1993) also provide an example for a positive victimology model of practice, and an individual therapy for recovering victims might also at times represent the practice of positive victimology (Ronel, 2008a).

Vectors of Positive Victimology

The very term *positive victimology* indicates the "positive" as an aspired direction. Consequently, there is a negative pole that this positive attempts to solve or sometimes even oppose. The spirit of victimology as a whole lies in this aspiration for the positive, and positive victimology emphasizes it. Victimization is a negative experience, and the field and science of victimology was constructed in an attempt to enhance some positive improvement, in theory, society, and law enforcement, and within individuals, families, and groups. In other words, victimology defines victimization at any level as negative—something that we wish to refrain from as much as possible—and aspires for a positive development, something that ought to be. Victimology by large, and especially positive victimology, attempts to create a movement from the "is," the victimization, to the wished, the positive, as much as possible. But what is the wished positive?

Deeply observing the negative to positive possibilities, we may draw several positive versus negative poles that may all represent a spectrum of positive victimology. In other words, we may draw a set of coordinates that go from the negative to the positive, which cover different aspects of victimology and its practices. Such a set of coordinates provides a pragmatic scheme that may assist in evaluating the positive potential and relevance of different interventions. Usually, no vector stands alone, but a set of vectors may represent any approach in victimology. Different theories, models, and interventions have different emphases of certain vectors. Locating different approaches on the overall vector scheme may assist in defining their presumptions and studying and comparing them. In addition, the definition of various vectors enables us to plan an intervention, either by reducing the negative (e.g., reducing risks), as many times as needed, or by promoting the positive, as it is believed here to provide a lasting effect (promoting likelihoods), or both, of course.

The first vector that I would like to describe here is, as I see it, the very basic of victimology: harm versus love. The harm of the victimization stands in the negative pole, and the vector goes to its positive direction of love via justice and healing. Harm may be self-harm, harmed caused by others, or harm that individual brings to others—any harm indicates a negative quality. When moving toward the positive pole, a sense of justice for victims is an important factor that might reduce the impact of the harm. Support is also a crucial factor, and it may be self-support or receiving support by others, and it is also marked by giving support. At the very positive pole, to my understanding, stands love, which opposes victimization. As said, I suggest here a line that goes from the negative experience of harm and victimization through justice and support and aspires for love. The more love we can provide or experience, the better the positive is represented; however, the sense of justice has its own role as well.

The second vector to be described here is that of social exclusion versus integration or sense of separation versus social unification. Since, as said, more often than not a sense of social separation and exclusion accompanies victimization, such an experience defines a negative pole. Consequently, the positive direction is that of social integration and an experience of social belonging and unification. Evaluating this vector requires an examination of both the vector of the individual within a social group and that of the wider context of that group. For example, a person may be well connected to a small supporting group that might be distanced from wider society. In such a case, the strong sense of unification within the small group might lead to a strong sense of social exclusion. On the contrary, a sense of integration with a group that is strongly integrated into society increases the sense of integration of its members, as is the case of various support groups (Kurtz, 1997).

Evaluating the relative strength of each vector (within the group and that of the group within society) can provide an assessment of the overall exclusion–inclusion status of individuals, as well as provide an evaluation of the value system of any theory or approach concerning social inclusion. For example, a battered women's shelter is a needed emergency intervention that provides an immediate security for battered women and within its walls provides a strong sense of social inclusion. However, residents of the shelter are cut off from their regular life and social connections; therefore, the shelter might increase their social exclusion (Saka and Kromer, n.d.). Of course, many times it is better than continuing with the risks outside the shelters. Nevertheless, positive victimology would suggest applying means of social inclusion of the residents to the wider society, as many times it actually happens.

Another vector that is important for healing is dependency and experience of powerlessness at a negative pole versus sense of independence and the exploring of personal strength at the positive pole. While any victimization is forced upon individuals and therefore involves some experience of powerlessness, the means individuals use for surviving it sometimes increase this sense to create a victim identity and what can be defined as secondary powerlessness (Ronel, 2008a). Consequently, a positive victimology response to victimization seeks both to increase the sense of autonomy and strength of the survivors and to increase individuals' ability to refrain from secondary powerlessness. Unfortunately, the negative pole might be represented by those interventions that admittedly or not keep the client in an inferior state in relation to the expert therapist (Saka and Kromer, n.d.). A positive direction in this vector is represented by victim's victimology (Ben-David, 2000) and by the strength perspective (e.g., Van Wormer and Davis, 2003).

The last vector that I want to draw—and the list here is an initial only and open to further development—is self-centeredness at the negative pole versus a growing ability to be other-centered or God-centered at the positive pole. Victimization, which many times forces individuals into an existential struggle for survival, keeps these individuals in a state of elevated self-centeredness (Ronel, 2008a). A sense of self in need of existential struggle leads to a marked self-centeredness. It does not necessarily say that these individuals are more egocentric than the average person—many times it is the opposite—however, they are very much self-occupied (with fear, interpersonal struggle, depression, anxiety, substance abuse or addiction, etc.). Therefore, healing and recovery indicate a movement out of this increased self-centeredness. This vector sets a recommendation for any intervention to target the self-centeredness of its clients and provide them with means of growing out of their self-centeredness toward others, toward life. Growing out of self-centeredness is to become less self-occupied and have an ability to step out of oneself (Ronel, 2008a). In addition, spiritually based interventions—such as 12-step groups—might provide their clients with a means to grow out of their self-centeredness toward God, as they understand God (Brende, 1995; Ronel, 2008b). In a way, this last vector is a basic one and any given vector can be related to it. For example, social alienation indicates or can increase a high self-centered experience, while social integration involves a degree of other-centeredness. Harming oneself or others obviously indicates a component of self-centeredness, while supporting others and experiencing interpersonal love indicates an ability to step out of self-centeredness. Correspondingly, a growth from dependence toward independence assists individuals to reduce their marked self-centeredness.

Conclusion

Positive victimology, as was described here, shares some assumptions with similar fields, such as positive criminology and positive psychology. Within these similarities, positive victimology is mostly victim oriented to represent Ben-David's (2000) idea of victim's victimology. While representing wider victimology in many of its aspects, positive victimology, by its very definition of *positive*, stresses a certain perspective and underlying assumptions, for example, the centrality of integration or the need to grow out of self-centeredness. As far as I see it, the main role of the definition of *positive victimology* is to emphasize several aspects and assumptions within victimology and describe aspects of victim assistance, recovery, and healing—all share the positive perspective. Since I defined this concept, some research has been conducted (e.g., Luria, 2012; Toren, 2015); however, it is only a start. The development of positive victimology into a valid field is dependent upon further research of its various assumptions, components, and practices.

References

Aharoni-Goldenberg, S., and Wilchek-Aviad, Y. (2008). Restitution: A multilateral penal approach. In N. Ronel, K. Jaishankar, and M. Bensimon (eds.), *Trends and Issues in Victimology* (pp. 88–111). Newcastle upon Tyne: Cambridge Scholars Publishing.

Balk, D. E. (1999). Bereavement and spiritual change. *Death Studies*, 23, 485–493.

Batson, N. (2013). The Creation of the Victimological Self [in Hebrew, English abstract]. Unpublished PhD dissertation. Ramat Gan, Israel: Bar-Ilan University.

Ben-David, S. (2000). Needed: Victim's victimology. In P. C. Friday and G. F. Kirchhoff (eds.), *Victimology at the Transition from the 20th to the 21st Century* (pp. 55–72). Monchengladbach, Germany: Shaker Verlag & WSVP.

Ben-David, S., and Goldberg, I. (2008). The relationship between childhood victimization, drug abuse and PTSD and adult delinquency in a prison population. In N. Ronel, K. Jaishankar, and M. Bensimon (eds.), *Trends and Issues in Victimology* (pp. 205–219). Newcastle upon Tyne: Cambridge Scholars Publishing.

Bitton, Y. (2008). Reclaiming power? Women victims of sexual violence and the civil legal system. In N. Ronel, K. Jaishankar, and M. Bensimon (eds.), *Trends and Issues in Victimology* (pp. 130–149). Newcastle upon Tyne: Cambridge Scholars Publishing.
Braithwaite, J., Ahmed, E., and Braithwaite, V. (2006). Shame, restorative justice and crime. In F. Cullen, J. Wright, and K. Belvins (eds.), *Taking Stock: The Status of Criminological Theory* (pp. 397–417). London: Transaction Publishers.
Brende, J. O. (1993). A 12-step recovery program for victims of traumatic events. In J. P. Wilson and B. Raphael (eds.), *International Handbook of Traumatic Stress Syndromes* (pp. 867–877). New York: Plenum Press.
Brende, J. O. (1995). Twelve themes and spiritual steps. In G. S. Everly Jr. and J. M. Lating (eds.), *Psycotraumatology* (pp. 211–229). New York: Plenum Press.
Brende, J. O., and McDonald, E. (1989). Post-traumatic spiritual alienation and recovery in Vietnam combat veterans. *Spirituality Today*, 41(3), 319–340.
Dancig-Rosenberg, H. (2008). Sexual assault victims: Empowerment or re-victimization? The need for a therapeutic jurisprudence model. In N. Ronel, K. Jaishankar, and M. Bensimon (eds.), *Trends and Issues in Victimology* (pp. 150–174). Newcastle upon Tyne: Cambridge Scholars Publishing.
Elisha, E., Idisis, Y., and Ronel, N. (2012). Window of opportunity: Social acceptance and life transformation in the rehabilitation of imprisoned sex offenders. *Aggression and Violent Behavior*, 17, 323–332.
Fattah, E. A. (2014). Under researched theoretical concepts in victimology—Proneness and vulnerability revisited. In P. Schafer and E. Weitekamp (eds.), *Establishing Victimology: Festscrift for Prof. Gerd Ferdinand Kirchhoff* (pp. 141–150). Monchengladbach, Germany: Hochschhule Niederrhein.
Fredrickson, B. L. (2001). The role of positive emotions in positive psychology: The broaden-and-build theory of positive emotions. *American Psychologist*, 56(3), 218–226.
Gottfredson, M. A., and Hirschi, T. (1987). *Positive Criminology*. Newbury Park, CA: Sage.
Groenhuijsen, M., and Letschert, R. (2014). Secondary victimization and the media: An international and comparative perspective. In P. Schafer and E. Weitekamp (eds.), *Establishing Victimology: Festscrift for Prof. Gerd Ferdinand Kirchhoff* (pp. 205–222). Monchengladbach, Germany: Hochschhule Niederrhein.
Hart, K. E., and Shapiro, D. A. (2002). Secular and spiritual forgiveness interventions for recovering alcoholics harboring grudges. Paper presented at the Convention of the American Psychological Association, Chicago.
Herman, J. (1992). *Trauma and Recovery: The Aftermath of Violence—From Domestic Abuse to Political Terror*. New York: Basic Books, Harper Collins.
Hulsmann, L. (2006). The problematic relationship between victims and criminal justice: How to prevent secondary victimization. In The XXII Post Graduate Course on Victimology, Victim Assistance, and Criminal Justice. Dubrovnik, Croatia: Inter University Center.
Kemmis, S., and McTaggart, R. (2000). Participatory action research. In N. K. Denzin and Y. S. Lincoln (eds.), *Handbook of Qualitative Research* (vol. II, pp. 567–605). Thousand Oaks, CA: Sage.
Kurtz, L. F. (1997). *Self-Help and Support Groups: A Handbook for Practitioners*. Thousand Oaks, CA: Sage.
Levy, I., and Ben-David, S. (2008). Blaming victims and bystanders in the context of rape. In N. Ronel, K. Jaishankar, and M. Bensimon (eds.), *Trends and Issues in Victimology* (pp. 175–191). Newcastle upon Tyne: Cambridge Scholars Publishing.
Lindgren, M., and Nikolić-Ristanović, V. (2011). *Crime Victims: International and Serbian Perspective*. Belgrade: Organization for Security and Cooperation in Europe, Mission to Serbia, Law Enforcement Department.
Luria, R. (2012). Implementation of due process of law upon victims of sexual assault within the criminal law system [in Hebrew, English abstract]. Unpublished PhD dissertation. Ramat Gan, Israel: Bar-Ilan University.

Luria, R., Ben-David, S., and Ronel, N. (2014). Positive victimology: The voice arising from the field. In P. Schafer and E. Weitekamp (eds.), *Establishing Victimology: Festscrift for Prof. Gerd Ferdinand Kirchhoff* (pp. 351–366). Monchengladbach, Germany: Hochschhule Niederrhein.
Marrone, R. (1999). Dying, mourning, and spirituality: A psychological perspective. *Death Studies*, 23, 495–519.
Ronel, N. (2006). When good overcomes bad: The impact of volunteers on those they help. *Human Relations*, 59(8), 1133–1153.
Ronel, N. (2008a). Grace therapy for recovering victims: A restorative 12-step based therapy. In M. S. Sundaram, P. K. Jaishankar, and S. Ramdoss (eds.), *Crime Victims and Justice: An Introduction to Restorative Principles* (pp. 399–408). New Delhi: Serial Publications.
Ronel, N. (2008b). The experience of spiritual intelligence. *Journal of Transpersonal Psychology*, 40(1), 100–119.
Ronel, N. (2012). Positive victimology in theory and practice. Paper presented at the Third Annual Conference of Victimology Society of Serbia: Victims and Contemporary Social Context: Theory, Practice, and Activism. Belgrade: Inter University Center.
Ronel, N. (2013a). From a criminal spin to positive criminology. In K. Jaishankar and N. Ronel (eds.), *Global Criminology: Crime and Victimization in a Globalized Era* (pp. 335–351). Boca Raton, FL: CRC Press.
Ronel, N. (2013b). Positive victimology in theory and practice. Presented at the Annual Post Graduate Course on Victimology, Victim Assistance, and Criminal Justice. Dubrovnik, Croatia: Inter University Center.
Ronel, N. (2014). Positive victimology in theory and practice. Presented at the Annual Post Graduate Course on Victimology, Victim Assistance, and Criminal Justice. Dubrovnik, Croatia: Inter University Center.
Ronel, N. (2015). How can criminology become positive? In N. Ronel and D. Segev (eds.), *Positive Criminology* (pp. 13–31). New York: Routledge.
Ronel, N., Ben-David, S., and Bensimon, M. (2012). Positive victimology—Struggling between "bad" and "good" (a round-table). In *The 14th International Symposium of the World Society of Victimology*, The Hague, Netherlands.
Ronel, N., and Elisha, E. (2011). A different perspective: Introducing positive criminology. *International Journal of Offender Therapy and Comparative Criminology*, 55(2), 305–325.
Ronel, N., Frid, N., and Timor, U. (2013). The practice of positive criminology: A Vipassana course in prison. *International Journal of Offender Therapy and Comparative Criminology*, 57(2), 133–153.
Ronel, N., and Toren, T.-Y. (2012). Positive victimology—An innovation or "more of the same"? *Temida*, 15(3–4), 171–180.
Saka, Y., and Kromer, J. (n.d.). "The mixed blessing": The influence of the shelter staying on battered women self perception. In M. Addad, Y. Wolf, and tova Rosenbaum (eds.), *Crime & Social Deviance* [in Hebrew, English abstract] (pp. 25–36). Ramat Gan, Israel: Bar-Ilan University.
Seligman, M. E. P., and Csikszentmihalyi, M. (2000). Positive psychology: An introduction. *American Psychologist*, 55(1), 5–14.
Shachaf-Friedman, E., and Timor, U. (2008). Family-group conferencing in Israel: The voices of victims following restorative justice proceedings. In N. Ronel, K. Jaishankar, and M. Bensimon (eds.), *Trends and Issues in Victimology* (pp. 57–87). Newcastle upon Tyne: Cambridge Scholars Publishing.
Sheldon, K. M., and King, L. (2001). Why positive psychology is necessary. *American Psychologist*, 56(1), 216–217.
Timor, U. (2008). An informal approach to delinquents and their victims: An alternative to standard punishment. In N. Ronel, K. Jaishankar, and M. Bensimon (eds.), *Trends and Issues in Victimology* (pp. 32–56). Newcastle upon Tyne: Cambridge Scholars Publishing.
Toren, T. Y. (2015). Theoretical and practical aspects of positive victimology. In N. Ronel and D. Segev (eds.), *Positive Criminology: The Good Can Overcome the Bad* (pp. 237–249). London: Routledge.

van Dijk, J. (2006). The mark of Abel: Reflections on the social labeling of victims of crime. Lecture delivered on the occasion of the official acceptance of the Pieter van Vollenhoven Chair in Victimology, Human Security and Safety at Tilburg University on November 24.

Van Wormer, K., and Davis, R. D. (2003). *Addiction Treatment: A Strengths Perspective.* Pacific Grove, CA: Brooks/Cole-Thomson.

Ward, T., Mann, R. E., and Gannon, T. A. (2007). The good lives model of offender rehabilitation: Clinical implications. *Aggression and Violent Behavior*, 12, 87–107.

Wexler, D. B. (2013). Getting and giving: What therapeutic jurisprudence can get from and give to positive criminology. Arizona Legal Studies. Retrieved from http://ssrn.com/abstract=2220509.

Interpersonal Cyber Crimes

IV

15

Generation Y and Online Victimization in Nigeria
How Vulnerable Are Younger Internet Users?

PHILIP NDUBUEZE

Contents

Introduction

Digital technology has produced a generation of people who have developed a strong sense of attachment to the Internet, computers, cell phones, and computer-mediated communications like emails, social networking sites, and instant messaging. This generation, often referred to as generation Y, is computer hypersensitive and Internet centric. They have a growing network of friends that they met for the first time online and with whom they sometimes make offline contacts. Young people normally shut out their parents or guardians, who are supposed to do the gatekeeping function and protect them from online predators.

On July 22, 2012, a 24-year-old young woman, Cynthia Osokogu, the only daughter of a retired army general, was reportedly murdered in cold blood in a hotel room in Festac town, Lagos, Nigeria, by two male undergraduate students whom she met on Facebook. The suspects were eventually tracked by the Nigerian police through the hotel's closed-circuit television (CCTV) camera footage and prosecuted (Usman, 2012). The murder of Miss

Osokogu has raised serious concerns about the safety of thousands of young Nigerians who interface with hitherto unknown persons on the Internet.

The Internet and other new technologies are a necessary evil in society (Shalhoub-Kevorkian and Berenblum, 2010). Teenagers use them to connect and socialize with their friends (Keith and Martin, 2005). Two-thirds of those within the age bracket of 12–15 and a quarter of the 8–11 age bracket frequent social networking sites (Spielhofer, 2010). Students, whether they are offenders or victims, do not want to be disconnected from their online social networks (Kraft and Wang, 2009). Internet traffic of the world is dominated by generation Y (Ndubueze, 2013). There is a surge on the number of young people who access the Internet and computer-mediated communications (Bowker, 2000; Hinduja and Patchin, 2007). Criminals have also found in the Internet and other computer-mediated communications a veritable platform for information exchange (Di Marco and Dimarco as cited in Holt, 2010). Hirtenlehner et al. (2012) identified four different patterns of stalking. One in 13 children who are between the ages of 11 and 16 have repeatedly been victims of cyber bullying in the past one year. One-quarter of children who are 14 years of age have arranged a face-to-face meeting with an online contact, while 15% of the 8- to 12-year-old bracket have done so (Spielhofer, 2010). Similarly, one in seven children between the ages of 10 and 17 are sexually solicited online (Iowa Internet Crime Against Children, 2009).

Despite the grave risk the Internet and computer-mediated communication platforms expose young people to, the subject matter of online victimization of young people and its intricacies have not been fully explored by researchers. This chapter attempts to fill that void by bringing to the fore the high vulnerability level of generation Y to online victimization. The chapter argues that younger Internet users are more venerable to online victimization than older Internet users, and that age correlates with victimization. It identifies factors responsible for this scenario and recommends strategies for reducing the online victimization rate of generation Y.

Conceptualizing Generation Y

The term *generation Y* is often used to refer to people born in the 1980s and later. Dacosta et al. (2012) observe that this category of people has been variously referred to as “the millennial generation,” “generation M,” “digital natives,” and “the net generation” in the literature.

People within this age bracket are technology sensitive and computer centric. They spend the better part of their day with their hands and eyes on computers and cell phones, texting, chatting, mailing, and messaging. In Nigeria today, perhaps because of the limited admission spaces in institutions of higher learning, coupled with the rising rate of youth unemployment, many youth who are not in school are either learning a trade or craft or hunting for job. Relatively, only a few are actively engaged in the labor force. Unlike the rest of the population, generation Y has spare time and capacity, which look for platforms for expression. Obviously, the Internet, and particularly social media, has become one of the preferred platforms for young people to express and engage themselves in a virtual world that beats the barriers of highly policed borders. Unfortunately, this engagement has not been all about work and leisure, but also of crime and criminality. Many young Nigerians have been victimized online, and many are increasingly being exposed to online victimization. The recent celebrated case of a young Nigerian woman who was trapped

Table 15.1 Online Character Index of Generations Y and X

Generation Y	Generation X
Computer/Internet centric	Computer/Internet centric
Internet adventurous	Internet cautious
Online friendly	Online nonfriendly
Online carefree	Online careful
Fun/compulsion-based surfing	Work/need-based surfing
Predators—insensitive	Predators—hypersensitive
Have short attention span	Have long attention span
Patient—deficit	Patient—full
Have less privacy concerns	Have high privacy concerns
Want immediate gratification	Can defer gratification
Trust indiscriminately	Trust discriminately
Need supervision	Self-regulated

via Facebook and eventually murdered in cold blood in a hotel room in Lagos is perhaps a classic example.

Furthermore, generation Y possesses some character traits that clearly distinguish it from generation X (comprising of those born earlier than the 1980s). This generational gap explains the difference in their approach to emerging technologies and their vulnerability to online victimization. These differences are highlighted in Table 15.1.

Moreover, in Nigeria certain socioeconomic factors account for the vulnerability state of younger Internet users. First is the increased admittance of young people into the virtual community. This is made possible by the recent crash in Internet access charges and the price of cell phones and SIM cards. Second, there is high youth unemployment; thus, some unemployed young adults hang out on the Internet as a pastime. Third, today, unlike a decade ago, in order to support their respective families, more women are engaged in the labor force. Thus, such women may not have time to closely supervise the activities of their youngsters as they otherwise would have done. Consequently, generation Y has spare time and capacity, which look for platforms for expression, and found the Internet as such a platform.

Mapping the Routine Activities of Generation Y in the Digital Age

Generation Y constitutes a unique breed of people whose routine activities have been greatly influenced by digital technologies. They are born in the digital era (within 18–29 years of age) and have been referred to as "digital natives," and opposed to their counterparts who were born earlier (aged 30 years and above), referred to as "digital immigrants" (DaCosta et al., 2012). Research has shown that there is a strong correlation between routine activities and lifestyles and criminal victimization. Miethe et al. (1987) in a study of 107,678 residents of 13 U.S. cities found that routine activities and lifestyle variables have a strong direct correlation with individual risk of property victimization. Pratt et al. (2010) found a correlation between users' routine activities online and Internet fraud victimization. Cuevas et al. (2007) noted that several studies have linked juvenile victimization to juvenile delinquency, and that in criminology the vulnerability of delinquent youth is usually attributed to their risky activities.

The results of more than 60 net generation focus groups of college students in many countries indicate that net generation students' behaviors are statistically significantly different (Ferris, 2012). They exploit multitasking opportunities with ease, are attached to social media, and seek immediate gratification from digital space (Gleason, 2012). A study by Zick (2010) revealed that in 2003–2005, adolescents spent on average more than six hours per day in leisure activities. Of this, about two-thirds was spent on passive leisure activities and less than one-third was spent on leisure activities that were likely to promote their personal growth. In the digitalized era, it is very probable that a large portion of the said two-thirds is spent online.

The digital age is awash with a free flow of information across age, class, geographic, racial, religious, sex, and time boundaries. The routine activities of generation Y in the digital space for the most part range from chats, instant messaging, and emailing to blogging, gaming, and phoning. While these activities in themselves are not necessarily harmful, they break the barriers of parental control and supervision and expose young adults to people whose intent may be malicious and criminal. Online predators exploit the naivety and quest for companionship of youngsters to victimize them. The Internet offers deviants, criminals, and terrorists a veritable platform to engage young people in a false friendship that offers them false hope and leaves their parents or guardians clueless about what is going on. Online predators exploit the anonymity the Internet guarantees to hide their true identity and criminal agenda until it is executed.

With the lax parental regulation, coupled with the relatively low level of digital literacy among parents, many young people loiter on cyber space, thereby exposing themselves to criminal victimization. Depression and feelings of boredom can also lead to compulsive use of the Internet by young people. Some youth resort to the Internet as a means of easing tension and bottled-up feelings of anxiety. Keeping a long list of Facebook friends on social media has become fashionable among young people. These young adults also media multitask. While surfing the net, they may be listening to music from their cell phones at the same time. Young people, unlike older people, seem to have less concern for privacy. Personal photos and profiles are posted indiscriminately online, unmindful of the fact that these could be used by criminal elements to victimize them.

Cyber cafes have remained one of the most popular Internet access location in Nigeria. This is more so because broadband Internet access is not so common among generation Y, who obviously do not have the financial wherewithal to service it. Conceptually, some of generation Y are concerned about their safety online, as Radda and Ndubueze (2013) found that fear of online victimization was high among undergraduates in Nigeria, and that fear of fraudulent mail was the most expressed fear. But in reality, these fears have not been able to dissuade them from their routine activities online, which oftentimes are foolhardy.

Age and Predatory Online Victimization

Studies have shown a strong correlation between age and criminal victimization (Zalaquett and Chatters, 2014). The safety of young people online in the digital age has raised fundamental security concerns across the globe. The last decade or so has seen a robust debate on the exposure of young people generally online and how this increased exposure is putting them at a pretty high risk of victimization. The Internet has become embedded in the social life of children and young people. Digital technologies, be it the Internet, instant messaging, email, or cell phone, have become part of the daily routine activities of young people, so much so that taking this away from them will amount to some kind of "digital banishment" or "digital ex-communication" for most of them. Parents, guardians, and teachers are worried about how much the emerging digital technologies distract young people from their academics and other meaningful activities. However, stakeholders are coming to terms with the sudden realization that the generation Y world is a world of digital tools. Thus, any attempt to separate them from these tools will be an effort in futility and may in fact be counterproductive. Apparently, the most that can be done is to educate them on the downsides of using digital tools and persuade them to be "digital wise."

The growing "digital addiction" among young people no doubt has some far-reaching implications for them and for society. Young people, unlike their older counterparts, are less calculative, less cautious, and therefore more prone to the deception and antics of online predators lurking in cyber space. Young people do not have the capacity that older people have to make sound judgments and wise choices. Their quest for immediate gratification and short patience span perhaps explain their hurried and reckless conduct online. They are often excited about the "freedom" of expression granted them by social media. Without caution and hesitation, they share some personal information, like their full names, mobile phone numbers, address, and photos with unknown persons, by implication unknowingly setting themselves up for both online and offline victimization.

Wolak et al. (2008) identified the most at-risk youth population to include those who have experienced offline physical or sexual victimization, parental alienation or conflict, depression, delinquent inclinations, relational problems, sexual orientation issues, and risky sexual behavior. In a study of 718 adolescents and teenagers aged 9–19 in Hong Kong using face-to-face interviews, Leung and Lee (2012) found that older boys with high family income are the adolescent group that is more likely to be harassed online. They argue that this is probably because they spend much time on social networking sites and prefer the online environment. They also found that older girls' personal information is frequently solicited online. O'Dea and Campbell (2012) argue that social networking sites account for much of teenagers' Internet usage and expose them to cyber bullying.

Furthermore, a survey by Qwest Communications Teens Council Program (as cited in Pragides, n.d.) revealed that teenagers are the latest victims of online identity theft. It identifies five factors that account for teen vulnerability to online identity theft: (1) They chat and sometimes meet with unknown persons through their social networking page. (2) They are ignorant of phishing scams. (3) They post their private particulars on several sites. (4) They save private information like their username, password, and social security number on their mobile phones. (5) They share their social security number while applying for jobs online.

Structure of Nigerian Virtual Community

The Nigerian society is undergoing very rapid structural changes. The past decade has been the most dramatic with the explosion of digital technologies. There is a growing migration from the analog platform to the digital platform in virtually every sector of the Nigerian society. The 2000s is marked by the "liberalization" of cell phones and Internet access.

Expectedly, the last half decade or so saw the admission of many young Nigerians into the virtual community. This admission was perhaps facilitated by the crash in price of cell phones, SIM cards, and airtime tariff. The proliferation of cyber cafes in major cities and towns, as well as university campuses, is also a contributing factor. Internet modems are much more affordable and common today. The fallout of the above scenario is increased Internet access points and options to Nigerians. The virtual window keeps widening as digital culture becomes increasingly embedded in the texture of the everyday life of the average Nigerian.

Social media and social networking sites are now very popular. Consequently, any Nigerian who is not enrolled in them is perceived to be old-fashioned and cranky. Perhaps due to peer pressure, many young Nigerians get enrolled into the virtual community without understanding its dynamics and intricacies. Membership to this community is relatively open, while the motivation for enrollment is mixed, ranging from work to leisure and from deviance to criminality. Apart from increasingly becoming an indispensable part of the life of the average Nigerian, the Internet and its associated culture has become a fashion of some sort. Fundamentally, this scenario has produced a bandwagon effect that sees certain people migrating from the analog space to the digital space from a purely fashion consideration rather than a need-based consideration.

Nowadays, BlackBerries, iPhones, and iPads have become increasingly popular and young people can connect to the Internet with these electronic devices away from home and far from the prying eyes of their parents or guardians. Some of these electronic devices were obtained from their parents, who seldom use them. In public places like markets, worship centers, airports, and motor parks, it is no longer uncommon to see young people carrying smart phones and sometimes iPads, oftentimes with their ear piece attached—all in a bid to stay connected to their friends and loved ones, most times out of an innate compulsion.

Categorization of Nigerian Virtual Community

The Nigerian virtual community can be divided into three mutually exclusive categories. This classification is by no means exhaustive, but a mere preliminary categorization based on the researcher's observation.

Category A: The Digital Affable

This category includes persons with a strong digital skill set. They are at home with their computers, cell phones, BlackBerries, and the Internet. The interface via social media and social networking sites. They have integrated digital tools into their daily lives and made them a part of their daily routine. They are perhaps the most vulnerable of online victimization. Most of generation Y and some of generation X belong to this category.

Category B: The Digital Enfeeble

These are weak in detail technologies. They use only the basic function of their cell phones and iPads. They are seldom on the Internet. They do not check their emails frequently. The digital enfeeble use digital technology tools only when they must. Even when they carry smart phones, they do so as a status symbol and know less than 30% of the phone's functions. In Nigeria, this category is generation X heavy.

Category C: The Digital Dumb

These ones are digitally cut off. They do not like digital tools and usually suffer "digital phobia." They avoid digital tools if they can, and when they must use them, they are assisted by a third party. This category will give their password to a trusted third party to help them make a withdraw from ATM machines. This category is dominated by the lower class and the elderly. They reside in rural and suburban areas and are not regularly in touch with digital technologies. They neither speak nor understand digital language.

Typology of Generation Y Internet Users

After years of observation and interaction with young Internet users in Nigeria, the researcher proposes a typology of generation Y users below:

Type I: Normal Users

Normal users use the Internet for their normal routine activities, like basic emailing, chatting, blogging, and research. They exercise moderation and do not stay on the Internet for long. They also exercise some degree of caution whenever online. Normal users use the Internet to connect with their friends and families. They also comb the Internet for academic resources, sports, and entertainment news. They differ from addicted users because their Internet usage is need based, focused, and rational. They differ from the aberrant and delinquent users because they do not engage in deviant and illegal activities online.

Type II: Addicted Users

Addicted users feel a strong compulsion to hang out and loiter on the Internet. They are online fun seekers and stay on the Internet to pass time. They engage in risky behaviors online, like extending and accepting friendship invitations to strangers and sharing their personal information online. Most youngsters start as normal users and if not properly supervised by their parents and guardians drift into addictive use. The scope and amount of data out there on the net is fascinating and for a young mind all the more engaging. The curious nature of the minds of young adults will keep them hanging out on the net in order to find answers for questions they may not freely and openly ask their parents or guardians. It will take repeated counseling to return an addicted user to a normal user.

Type III: Aberrant Users

Aberrant users use the Internet to commit deviant acts like bullying, harassing, and stalking their peers and others. They visit X-rated sites like pornography sites and also disseminate X-rated materials to their peers and others. Users in this category knowingly access and download pirated music and software online. They also hack others' computers, not necessarily for personal gain, but just to assert their technology ingenuity and

Internet wizardry. The Internet obviously contains both healthy and harmful information. Thus, user discretion is required. When a young adult chooses to repeatedly visit sites with information harmful to his or her well-being, he or she gradually drifts into aberrant use. Similarly, the use of the Internet for perpetrating misdemeanors can also be considered aberrant.

Type IV: Delinquent Users

Delinquent users are those who use the Internet to pursue criminal ends. The activity of this category of Internet users includes identity theft, phishing scams, and various forms of online advance fee fraud, otherwise called "yahoo-yahoo" or "419" in Nigeria. This is common among delinquent undergraduate students in Nigeria and some young school leavers. They use email harvesters and key loggers to access people's email addresses and send them all sorts of fraudulent mails with bogus claims. Delinquent users constitute a serious threat to cyber security. Most policing and regulatory efforts are focused on how to rid the cyber space of delinquent users who technically constitute a serious threat to normal and addictive users. They have an above-average Internet skill set that allows them to navigate their way around the virtual world while masking their real identity. They are dangerous social network friends and operate in a covert and clandestine pattern.

Discussion and Conclusion

The lifestyle exposure theory constitutes the theoretical orientation of this chapter. Hindelang et al. (1978) developed the lifestyle exposure theory. They posit that sociodemographic characteristics like age, gender, marital status, and income produce different role expectations, and thus different lifestyles that eventually expose people to risk and ultimately account for differences in the chances of been victimized. By "lifestyle," they mean routine daily activities, be they vocational or leisure related. The theory argues that as the child enters late adolescence, his or her activities are removed from the institutional control of the family and school. This, by extension, exposes the child to victimization. Conversely, older people whose lifestyle is different are less likely to be victimized by crime.

Those of generation Y are technology-savvy and have integrated digital technologies in virtually every aspect of their lives. They store books, movies, music, dictionaries, and novels on their mobile phones and computers. They hang out with friends on social media and, by implication, increase their chances of online victimization. Moreover, their chances of online victimization are execrated by the fact that they accept friendship invitations from hitherto unknown people and are quick to disclose some of their personal information to such people. Because criminal elements are on the prowl in cyber space, young adults are perhaps the most vulnerable group of online users.

The bandwagon migration to cyber space by young people is on the increase. While the virtual world offers young people a platform for socializing and leisure, it offers criminals and deviants a flock of soft targets who they hit in their most unguarded moments. Young people have little or no privacy concerns online. The sharing of private information on social networking websites is probably one of the major factors accounting for the increased vulnerability of generation Y online. This risky and reckless habit of young people online makes them all the more vulnerable.

The Internet and computer-mediated communications have changed the scope and tenor of victimology. Obviously, online victimization is one subject matter that will continue to engage researchers worldwide. Young people are increasingly depending on the Internet the world over, a dependence that has increased their vulnerability to online victimization. This chapter tried to establish a nexus between age and online victimization. It argued that the character traits of generation Y coupled with their routine activities and lifestyles make them more susceptible to cyber victimization.

To close the vulnerability window of generation Y to online victimization, urgent intervention is required on all fronts. National governments should establish more task forces to protect children and young people against Internet crimes. Furthermore, Internet service providers (IPSs) should cooperate with law enforcement agencies to police Internet users and alert relevant law enforcement agents once users cross the line of online ethics. In addition, they should be on the lookout for pedophiles that lurk around the Internet with a view to preempting their nefarious activities. Similarly, cyber cafe proprietors also occupy a strategic position in the prevention of online victimization. The role of third parties in the prevention of cyber crime in Nigeria has been explored in a recent study (Ndubueze and Igbo, 2014). Parents should closely monitor the online activities of their children and take time to educate them on the dangers on online adventurism. The various ministries of education should make "Internet education" a critical component of the computer education being taught in schools. There is a need for increased awareness on the downside of digital technology among young people. Above all, an attitude change is required for the message of safe Internet use to resonate with the critical mass of youngsters who dance their Sabbath in virtual space.

Recommendations

The efforts of law enforcement and regulatory agencies to secure cyber space should not be generic and wholesale. Such efforts should be generation specific and pay special attention to the most vulnerable age group: generation Y. These young adults by virtue of their risky routine activities online are prone to different forms of online victimization. In other words, cyber security policies should be youth sensitive.

The government, and particularly the youth development ministry, should think of how to meaningfully engage the youth online since it is in this space where they spend most of their leisure time. More sensitization to the activities, techniques, and tricks of online predators will go a long way in insulating this most vulnerable group.

Above all, increased and sustained surveillance of cyber space will help in detecting the changing strategies of criminal elements who lurk the Internet. There should be collaboration among all stakeholders in policing the increasingly criminogenic cyber space. This way, we will make remarkable progress in our effort to secure the cyber space and apprehend and prosecute cyber offenders.

References

Bowker, A. L. (2000). The advent of the computer delinquent. *FBI Law Enforcement Bulletin*, 69(12).
Cuevas, C. A., Frankelhor, D., Turner, H. A., and Ormrod, R. K. (2007). Juvenile delinquency and victimization: A theoretical typology. *Journal of Interpersonal Violence*, 22(12), 1581–1602.

DaCosta, B., Kinsell, C., and Nasah, A. (2012). Millennials are digital natives? An investigation into digital propensity and age. In S. P. Ferris (ed.), *Teaching, Learning and Net Generation: Concepts and Tools for Reaching Digital Learners* (pp. 90–106). Hershey, PA: IGI Global.

Ferris, S. P. (ed.). (2012). *Teaching, Learning and the Net Generation: Concepts and Tools for Reaching Digital Learners*. Hershey, PA: IGI Global.

Gleason, J. P. (2012). Interactivity and its effect on student learning outcomes. In S. P. Ferris (ed.), *Teaching, Learning and the Net Generation: Concepts and Tools for Reaching Digital Learners* (pp. 129–149). Hershey, PA: IGI Global.

Hindelang, M., Goffredson, M., and Garafalo, J. (1978). *Victims of Personal Crime: An Empirical Foundation for a Theory of Personal Victimization*. Cambridge, MA: Ballinger.

Hinduja, S., and Patchin, J. W. (2007). Offline consequences of online victimization: School violence and delinquency. *Journal of School Violence*, 6(3), 89–112.

Hirtenlehner, H., Starzer, B., and Weber, C. (2012). A differential phenomenology of stalking: Using latent class analysis to identify different types of stalking victimizations. *International Review of Victimology*, 18(3), 207–227.

Holt, T. J. (2010). Examining the role of technology in the formation of deviant subcultures. *Social Science Computer Review*, 28(4), 446–481.

Iowa Internet Crime Against Children. (2009). Taskforce. Retrieved February 24, 2009, from http://www.iaicac.org/Pages/welcome.aspx.

Keith, S., and Martin, M. (2005). Cyber-bullying: Creating a culture of respect in a cyber world. *Reclaiming Children and Youth*, 13(4), 224–228.

Kraft, E. M., and Wang, J. (2009). Effectiveness of cyber bullying prevention strategies: A study on students' perspectives. *International Journal of Cyber Criminology*, 3(2), 513–535.

Leung, L., and Lee, P. S. N. (2012). The influence of information literacy, Internet addiction and parenting styles on Internet risks. *New Media & Society*, 14(1), 117–136.

Miethe, T. D., Stafford, M. C., and Long, J. S. (1987). Social differentiation in criminal victimization: A test of routine activities/lifestyle theories. *American Sociological Review*, 52(2), 184–194.

Ndubueze, P. N. (2013). Social values and the yahooboys' subculture in Nigeria: Towards a paradigm shift for national value re-orientation. *Nigerian Journal of Sociology and Anthropology*, 11(1), 101–113.

Ndubueze, P. N., and Igbo, E. U. M. (2014). Third parties and cyber-crime policing in Nigeria: Some reflections. *Policing: A Journal of Policy and Practice*, 8(1), 59–68.

O'Dea, B., and Campbell, A. (2012). Online social networking and the experience of cyber-bullying. *Study in Health Technology Information*, 181, 212–217.

Pragides, B. (n.d.). Teens the latest victims of online identity theft. Retrieved January 4, 2014, from http://ezinearticles.com/?Teenagers---The-Latest-Victims-Of-Online-Identity-Theft&id=636577.

Pratt, T. C., Holtfreter, K., and Reisig, M. D. (2010). Routine online activity and Internet crime targeting: Extending the generality of routine activity theory. *Journal of Research in Crime and Delinquency*, 47(3), 267–296.

Radda, S. I., and Ndubueze, P. N. (2013). Fear of on-line victimization among undergraduate students: A comparative study of two selected urban universities. *African Journal of Criminology and Justice Studies*, 7(1/2), 35–46.

Shalhoub-Kevorkian, N., and Berenblum, T. (2010). Panoptical web: Internet and victimization of women. *International Review of Victimology*, 17, 69–95.

Spielhofer, T. (2010). Child online risk and safety: A review of the available evidence. UK Council for Child Internet Safety. Retrieved from http://www.saferinternet.org.uk/content/childnet/safterinternetcentre/downloads/Research_Highlights/NFER_Childrens_Online_Safety_Report_final_Mar_2010.pdf.

Usman, E. (2012). How ex-general's daughter, Cynthia, was killed by Facebook 'friends'.

Vanguard Online. Retrieved from http://www.vanguardngr.com/2012/08/how-ex-generals-daughter-cynthia-was-killed-by-facebook-friends/.

Wolak, J., Finkelhor, D., Mitchell, K. J., and Ybarra, M. I. (2008). Online "predators" and their victims: Myth, realities, and implications for prevention and treatment. *American Psychologist*, 63(2), 111–128.
Zalaquett, C. P., and Chatters, S. J. (2014). Cyberbullying in college: Frequency, characteristics, and practical implications. *SAGE Open*, 4. DOI: 1177/21582440414526721.
Zick, C. D. (2010). The shifting balance of adolescent time use. *Youth and Society*, 41(4), 569–596.

Sexting among Teens

Are they Victims or Offenders?*

16

DEBARATI HALDER AND K. JAISHANKAR

Contents

Introduction

Since the beginning of the technology era, the United States and the United Kingdom, along with prominent European and Asian techno-savvy countries, took measures to protect children, teenagers, and young adults from being victims of sexual exploitation in the systems of information technologies. Each of these laws maintained distributing pictures of minors

* Earlier published as "Teen Sexting: A Critical Analysis on the Criminalization Vis-a-Vis Victimization Conundrums" by the authors in *VFAC Review*, July/August 2014, Issue 6. Republished with permission from the Cybercrime Forum, Korean Institute of Criminology.

engaged in sexual activities would constitute an offense.[*] However, most of these laws do not mention the category of the recipients; rather, the word *distribution* is used in broader terms to indicate general recipient, including children and adults. The European Union (EU) convention on cyber crime was the first universal document to declare offenses related to child pornography a penal act.[†] Following the EU convention, many cyber-savvy countries enacted their own domestic laws to prevent online child pornography suiting the needs of the modern digital age. But "sexting"[‡] (Roberts, 2005; Jaishankar, 2009; Reyns et al., 2011; Albury and Crawford, 2012; Agustina and Gómez-Durán, 2012; Ahern and Mechling, 2013; Drouin et al., 2013; Walker et al., 2013; Chalfen, 2014; Döring, 2014), the new generation pornography, defies major antipornography initiatives started by world leaders.

Sexting or "auto pornography" (Humbach, 2010)[§] by "gizmo-freak" teenagers has put a question mark on the usage of antipornography laws toward the creators: teenage girls and boys. Various judgments on sexting have created confusion among the prosecutors, judges, antipornography advocates, and parents of teenagers as to the effect of sexting and its clash with personal freedoms. The situation looks as though the interpretation of the antipornography laws has suddenly been jolted by the hard reality that the victims are perpetrators themselves. The teens use sexting to impress their boyfriends or girlfriends, never knowing that it can constitute a felony (Rosen, 2009). It was only in the first part of 2009 that the menace of sexting began to be recognized. The reports on prosecution response to charges of sexting since April 2009 have become an eye-opener as to how the antipornography laws and policy guidelines of the United States need to be used for the betterment of children of the information technology era.

In the beginning, sexting was considered a new-found way of fun for techno-savvy adolescent children; parents, caregivers, and the legal and justice system felt simple warnings or counseling would be sufficient to teach these children. However, the refusal of three Pennsylvania teenagers to undergo an educational program, which was suggested by District Attorney George Skumanick,[¶] and the consequences thereof sparked huge debates in the United States on the clash of freedoms and legal charges, reiterating the need to treat

* 18 USC §2252A, discusses "certain activities relating to material constituting or containing child pornography" and states in paragraph 2 that any person who "knowingly receives or distributes any child pornography that has been mailed, or using any means or facility of interstate or foreign commerce shipped or transported in or affecting interstate or foreign commerce by any means, including by computer; or any material that contains child pornography that has been mailed, or using any means or facility of interstate or foreign commerce shipped or transported in or affecting interstate or foreign commerce by any means, including by computer" shall be punished for committing the offense of child pornography. In the United Kingdom, the Protection of Children Act of 1978, in Section 1, says, "It is an offence for a person—(a) to take, or permit to be taken or to make, any indecent photographs or pseudo-photographs of a child; (b) to distribute or show such indecent photographs or pseudo-photographs." Among Asian countries, India and the Philippines have stringent laws to prevent the distribution of child pornography, including the Information Technology Act of 2008 for India and Republic Act 9775, also known as the Anti-Child Pornography Act of 2009, for the Philippines.

† Title 3, Article 9 of the EU convention, 2001, speaks about offenses related to child pornography.

‡ The word *sexting* was first used in early 2005 in the *Sunday Telegraph Magazine* to describe the new way of interaction between teenagers, which combines sexual images and mobile phone texts.

§ Humbach (2010) first used the word *auto pornography* to analyze self-nude photography.

¶ In late 2008, a Pennsylvania school reported cell phone photos of scantily clad teenagers being "traded" by teenage boys. In early 2009, Wyoming County District Attorney George Skumanick warned these teenagers, including the girls who created and sent these self-semi-nude images to their friends, with threats that they can be booked under child pornography laws. He asked them to undergo a five-week educational program as "punishment." But three of the girls and their parents, with the aid of the American Civil Liberties Union, protested Skumanick's views, stating that those photos of the girls cannot be called "child porno photos" and Skumanick's warning went against their (the girls') civil rights (Sanchez, 2009).

juvenile offenders of Internet crime differently. However, the later part of 2009 saw the affirmation of the criminal conviction of an 18-year-old boy by the Iowa Supreme Court (Legal Profession Blog, 2009), which further brings up the question, what constitutes sexting to be considered a felony? This chapter analyzes these questions in detail and examines the impact of sexting on judges, prosecutors, law enforcement personnel, jurists, parents, and accused children overall.

The chapter is divided into four parts. Part I explores the nature of sexting and tries to find answers to a few questions: Why is sexting preferred by teenagers? Do all sorts of sexting fall under the offense of obscenity or the category of child pornography? Is sexting synonymous with child pornography? Part II discusses the legal issues of sexting. The thread, what sorts of sexting fall under the category of felony, is pulled in this part also and is discussed from a legal angle with the help of reported cases on sexting. This part delves into the question of whether present federal child pornography laws, as are used in the United States, are effective in dealing with this new type of adolescent sexual prank. Does the First Amendment guarantee or encourage sexting? (McLaughlin, 2012). What is the responsibility of law and justice machinery in such cases? If convicted, how should the juvenile be treated? How can the laws be used to prevent the younger generation from misusing information technology such as mobile phones and web cams?

Part III discusses the responsibility of peers and parents. How much are the parents, as well as schools, responsible for preventing sexting? Can special education really help? Do children need to know the legal consequences of sexting? What is the effect of sexting? Who are the victims and how should they be treated? Also in this part, we return to the legal analysis of the present management of sexting cases by judges and prosecutors. This would be more an analysis on the future effects of present judgments on sexting and a possible global response to the issue. This chapter concludes with a model policy guideline for managing sexting (Part IV).

Part I: Analyzing Sexting

Defining *Sexting*

Sexting simply means sending and consequently receiving text messages carrying sexual expressions and sexual images through mobile phones. Even though technically sexting may mean any such electronically communicated text message, which can include email messages as well as mobile phone messages, the term *sexting* is popularly used for indicating mobile phone text messages only. Such sexually explicit communications have existed since the beginning of the web era, where communicating partners can be (1) only adults, (2) adults and children, (3) only adolescent teens, or (4) adults and teens. However, usage of the term *sexting* for the purpose of sending sexual text messages through mobile phones became widely famous after a section of media started using the term to highlight the perils of sexual interaction through technology among teens (Roberts, 2005). Presently, *sexting* is used to mean text messages that include individuals' (teens especially) nude pictures or naked private parts, like breasts and genitals, or even sexually compromising positions of two partners, captured by one of the partners with the help of a mobile camera, and sending the same to others, who are mostly the creator's friends, belonging to the same age group, via mobile phone or email messages, or uploading these messages from camera phones to social networking sites. *Sexting*, for the purpose of mobile phone texting, has been defined by many in different ways. As per MySecureCyberspace (2012), *sexting* means "the trend of sending each other sexually explicit or suggestive content, usually photographs." Jaishankar (2009, p. 21) defines *sexting* as "self photographing nude body or body parts and sending to others, as well as texting obscene words to known persons (in most cases) using mobile phone."

While sexting can take place consensually between people who are in a relationship, it also occurs unknowingly or against the wishes of a person who is the subject of the content (MySecureCyberspace, 2012). Hence, sexting can be defined as an electronic communication that "includes a variety of risqué stunts." Nude pictures of a girl sent to her boyfriend by herself, as well as capturing indecent images in a locker room by a stranger and then distributing them to a vast audience, can be termed sexting. This is a popular trend among teens to flirt electronically (MySecureCyberspace, 2012). According to Jayne Hitchcock, president of Working to Halt Online Abuse (WHOA) (www.haltabuse.org), sexting happens "when some one sends a nude or semi nude picture via cell phone" (Personal Communication, June 19, 2012). Goldstein (2009) strongly agrees to call it "self-produced child pornography" when adolescents take pictures of themselves bare bodied or involved in sexual activities with other adolescents, and then send them to others by text messages, emails, and so forth. Rosen (2009) calls it "a new and growing social phenomenon." He describes sexting as an adolescent behavior of sending or receiving snapshots or video clips either of themselves or of other teens and then spreading them to the wider audience from their mobile phones or "handheld PDAs like a Blackberry" (Rosen, 2009).

Wilson (2008) points out that sexting is mainly done by schoolchildren. Levine (2009) feels sexting is "sending or posting soft-core photo or video self-portraits," and she says it is "dangerous." Given the amount of reported cases that we are going to analyze later in this chapter, and scrutinizing the experts' views that we have used above to define *sexting*, we deduct that sexting, as used in the web 2.0 era, indicates involvement of schoolchildren of adolescent age. Shellenbarger (2009) analyzed sexting and very aptly described it as kid's "mating calls." Commenting on the nature of sexting, she further feels that sexting can be called "today's version of streaking, skinny-dipping and mooning pranks used by previous generations to get attention or have fun" (Shellenberger, 2009).

Nature of Sexting

From the above definitions of *sexting*, we can conclude that sexting is the digital way of traditional "sexy prank talks" between teens who are either interested in each other or simply want to impress others. This can be considered a new form of child pornography only in certain situations (Wilson, 2008), which we will be discussing in later paragraphs. We find that "sexting among teens" has certain unique characteristics that differentiate it from traditional forms of child pornography:

- Sexting is done by teenagers of adolescent age (13–18).
- In cases of sexting among teens, both the original creators and the original recipients are teens. In other words, in such cases, adults are not participants.
- A mobile phone with a camera is the main device used for sexting.
- Adolescent teens take pictures of their nude bodies or bare private parts or genitals only and send them to their friends either with some written text messages or without any message as such.

- This may even include taking pictures in compromising positions and sending them to others.
- The majority of sexting cases first start among boyfriends or girlfriends either on demand or to impress the other person.
- It can also be done by a teen taking pictures of other friends, including himself or herself, and sending them to a large number of friends.
- In some cases, the self-captured or received pictures are distributed to known or even unknown individuals either by cell phone or by email and social networking sites. It is only in this stage that any adult receiver, who receives the message in bulk, accidentally becomes a participator. But the adult is never the first recipient.
- Such distribution can happen even to take revenge due to breaking of an emotional relationship.
- Sexting is mainly done by and among children of the same school; however, sometimes there can be involvement of children of different schools when they know the sender personally or through social networking sites, or even when the angry teen wants to spread the picture to a wider audience randomly.
- Sexting is done by teenagers who do not know that it can create legal trouble.
- Sexting can create terrible mental trauma on the creator as well as the recipient. It can even lead the creator to commit suicide. It can also lead some recipients to turn into instant bullies toward the creator.

Sexting and Child Pornography

From the characteristics of sexting that we have just discussed above, it may seem that sexting is a new form of child pornography (Humbach, 2010). For this very purpose, we need to have a short discussion of child pornography from the American legal point of view. The concept of illegal child pornography in the United States has gone through various tests since the inception of the digital era. Child pornography laws were mainly created to prevent sexual exploitation and sexual abuse of children while photographing or capturing video clippings of a minor's pornographic images.* Retaining the underlying need to prevent child sexual abuse and child sexual exploitation, the federal law has been amended to suit the need of the digital era, and the present law on pornography clarifies child pornography as below:

> "Child pornography" means any visual depiction, including any photograph, film, video, picture, or computer or computer-generated image or picture, whether made or produced by electronic, mechanical, or other means, of sexually explicit conduct, where—
>
> A. the production of such visual depiction involves the use of a minor engaging in sexually explicit conduct;
> B. such visual depiction is a digital image, computer image, or computer-generated image that is, or is indistinguishable from, that of a minor engaging in sexually explicit conduct; or
> C. such visual depiction has been created, adapted, or modified to appear that an identifiable minor is engaging in sexually explicit conduct.†

* *New York v. Ferber*, 458 U.S. 747, 764–65 (1982).

† Paragraph 8 of 18 USC §2256.

Hence, to be classified as child pornography, any image must fulfill four basic needs:

1. Clarification of conduct: It should be a visual depiction of sexually explicit conduct.
2. Who should be involved? The production of such a visual depiction must involve minors who are engaged in sexually explicit conduct.
3. What should be shown? Such a digital image shows minors involved in sexually explicit conduct. The code has thus used the very strong phrase "indistinguishable from."
4. Clear clarification of only minors: The last paragraph (C) further adds that to qualify as child pornography, the visual depiction must have been created, modified, or adapted to appear that the person involved in it is an identifiable minor.* This provision is meant to particularly distinguish such pornographies that are camouflaged child pornographies, that is, where younger-looking young adult actors are used for creating such visual depiction† and prevent only such visual depictions where minor participators can be identified.

Here, we must note that these laws mention nothing about the creator or distributor of these pornographic images. It is always presumed that the child pornographic images, the sexually explicit conduct of the child models, and the images of the private body parts or genitals of the children for the purpose of child pornography are captured, created, edited, or distributed by adults only. Needless to say, sexting among teens being a very recent phenomenon, no lawmaker felt that child pornography can be created by teenagers also. We understand that this very truth has encouraged the tendency to confuse sexting among teens with traditional child pornography, which involves adult–child interactions. This is evidenced in most cases of sexting. For instance, Skumanick warned the students that sexting can amount to child pornography, as he felt the conduct of the teenagers in capturing and distributing self-semi-nude images amounts to "traditional child pornography" (Humbach, 2010). Sexting among teens creates more legal confusions when the images depict two teenagers involved in compromising positions; this may perfectly attract sexually explicit conduct for the purpose of constituting child pornography. The term *sexually explicit conduct* for the purpose of Internet child pornography has been defined by paragraph 2B of 18 USC §2256.

Humbach (2010) calls *sexting* auto pornography and feels that when it is only self-nude or seminude photography, it need not be called child pornography for reasons of penal sanctions and issues of First Amendment protection. We support Humbach's (2010) view that sexting cannot be synonymous with child pornography for reasons of penal sanctions; however, we oppose terming *sexting* auto pornography. We feel that the word *pornography* carries very strong legal meaning, and it is not suitable for describing sexting among teens when the main motive is not any commercial purpose, but only adolescent sexual gratification. We can therefore conclude that the act of sexting by teens, which involves self-image capturing and sending it to a particular individual who is also a teen, with an intention to impress him or her, may not always be synonymous with child pornography

* Paragraph 8 of 18 USC §2256.

† Criminal Resource Manual 2467 Keeney Memorandum—Recent Amendments to the Federal Child Pornography and Abuse Statutes—18 U.S.C. § 2252A, retrieved July 15, 2013, from http://www.justice.gov/usao/eousa/foia_reading_room/usam/title9/crm02467.htm.

for penal purposes. However, it may amount to another form of digital-aided adolescent sexual behavior.

Part II: Legal Treatment of Sexting

When Is Sexting Illegal?

According to Wilson, "although in this context sexting is generally done between school friends, it's important to note that no matter the circumstance, it is illegal to possess, distribute or manufacture pornography involving anyone less than 18 years of age. Therefore, students who are minors themselves and are found distributing or possessing such images can be found guilty of child pornography ... and can face up to 10 years in prison" (Wilson, 2008). Sexting, having characteristics of child pornography, is being legally considered as a new form of child pornography. From the various reported cases,* it can be seen that sexted messages are being misused by being distributed either through similar Short Message Services (SMSs) or through emails or social networking websites to a wider audience to harass the original sender. Almost every state in the United States has penalized production, distribution, and private possession of child pornography,† besides the existing federal laws‡ penalizing such actions. The two important cases that paved the way for framing sexting as child pornography are *Osborne v. Ohio* (495 U.S. 103 [1990]) and *Ashcroft v. Free Speech Coalition* (535 U.S. 234 [2002]). A critical scrutiny of the judgments of these two cases would reveal why sexting is considered by many to be illegal.

Journey from *Osborne* to *Ashcroft*

In the case of *Osborne v. Ohio*, Osborne was convicted for possessing photographs depicting a nude male adolescent posed in a sexually explicit position. He was convicted for violating the Ohio statute prohibiting any person from possessing or viewing any material or performance showing a minor who is not his child or ward in a state of nudity unless (1) the material or performance is presented for a bona fide purpose by or to a person having a proper interest therein, or (2) the possessor knows that the minor's parents or guardian has consented in writing to such photographing or use of the minor. The Ohio Supreme Court affirmed the conviction, rejecting Osborne's plea that the First Amendment forbids the state's statutes prohibiting private possession of child pornography.§ The court also upheld that the statute is not unconstitutionally overbroad,¶ stating that "since, in light of its specific exceptions, it must be read as only applying to depictions of nudity involving a lewd exhibition or graphic focus on the minor's genitals, and since scienter is an essential

* The cases are discussed later in the case study section.

† States like Alaska, Arizona, California, Florida, Colorado, Iowa, and Michigan have very stringent laws against child pornography, including the creation and distribution of it.

‡ 18 USC, Part I, Chapter 110, discusses and penalizes child pornography under §2252A. Further, under the Adam Walsh Child Protection and Safety Act of 2006, including the Sex Offender Registration and Notification Act (SORNA), it is mandatory for states to impose registration requirements on anyone 14 years or older who is convicted of a child pornography offense.

§ Retrieved July 15, 2013, from http://www.law.cornell.edu/supct/html/historics/USSC_CR_0495_0103_ZS.html.

¶ Retrieved July 15, 2013, from http://www.law.cornell.edu/supct/html/historics/USSC_CR_0495_0103_ZS.html.

element of the offense."[*] But it must be remembered that *Osborne* was decided in 1990, when digital communication of a sexual nature between teenagers using mobile phones or the Internet was not as alarming as it is now. *Osborne* was decided keeping in view the safety of children and question of sexual abuse and sexual exploitation of children, following the path paved by *New York v. Ferber* (458 U.S. 747, 758).[†] In this case, the court gave priority to prevention of sexual abuse, rather than the expanding right to speech and expression under the First Amendment guarantees. Since then, it has been firmly established that possession of child pornographic images by any individual, irrespective of his or her age, would be considered illegal.

Ashcroft v. Free Speech Coalition[‡] clarified what sorts of child pornographic images, which are created digitally, may not amount to illegal possession of child pornography. This is a landmark case that legalized adults' right to view and possess pornography, which is not forbidden by either *Miller*[§] or *Ferber*.[¶] The suit questioned the legal validity of the Child Pornography Prevention Act of 1996 (CPPA). This act stretched the prohibition limit on child pornography to cover not only pornographic images created by using actual children, but also (1) "any visual depiction, including any photograph, film, video, picture, or computer or computer-generated image or picture" that "is, or appears to be, of a minor engaging in sexually explicit conduct" (§2256(8)(B)),[**] and (2) any image that is sexually explicit and is "advertised, promoted, presented, described, or distributed in such a manner that conveys the impression" that it portrays "a minor engaging in sexually explicit conduct" (§2256(8)(D)).[††] The two sections discussed here, which constitute the soul of CPPA,[‡‡] therefore ban "virtual pornography," which is created not with actual minors, but with "youthful looking adults" or "computer imaging technology," and this ban is aimed at preventing the production or distribution of pornographic images or material that technically qualify as child pornography. The court held these two sections were "overboard" and CPPA is inconsistent with *Miller*,[§§] as it covers images that are not obscene as per *Miller*'s test;[¶¶] neither was it deemed consistent with *Ferber*.[***]

* Retrieved July 15, 2013, from http://www.law.cornell.edu/supct/html/historics/USSC_CR_0495_0103_ZS.html.

† Retrieved July 15, 2013, from http://www.law.cornell.edu/supct/html/historics/USSC_CR_0458_0747_ZS.html.

‡ 535 U.S. 234 (2002).

§ *Miller v. California*, 413 U.S. 15 (1973). In this case, the appellant was convicted for mailing sexually unsolicited material. This action of the appellant was in violation of a California statute. Miller's case established certain landmark criteria for judging obscenity in the United States. It was held that obscene material is not protected by the First Amendment. Also, this judgment set up a three-layer assessment test for obscenity, which is as follows: "(a) whether 'the average person, applying contemporary community standards' would find that the work, taken as a whole, appeals to the prurient interest, Roth, supra, at 489, (b) whether the work depicts or describes, in a patently offensive way, sexual conduct specifically defined by the applicable state law, and (c) whether the work, taken as a whole, lacks serious literary, artistic, political, or scientific value. If a state obscenity law is thus limited, First Amendment values are adequately protected by ultimate independent appellate review of constitutional claims when necessary" (pp. 24–25). Retrieved August 5, 2013, from http://www.law.cornell.edu/supct/html/historics/USSC_CR_0413_0015_ZS.html.

¶ *New York v. Ferber*, 458 U.S. 747, 758.

** 18 USC, Part I, Chapter 110, §2256(8)(B).

†† 18 USC, Part I, Chapter 110, §2256(8)(D).

‡‡ The CPPA stressed that these two sections of 18 USC, Part I, Chapter 110, be made the main pillars for judging child pornography cases.

§§ *Miller v. California*, 413 U.S. 15 (1973).

¶¶ Retrieved July 15, 2013, from http://www.law.cornell.edu/supct/html/historics/USSC_CR_0458_0747_ZS.html.

*** *New York v. Ferber*, 458 U.S. 747, 758.

These two cases, armed with *Miller* and *Ferber*'s decisions, had established that distribution or possession of child pornography, when created with actual children, can be an illegal activity. Sexting is typically created with children and by children. However, in some cases, adult participation in possessing the images after they have been distributed on the Internet by children cannot be ruled out. This makes the issue more critical, and therefore compels law enforcers to think that sexting, which includes possession of child pornographic images, is a criminal liability.

Pulling the thread from the above paragraph, we argue that there lies serious confusion as to whether sexting can be framed as child pornography when the question of "storing" and "distribution" arises, and whether the teens who are participating in creating, sending, possessing, and even distributing the sexted images can be convicted under regular child pornography law. As we have mentioned earlier, surprisingly, the federal laws or even the judicial decisions do not mention whether the case can be framed under regular child pornography laws and the accused can be convicted for charge of creation or possession of images when the sender and recipient are both children under 18. We use the word *surprisingly* here because sexting between teens can be traced back to 2002 or even earlier, when *Ashcroft* was decided. This confusion compels us to strengthen our argument that sexting between minors is not child pornography in the true sense for the purpose of stronger punishment prescribed by federal law.* The law has failed to keep pace with the rapidly growing Internet generation. The digital pranks of a child cannot be subjected to stringent laws that are mainly meant for adults.

Judicial Confusion

A series of sexting cases has come up with judicial decisions. We will take them up as case studies for studying the judicial confusion for treating sexting cases, along with the Skumanick case, which is a landmark case in sexting.

Case Study 1

In the case of AH (*A.H. v. State*, 949 So. 2d 234, 235–36 [Fla. App. 2007]), two 17-year-old teenagers of Florida took 100 photographs of themselves naked and engaging in unspecified

* §2252A of 18 USC, Part I, Chapter 110, states punishments for child pornography in subsection (b), which runs as follows:
(1) Whoever violates, or attempts or conspires to violate, paragraph (1), (2), (3), (4), or (6) of subsection (a) shall be fined under this title and imprisoned not less than 5 years and not more than 20 years, but, if such person has a prior conviction under this chapter, section 1591, chapter 71 section 1591, chapter 71, chapter 109A, or chapter 117, or under section 920 of title 10 (article 120 of the Uniform Code of Military Justice), or under the laws of any State relating to aggravated sexual abuse, sexual abuse, or abusive sexual conduct involving a minor or ward, or the production, possession, receipt, mailing, sale, distribution, shipment, or transportation of child pornography, or sex trafficking of children, such person shall be fined under this title and imprisoned for not less than 15 years nor more than 40 years.
(2) Whoever violates, or attempts or conspires to violate, subsection (a)(5) shall be fined under this title or imprisoned not more than 10 years, or both, but, if such person has a prior conviction under this chapter, chapter 71, chapter 109A, or chapter 117, or under section 920 of title 10 (article 120 of the Uniform Code of Military Justice), or under the laws of any State relating to aggravated sexual abuse, sexual abuse, or abusive sexual conduct involving a minor or ward, or the production, possession, receipt, mailing, sale, distribution, shipment, or transportation of child pornography, such person shall be fined under this title and imprisoned for not less than 10 years nor more than 20 years.
(3) Whoever violates, or attempts or conspires to violate, subsection (a)(7) shall be fined under this title or imprisoned not more than 15 years, or both.

but lawful sexual behavior (Humbach, 2010). The two were subsequently charged with "promoting a sexual performance of a child" by "producing, directing or promoting a photograph or representation that they knew to include the sexual conduct of a child," a second-degree felony under Florida law. The defendant AH was adjudged delinquent and the judgment was upheld in appeal. The appeals court held that even if sexual intercourse between the two minors can be assumed legal, the defendant's act of self-pornography is not protected by the state constitutional right of privacy.*

Case Study 2

A 15-year-old girl in Ohio sent nude photos of herself through her mobile phone to others. In this case, she was charged with "illegal use of a minor in nudity-oriented material." The charges were based on Ohio state statute (Ohio Revised Code Annotated §2907.323(A)(3)), which was previously upheld by the U.S. Supreme Court in the case of *Osborne v. Ohio*. The court, however, held that to be constitutional, this statute must be limited to pictures that involve "a lewd exhibition" or "graphic focus on a minor's genitals" (Zimmer, 2008; Humbach, 2010). But the prosecutor used this statute and proceeded. The girl, in order to avoid conviction on charges that could lead to her having to register as a sex offender for 20 years, agreed to enter a plea to a lesser felony. The court refused such a plea and put the case over for six months on the condition that the accused abide by the conditions set by the prosecutor. But the girl was caught violating one of the conditions and was sentenced.

Case Study 3

In New Jersey, a 14-year-old girl was arrested on child pornography charges after the National Center for Missing and Exploited Children reported her to the authorities for the self-nude pictures she had posted on Myspace. In this case, the girl was charged with possessing and distributing child pornography. The prosecutor offered a condition to the girl to undergo six months of counseling and probation and to "stay out of trouble," to avoid conviction that might have led to her being registered as a sex offender.

Case Study 4

In Nebraska, a high school freshman student was convicted and sentenced to 12 months probation for sending nude photos to a 13-year-old girl. This case also included "20 hours of community service, counseling as directed by the probation department, no contact with the victim, a strict curfew and no use of a cell phone during his probationary term" as part of the sentence (Graham, 2009).

Case Study 5

In Vermont, an 18-year-old boy pleaded guilty to reduced charges in a case where he allegedly directed two teenage girls to send him their videotaped nude sexual images. In this case, the boy was sentenced to "two years in prison but will serve 90 days after pleading guilty to two counts of committing a prohibited act and one count of lewd and lascivious conduct" (eCampus News, 2009). This was done as Vermont had passed a law "decriminalizing sexting" "that allows minors charged with a first offense of 'sexting' to be declared delinquent in juvenile court and sent to a diversion program, not prosecuted as adults or put on the state's sex offender registry" (eCampus News, 2009).

* §2252A of 18 USC, Part I, Chapter 110.

Case Study 6

In Iowa, the Supreme Court affirmed a criminal conviction of an 18-year-old boy for "distribution of obscene material to a minor." In this case, the boy had sent a photograph of his erect penis to a 14-year-old female. The photo (along with a photograph of his face and an "I love you") was sent in response to her repeated request for the same, although she testified that she had sought a photo of his penis in a nonerect condition (Legal Profession Blog, 2009). "The court concluded that the jury could properly find the photo obscene based on the instructions of the judge" (Legal Profession Blog, 2009).

Case Study 7

> In Wisconsin, a 17-year-old boy recently was charged with child pornography, sexual exploitation of a child and defamation for allegedly posting nude photos of his 16-year-old ex-girlfriend on his MySpace page. The girl had taken the pictures with her cell phone at her mother's home and e-mailed them to the boyfriend, authorities said. (Wilson, 2009)

Case Study 8

All these cases we have discussed above show the tendency of booking the minor accused as an offender, be it for a lesser felony or as a delinquent fit to counseling. The case of Skumanick (Humbach, 2010), however, can be considered a landmark case as to whether sexting between minors can really be synonymous with child pornography and whether it attracts First Amendment protection. In this case, some teen girls were involved "whose candid photos were found by Tunkhannock School District officials on the phones of male students last year." When reported, District Attorney George Skumanick threatened the girls with prosecution for child pornography charges "unless they agreed to participate in a five-week 'educational' program." All but three girls agreed to go for the educational program. The three girls sought to fight for their civil rights with the help of the American Civil Liberties Union. In March 2009, a federal judge issued a restricting order on Skumanick from prosecuting these three girls as offenders under child pornographic laws. "U.S. District Judge James Munley said he was issuing a restraining order on Wyoming County District Attorney George Skumanick because his proposed action would violate freedom of speech and parental rights" (Humbach, 2010).

The above case studies of judicial decisions show that accused minors of sexting cases are treated no less than sex offenders, even if they are referred for a lesser felony or probation and counseling. A marked difference between the traditional idea of child pornography and sexting between minors lies in the point that the production of sexting may not happen as part of child abuse or child sexual exploitation. As we have already mentioned, except in some rare cases, the creator of the sexted images himself or herself volunteered to be exposed, and the recipient is also a minor whom the creator himself or herself chooses. As Skumanick rightly feared to support his argument for prosecuting the children under child pornography, this may lead to more trouble when such images reach adults who may misuse them. But apprehension of such kind may not help in any way to restrain the adolescents by stronger laws.

Most of these reported cases speak about production of self-nude pictures, naked genitals, or lawful sexual acts, which, even though they attract the penal sanctions of child pornography laws, we must remember that none of these cases speak about capturing such nude photos by others and without consent of the child in question. These are neither voyeurism nor capturing sexual images of children by adults for commercial or noncommercial purposes. But they are "self-imaging" by adolescents who want to impress others of their own age group. Hence, we argue that such production and distribution cannot attract any penal action, especially when the teenagers are ignorant of the fact that these may lead to legal trouble when done by or with adults. However, it needs to be noted that in 2012, 13 states in the United States had introduced bills for regulating sexting-related issues. As was shown by Hinduja and Patchin (2013), 19 states, Arizona, Arkansas, Connecticut, Florida, Georgia, Hawaii, Illinois, Louisiana, Nebraska, Nevada, New Jersey, New York, North Dakota, Pennsylvania, Rhode Island, South Dakota, Texas, Vermont, and West Virginia, have laws related to sexting. While sexting has been considered an issue of legal concern in the United States, in Asian countries, the issue still needs to be focused by law. In India, even though the term *sexting* has not been recognized by any law as a penal offense or even an issue to be legally concerned about, there are two specific provisions that broadly touch upon the issue; Section 67B of the Information Technology Act of 2000 (amended in 2008) makes creating, publishing, or transmitting material depicting children in sexually explicit acts as punishable offences. This provision also includes grooming of children for the purpose of creation of child pornographic materials, as well as recording of one's own sexual abuse or that of others.* However, while this provision was exclusively meant for regulating child pornography as included in the Information Technology Act, in 2012 a new law, the Protection of Children from Sexual Offences Act, was created to address sexual offenses against children exclusively by the government of India. In this law, Section 11 addresses using children for sexual harassment purposes, and this also includes compelling, grooming, or making the children show their private parts for sexual gratification through digital media. Section 13 of this law further makes it punishable to use children for pornographic purposes, and Section 15 makes it an offense to store any digital child pornographic material for any commercial purposes by any person.† But all of these laws predominantly cover child pornography and the issue of sexting particularly. Similarly, in South Korea, the Act of Protection of Children and Juveniles from Sexual Abuse (2011) addresses the issues of creation, distribution, production, and storage of child pornographic materials and abuse of children for the same purpose; however, like India, South Korea does not have any specific laws for addressing sexting or sexting-related abuses or harassments.

* Section 67B of the Information Technology Act of 2000 (amended in 2008) states as follows:
Whoever,—
(a) publishes or transmits or causes to be published or transmitted material in any electronic form which depicts children engaged in sexually explicit act or conduct or (b) creates text or digital images, collects, seeks, browses, downloads, advertises, promotes, exchanges or distributes material in any electronic form depicting children in obscene or indecent or sexually explicit manner or (c) cultivates, entices or induces children to online relationship with one or more children for and on sexually explicit act or in a manner that may offend a reasonable adult on the computer resource or (d) facilitates abusing children online or (e) records in any electronic form own abuse or that of others pertaining to sexually explicit act with children, shall be punished on first conviction with imprisonment of either description for a term which may extend to five years and with a fine which may extend to ten lakh rupees and in the event of second or subsequent conviction with imprisonment of either description for a term which may extend to seven years and also with fine which may extend to ten lakh rupees: Provided that the provisions of section 67, section 67A and this section does not extend to any book, pamphlet, paper, writing, drawing, painting, representation or figure in electronic form— (i) The publication of which is proved to be justified as being for the public good on the ground that such book, pamphlet, paper writing, drawing, painting, representation or figure is in the interest of science, literature, art or learning or other objects of general concern; or (ii) which is kept or used for bonafide heritage or religious purposes. Explanation: For the purposes of this section, "children" means a person who has not completed the age of 18 years.

† See Sections 11, 13, and 14 of the Protection of Children from Sexual Offences Act of 2012. Retrieved July 11, 2014, from http://wcd.nic.in/sites/default/files/childprotection31072012.pdf

Even though "ignorance of the law is no excuse," children, who are not expected to know the consequences, must be taught the basic laws first, in order to be aware of the consequences of their "sexual whims and fancies." Branding these teens as "delinquents" and pulling them to the courts or police stations may be a deterrent for other teenagers who will be afraid of trying such adventurous acts in the future. But the question is, can the legal sanctions, which are meant for adults, really help to make children understand the consequences of such typical adolescent misdeeds? We discuss this in detail in Part III.

Part III: Management of Sexting

Criminalization Will Have Adverse Impact

The majority of reported cases show that sexting is done by two or more teenagers who know each other either through school or as neighbors. However, in this age of cyber generation, soon sexting will be a favorite way of communication with "virtual friends." Some reported cases do show that the creator has communicated with sexting messages to his or her virtual friends, as was the case for the Pennsylvania students, where the girls had sent seminude images to their friends (Humbach, 2010). There are also reports that sexting messages are extracted from the cell phone by the creator herself and have been floated on social networking websites like Myspace or Facebook (Goldstein, 2009). The question is thus, who is responsible for teaching these hi-tech adolescent children to stop misusing the digital media? We rule out the strict legal machinery at the beginning from this list. Adolescents do have a right to explore their own sexuality, as well as to know and learn about the opposite sex's physiology (Goldstein, 2009). Indeed, sexting is not the best way to learn, but at the same time, strong legal punishment may lead to a multitude of problems. The children who are involved in it may never understand the legal implications burdened upon them. Many states in the United States have developed antisexting laws, which give a picture that sexting is indistinguishable from child pornography. But as we have already argued that sexting cannot be synonymous with child pornography, the success rate of these laws in preventing sexting remains doubtful; the Skumanick case (Humbach, 2010) is an eye-opener in this regard. The strict legal approach will make the teens more averse toward adhering to the laws; furthermore, it will encourage the "offending" children to commit more such mischievous deeds, which will immediately turn the media spotlight toward them.

Why Judicial Punishment May Fail

To strengthen our argument against the usage of child pornography laws for sexting cases, we further reiterate the fear that if the adolescent is charged and subsequently arrested for sexting, it may prove more dangerous. Children of the digital era are well versed in practical as well as theoretical usage of electronic technology. The cases cited in this chapter show that in some cases, the "offender" has been sentenced to be in probation or even termed a juvenile delinquent. In certain cases, they have also been ordered to stay without mobile phones for days and do community service. But can this prevent the adolescent from being an offender again? Even if he or she is, in the case of a serious charge, kept in a juvenile home, in probation, or secluded from other children, including his or her mobile devices, he or she can always teach other children to do such "mischief." The child can become a hi-tech guru who will spread the message of how not to be caught while sexting. In such cases, the aim of the law, as well as the judicial decision regarding the offending child, will hopelessly fail. We may pull the example of the first teen who spread a computer virus in the 1980s. He set an example for other kids of how to quickly become famous. Similarly, the newspaper reports, media spotlight, and even Internet research of the offending sexter may motivate other children to follow the same mischievous way to get "sudden fame."

Can School Policy Guidelines Help?

We feel that school counseling can be a better option than criminalization of sexting. The message that sexting can be dangerous and may lead to legal problems must be conveyed by the school counselors first. Since most of the sexting partners are schoolmates, the responsibility lies with the school administration to teach children about the negative effects of conveying emotional interests through sexting. After reviewing the literature on the roles played by the schools (Kolb, 2009), we are of the opinion that this challenge of the digital age can be better tackled by schools as school bullying cases. Even though sexting cannot be categorized as cyber bullying, some reports show that sexting may lead to severe school bullying and cyber bullying as well. In a report (Randi, 2010), a Florida girl was reported to have committed suicide after she was severely bullied by her school and classmates over her topless photo. The report says that she had captured her own topless photo and sent it to a boy she liked. But the sexted message was received by someone else who was using the boy's mobile, and he distributed the picture to other school kids (Randi, 2010). In an Ohio case (Celizic, 2009), sexting and subsequently cyber bullying claimed the life of 18-year-old high school student Jessica Logan. Logan had sent her nude photos to her boyfriend, another teen. After they broke up, the boy, in a spate of anger and frustration, distributed his ex-girlfriend's nude photos to the junior students of the school where Logan was a student. Logan was severely bullied by her schoolmates and finally committed suicide. This case sets an example as to how sexting can pull in other adolescent behavioral problems, like school bullying and teasing. There are thousands of such incidences of sexting leading to subsequent school bullying of the photographed victim happening in the United States nowadays. Many schools in the United States have developed policy guidelines whereby school bullying is termed a good reason for suspending the child. But at the same time, as we have mentioned earlier, sexting cannot be a good reason to terminate the studentship of the child. Thorough counseling to prevent the child from posting self-nude or seminude pictures needs to be a part of the school curriculum.

While reviewing the literature, we noticed numbers of "feedback" to blogs or reports on sexting. One such feedback of the blog of Liz Kolb (2009) correctly points out that schools must stop banning cell phones on campus. Usage of mobile phones by people of all ages, including children, has become a part of modern life; hence, banning mobile phones may not help. The teachers must get to know the present trend of the usage of these phones, in order to teach the children in their own language (Kolb, 2009). We insist upon school policy guidelines toward prevention of sexting rather than anti–child pornography laws. Many schools in the United States have started taking initiatives to educate students about the dangers of mobile phone technology. However, as has been pointed out by researchers, taking precautionary steps against sexting does not mean banning of cell phones on the school campus alone (Kolb, 2009). Texting during class hours can be caught, and the wrongdoer can be given counseling or moral punishment immediately. But sexting includes taking pictures of one's self. Indeed, placing a camera phone within one's clothes and capturing images during class hours cannot be ruled out, but the majority of the reported sexting cases prove that these pictures are taken either in a secluded place or in the bathroom, where there is no elderly supervision. Such activities can be compared to adolescent sexual behaviors like secret masturbation or peeping under the skirts of girls. Sexting in school can only be prevented if it is considered an "adolescent obsession" and properly counseled.

Counseling the Parents

Sexting from home is also a growing problem, much like sexting from school premises. Counselors advise that parents should not become hyper by seeing such cell phone activities (Wilson, 2008). Every parent must understand that children must be given the full right to explore adolescent sexuality in a very careful way. This could be done through school counseling, parental pep talks, and giving the child thorough information about human sexual behavior, the reproductive system, the pros and cons of emotional relationships, the precautionary steps to be adopted while floating personal messages with images to friends, and so forth. Children must be told about the consequences of sexual obsession through sexting by giving examples of adult–child pornographic crimes, especially where distribution of the material to the wider public is involved. The law will then play the role of guardian and not a fear-creating or hate-mongering object. It is only when the children understand the negative consequences before creating the offense itself that the success of anti–child pornography laws will be proved.

Part IV: A Model Policy Guideline

Sexting is the new phenomenon of the digi-kids. We are of the opinion that no law targeted to control child pornography can prevent teen-to-teen sexting. Even if such laws are adopted in a new language, the ultimate purpose of the law will fail. The adolescent queries of the child cannot be suppressed with the fear of law. However, we propose a child-friendly policy guideline for preventing sexting among teens. Below we have framed out the model policy guideline:

Name: Model policy guideline for preventing sexting among teenagers.

Purpose: As the name suggests, this policy guideline will work toward preventing sexting using mobile phones among teenagers.

Scope of the policy guideline: This guideline will be used only for sexting cases where the original creator or sender and the original receiver are both teens (children under 18 years of age).

Definition: This chapter will contain the accepted legal definitions of *children*, *nude photo*, and so forth, and develop universally accepted definitions of *capturing of images*, *sexting*, and *distribution of sexted images* for the purpose of this policy guideline only.

Role of the school:

1. Every school must have its own counselor who should be an expert in treating those children who are caught in digital obsession.
2. The schools must have counseling sessions as a part of their daily or weekly curriculum.
3. The teachers must also accompany children when such counseling sessions take place.
4. The schools must not indulge in corporal punishment toward the sexter.
5. For a first-time sexter, the school must arrange for a thorough individual counseling session for the child, where the student's guardian's presence is compulsory.
6. The school in no way should contact the media to highlight the issue.
7. For a second-time sexter, he or she must be taken to the district attorney's office, accompanied by the school counselor, teacher, and guardian, and the district attorney will impart counseling on the legal implications of sexting as to how it can lead to offenses like child pornography when the message is accidentally received by a pedophile, and so forth.
8. Schools must arrange for talks on cyber safety for children weekly or monthly by calling in renowned cyber crime counselors or experts.

Categories of the creator or sender and receiver: The policy guideline should also demarcate categories of the creator or sender and receiver; for instance, the original creator or sender of the sexted self-nude pictures and the original receiver of the same may be categorized as "first category sexters," those children who receive the sexted messages from the original receiver may be called "second category receivers," those who receive the sexted images from the original receiver and then subsequently send them to others may be called "second category of sexters," and so forth.

Treatment:* The policy guideline can have the following treatments for the sexters:

1. If caught during class hours, he or she must be told to temporarily leave the cell phone with the school administration and attend a compulsory counseling session after school hours.
2. He or she must completely delete the captured images from the mobile phone.
3. If he or she is a first-time sexter, thorough counseling by the school administration would be enough.
4. His or her parents must be called in for a parent–child teacher session to discuss and teach the student about the perils of sexting.
5. In case of a second-time sexter, he or she must be taken to the district attorney's office.
6. He or she must be involved in counseling other sexters, where he or she can share his own experience of counseling and its positive effects.
7. He or she must be told to write essays as to why sexting is dangerous. The schools can arrange for a competition for such essays without hurting the sexter's emotions and public image. This will encourage the particular student to understand the gravity of the situation, as well as spreading awareness to others.

* We do not wish to use the term *punishment*; on the contrary, we will use the term *treatment* to indicate what should be done to sexters.

Conclusion

Sexting among teens is becoming an obsession. The sooner the myth that sexting helps ego boosting is broken, the sooner the children will be out of danger, which may even lead to problems of child pornography. Truly, children are becoming more mature than adults in understanding the various tricks of digital technology. But at the same time, such maturity cannot be controlled by laws that term all sorts of distribution of pornographic images as crimes without differentiating between the sender's and recipient's age, laws drafted in language that is beyond the child's understanding. We strictly opine that sexting, when exchanged between minors, can never be termed a crime in the strictest meaning, and child-friendly policy guidelines are the need of the day to tackle this "child's play."

References

Agustina, J. R., and Gómez-Durán, E. L. (2012). Sexting: Research criteria of a globalized social phenomenon. *Archives of Sexual Behavior*, 41, 1325–1328.

Ahern, N., and Mechling, B. (2013). Sexting: Serious problems for youth. *Journal of Psychosocial Nursing and Mental Health Services*, 51(7), 22–30.

Albury, K., and Crawford, K. (2012). Sexting, consent and young people's ethics: Beyond Megan's story. *Journal of Media & Cultural Studies*, 26, 463–473.

Celizic, M. (2009). Her teen committed suicide over 'sexting': Cynthia Logan's daughter was taunted about photo she sent to boyfriend. June 3. Retrieved from http://www.today.com/id/29546030#.VACcu8WSzbw.

Chalfen, R. (2014). Sexting at a young age. In M. Ball and G. Smith (eds.), *A Revealing Overview: Working with Images: Practices of Visualisation, Representation & Pattern Recognition*. New York: Sage. Retrieved from https://sites.google.com/a/temple.edu/richard-chalfen-ph-d/sexting-at-a-young-age.

Döring, N. (2014). Consensual sexting among adolescents: Risk prevention through abstinence education or safer sexting? *Cyberpsychology: Journal of Psychosocial Research on Cyberspace*, 8(1), article 9. Retrieved from http://www.cyberpsychology.eu/view.php?cisloclanku=2014031401&article=9.

Drouin, M., Vogel, K. N., Surbey, A., and Stills, J. R. (2013). Let's talk about sexting, baby: Computer-mediated sexual behaviors among young adults. *Computers in Human Behavior*, 29, A25–A30.

eCampus News. (2009). Vermont teen sentenced to prison in 'sexting' case. September 4. Retrieved from http://www.ecampusnews.com/policy/litigation/vermont-teen-sentenced-to-prison-in-sexting-case.

Goldstein, L. (2009). Documenting and denial: Discourses of sexual self exploitation. *Jump Cut: A Review of Contemporary Media*, 51. Retrieved from http://ejumpcut.org/archive/jc51.2009/goldstein/index.html.

Graham, F. (2009). Student gets year probation for 'sexting'. *North Platte Bulletin*, December 5. Retrieved from http://www.northplattebulletin.com/index.asp?show=news&action=readStory&storyID=16546&pageID=3.

Hinduja, S., and Patchin, J. W. (2013). State sexting laws: A brief review of state sexting laws and policies. February. Retrieved from http://cyberbullying.org/state-sexting-laws.pdf.

Humbach, J. A. (2010). "Sexting" and the First Amendment. *Hastings Constitutional Law Quarterly*, 37, 433. Retrieved from http://digitalcommons.pace.edu/cgi/viewcontent.cgi?article=1594&context=lawfaculty.

Jaishankar, K. (2009). Sexting: A new form of victimless crime. *International Journal of Cyber Criminology*, 3(1), 21–25.

Kolb, L. (2009). Sexting & texting; schools role. February 20. Retrieved from http://www.cellphone-sinlearning.com/2009/02/sexting-texting-schools-role_20.html.
Legal Profession Blog. (2009). Sexting conviction upheld. September 18. Retrieved from http://law-professors.typepad.com/legal_profession/2009/09/sexting-conviction-upheld.html.
Levine, J. (2009). What's the matter with teen sexting?. February 10. Retrieved from http://prospect.org/article/whats-matter-teen-sexting.
McLaughlin, J. H. (2012). Exploring the First Amendment rights of teens in relationship to sexting and censorship. *University of Michigan Journal of Law Reform*, 45, 315–350. Retrieved from http://repository.law.umich.edu/cgi/viewcontent.cgi?article=1070&context=mjlr.
MySecureCyberspace. (2012). Sexting. Carnegie Mellon University. Retrieved from http://www.mysecurecyberspace.com/encyclopedia/index/sexting.html.
Randi, K. (2010). How a cell phone picture led to girl's suicide. CNN, October 7. Retrieved from http://edition.cnn.com/2010/LIVING/10/07/hope.witsells.story.
Reyns, B. W., Burek, M. W., Henson, B., and Fisher, B. S. (2011). The unintended consequences of digital technology: Exploring the relationship between sexting and cybervictimization. *Journal of Crime and Justice*, 36(1), 1–17.
Roberts, Y. (2005). The one and only. *Sunday Telegraph Magazine*, July 31, p. 22.
Rosen, D. (2009). Sexting: The latest innovation in porno? March 25. Retrieved from http://www.counterpunch.org/2009/03/25/sexting-the-latest-innovation-in-porn.
Sanchez, J. (2009). Federal judge blocks teen "sexting" charges. March 31. Retrieved from http://arstechnica.com/tech-policy/2009/03/judge-blocks-teen-sexting-charges.
Shellenbarger, S. (2009). Why do teens engage in sexting? June 15. Retrieved from http://blogs.wsj.com/juggle/2009/06/15/why-do-teens-engage-in-sexting.
Walker, S., Sanci, L., and Temple-Smith, M. (2013). Sexting: Young women's and men's views on its nature and origins. *Journal of Adolescent Health*, 52, 697–701.
Wilson, L. (2008). Sexting and minors: Child pornography, not child's play. October. Retrieved from http://blog.lawinfo.com/2008/10/08/sexting-and-minors-child-pornography-not-childs-play.
Zimmer, R. (2008). Hottinger: Law didn't anticipate cell phone photo case (video): If teen convicted, judge would have flexibility on sex offender registration. October 8. Retrieved from http://uk.legal.narkive.com/CT2WrWlz/hottinger-law-didn-t-anticipate-cell-phone-photo-case-video-usa.

17

Cyber and Mobile Phone Bullying Victimization among Youth in Singapore

An Exploration of Correlates

THOMAS J. HOLT, GRACE CHEE,
AND ESTHER NG

Contents

Introduction

Over the past few decades, bullying has been identified as one of the most significant problem behaviors confronting children and adolescents (Olweus, 1991). Bullying behaviors typically involve persistent physical, verbal, or emotional harassment of one individual over another, often accompanied by a power imbalance that negatively impacts the intended target (Dake et al., 2003; Espelage et al., 2004). The increased use of technology among youth populations has facilitated the emergence of so-called cyber bullying, where cell phones, email, and other forms of computer-mediated communications (CMCs) allow individuals to create and send harassing messages or rumors about victims in a distributed fashion (Berson et al., 2002; Hinduja and Patchin, 2008; Holt and Bossler, 2007; Twyman et al., 2010; Ybarra and Mitchell, 2004). Additionally, many who experience cyber bullying also report concurrent bullying victimization in the real world (Erdur-Baker, 2010; Hinduja and Patchin, 2008; Kowalski and Limber, 2007; Ybarra and Mitchell, 2004).

The growing research on cyber bullying has, however, provided limited information on the prevalence of this problem in Asian populations (Hokoda et al., 2006; Huang and Chou, 2010; Li, 2006; Wong et al., 2008). This is problematic given the rapid expansion and adoption of technology within these countries, coupled with access to high-speed Internet connectivity. Furthermore, few researchers have considered how cyber bullying victimization may be accounted for through criminological theory in an international context. One of the most commonly tested frameworks regarding online victimization is the routine activities theory (Cohen and Felson, 1979), which argues that victimization is most likely when individuals are placed in high-risk situations, in close proximity to motivated offenders, appear to be attractive targets, and lack a capable guardian (Cohen and Felson, 1979). In addition, individuals who engage in criminal and deviant behavior are at an increased risk of victimization as they increase both their proximity to motivated offenders and the probability of retaliation, while also decreasing social guardianship by associating with delinquent others (Jensen and Brownfield, 1986; Lauritsen et al., 1992; Zhang et al., 2001).

Given that cyber bullying victimization rates appear to be similar cross-nationally (Beran and Li, 2008; DeVoe et al., 2011; Erdur-Baker, 2010; Jones et al., 2013; Li, 2008; Thorp, 2004), it is theoretically plausible that routine activities would be fruitful to explain bullying victimization via the Internet and mobile phones in a juvenile sample from Asia. To address this gap in the literature, this study considers the applicability of elements of the routine activities theory with a nationally representative sample of youth in Singapore. Citizens of this country have a high degree of access to computers, technology, and high-speed Internet connectivity (CIA, 2007; Liau et al., 2005). As a result, this juvenile population should have exposure to technology and prospective experiences with bullying on- and offline. The findings of this study will be discussed in depth, along with implications for criminologists, mental health professionals, and educators.

Routine Activities Theory and Cyberbullying Victimization

The routine activities theory has been applied to a wide range of person and property-based crimes in the real world (Cohen and Felson, 1979; Lauritsen et al., 1992; Meithe and Meier, 1994), and to a small number of cyber crime victimization experiences (see Holt and Bossler, 2014 for review). This theory posits that victimization occurs when a motivated offender, suitable target, and lack of guardian converge in time and space, usually in some sort of risky or criminogenic environment (Cohen and Felson, 1979). Though virtual environments do not always necessitate a true temporal interaction between victim and offender (see Yar, 2005), they do enable access to and interactions with victims nearly 24 hours a day. With regard to cyber and mobile phone bullying victimization, CMCs like email and text messaging provide bullies a platform to interact with victims from any location at any time because they may see or read the message (Hinduja and Patchin, 2008). In fact, the devices used to connect to the Internet serve as a point of victim exposure to motivated offenders throughout the day, outside of school hours. The Internet, computers, and mobile phones increase victim exposure to offenders, as they can be contacted at any time through this technology.

Research applying this theory to cyber bullying victimization suggests that there are various points of exposure that may increase an individual's proximity to motivated offenders (Bossler et al., 2010; Holt and Bossler, 2009; Marcum, 2010). There are also certain behavioral and demographic characteristics that may make an individual a more attractive target to bullies (Erdur-Baker, 2010; Hinduja and Patchin, 2008; Holt et al., 2013; Kowalski and Limber, 2007; Turner et al., 2012; Ybarra and Mitchell, 2004). Guardianship factors are, however, inconsistent in affecting the risk of victimization: limited evidence suggests social and technical guardians may either have no effect on or increase the risk of victimization (Bossler et al., 2012; DeHue et al., 2008; Holt and Bossler, 2009; Marcum, 2008). Due to the inconsistent findings regarding guardianship measures, this study focuses on factors that increase exposure to motivated offenders and target attractiveness. These variables are more consistently operationalized and should provide a point of direct comparison in a cross-national context.

To that end, exposure to motivated offenders in online spaces should directly increase the risk of cyber bullying victimization. In online environments, offenders may only be able to target individuals on the basis of their use of various pieces of technology (Yar, 2005). As a result, youth who have the ability to access the Internet while at school and at home should increase the risk of cyber bullying. In much the same way, mobile phone ownership may be associated with mobile phone bullying victimization, though it is possible that this relationship may be nonsignificant due to the relatively necessary relationship between these two items.

Though access to technology is important as a point of exposure to motivated offenders, prior research has demonstrated that individual online behaviors are critical risk factors for online harassment and cyber bullying victimization (Berson et al., 2002; Hinduja and Patchin, 2008; Holt and Bossler, 2007; Twyman et al., 2010; Ybarra and Mitchell, 2004). The more time individuals spend in various online environments, including chat rooms, instant messaging systems, bulletin board systems, email, and blogging sites, the more increased is their potential exposure to offenders. In addition, these environments provide offenders with immediate avenues to send threatening or hurtful messages to their target (Hinduja and Patchin, 2008; Holt and Bossler, 2007; Marcum, 2010; Marcum et al., 2010; Ybarra et al., 2007). In much the same way, the more time individuals spend texting via mobile phones, the more increased their exposure may be to motivated offenders and the likelihood of victimization (Holt et al., 2013).

Beyond proximity to offenders, there are multiple demographic factors that may make a target more attractive to bullies. Specifically, youth who experience bullying in the real world may be a more readily identified target in online spaces. Bullies may already realize their victim's social marginalization or personal shortcomings, making them an attractive target for bullying in multiple environments. To that end, prior research demonstrates that individuals who are bullied in the real world report experiences with cyber bullying victimization at higher rates (Erdur-Baker, 2010; Hinduja and Patchin, 2008; Holt et al., 2013; Kowalski and Limber, 2007; Turner et al., 2012; Ybarra and Mitchell, 2004).

The attitudes that youth hold toward their school experience, sometimes referred to as school adjustment, may also be associated with risks for cyber bullying victimization (Beran and Li, 2007; Forero et al., 1999; Holt et al., 2013; Nansel et al., 2001; Sourander et al., 2000; Wolke et al., 2000). Youth with poor school adjustment are more likely to receive low grades and underperform in the classroom, and have fears regarding their school environment due in part to social isolation and marginalization while on campus (Esbensen and Carson, 2009; Glew et al., 2005; Patchin and Hinduja, 2010; Sourander et al., 2010). As a consequence, poor school adjustment appears to increase an individual's perceived attractiveness as a target for bullies on- or offline (Beran and Li, 2007; Forero et al., 1999; Holt et al., 2013; Nansel et al., 2001; Sourander et al., 2000; Wolke et al., 2000).

Bullying research has also found a mixed relationship between age and victimization, though the general age of youth in bullying studies is limited (see Tokunaga, 2010 for review). Youths between the ages of 10 and 15 appear to report higher rates of victimization (Cassidy et al., 2009; Kowalski and Limber, 2007; Williams and Guerra, 2007; Ybarra et al., 2007). This may stem from differential access to technology based on the age of the user;

parents and guardians are more likely to restrict access to computers and mobile phones for young children (Smith et al., 2008). Thus, it is plausible that somewhat older youth may be more likely to experience cyber bullying victimization than others.

Finally, the literature is mixed regarding the gendered nature of cyber bullying victimization. A small number of studies have found that females are more likely to report cyber bullying victimization (Bossler et al., 2012; Navarro and Jasinski, 2013; Wade and Beran, 2011), though several researchers have found no significant differences between boys' and girls' rate of victimization (Beran and Lee, 2007; Hinduja and Patchin, 2008; Li, 2006; Tokunaga, 2010; Wolack et al., 2007; Ybarra, 2004). As a result, it is plausible that females may report a higher risk of victimization in online spaces.

Data and Methods

This study utilized data from a self-report survey collected from one primary (n = 680) and eight secondary schools (n = 3382) in Singapore in 2006. These schools were located across the country, and incorporated students from all social, economic, and cultural backgrounds. This sample was developed to understand the prevalence and incidence of both real-world and cyber bullying across Singapore. Due to missing data, the total sample size for cyber bullying victimization is n = 3223 for mobile phone bullying victimization. This sample is, however, in keeping with the demographic composition (56% male, 44% female) of the larger data set and the youth population of Singapore generally (CIA, 2007).

Dependent Variables

To assess *cyber bullying victimization*, a scale for bullying experiences in chat rooms, email, computer instant messaging, bulletin board systems, and newsgroups was created ($\alpha = 0.921$). Due to limited variation in the frequency of bullying experiences, this was collapsed into a binary (0 = no, 1 = yes) response with 18.9% of the sample reporting cyber victimization (see Table 17.1 for details). A two-item scale ($\alpha = 0.806$) was created to measure *mobile phone bullying victimization* through mobile phone text messages and mobile multimedia (MMS) messages. This scale was also turned into a binary measure, with 17.7% of the sample reporting mobile phone bullying victimization.

Independent Variables

Access to Technology

Three measures of access to technology were included in the models. To measure students' access to Internet usage at school (*school Internet use*), students were asked, "Can you use the Internet to 'chat,' send emails, instant messages, or post on web pages in school?" (0 = no, 1 = yes). Similarly, students were also asked, "Can you use the Internet to 'chat,' send emails, instant message, or post on web pages at home?" (0 = no, 1 = yes) (*home Internet usage*). Seventy percent of the youth indicated having access to the Internet at home, whereas only 37.7% indicated Internet access at school. Furthermore, for its expected connection to mobile phone victimization, students were asked, "Do you have your own mobile phone?" (0 = no, 1 = yes) (*mobile phone ownership*). The majority of

Table 17.1 Descriptive Statistics

Dependent Variables	*M*	SD	Min	Max
Cyber victimization	0.189	0.392	0	1
Mobile victimization	0.177	0.376	0	1

	Cyber Model			Mobile Model				
Independent Variables	*M*	SD	*N*	*M*	SD	*N*	Min	Max
School Internet use	0.377	0.485	3223	0.377	0.485	3233	0	1
Home Internet use	0.702	0.457	3223	0.701	0.458	3233	0	1
Mobile phone ownership	0.760	0.427	3223	0.759	0.428	3233	0	1
Chat room use	1.463	0.916	3223	1.467	0.920	3233	1	4
Email use	1.822	0.980	3223	1.827	0.983	3233	1	4
IM use	2.332	1.266	3223	2.333	1.266	3233	1	4
Bulletin board use	1.279	0.687	3223	1.282	0.692	3233	1	4
Blog use	1.504	0.909	3223	1.505	0.910	3233	1	4
MMS texting	1.409	0.823	3223	1.410	0.825	3233	1	4
Physical bullying	2.136	2.219	3223	2.143	2.223	3233	0	10
School adjustment	2.783	1.312	3223	2.778	1.312	3233	1	7
Class level	0.839	0.367	3223	0.839	0.367	3233	0	1
Gender	0.446	0.497	3223	0.445	0.497	3233	0	1

students indicated that they owned a mobile phone (cyber model mean = 0.76, SD = 0.427; mobile phone model mean = 0.759, SD = 0.428).

Online Routine Behaviors

To further examine students' relationship with technology, they were asked how often (1 = rarely or never, 2 = one or two times per week; 3 = three or four times per week; 4 = almost every day) they used various forms of technology that could increase their exposure to motivated offenders. Specifically, they were asked how often they entered chat rooms (*chat room use*), sent emails (*email use*), sent computer instant messages (*IM use*), posted on bulletin boards (*bulletin board use*), wrote on blogs (*blog use*), and sent multimedia messages (*MMS texting*) in the last year. The majority of Singapore youth (75.1%) indicated they rarely or never used a chat room. Similarly, 81.9% indicated they rarely or never used an online bulletin board. Seventy-one percent (71.5%) and 74.6% of the respondents indicated they never or rarely used an online blog and or sent MMS texts, respectively. Email and IM usage were reported at much higher rates: half (51.7%) of respondents indicated they used email at least once or twice per week, and more than half, 60.3% of respondents, reported they used IM at least once or twice a week; 28.8% indicated that they did so every day.

Target Suitability

To assess the role of target suitability in this model, we included four variables associated with bullying victimization: (1) whether the student had been physically bullied (*physical bullying*),

(2) his or her school adjustment (*school adjustment*), (3) his or her year in school (*class level*), and (4) gender (*gender*). For *physical bullying*, students were asked how often any of five events happened over the past 12 months: (1) "being teased in an unpleasant way," (2) "being called hurtful names," (3) "being left out of things on purpose," (4) "being threatened with harm," and (5) "being hit or kicked" (0 = never, 1 = sometimes, 2 = often). A *physical bullying* scale was created by adding the responses to the five items, creating a reliable scale ($\alpha = 0.803$) that ranges from 0 (indicated no reported bullying) to 10 (all types of bullying occurring often; cyber model mean = 2.136, SD = 2.219; mobile phone model mean = 2.143, SD = 2.223).

In order to examine school adjustment (*school adjustment*), a seven-item Likert-type scale question with pictorial responses was used. Specifically, students were presented with the statement "Now look at these pictures and place a circle around the letter under the face which is most like you when you are at school?" with seven pictures indicating varying levels of happiness (1 = very happy to 7 = very sad). The use of visual measures is debated in the literature (Chambers and Craig, 1998; Davies and Brember, 1994; Reynolds et al., 2008), though the range in age and reading comprehension of the respondents makes this a more useful measure to capture responses. The mean answer for students on the scale indicated most students were generally content (cyber model mean = 2.783, SD = 1.312; mobile phone model mean = 2.778; SD = 1.312).

School level (*class level*) (0 = secondary school, 1 = primary school) and gender (*gender*) (0 = male, 1 = female) were both measured dichotomously. The majority of students surveyed were from secondary schools (83.9%), reflecting a slightly older population. The final sample was approximately 56% male and 44% female, which is similar to that of the nation's population of male (51.7%) and female (48.3%) youth (CIA, 2007).

Findings

Two binary logistic regression models were estimated for cyber bullying and mobile phone bullying victimization, respectively, due to the use of dichotomous dependent variables with limited variation. In the model for cyber bullying victimization (see Table 17.2), the ability to access the Internet from home increases the risk of cyber bullying victimization. Those youth who spend more time in every form of electronic communication were also significant, except for MMS texting. Thus, an individual's proximity to motivated offenders in online environments appears to significantly increase the likelihood of victimization (see also Holt and Bossler, 2007; Holt et al., 2013; Marcum et al., 2010).

Several variables for target attractiveness were also associated with an increased risk of victimization. Youth who were bullied in the real world were more likely to report cyber bullying victimization, as were those who reported negative school adjustments. Finally, females and younger students were more likely to report experiencing cyber bullying victimization. Given that gender was a significant predictor for target attractiveness (see also Holt and Bossler, 2007; Tokunaga, 2010), we partitioned the model into males and females to assess any significant differences between the sexes (see Table 17.2, Model 2). Though there are different variables that are significant for males and females, we used equality of coefficient tests (Paternoster et al., 1998) to determine any statistically significant differences between the sexes. The results indicate that males who blogged and sent MMS text messages frequently were more likely to experience cyber bullying victimization. School level was also significantly different between the sexes, such that females in earlier grades

Table 17.2 Cyberbullying Victimization Regression Model

	Model 1		Model 2		
			Male	Female	
	(n = 3223)		(n = 1785)	(n = 1438)	
	B	SE	Exp. B	Exp. B	Exp. B
Home Internet use	0.383	0.135	1.467**	1.780**	1.237
School Internet use	0.127	0.103	1.135	1.065	1.200
Mobile phone ownership	−0.176	0.126	0.839	0.821	0.835
Chatroom	0.125	0.052	1.133*	1.095	1.164
Email	0.110	0.056	1.116*	1.071	1.162
Computer IM	0.220	0.050	1.246**	1.301**	1.183*
Bulletin boards	0.183	0.072	1.201*	1.273	1.100
Blogs	0.139	0.015	1.149*	**1.191***	**1.137**
MMS	0.043	0.059	1.044	**1.101**	**1.001**
Traditional bullying	0.235	0.021	1.265**	1.265**	1.280**
School adjustment	0.078	0.036	1.081*	1.056	1.114
School level	−0.097	0.031	0.908**	0.900	0.928*
Gender	0.282	0.100	1.326**	—	—
Pseudo-R^2	0.160			0.191	0.129

Note: Model 1: Chi-square = 336.822**, −2LL = 2790.487. Model 2: Male model: Chi-square = 221.460**, −2LL = 1466.559. Female model: Chi-square = 122.456**, −2LL = 1315.036. Any significant differences ($z \geq 1.96$) between the partitioned models are noted in bold text. SE = standard error; Exp. = experiment.

*$p \leq 0.05$, **$p \leq 0.01$.

were more likely to be victimized. This finding is in keeping with the literature regarding gender differences in the likelihood of cyber bullying victimization (see Bossler et al., 2012; Navarro and Jasinski, 2013; Wade and Beran, 2011).

An additional set of regression models was conducted for mobile phone bullying victimization (see Table 17.3, Model 1), which indicates there are some differences in the risk factors for mobile phone bullying relative to cyber bullying victimization. Specifically, cell phone ownership was correlated with victimization, as was time spent blogging and sending MMS texts. Spending less time in IM chats was also correlated with the risk of mobile phone victimization, which may reflect increased time in other online environments. Thus, exposure and proximity to motivated offenders appears to increase the risk of mobile phone bullying victimization.

The target attractiveness variables were similar for both the mobile phone and cyber bullying victimization models. Those youth who are bullied in the real world were also more likely to report mobile phone bullying (see Holt et al., 2013), as were those youth with poor school adjustments. In addition, mobile phone bullying victimization was also more likely for females. Due to the significance of gender, two additional regression models were conducted and partitioned based on the gender of the respondent. Equality of coefficient tests were also conducted, and while there were significant variables in each model, none of these differences were statistically significant between the two models. As a result, gender is a significant predictor, but there appear to be no statistically significant factors that increase the risk of victimization between males and females in this sample.

Table 17.3 Mobile Phone Bullying Victimization Regression Model

	Model 1		Model 2		
			Male	Female	
	(n = 3233)		(n = 1793)	(n = 1440)	
	B	SE	Exp. B	Exp. B	Exp. B
Home Internet use	−0.036	0.131	0.965	0.990	0.962
School Internet use	0.054	0.109	1.056	1.010	1.092
Mobile phone own	0.987	0.157	2.683**	3.071**	2.178**
Chatroom	0.101	0.057	1.106	1.035	1.192*
Email	0.089	0.060	1.094	1.100	1.075
Computer IM	−0.142	0.052	0.868**	0.842*	0.915
Bulletin boards	0.091	0.078	1.096	1.121	1.061
Blogs	0.141	0.060	1.152*	1.286**	1.030
MMS	0.369	0.057	1.447**	1.619**	1.288**
Traditional bullying	0.234	0.022	1.287**	1.288**	1.314**
School adjustment	0.092	0.038	1.097*	1.070	1.131*
School level	0.033	0.031	1.033	0.969	1.122*
Gender	0.491	0.105	1.634**	—	—
Pseudo-R^2	0.167			0.205	0.131

Note: Model 1: Chi-square = 340.215**, −2LL = 2602.434. Model 2: Male model: Chi-square = 222.077**, −2LL = 1279.986. Female model: Chi-square = 123.746**, −2LL = 1303.441. There were no significant differences ($z > 1.96$) between the partitioned models.

*$p < 0.05$, **$p < 0.01$.

Discussion and Conclusion

As researchers increasingly focus on the problem of cyber bullying, there is a need to identify the risk factors associated with victimization among vulnerable populations. Limited research suggests that routine activities theory may be able to account for bullying victimization (e.g., Holt et al., 2013; Holt and Bossler, 2007; Marcum et al., 2010). Few studies have, however, examined these issues in a cross-national context, especially within Asian nations that have greater Internet connectivity (CIA, 2007). Thus, this study utilized a sample of youth from Singapore to identify the correlates of cyber bullying and mobile phone bullying victimization.

The findings suggest that individual behaviors that increase an individual's exposure and proximity to motivated offenders increased the risk of both cyber and mobile phone bullying victimization. Youth with access to the Internet at home increased the risk of cyber bullying victimization, while mobile phone ownership was associated with the risk of mobile phone bullying victimization. The frequency of use of various forms of CMCs also affected the risk of bullying victimization by increasing overall exposure to motivated offenders (Hinduja and Patchin, 2008; Holt and Bossler, 2007; Marcum, 2008; Marcum et al., 2010; Ybarra and Mitchell, 2008). Thus, this study reinforces previous research that time spent in online environments increases the risk of victimization by increasing a victim's potential to receive and read messages from bullies.

Target suitability also differentially increases risk of victimization. In particular, those youth who experience traditional bullying in the real world were also more likely to report both cyber and mobile phone bullying victimization (Hinduja and Patchin, 2008; Kim et al., 2005; Klomek et al., 2008; van der Wal et al., 2003). Bullying victimization in the real world may increase a victim's proximity to bullies in virtual spaces, as the victim is a known entity to his or her bully in the real world and becomes a suitable target online (Beran and Li, 2008; Hinduja and Patchin, 2008; Holt et al., 2013; Ybarra and Mitchell, 2004).

In addition, females and those with negative affect while at school are more likely to experience both cyber and mobile phone bullying (Hinduja and Patchin, 2008; Kim et al., 2005; Klomek et al., 2010; Ybarra and Mitchell, 2008; van der Wal et al., 2003). These findings are consistent with the larger research literature on cyber bullying (Hinduja and Patchin, 2008; Klomek et al., 2010; Navarro and Jasinski, 2013; Wade and Beran, 2011), including cross-national studies on victimization (Holt et al., 2013; Kim et al., 2005; Li, 2008). This relationship may stem from the fact that females typically engage in verbal and psychological bullying behaviors relative to males, who tend to perform acts of physical bullying and violence (see Tokunaga, 2010).

Despite the significant relationship between gender and victimization, there were few significant differences between the correlates for males and females generally. The results indicate that males who spend more time online were more likely to experience cyber bullying victimization. This is sensible in relation to prior research on the routine activities theory and bullying victimization generally (see Holt and Bossler, 2007; Holt et al., 2013; Marcum et al., 2010). Younger females were more likely to be victimized, which may stem from differential access to technology. Specifically, youth tend to obtain access to technology as they age, and those who acquire phones and Internet access may be more likely to engage in bullying at an early age (Hinduja and Patchin, 2010; Tokunaga, 2010).

Taken as a whole, this study demonstrates that the predictors for bullying victimization do not differ based on geographic differences (Hinduja and Patchin, 2008; Huang and Chou, 2010; Klomek et al., 2010; Li, 2006; Ybarra and Mitchell 2008). In addition, the relationship between traditional bullying, technology use at school and at home, and affect suggests a need for intervention strategies that involve both schools and parents generally (Nansel et al., 2001, 2003; Hinduja and Patchin, 2008). School administrators and counselors must implement programs to diminish bullying in the school, which may in turn diminish the risk of cyber and mobile phone bullying (Hinduja and Patchin, 2008; Marcum, 2008; Marcum et al., 2010). Such programs must be implemented at early ages so as to demonstrate the negative consequences that may result from both victimization and offending in order to reduce the prevalence of bullying generally (Marcum, 2010; Tokunaga, 2010).

At the same time, parents must manage their child's access to technology due to the relationship between home Internet access, frequency of CMC use, and mobile phone access. For instance, supervising online activities through the use of filtering software and placing computers in public spaces within the home may help increase communication between parents and children about appropriate online activities (Hinduja and Patchin, 2008; Marcum et al., 2010). Mobile phone management must also be encouraged and enforced despite the portability and lack of interception capabilities afforded by these devices. This may help to reduce exposure to motivated offenders while online and affect the likelihood of victimization. Finally, parents must recognize changes in affect or mood, a lack of appetite, and other physical symptoms that could indicate a child may be experiencing bullying on- or offline (Nansel et al., 2001, 2003; Hinduja and Patchin, 2008; Ybarra and Mitchell, 2004). In turn, this may help to diminish the risk of bullying victimization in both real and virtual spaces.

There are, however, several limitations of this study that must be considered. Specifically, this study did not include measures for guardianship factors that may reduce the risk of victimization (Holt and Bossler, 2009; Marcum, 2010). Guardianship is one of the key components of the routine activities theory; thus, future study is needed to identify appropriate measures that capture technical guardianship effectively. Additionally, the cross-sectional nature of this data makes it difficult to identify the causal order of the relationships identified in this study. Furthermore, this study utilized a binary measure of victimization rather than distinguishing between minor and serious forms of cyber and mobile phone bullying victimization. Thus, further study is needed to consider the relationships between various forms of bullying victimization in online environments. Such research is vital to improve our general understanding of the impact of bullying victimization around the world.

References

Beran, T., and Li, Q. (2005). Cyber-harassment: A new method for an old behavior. *Journal of Educational Computing Research*, 32(3), 265–277.

Beran, T., and Li, Q. (2007). The relationship between cyber bullying and school Bullying. *Journal of Student Wellbeing*, 1, 15–33.

Berson, I. R., Berson, M. J., and Ferron, J. M. (2002). Emerging risks of violence in the digital age: Lessons for educations from an online study of adolescent girls in the United States. *Journal of School Violence*, 1, 51–71.

Bossler, A. M., and Holt, T. J. (2010). The effect of self-control on victimization in the cyberworld. *Journal of Criminal Justice*, 38(3), 227–236.

Bossler, A. M., Holt, T. J., and May, D. (2012). Predicting online harassment victimization among a juvenile population. *Youth and Society*, 44(4), 500–523.

Cassidy, W., Jackson, M., and Brown, K. (2009). Sticks and stones can break my bones, but how can pixels hurt me? Students' experiences with cyber-bullying. *School Psychology International*, 30, 383–402.

Central Intelligence Agency (CIA). (2007). The world factbook. Singapore, 2006. Retrieved from http://www.umsl.edu/services/govdocs/wofact2006/geos/sn.html.

Chambers, C. T., Craig, K. D. (1998). An intrusive impact of anchors in children's faces pain scales. *Pain*. 78(1), 27–37.

Cohen, L. E., and Felson, M. (1979). Social change and crime rate trends: A routine activity approach. *American Sociological Review*, 44, 588–608.

Dake, J. A., Price, J. H., and Telljohann, S. K. (2003). The extent and nature of bullying at school. *Journal of School Health*, 73(5), 173–180.

Davies, J., and Brember, I. (1994). The reliability and validity of the 'Smiley' scale. *British Educational Research Journal*, 20(4), 447–454.

Dehue, F., Bolman, C., and Vollink, T. (2008). Cyberbullying: Youngsters' experiences and parental perception. *CyberPsychology and Behaviour*, 11, 217–223.

DeVoe, J.F., Bauer, L., and Hill, M.R. (2011). Student victimization in U.S. schools. November. Washington, DC: National Center for Education Statistics, U.S. Department of Education.

Erdur-Baker, Ö. (2010). Cyberbullying and its correlation to traditional bullying, gender, and frequent and risky usage of internet mediated communication tools. *New Media and Society*, 12, 109–126.

Esbensen, F. A., and Carson, D. C. (2009). Consequences of being bullied: Results from a longitudinal assessment of bullying victimization in a multisite sample of American students. *Youth and Society*, 41(2), 209–233.

Espelage, D. L., Mebane, S. E., and Swearer, S. M. (2004). Gender differences in bullying: Moving beyond mean level differences. In D. L. Espelage and S. M. Swearer (eds.). *Bullying in American Schools: A Social-Ecological Perspective on Prevention and Intervention*. Mahwah, NJ: Lawrence Erlbaum Associates.

Forero, R., McLellan, L., Rissel, C. and Bauman, A. (1999) Bullying behaviour and psychosocial health among school students in New South Wales, Australia: Cross sectional survey. *British Medical Journal*, 319, 344–348.

Glew, G. M., Fan, M., Katon,W., Rivara, F. P., and Kernic, M. A. (2005). Bullying, psychosocial adjustment, and academic performance in elementary School. *Archives of Pediatrics Adolescent Medicine*, 159(11), 1026–1031.

Hinduja, S., and Patchin, J. W. (2008). *Bullying Beyond the Schoolyard: Preventing and Responding to Cyber Bullying*. Thousand Oaks, CA: Corwin.

Hinduja, S. and Patchin, J. W. (2010). Bullying, cyberbullying, and suicide. *Archives of Suicide Research*, 14(3), 206–221.

Hokoda et al., (2006). School bullying in Taiwanese adolescents. *Journal of Emotional Abuse*, 6(4), 70–90.

Holt, T. J., and Bossler, A. M. (2007). Examining the applicability of lifestyle-routine activities theory for cyber crime victimization. *Deviant Behavior*, 30, 1–25.

Holt, T. J., and Bossler, A. M. (2009). Examining the applicability of lifestyle routine activities theory for cybercrime victimization. *Deviant Behavior*, 30(1), 1–25.

Holt, T. J., and Bossler, A. M. (2014). An assessment of the current state of cybercrime scholarship. *Deviant Behavior*, 35(1), 20–40.

Holt, T. J., Chee, G., Ng, E., and Bossler, A. M. (2013). Exploring the consequences of bullying victimization in a sample of Singapore youth. *International Criminal Justice Review*, 23, 5–24.

Huang, Y., and Chou, C. (2010). An analysis of multiple factors of cyberbullying among junior high school students in Taiwan. *Computers in Human Behavior*, 26(6), 1581–1590.

Jensen, G. F., and Brownfield, D. (1986). Gender, lifestyles, and victimization: Beyond routine activity. *Violence and Victims*, 1, 85–99.

Jones, L. M., Mitchell, K. J., and Finkelhor, D. (2013). Online harassment in context: Trends from three youth internet safety surveys (2000, 2005, 2010). *Psychology of Violence*, 3, 53–69.

Kim, Y. S., Koh, Y. J., and Leventhal, B. (2005). School bullying and suicidal risk in Korean middle school students. *Pediatrics*, 115, 357–363.

Klomek, A., Sourander, A., and Gould, M. (2010). The association of suicide and bullying in childhood to young adulthood: A review of cross-sectional and longitudinal research findings. *Canadian Journal of Psychiatry*, 55, 282–288.

Klomek, A. B, Marrocco, F., Kleinman, M., Schonfeld, I. S., Gould, M. S. (2008). Peer victimization, depression, and suicidiality in adolescents. *Suicide and Life-threatening Behavior*, 38, 166–180.

Kowalski, R. M., and Limber, S. P. (2007). Electronic bullying among middle school students. *Journal of Adolescent Health*, 41, S22–S30.

Lauritsen, J. L., Laub, J. H., and Sampson, R. J. (1992). Conventional and delinquent activities: Implications for the prevention of violent victimization among adolescents. *Violence and Victims*, 7, 91–108.

Li, Q. (2006). Cyberbullying in schools: A research of gender differences. *School Psychology International*, 27(2), 157–170.

Li, Q. (2008). Cyberbullying in schools: An examination of preservice teachers' perception. *Canadian Journal of Learning and Technology*, 34(2), 75–90.

Liau, A. K., Khoo, A., and Hwaang, P. (2005). Factors influencing adolescents' engagement in risky Internet behavior. *Cyberpsychology*, 8, 513–520.

Marcum, C. D. (2008). Identifying potential factors of adolescent online victimization for high school seniors. *International Journal of Cyber Criminology*, 2, 346–367.

Marcum, C. D. (2010). Assessing sex experiences of online victimization: An examination of adolescent online behaviors utilizing routine activity Theory. *Criminal Justice Review*, 35(4), 412–437.

Marcum, C. D., Higgins, G. E., and Ricketts, M. L. (2010). Potential factors of online victimization of youth: An examination of adolescent online behaviors utilizing routine activity theory. *Deviant Behavior*, 31, 381–410.

Miethe, T. D., and Meier, R. F. (1994). *Crime and Its Social Context*. Albany, NY: SUNY Press.

Nansel, T. R., Overpeck, M., Pilla, R. S., Ruan, W. J., Simons-Morton, B., and Scheidt, P. (2001). Bullying behaviors among U.S. youth. *JAMA*, 285, 2094–2100.

Nansel, T. R., Overpeck, M. D., Haynie, D. L., Ruan, W. J., and Scheidt, P. C. (2003). Relationships between bullying and violence among US youth. *Archives of Pediatric Adolescent Medicine*, 157, 348–353.

Navarro, J. N., and Jasinski, J. L. (2013). Why girls? Using routine activities theory to predict cyberbullying experiences between girls and boys. *Women and Criminal Justice*, 23, 286–303.

Olweus, D. (1991). Bully/victim problems among schoolchildren: Basic facts and effects of a school based intervention program. In D. J. Pepler and K. H. Rubin (eds.), *The Development and Treatment of Childhood Aggression* (pp. 15–24). Hillsdale, NJ: Lawrence Erlbaum Associates.

Patchin, J. W. and Hinduja, S. (2010). Changes in adolescent online social networking behaviors from 2006 to 2009. *Computers and Human Behavior*, 26, 1818–1821.

Paternoster, R., Brame, R., Mazerolle, P., and Piquero, A. (1998). Using the correct statistical test for the equality of regression coefficients. *Criminology*, 36(4), 859–866.

Reynolds B, Penfold R. B., Patak, M. (2008). Dimensions of impulsive behavior in adolescents: Laboratory behavioral assessments. *Experimental and Clinical Psychopharmacology*, 16(2), 124–31.

Smith, P. K., Mahdavi, J., Carvalho, M., Fisher, S., Russell, S., and Tippett, N. (2008). Cyberbullying: Its nature and impact in secondary school pupils. *Journal of Child Psychology and Psychiatry*, 49,(4), 376–385.

Sourander, A., Brunstein-Klomek, A., Helenius, H., Ikonen, M., Lindroos, J., Luntamo, T., Koskelainen, M. (2010). Psychosocial risk factors associated with cyberbullying among adolescents: A population-based study. *Archives of General Psychiatry*, 67(7), 720–728.

Sourander, A., Helstelä, L., Heleinus, H. and Piha, J. (2000) Persistence of bullying from childhood to adolescence–a longitudinal 8-year follow-up study. *Child Abuse Neglect*, 24, 873–881.

Thorp, D. (2004). Cyberbullies on the prowl in schoolyard. July. *The Australian*.

Tokunaga, R. S. (2010). Following you home from school: A critical review and synthesis of research on cyberbullying victimization. *Computers in Human Behavior*, 26(3), 277–287.

Turner et al., (2010). Poly-victimization in a national sample of children and youth. *American Journal of Preventive Medicine*, 38, 323–325.

Twyman, K., Saylor, C., Taylor, L. A., and Comeaux, C. (2010). Comparing children and adolescents engaged in cyber bullying to matched peers. *Cyberpsychology, Behavior, and Social Networking*, 13, 195–199.

Wade, A., and Beran, T. (2011). Cyberbullying: The new era of bullying. *Canadian Journal of School Psychology*, 26, 44–61.

Williams, K. R., and Guerra, N. G., (2007). Prevalence and predictors of internet bullying. *Journal of Adolescent Health*, Dec;41(6 Suppl 1):S14–21.

Wolak, J., Mitchell, K., Finkelhor, D., (2007). Unwanted and wanted exposure to online pornography in a national sample of youth Internet users. *Pediatrics*, 119, 247–257.

Wolke, D., Woods, S., Bloomfield, L., and Karstadt, L. (2000). The association between direct and relational bullying and behaviour problems among primary school children. *Journal of Child Psychology and Psychiatry*, 41, 989–1002.

Wong, D. S. W., Lok, D. P. P., Lo, T. W., and Ma, S. K. (2008). School bullying among Hong Kong Chinese primary schoolchildren. *Youth and Society*, 40, 35–54.

Yar, M. (2005). The novelty of 'cybercrime': An assessment in light of routine activity theory. *European Journal of Criminology*, 2, 407–427.

Ybarra, M., Mitchell, K., and Wolak, J. (2008). How risky social networking sites: A comparison of places online where youth sexual solicitation and harassment occurs. *Pediatrics*, 121, e350–e357.

Ybarra, M. L. (2004). Linkages between depressive symptomatology and internet harassment among young regular internet users. *Cyberpsychology and Behavior*, 7, 247–257.

Ybarra, M. L., and Mitchell, J. K. (2004). Online aggressor/targets, aggressors, and targets: A comparison of associated youth characteristics. *Journal of Child Psychology and Psychiatry*, 45, 1308–1316.

Ybarra, M. L., Mitchell, K. J., Finkelhor, D., and Wolak, J. (2007). Internet prevention messages: Targeting the right online behaviors. *Archives of Pediatrics & Adolescent Medicine*, 161, 138–145.

Zhang, L., Welte, J. W., and Wiecxorek, W. F. (2001). Deviant lifestyle and crime victimization. *Journal of Criminal Justice*, 29, 133–143.

Assessment of Cyber Criminology

Obstacles, Challenges, and Promising Paths of the New Science of Cyber Crime*

18

BRIE DIAMOND AND
MICHAEL BACHMANN

Contents

Introduction

Computers have become an integral part of every aspect of our lives. Computer technologies are relied on for nearly everything we do, and we live in societies that are fundamentally dependent on digital infrastructure for their continued functioning. Increasingly, this mission-critical nature of computer networks for nearly all industry sectors, combined with the wealth of personal information that is being put online, has bred a new type of dangerous criminal—one that is targeting computers to steal our information, finances, and personal identifications (Bachmann and Corzine, 2009; Furnell, 2002; Holt, 2010; Jaishankar, 2007, 2008; Jewkes, 2007; Nhan and Bachmann, 2010; Yar, 2006). The Office of the President of the United States (White House, Office of the Press Secretary, 2009, para. 18) suggests that the threat posed by these cyber criminals "is one of the most serious economic and national security challenges."

Today, governments around the globe struggle to employ effective countermeasures against cyber attacks. The implementation of such countermeasures is increasingly facilitated by the vast amount of scientific knowledge about the technical details of the various attack methods (Amoroso, 2011). Unfortunately, the guidance provided by these studies is limited to details on the methods of attack and is left lacking insight about who the attackers are and how they differ from "traditional" criminals. This situation persists despite the

* This chapter was earlier published as Diamond, B., and Bachmann, M. (2015). Out of the beta phase: Obstacles, challenges, and promising paths in the study of cyber criminology. *International Journal of Cyber Criminology*, 9(1), 24–34. Reproduced with permission.

concerted efforts of a small number of dedicated scholars from around the globe (among them, Bachmann, Brenner, Hinduja, Holt, Jaishankar, Jewkes, Kilger, Nhan, Turgeman-Goldschmidt, Patchin, Wall, and Yar, to name but a few) advancing a newly developing field of criminological study called *cyber criminology* (Jaishankar, 2007).

For the past eight years, the young discipline has grown with the contribution of many experts, including the exceptional efforts of its founder, K. Jaishankar, who defined cyber criminology as "the study of causation of crimes that occur in the cyberspace and its impact in the physical space" (Jaishankar, 2007, p. 1). This definition accounts for the multidisciplinary nature of the field that relies upon insights from both the social (criminology and sociology) and computer sciences. Also, Jaishankar (2008) has introduced the first theory (space transition theory of cyber crimes) exclusively developed to explain offending in cyber space and has founded the first academic journal dedicated to the criminological study of cyber crimes, the *International Journal of Cyber Criminology*, http://www.cybercrimejournal.com (Jaishankar, 2007). With the contributions of international experts, this ranked journal with high-quality articles and rigorous peer review has grown as a core outlet in the field of cyber criminology.

These and similar efforts aside, the fact remains that cyber criminology is largely ignored or marginalized by mainstream criminology, and that many criminologists refrain from examining this important, future-oriented issue. Whether it be that they are lacking the necessary understanding of technology, are intimidated by the jargon of the field, or continue to fail to realize the full extent of societal implications of this new type of crime, the lack of consideration is troubling. Others become discouraged by the multitude of methodological problems involved in conducting quantitative studies of cyber offenders, particularly when attempting to generate representative samples of online offenders. Also, major criminological associations (e.g., the American Society for Criminology [ASC]) continue to marginalize cyber criminological studies in their annual conferences, and partly due to the many unresolved methodological problems, cyber crime researchers face significant difficulties in getting their manuscripts accepted by top-tier criminological journals. Taken together, these problems systematically discourage many from studying the problems and, in turn, result in still limited, albeit rapidly increasing, numbers of annual publications.

The chapter addresses many of the main problems facing cyber criminologists today. It intends to shed a light on the difficulties and suggests ways to overcome them. The strengths and weaknesses of potential methods are analyzed, and their implications for the interpretation and generalization of results are considered. Suggestions for future research are provided. The presentation seeks to spark a conversation with the audience about promising solutions to some of the current problems and potential approaches of how to create standards for future research in this new area of criminology.

Issues in Defining Cyber Crime

The difficulties surrounding the study of cyber crime begin at the definitional level. Should cyber crime be conceptualized as a brand new crime type or traditional crimes pursued through a new medium? Researchers such as Grabosky (2001) adhere to the former definition and regard cyber crimes to be motivated by the same basic human emotions—greed, lust, and revenge—that underlie crimes committed in real space. Along the same lines, Thomas and Loader (2000, p. 3) define cyber crime as "computer-mediated activities which are either illegal or considered illicit by certain parties and which can be conducted through global electronic networks." However, others have argued that many cyber crimes fail to conform to the traditional model of crime. Furnell (2002) suggests a two-pronged understanding of cyber crimes—*computer-assisted* and *computer-focused* crimes. Furnell views the former, computer-assisted crimes to be "old wine in new bottles" (to use the nomenclature expressed in Grabosky, 2001), wherein crimes such as credit card fraud and cyber terrorism are committed through the use of information and communications technology (ICT), but are still capable of being conducted via traditional methods. Conversely, computer-focused crimes, such as hacking and website defacement, represent new crimes unparalleled in conventional crimes that necessitate the use of ICT—without which these crimes would not exist. Likewise, Smith and colleagues (2004) draw a distinction between those crimes that use ICT in the commission of the offense and those that are directed squarely at such technologies. Also, cyber criminologists like Wall (1999), Yar (2005), and Jaishankar (2008, 2011) ascertain that cyber crime is a new form of crime. Jaishankar (2008, p. 291) explains,

> Even though some researchers feel cyber crimes as a case of "old wine in new bottles" (Grabosky, 2001), "old wine in bottles of varying and fluid shape" (Yar, 2005), or "new wine in no bottles" (Wall, 1999), cyber crimes are still different from the crimes of physical space. There exists a fine line of demarcation between the crimes of physical space and crimes of cyberspace. The demarcation lies in the "involvement of the virtual cyber medium" (Pati, 2003), "lack of geographical boundaries" (Hafner and Markoff, 1995; Mitra, 1999), and "their occurrence in a diffuse, fluid, evolving" (Brenner, 2004) and "spatiotemporally disorganized environment" (primarily the collapse of spatial–temporal barriers, many-to-many connectivity, and the anonymity and plasticity of online identity) (Yar, 2005; Williams, 2005). Yar (2005) ascertains after analyzing cyber crime with routine activities theory that cyber crime is a new and distinctive form of crime. Cyber crime is an entirely new form of crime.

However, studies of cyber crime suffer from many of the same definitional issues common to other subdisciplines in the field. White-collar crime, as Smith and colleagues point out (2004, p. 10), has come to include a variety of crimes that "include any acts of occupational deviance involving a breach of the law or ethical principles"—a definition that inhibits clarity across research endeavors. Likewise, the study of sex offending, which can entail a wide range of criminal conduct—with distinct motives and a wide range of harm to victims and society—is analogous to the difficulties surrounding cyber crime research, which can run a similar gamete of human behavior.

Dearth of Data

The problems arising from the wide range of criminal behavior encapsulated by the term *cyber crime* are not aided by the veritable lack of data available to scrutinize these crimes. Most of the data on cyber crime come from either agency or victimization surveys. Beginning in 2004, the Census of State and Local Law Enforcement Agencies, representing more than 20,00 agencies across the United States, asks whether these agencies perform cyber crime investigations on a regular basis (U.S. Department of Justice, 2004). A similar survey of campus law enforcement agencies makes the same inquiries of campus agencies and shows that more than half of these agencies have individuals designated to handle cyber crimes on campus (U.S. Department of Justice, 2004–2005). Likewise, the Law Enforcement Management and Administrative Statistics (LEMAS) survey asks whether agencies handle cyber crimes via a specialized unit, designated personnel, or if they do not have any special way to handle such crimes (U.S. Department of Justice, 2007). While datasets such as these give a base understanding of the law enforcement resources dedicated to cyber crime, they do not provide much depth into the prevalence of or official handling of such crimes—let alone offender characteristics.

A handful of datasets provide victimization information, and even fewer use offender reports of cyber crime. Since 2006, the National Crime Victimization Survey (NCVS) (U.S. Department of Justice, 2012a), a representative sample of U.S. households, has inquired about cyber crime victimization against members over the age of 12. Unfortunately, this single question does not disaggregate cyber crime into its various categories, making the usefulness of this measure rather superficial. The Identity Theft Supplement of the NCVS collected in 2012 (U.S. Department of Justice), representing household members 16 years of age and older, however, does delve expressly into hacking in regard to identity theft victimization. Specifically, it asks victims of identity theft if the misuse of their personal information came to their attention due to "suspicious computer activity including email hacked." Beyond these few examples, little large-scale effort has been made to document the prevalence of cyber crime victimization.

If victimization data are rare, information on cyber crime offenders is virtually nonexistent. The Survey of Inmates in State and Federal Correctional Facilities (U.S. Department of Justice, 2004) collects data on whether inmates used computers in the commission of a range of offenses, including identity theft, obscene communication, copyright infringement, forgery, and sabotage of a computer or computer system. These data, while representing an ability to delve into cyber crime offender characteristics, highlight the nascent focus on this type of crime. What exists beyond these few examples is largely small, convenient samples of college students reporting on their involvement in minor forms of cyber crime, such as digital piracy (see Gunter, 2011; Higgins and Makin, 2004; Morris and Blackburn, 2009). These data represent the bulk of cyber crime research and its application of criminological theories.

Theoretical Issues

Flowing from the contention over the definition of *cyber crime* and the lack of data on the topic, theoretical advancement has been lacking. The debate over whether cyber crime is a new type of crime or old crimes committed in new ways is mirrored in the theoretical literature. Scholars disagree as to whether our current sociologically driven theories are capable of properly accounting for criminal behavior committed in the virtual realm. While some have proposed theories such as routine activities and social learning to be adaptable to cyber crime, others have argued that a fresh theoretical approach is warranted (Jaishankar, 2008).

The problems underlying cyber criminology are two-pronged (Yar, 2005). First, many of the correlates of crime established through traditional criminology are irrelevant in regard to cyber crime. Most cyber crimes still tend to be committed by young males; however, due to the very nature of this class of crime, cyber criminals tend to be well-educated members of the middle or upper-middle class (Bachmann, 2010; Pratt et al., 2010; Smith et al., 2004; Yar, 2006). The "usual suspects" of many criminological theories—minority, poorly educated offenders from the lower class—are simply priced and skilled out of computer-related crimes. Likewise, the traditional victim–offender relationship, where individuals tend to know and share many common characteristics with an offender, is largely irrelevant.

In a similar vein, the physical aspects of traditional crimes that have shaped criminological theory bear little to no importance in regard to cyber crimes. Flowing from the work of Shaw and McKay (1942), criminological theories have long since relied on the confluence of offenders and victims in time and space. The rich imagery of the zone in transition—replete with characters interacting on disordered, volatile streets—sparked a wave of theories focused on the impact of the physical, social environment on human behavior. These theorists had street crimes—strong-arm robberies and residential burglaries—in mind when developing these explanations and could hardly have anticipated a genre of deviance almost completely detached from the physical environment.

Cyber crimes offer a unique opportunity for offenders to gain access to what would *sans* Internet be inaccessible victims. So the question remains: Can our traditional criminological theories be transposed to the virtual world? Some see our current theories as being of little utility, though attempts have been made to apply routine activity theory (RAT) to cyber crime. The problem for RAT is the heavy emphasis on the convergence of offenders and victims in physical space (see Cohen and Felson, 1979). Yar (2005) argues that the "antispatial" (quoting Mitchell, 1995) nature of cyber crime can be rectified within the existing theory.

The amorphous virtual environment may be less of an issue for the study of cyber crime than it seems. While, as Yar (2005) points out, it is impossible to predict the convergence of motivated offenders and suitable targets in the online environment, so it is largely impossible to pinpoint the convergence of these actors in real space. The Internet may be "populated 24/7," but there are still times of greater traffic—introducing more offenders and targets—that may still be predictive of victimization. Regardless, most research on RAT focuses not on the physical convergence of offenders and targets, but on the characteristics of suitable targets and their lack of guardianship. This situational foreground is the true power and focus of RAT. Likewise, applications of RAT to cyber crime should be less concerned with the fittingness of the virtual environment to the theory, and focus instead on what cyber criminals view to be a suitable target and what guardianship is deemed adequate to reduce the chances of victimization.

Yar (2005) surveys the aspects of a suitable target (proximity, exposure, attractiveness, and guardianship) outlined in RAT and concludes that these categories have mixed applicability to the virtual environment. Obviously, the idea of physical proximity is problematic for the theory, but he also dismisses the concept of exposure (visibility, as he refers to it) as being a constant and a requirement of involvement in the online environment. Yes, visibility is inherent on the Internet, but how does this differ from the inherent visibility of most individuals in the physical world? Exposure exists more along a continuum, so that the amount of exposure to motivated offenders is what matters. Likewise, the more prominent an individual's presence on the Internet and across a range of websites, the greater the opportunity for his or her victimization, thus making him or her a more visible and suitable target. This position is supported by recent RAT research on online financial fraud (Pratt et al., 2010). Likewise, researchers have shown that online harassment victimization depends on the amount of time spent in chat rooms and engaged in instant messaging (Holt and Bossler, 2008). The ideas of attractiveness and capable guardianship translate nicely to suitable targets in the online environment. Those individuals or organizations that pose a financial benefit (e.g., intellectual property) or an affiliation of interest to an offender (e.g. religious, sexual, or racial) will likely be deemed more attractive targets. Finally, the concept of capable guardianship translates to the virtual environment as well. Yar (2005) explains how guardianship takes on two forms: social guardianship, such as the presence of network administrators or online citizens calling out cyber offenders, and physical guardianship, such as antivirus software and firewalls.

In the end, Yar (2005) considers RAT to be of limited utility to the explanation of cyber crime. This seems largely due to the nonphysical nature of the online environment and the inability to predict when and where offenders will come into contact with suitable targets. RAT, however, is a policy-focused theory that quibbles less about the environmental background that these actors move through and focuses more on the characteristics of individuals that increase their risk of victimization. As such, ignoring the role of physical proximity that is so important to crimes committed in real space, but appreciating the ways that online exposure, target attractiveness, and the absence or weakness of social or physical guardianship shape the victimization risk of online entities has a distinct probability of explaining crime in virtual space.

Other existing theories seem less capable of explaining cyber crime. One of the most important predictors of street-level offending, low self-control, is unlikely to be applicable to individuals who are capable of pursuing higher levels of education and employment. One would expect the findings to be quite similar to the nonsignificance of low self-control in predicting corporate crime (Simpson and Piquero, 2002). Holt and colleagues (2011), however, have uncovered a small, yet significant influence of low self-control on offenses committed by teenagers, such as pirating media or software, hacking, and viewing sexual material—a group of individuals and behaviors with a stronger link to the desire for immediate gratification than perhaps more serious forms of cyber crime (see also Higgins, 2004; Higgins and Makin, 2004). Further, the plausability of stressful life experiences being the motivation behind these crimes seems tenuous as well (although, in regard to cyber bullying, see Patchin and Hinduja, 2011).

Some indications have been made, however, that social learning principles may be important in cyber offending (Holt and Bossler, 2008; Holt et al., 2010, 2011; Morris, 2011; Morris and Blackburn, 2009; Morris and Higgins, 2010). Namely, association with delinquent peers appears to predict involvement in computer hacking, digital piracy, and online harassment victimization. Holt et al. (2010) show that while differential association with cyber offenders is the most influential social learning principle, the remaining aspects of imitation, differential reinforcement, and pro-delinquent definitions significantly influence cyber crime involvement. Likewise, findings from a survey of roughly 800 college students suggest that hackers may engage in some of Sykes and Matza's (1957) techniques of neutralization, such as denial of injury or victim blaming, to justify their behavior (Morris, 2011). In conclusion, it appears that many of our existing theories can be successfully applied to various forms of cyber crime, apart from exclusive theories on cyber crime, such as the space transition theory (Jaishankar, 2008). What needs to be done now is more systematic research into which theories operate best upon which categories of cyber crime and for which types of offenders.

Teaching Issues

Cyber crime courses are ones of particular interest to modern-day students of numerous disciplines. However, programs attempting to offer such courses find themselves encountering a number of issues. Historically, college classes focused solely on cyber forensics, the practical implementation of cyber crime investigation, rather than the theoretical discipline of cyber criminology (Jaishankar, 2010). Melding the two focuses of cyber forensics and cyber criminology would lead to a more holistic educational experience for students in the field. To this end, the University of Alabama now offers a minor in cyber criminology that exposes students to the law enforcement practices, theoretical explanations, computer science ethical issues, and cyber law surrounding cyber crime (for further information, see http://courseleaf.ua.edu/artssciences/criminaljustice/#cybercrimitext). Fortunately, other undergraduate and graduate courses are already offered all over the globe and more are currently being developed. It appears that the issue of cyber crime and our understanding of its societal implications are slowly moving outside of the narrow confines of computer sciences. With more social science departments incorporating the issue into their programs, the hope remains that a next generation of social scientists will devote more attention to this pressing, vast, and growing problem. The primary challenge for such programs will be to strike an appropriate balance in incorporating technological aspects, since many students in these fields are easily intimidated by the technical intricacies involved in the commission of many cyber crimes.

Publication Issues

Some of these theoretical endeavors have made their way into mainstream criminology journals, but most research on cyber crime is relegated to edited book volumes and more obscure journals or journals outside of the field altogether (Jaishankar, 2010). Further, few cyber crime–specific peer-reviewed journals exist for authors to disseminate their work to other cyber criminologists—the *International Journal of Cyber Criminology* being the most prominent. The choices of outlets are expanding, however, with new journals such as the *Journal of Technology and Crime* being established. As federal interest in preventing cyber crime continues to grow, and with it the amount of data for analysis, hopefully we will see the numbers of top-tier cyber crime publications grow and the prestige of these specialized journals rise. As it stands, the more creative and less conventional methodological approaches necessitated for many especially quantitative cyber crime studies render placing these studies in top-tier journals difficult. Currently, the gradual shift of the federal level away from terrorism and toward cyber crime is already being reflected in a surge of edited and sole-authored book publications on cyber crime–related issues. The range of topics addressed in these recent books includes classic cyber criminological studies, as well as homeland and critical infrastructure protection from digital threat assessments, and cyber terror and cyber warfare–related issues.

Conclusion

In spite of the various issues mentioned, it should be noted that cyber criminology has come a long way during the short time since its conceptual inception (Jaishankar, 2007), and its developmental pace continues to accelerate. As evermore spectacular high-dollar and high-impact cyber crime heists (Douglas and Timberg, 2014), vulnerabilities, and surveillance issues (McManus, 2014) continue to grip the attention of mainstream media, society at large is becoming more aware of the severity and dangerousness of cyber crimes and related issues. The young discipline of cyber criminology is already benefiting from this increasing awareness. More social scientists are beginning to examine cyber criminological topics and aspects, and it is safe to predict that greater numbers will follow in the years to come. Just as its subject of study, cyber criminology will become more mainstream within criminology. Hopefully, this predictable growth of the field will bring with it solutions to some of the basic problems outlined in this chapter that are currently still plaguing this young discipline.

References

Amoroso, E. G. (2011). *Cyber Attacks: Protecting National Infrastructure*. Burlington, MA: Elsevier.

Bachmann, M. (2010). Deciphering the hacker underground: First quantitative insights. In T. Holt and B. Schell (eds.), *Corporate Hacking and Technology-Driven Crime: Social Dynamics and Implications* (pp. 105–127). Hershey, PA: IGI Global.

Bachmann, M., and Corzine, J. (2009). Insights into the hacking underground. In T. Finnie, T. Petee, and J. Jarvis (eds.), *The Future Challenges of Cyber Crime*, vol. 5: *Proceedings of the Futures Working Group* (pp. 31–41). Quantico, VA: Federal Bureau of Investigation.

Brenner, S. (2004). Toward a criminal law for cyberspace: Distributed security. *Boston University Journal of Science & Technology Law*, 10(2), 1–112.

Cohen, L. E., and Felson, M. (1979). Social change and crime rate trends: A routine activity approach. *American Sociological Review*, 44, 588–605.

Douglas, D., and Timberg, C. (2014). Target breach could represent leading edge of wave of serious cybercrime. *Washington Post*, February 9. Retrieved October 12, 2014, from http://www.washingtonpost.com/business/economy/target-breach-could-represent-leading-edge-of-wave-of-serious-cybercrime/2014/02/09/dc8ea02c-8daa-11e3-833c-33098f9e5267_story.html.

Furnell, S. (2002). *Cyber Crime: Vandalizing the Information Society*. London: Addison Wesley.

Grabosky, P. N. (2001). Virtual criminality: Old wine in new bottles? *Social and Legal Studies*, 10(2), 243–249.

Gunter, W. D. (2011). Criminological predictors of digital piracy: A path analysis. In K. Jaishankar (ed.), *Cyber Criminology: Exploring Internet Crimes and Criminal Behavior* (pp. 173–191). Boca Raton, FL: CRC Press.

Hafner, K., and Markoff, J. (1995). *Cyberpunks: Outlaws and Hackers on the Computer Frontier*. Toronto: Simon and Schuster.

Higgins, G. E. (2004). Can low self-control help with the understanding of the software piracy problem? *Deviant Behavior*, 26(1), 1–24.

Higgins, G. E., and Makin, D. A. (2004). Does social learning theory condition the effects of low self-control on college students' software piracy? *Journal of Economic Crime Management*, 2, 1–22.

Holt, T. J. (2010). *Crime On-Line: Correlates, Causes, and Context*. Raleigh, NC: Carolina Academic Press.

Holt, T. J., and Bossler, A. M. (2008). Examining the applicability of lifestyle-routine activities theory for cyber crime victimization. *Deviant Behavior*, 30(1), 1–25.

Holt, T. J., Bossler, A. M., and May, D. C. (2011). Low self-control, deviant peer association, and juvenile cyberdeviance. *American Journal of Criminal Justice*, 37(3), 378–395.

Holt, T. J., Burruss, G. W., and Bossler, A. M. (2010). Social learning and cyber-deviance: Examining the importance of a full social learning model in the virtual world. *Journal of Crime and Justice*, 33(2), 31–61.

Jaishankar, K. (2007). Cyber criminology: Evolving a novel discipline with a new journal. *International Journal of Cyber Criminology*, 1(1), 1–6.
Jaishankar, K. (2008). Space transition theory of cyber crimes. In F. Schmalleger and M. Pittaro (eds.), *Crimes of the Internet* (pp. 283–301). Upper Saddle River, NJ: Prentice Hall.
Jaishankar, K. (2010). The future of cyber criminology: Challenges and opportunities. *International Journal of Cyber Criminology*, 4(1/2), 26–31.
Jaishankar, K. (2011). *Cyber Criminology: Exploring Internet Crimes and Criminal Behavior.* Boca Raton, FL: CRC Press.
Jewkes, Y. (2007). *Crime Online*. Cullompton, UK: Willan.
McManus, D. (2014). Edward Snowden: A whistle-blowing outlaw, now with a Pulitzer Prize to his name. *Los Angeles Times*, April 14. Retrieved October 12, 2014, http://www.latimes.com/opinion/opinion-la/la-ol-pulitzer-prize-edward-snowden-nsa-20140414,0,3959573.story.
Mitchell, W. J. (1995). *City of Bits: Space, Place, and the Infobahn*. Cambridge, MA: MIT Press.
Mitra, A. (1999). Cybernetic space: Our new dwelling place. Presented at Proceedings of the Hawaii International Conference on Social Sciences, Honolulu, June 12–15, 2003. Retrieved December 20, 2006, from www.hicsocial.org/Social2003Proceedings/AnandaMitra.pdf.
Morris, R. G. (2011). Computer hacking and the techniques of neutralization: An empirical assessment. In T. J. Holt and B. H. Schell (eds.), *Corporate Hacking and Technology-Driven Crime: Social Dynamics and Implications* (pp. 1–17). Hershey, PA: IGI Global.
Morris, R. G., and Blackburn, A. G. (2009). Cracking the code: An empirical exploration of social learning theory and computer crime. *Journal of Crime and Justice*, 32(1), 1–34.
Morris, R. G., and Higgins, G. E. (2010). Criminological theory in the digital age: The case of social learning theory and digital piracy. *Journal of Criminal Justice*, 38(4), 470–480.
Nhan, J., and Bachmann, M. (2010). Developments in cyber criminology. In M. Maguire and D. Okada (eds.), *Critical Issues of Crime and Criminal Justice: Thought, Policy, and Practice* (pp. 164–177). Thousand Oaks, CA: Sage.
Patchin, J. W., and Hinduja, S. (2011). Traditional and nontraditional bullying among youth: A test of general strain theory. *Youth and Society*, 43(2), 727–751.
Pati, P. (2003). Cyber crime. Retrieved December 15, 2006, from http://www.naavi.org/pati/pati_cybercrimes_dec03.htm.
Pratt, T. C., Holtfreter, K., and Reisig, M. D. (2010). Routine online activity and Internet fraud targeting: Extending the generality of routine activity theory. *Journal of Research in Crime and Delinquency*, 47(3), 267–296.
Shaw, C. R., and McKay, H. D. (1942). *Juvenile Delinquency in Urban Areas*. Chicago: University of Chicago Press.
Simpson, S., and Piquero, N. L. (2002). Low self-control, organizational theory, and corporate crime. *Law and Society Review*, 36(3), 509–548.
Smith, R. G., Grabosky, P., and Urbas, G. (2004). *Cyber Criminals on Trial.* Cambridge: Cambridge University Press.
Sykes, G. M., and Matza, D. (1957). Techniques of neutralization: A theory of delinquency. *American Sociological Review*, 22, 664–670.
Thomas, D., and Loader, B. (2000). Introduction. In D. Thomas and B. Loader (eds.), *Cyber Crime: Law Enforcement, Security and Surveillance in the Information Age* (pp. 1–13). London: Routledge.
U.S. Department of Justice, Bureau of Justice Statistics. (2004). Survey of inmates in state and federal correctional facilities, 2004. ICPSR04572-v1. Ann Arbor, MI: Inter-University Consortium for Political and Social Research [distributor]. DOI: 10.3886/ICPSR04572.v1.
U.S. Department of Justice, Office of Justice Programs, Bureau of Justice Statistics. (2004–2005). Survey of campus law enforcement agencies, 2004–2005: [United States]. ICPSR27261-v1. Ann Arbor, MI: Inter-University Consortium for Political and Social Research [distributor]. DOI: 10.3886/ICPSR27261.v1.

U.S. Department of Justice, Office of Justice Programs, Bureau of Justice Statistics. (2007). Law enforcement management and administrative statistics (LEMAS), 2007. ICPSR31161-v1. Ann Arbor, MI: Inter-University Consortium for Political and Social Research [distributor]. DOI: 10.3886/ICPSR31161.v1.

U.S. Department of Justice, Office of Justice Programs, Bureau of Justice Statistics. (2012a). National crime victimization survey, 2012. ICPSR31202-v2. Ann Arbor, MI: Inter-University Consortium for Political and Social Research [distributor]. DOI: 10.3886/ICPSR34650.v1.

U.S. Department of Justice, Office of Justice Programs, Bureau of Justice Statistics. (2012b). National crime victimization survey: Identity theft supplement, 2012. ICPSR34735-v1. Ann Arbor, MI: Inter-University Consortium for Political and Social Research [distributor]. DOI: 10.3886/ICPSR34735.v1.

Wall, D. S. (1999). Cyber crimes: New Wine, no bottles? In P. Davies, P. Francis, and V. Jupp (eds.), *Invisible Crimes: Their Victims and Their Regulation* (pp. 105–139). London: Macmillan.

White House, Office of the Press Secretary. (2009). Remarks by the president on securing our nation's cyber infrastructure [Press release]. Retrieved October 12, 2015, from http://www.whitehouse.gov/the-press-office/remarks-president-securing-our-nations-cyber-infrastructure.

Williams, M. (2005). Cyber crime. In J. Mitchell Miller (ed.), *Encyclopaedia of Criminology*. London: Routledge.

Yar, M. (2005). The novelty of "cyber crime": An assessment in light of routine activity theory. *European Journal of Criminology*, 2, 407–427.

Yar, M. (2006). *Cybercrime and Society*. London: Sage.

Epilogue

NATTI RONEL*

Criminal behavior is a behavior or chain of behaviors related to people. Usually, we tend to describe criminal acts by emotion-raising titles and labels, to hold certain myths concerning these behaviors, to attempt to impose regulations and laws that may be more or less efficient to reduce crime, and to socially react to those involved, both as criminals and as victims, as though they fully represent the master status we attach to these scenes. But, beyond all these and other reactions, crime is between people, and it affects the lives of people, individuals or groups, criminals or victims, at any level. Sometimes, it is a private event between individuals, who closely know each other, as is the case in domestic violence; however, other times it may happen in the public sphere, but still, it is between involved people. Even when we consider the newly defined *green criminology*, where crime is against the environment, still people are involved as criminals and as affected victims, since these acts have lasting effects on the lives of a great mass of individuals. Whenever and wherever we approach it, crime is an interpersonal event, and we have to be reminded of this simple fact time and again.

The wish for simplicity tends to divide the criminal scene into the "pure criminal" and the "pure victim." Even when we clearly know that it is rarely that simple, such a description is almost inevitable. It assists us to gain a sense of control over criminality (mostly illusionary control) and to justify the legal and social reactions. Nevertheless, interpersonal encounters are never as simple, and crime, as an interpersonal occurrence, is not distinct. In any case, victims are never to be blamed for the criminal act imposed on them; however, many times individuals who perform criminal activities might be recovering victims as well, and an individual who at a given moment experienced victimization can be an aggressor in other cases. Criminal behavior is a nonsimple, confusing, interpersonal event.

The up-to-date understanding of the complexity of crime reveals areas of criminality and populations that traditionally were less known or even were not considered criminals. For example, domestic violence, a well-established field of study and practice, is a relatively new one, representing new understandings. Sexual offenses and trafficking of individuals also exemplify such relatively new recognized and defined domains of practice and study that recently became well established. Within these examples, we see that the new understanding contains a simultaneously new consideration of women, children, and minorities as vulnerable groups that are widely affected by crime. As said, currently it is an established known fact; however, it is still relatively new and developing knowledge.

Crime is a human act in between people. While offending is human and universal, struggling against it, or beyond it, is no less universal and human. New opportunities for crime are also new opportunities for human growth out of it. I hope that the chapters of this book, edited by Jaishankar, will contribute to our understanding of these new opportunities that represent the old—our old and lasting ability to be fully human.

* Professor Natti Ronel, head of the Department of Criminology, Bar-Ilan University, Ramat Gan, Israel, was the program chair of the Second International Conference of the South Asian Society of Criminology and Victimology (SASCV), conducted January 11–13, 2013, in Kanyakumari, India.

Index

J

K

L

M

T

U

V

W

Y

Z

For Product Safety Concerns and Information please contact our EU representative GPSR@taylorandfrancis.com Taylor & Francis Verlag GmbH, Kaufingerstraße 24, 80331 München, Germany

Batch number: 10732714

Printed by Printforce, the Netherlands